# A GAME CALLED
# SALISBURY

## The Spinning of a
## Southern Tragedy and
## The Myths of Race

### SUSAN BARRINGER WELLS

ISBN  0-7414-4425-9


*Published by:*

PUBLISHING.COM

*1094 New DeHaven Street, Suite 100*
*West Conshohocken, PA 19428-2713*
*Info@buybooksontheweb.com*
*www.buybooksontheweb.com*
*Toll-free  (877) BUY BOOK*
*Local Phone (610) 941-9999*
*Fax  (610) 941-9959*

*Printed in the United States of America*

*Printed on Recycled Paper*

*Published  December 2007*

To My Aunt,
Nellie Jewel Barringer Troxell


*And to*:

Isaac Lyerly, Nease Gillespie, Augusta Lyerly,
Della Dillingham, Mary Lyerly, Jack Dillingham,
Addie Lyerly, John Gillespie, John Lyerly,
Harrison Gillespie, Janie Lyerly, James Gillespie,
Alice Lyerly, George Ervin, and Henry Lee Gillespie

*It is with no pleasure I have dipped my hands in the corruption here exposed. Somebody must show that the Afro-American race is more sinned against than sinning....*

— Ida B.Wells,
*Southern Horrors: Lynch Law in All Its Phases*, 1892

# Contents

# Preface

When retired UNC History professor William Powell was a boy, his parents would stop and recite the story of the 1906 axe murders every time they drove by the old Lyerly home place in Rowan County, North Carolina. Years later, Powell would retell that story to his students, again and again.

I didn't hear it myself until about ten years ago when I was researching my family history. It was then I found out four in my great grandfather's family had been axe murdered. Then I found out three of their sharecroppers—Nease Gillespie, John Gillespie and Jack Dillingham—were lynched for it. And then I found a noose.

It had been hanging on a nail in another ancestor's old well house for about a hundred years, before I snuck it out of there, just as the Department of Transportation was about to raze the place to widen Highway 70.

Then I learned about the 1898 propaganda campaign that had sparked more than a few acts of violence in Rowan County and elsewhere. It told me just how much I'd never been taught about our state's black history and made me want to know much more.

Looking for descendants of the lynching victims led to my first ever visit to a southern black church, whose congregation introduced me to Nease Gillespie's family.

One of them just happened to take William Powell's History Course at UNC. On one of those days after William recounted the story to his students, Sharon stopped to talk to him before leaving class and told him of her relationship to Nease.

I've since learned that the rope was not my great grandfather's only souvenir. In his desk drawer—my mother told me her mother told her—he kept fingernails from one of the victims. Not knowing exactly how to process that piece of information at first, it sat on the surface of my brain some time before sinking in. I think it was while talking to Sharon on the phone one day that it hit me—those body parts may have belonged to *her* great grandfather.

While looking for Nease's family, I ran into relatives of my own I never knew I had, regained others I'd "lost" for years, and found an ancestry richer than I'd imagined. Some of it, a DNA test revealed, is African.

Some time in the midst of my investigation, and before learning of my African ancestry, I began to question the concept of race and just what exactly these "races" were supposed to be. The traditional answers, I found, were far from the truth I soon discovered.

After learning there was such widespread interest in the Lyerly story and about the many misconceptions surrounding it and the concept of race, I decided to publish my findings.

Besides the axe murder, the book is about two lynchings and what caused them. It's also about my family and a little about me. Mainly, it's about who told the stories, why they spun them the way they did, and how their lies have hurt us all. Most important, it's about what's happening right now.

# NOTE TO READERS

## *On Sources*

Because knowing *who* said *what* is vital to this story, sources are identified frequently within the text. I tried to make the others easier to distinguish by using letters, as well as numbers, for reference. Also, *N&O* is used consistently within the text to abbreviate the *Raleigh News and Observer* to avoid confusing it with another primary source, the *Charlotte Observer*.

Though some women reporters were working in the early 1900s in the South, most, if not all telling this story were men. For that reason, "he" instead of "he or she" is used in reference to an unknown reporter. It doesn't mean anything; it's just easier. The words "black" and "white" are used, reluctantly, for the same reason. Less acceptable quoted terms are left as they are.

The strong influence of politics on the press in the early 1900s makes it impossible to rely completely on what any paper said about this story. Therefore everything coming from news sources should be read as "reportedly" or "allegedly" whether specifically labeled that way or not. Those reporting the story elevated a lot of hearsay to the status of "evidence."

What happened, for sure, is pretty much covered in the short introduction, along with what is documented by historians in chapters VI and XXV, and scattered elsewhere throughout the book.

The rest is left for the reader to decide.

## *On Politics*

Southern Democrats who promoted the agenda of white supremacy, often called "Dixiecrats," should not be confused with members of the current National Democratic Party or other Democrats who abhorred this agenda during Jim

Crow's rule of the South. Before and during Reconstruction, right after the Civil War, the black community saw the Republican party as their champions and protectors, but that scenario changed as Jim Crow's influence over the South increased.

After President Johnson signed Civil Rights legislation in the 1960s, many Dixiecrats moved to the Republican Party, and then the two parties, for the most part, reversed roles on racial and other issues. This explains why the Republican Party was once favored, as a whole, by the black community, which now pretty much votes the Democratic ticket.

# Main Characters

## I. 1906 MURDERS

**A. SCENE OF LYERLY MURDERS: Unity and Neighboring Townships in Rowan County, North Carolina**

**1. Murder Victims – Couple and Their Two Youngest Children**

ISAAC LYERLY, age 68
AUGUSTA BARRINGER LYERLY, age 42
JOHN H. LYERLY, age 8
ALICE LYERLY, age 6

**2. Survivors – Isaac and Augusta's Oldest**

MARY A. LYERLY, age 17
ADDIE L. LYERLY, age 14
JANIE E. LYERLY, age 10

**3. Suspects**

NEASE GILLESPIE (alias Mich or Mitchell Graham), age 55
JOHN GILLESPIE, age 14 or 15 – Nease's son
HENRY LEE GILLESPIE, age 18-20 – Nease's son
GEORGE ERVIN, age 29-30
JACK DILLINGHAM, late 20s or early 30s, from Virginia
DELLA YOUNG DILLINGHAM, Jack's wife

**4. Witnesses Incarcerated**

FANNIE GILLESPIE, age 53 – Nease's wife and/or long-time companion
HENRY MAYHEW, age 10 or 11 – Fannie's son, Nease's step-son

## 5. Neighbors Known to be Related to Isaac or Augusta

JOSEPH GRAHAM LYERLY, age 40 – Isaac's oldest son by
first wife – lived ½ mile east of Isaac
SALLIE (SARAH) LYERLY – Isaac's sister, married first
cousin W.C. Lyerly – lived 1 mile south of Isaac
CATHERINE LYERLY WALTON – Isaac's sister, lived near
Sallie with adult son, Emmanuel Walton
W. P. (Pless) BARBER & MARTHA WALTON (Isaac's niece)
– married couple lived about 1 mile west of Isaac
EMMANEUL (Mann) WALTON – Isaac's nephew, lived about
1 mile south of Isaac
EDGAR A. (Ed) BARBER – Isaac's nephew and local constable
GEORGE A. RUFTY – Isaac's cousin, kept souvenirs from
lynching
JOHN REDWINE BARRINGER – Augusta's brother

## 6. Other Neighbors

ROBERT F. (Filmore) COOK – lived 3/4 to 1 mile, probably
south, of Isaac near Sallie Lyerly – in 1900 lived north of Isaac
near Matt Webb
MATT LEE WEBB, age 23 – Mary Lyerly's forbidden beau,
lived about 1 mile north of Isaac
LEROY POWLAS – lived about 1 mile east of Isaac, Henry Lee
Gillespie and George worked for him
EMMA GILLESPIE – Henry Lee Gillespie's wife
ELLA CHAMBERS – friend of Graham/Gillespie family
RICHARD GRAHAM – said to have supported John Gillespie's
alibi
DICK FILE – lived about 1 mile northwest of Isaac

## 7. County Officers

EDGAR A. (Ed) BARBER – constable
EDWARD JED (E.J) ROSEMAN – Isaac's grand nephew
DEPUTY CHARLES GOODMAN – drove Henry Mayhew to
town

## 8. Physicians

DR. CHENAULT – lived in next township, attended to Alice
Lyerly's wounds after murders
DR. DORSETT – coroner

## B. SALISBURY SCENE

### 1. Officials

SHERIFF DAVID R. JULIAN – father of Deputy Julian &
editor John Moose Julian
DEPUTY DAVID W. JULIAN – son of the sheriff, brother of
editor John Moose Julian
DEPUTY J. HODGE KRIDER – jailer
J. FRANK MILLER – Chief of Police – cousin of reporter
Thomas Bost
ARCHIBALD HENDERSON BOYDEN – Mayor, nicknamed
"Baldy" one of first members of the Ku Klux Klan in North
Carolina, cousin of John Steele Henderson
WILLIAM CICERO HAMMER – State Solicitor/Prosecutor,
editor/owner of *Asheboro Courier* newspaper
BENJAMIN FRANKLIN LONG – judge called for August 6
special term – Statesville resident
ROBERT BROADNAX GLENN – governor, Democratic Party,
succeeded Charles B. Aycock, both staunch white supremacists
GARLAND S. FERGUSON – judge presiding over regular
August term, Rowan County

### 2. Attorneys

THEODORE F. KLUTTZ – former U.S. Congressman, assisted
prosecution of murder suspects and defense of lynching suspects,
father of *Observer* reporter Theo F. Kluttz, Jr.
JAKE F. NEWELL – prominent Republican, nicknamed "silver-
haired orator," defended murder suspects
LEE S. OVERMAN – U.S. Senator – pleaded with mob, editor
Julian's legal mentor
JOHN STEELE HENDERSON – cousin to Mayor Boyden,
wrote news of Lyerly case in letters to his wife

## 3. Reporters

JOHN MOOSE JULIAN – editor of *Salisbury Post*, sheriff's son, state and local Democratic legislator
HENRY EDWARD COWAN (H.E.C.) BRYANT – nicknamed "Red Buck," reporter for *Charlotte Observer*
JOHN CHARLES MCNEILL – lawyer, poet, and reporter for *Charlotte Observer*
JOSEPH PEARSON CALDWELL – editor of *Charlotte Observer*, brother-in-law of Theo F. Kluttz Sr.
THEODORE F. KLUTTZ, JR. – reporter for *Charlotte Observer*, nephew of Caldwell
WILLIAM THOMAS (Tom or W. T.) BOST – Isaac's former neighbor, *Observer's* Salisbury correspondent
JOHN MITCHELL, JR. – editor of *Richmond Planet*, one of few African American papers left in the South in early 1900s
JOSEPHUS DANIELS – owner/editor of *Raleigh News and Observer* – one of South's most famous and radical racists

## 4. Suspected Lynchers and Residence

GEORGE HALL – Spencer, Rowan County
FRANCIS CRESS – Salisbury
GEORGE GENTLE – Franklin Township, neighborhood next to Isaac's
HENRY GOODMAN – Salisbury or elsewhere in Rowan County
BUD BULLYBOY – probably neighborhood near Isaac's
JOHN CAUBLE – Salisbury
ALEX JACKSON – Faith
THE MAN IN THE PANAMA HAT – mystery man, "interloper," possibly John Redwine Barringer

# II. 1902 CASE

## A. DECEASED OR VICTIM

CORNELIA BENSON, age 27

## B. CORNELIA'S RELATIVES

WILLIAM A. BENSON – brother
LAURA BENSON – sister-in-law
NANCY BENSON – mother
SAMUEL AND SIDNEY BENSON – nephews, William and
Laura's sons

## C. ACCUSED OF MURDERING CORNELIA

JAMES GILLESPIE, age 11
HARRISON GILLESPIE, age 13

## D. RELATIVES OF ACCUSED, LIVING IN SAME HOUSEHOLD

STOKES COWAN – stepfather, next door neighbor of Bensons
ANNA GILLESPIE COWAN – Stoke's wife and Harrison's
mother
SUSANNA GILLESPIE – Anna's sister and James' mother

## E. OFFICIALS

SHERIFF D. R. JULIAN
DEPUTY DAVID JULIAN
JAILER J. HODGE KRIDER
MAYOR A. J. BOYDEN
DEPUTY ABNER RICE
DEPUTY JOE CARSON
JUDGE THOMAS J. SHAW

## F. ATTORNEYS

LEE S. OVERMAN
WALTER MURPHY
SOLICITOR (STATE PROSECUTOR) W. C. HAMMER

## G. GOVERNOR

CHARLES BRANTLEY AYCOCK

## H. LYNCHING SUSPECT

TOM SPARNELL – Salisbury barkeeper

## I. REPORTERS

THEO. F. KLUTTZ, JR. – *Charlotte Observer*
JOHN MITCHELL, JR. – *Richmond Planet*
JOSEPHUS DANIELS – *Raleigh News and Observer*
UNIDENTIFIED – *Salisbury Sun*

# INTRODUCTION

*Children have never been very good at listening to their elders,
but they have never failed to imitate them.*

— James Baldwin

ON THE SWANNANOA RIVER, ASHEVILLE, N.C.

On a warm summer day in western North Carolina, Embler Kibler came running home from play with an ugly red mark around his neck and his face discolored. Embler's older friend Jack McClay had brought a rope with him that day and suggested they play a new game. Jack had appointed himself executioner.

Embler's older playmate, Porter Claxton, was able to dodge eleven-year-old McClay when Jack first tried to loop the noose around his neck, but Embler, only six years old, could not escape. After tightening the knot at the little boy's throat, Jack tied the loose end to a nail driven into the wall on the porch where the children were playing. Then Jack and Porter ran off and left Embler hanging there with only his toes touching the floor. Though it must have seemed like an eternity to Embler, only minutes passed before he was able to struggle free. A Raleigh reporter commented the next day about the close call: "Had the rope been fastened more securely," he said, "the practical joke might have proven fatal." [1]

Embler's father swore out a warrant.

On August 10, 1906 Jack McClay was brought before the magistrate in Asheville. The red marks, still showing on Embler's neck, and the rope were offered as evidence. When questioned, Jack explained that they were just playing a game called "Salisbury." [2]

A few days later, a group of Raleigh youths decided to lynch a black woman. Carefully plotting their scheme, the group agreed on a signal and hustled up a heavy rope. Then, after successfully lassoing the head of their intended victim, the boys demanded she "tell all she knew regarding certain affairs of the place." The woman's screams, luckily, summoned help and saved her. "There is no doubt," said a Greensboro newsman, "that the situation was occasioned by the activity of the recent lynchers at Salisbury." [3]

The following week, yet another group of would-be lynchers, this time from Greensboro, congregated in the vicinity of South Elm and Lee Streets. These boys, "not to be outdone by the urchins of any [other place] in the state or country," approached the task strategically. It was soon decided that the victim would come from among their own group, and they drew straws to see who would play the officers, the mob leaders, and "the murderer" (the one who would be hanged). But when the holder of the short straw backed out, the gang of boys begat plan B—they'd have to catch a black kid to take his place. So they fixed up a box to represent the jail and decided that the "officers" would capture "a nigger" to play the murderer. The role of mob leader was the most coveted. "I don't want to be the officer," one boy insisted, "you bet I'm going to do business; I am the ringleader...come on; let's catch a nigger. There goes one now." [4]

Outnumbered by the group, the black boy was easily captured, but the rest didn't go smoothly at all. "The negro boy objected to being hung and made a stiff fight for liberty. In fact, the assailants never did get him to 'jail'," and fearing all the ruckus had attracted the police, the boys soon dispersed. [5]

ෆ୨౩

"The entire civilized world had its eyes on Salisbury last week," said the *Charlotte Observer* on August 15th. The story made headlines across the country—few failed to at least mention the mass lynching that took place just outside the city on August 6th. On that infamous Monday night around eleven, a mob of 200 to 500 men, observed by as many as 5000 spectators—men, women, and children—stormed the Rowan County jail in downtown Salisbury and dragged from the third floor and into the street three of its prisoners. This was no child's play. Accused, but not convicted of axe-murdering four white family members, these three were condemned by a mob, marched to the edge of town, and lynched. Their hanging bodies were riddled with bullets and carved by knives. Some newspapers said the mutilation began during the march. Despite the torture, and before slowly choking to death, the victims denied any involvement in the axe murders. One of them was only fifteen.

Perhaps to their credit, Salisbury, Governor Glenn, and the entire state of North Carolina was considerably embarrassed over the incident—enough to make a few changes in the law. The state, historically speaking, is proud of how it conducted its affairs during the aftermath. And at least one southern writer saw the 1906 lynching as a "turning-point" in the attitudes of North

Carolina officials and the public—one that led to the demise of mob violence in the state. [6]

Things did appear so, especially the way the press portrayed them. Judge Benjamin Franklin Long had harshly condemned the lynching the next day, and several white men were quickly arrested to quell the growing public outrage. Long was praised by many, including at least one black newspaper, for his apparent resolve to punish all who were involved in the crime. [7] But did Long, Glenn, and Salisbury do what they could to prevent the lynching? And were there any serious consequences for those involved?

Despite the favorable historical assessment of the outcome of the double tragedy, no thorough investigation was conducted at the time or since. And many questions have remained unanswered throughout the century. Some, like—what could drive men, some of them "good citizens," to resort to murder and mob violence—can be explained. Others are not so easy. Too much time has passed, and those who may have answers are no longer alive to ask. So we may never know if those lynched for the Lyerly murders were guilty or innocent. But if they didn't do it, who *did* kill my relatives?

Like the contents of an unkempt crate of ropes and strings, the elements in this plot are jumbled in a tangled mess. But if all the knots and twists won't unwind, the loose ends can still be connected and ties made to the tragedy's historical setting. Zooming in on 1906 magnifies the dual drama as a horrible, isolated incident, but stepping back and viewing the whole performance from a distance, brings it into clearer focus. From that perspective, it looks more like a remake of any scene from an extended tragedy that began just a few years earlier. That infernal play—the reign of Jim Crow—enjoyed far too long a run in the South, and some of its villains are among the most revered men in North Carolina history.

# BOOK ONE

## MOST BRUTAL MURDER
## IN ROWAN COUNTY HISTORY

MAP OF BARBER JUNCTION WITH LYERLY HOME
ON STATESVILLE ROAD (OLD U.S. 70)

# I

# FRIDAY THE THIRTEENTH

## JULY, 1906

*An event has happened, upon which it is difficult to speak, and impossible to be silent.*

— Edmund Burke

ISAAC LYERLY

The "most brutal in Rowan County history." That's how the papers described the massacre of my great grandfather's sister, Augusta Barringer Lyerly, her husband, Isaac, and their two youngest children. As murders go, they don't get much grislier, and nothing catches the attention of the public or the press like the horrifying details of an axe murder.[1] Adding to the mystique of this one is the night it happened: Friday the thirteenth—July, 1906.

The feeding frenzy began the next day. News of the slaughter summoned the press and a large crowd of curious and concerned neighbors—though the main attraction, at that time, may have been less about what and more about who.

Born into prominent, land-wealthy families, the Lyerlys and the Barringers were white—or mostly white. Isaac and Augusta were third and fourth generation descendants of German immigrant pioneers. These settlers, along with the Scotch, Irish, Dutch, and a Prussian or two, had colonized most of Rowan County—once the natives were run off and silenced—around the middle of the eighteenth century.

The suspects, on the other hand, were *not* mostly white and not, officially, descended from prominent white families. Nease Gillespie, John Gillespie, and Jack Dillingham, three of the six so-called "Negro" or "Mulatto" laborers accused of the crime, were lynched mostly because of who they weren't. More than likely descendants of slaves, the Gillespies and Dillinghams were of mixed descent—African and European—known officially as "Mulattos" *before* the twentieth century. In 1900, the revised reporting standards of the U.S. Census had tried to erase the evidence, and therefore the cause, of this mixed heritage, by lumping all mulattos and blacks into one category— "Negroes" —covering up many years of the crime of rape against black women by white men.

At the height of the reign of Radical Racism, 1906 was situated right in the middle of "one of the most racially troubled periods ever."[2] One historian called it the "worst of times."[3] Decades earlier, Emancipation and Reconstruction had given the so-called "New Negro" a taste of freedom, and naturally, as time went on, he grew hungry for more—for political, civil, and economic equality. But some whites feared all this would lead to "social equality," code words for interracial sex and marriage.

Thus the black male, taking the hit for white hypocrisy, became the new boogeyman, more specifically, an "incubus—a winged demon that has sexual intercourse with women while they sleep."[4] This bedeviled transformation didn't happen overnight, but it damned near did. Things hadn't gotten so out of hand until the 1890s, when whites' heretofore smoldering fears of sexual revenge from blacks were ignited and fueled by a few politicians who exploited them all (the blacks, the whites, and their fears) for personal economic and political gain. Propaganda was the igniter, and newspapers provided politicians with the consummate kindling for the flames that followed. To keep blacks in their place and out of politics and the newly developing industrial labor force, white publishers and editors actively discouraged racial cooperation by creating distrust and hatred of blacks. But the fire's residual ashes—violent acts such as lynching—exceeded the intended suppression of black ambitions.

Though not meant to produce such barbarous outcomes, it was, nevertheless, a systematic and calculated plot to dehumanize, and subsequently disfranchise, an entire segment of the South's citizenry. The role of the white press was to sensationalize and fabricate black crimes and, at the same time, downplay and ignore black accomplishments. And so *many* black successes, talents, and achievements were excluded from history for more than a century. Blacks and whites, even today, know little about them. Adding injury to insult, "Popular fiction denigrating blacks flooded the market."[5] Succumbing to this brainwashing, many whites were deceived, either by the sophisticated tactics or their own ignorance—or both. Some were just plain cowards, while more than a few had good reason to fear the consequences of bucking the new system of so-called separate, but equal.

The fear of racial retaliation in the days that followed was not totally unfounded. Some blacks didn't just sit back and accept their fate. It was an incredibly bitter pill to swallow, having finally gained some freedoms and rights after centuries of abuse and exploitation, and then having lost them almost overnight. It's like the blind peanut vendor in Frazier's *Cold Mountain* told Inman when he asked him what he'd pay to have his sight back for ten minutes. "I fear it might turn me hateful," he replied. "It's having a thing and the loss I'm talking about."

The threat was not nearly as prevalent as whites were led to believe. Most blacks were simply bogged down in basic survival mode. Even so, though very few fought back, most were seen as suspicious.

And so it came to pass that all people of color bore the blame for just about everything that went wrong. As America entered the twentieth century, "a malicious negrophobia—a pathological fear and hatred of blacks—had gripped the country." [6]

BARBER JUNCTION DEPOT

Compared to eastern North Carolina, where the worst of the state's racial strife had played out a few years earlier, the Piedmont region in 1906 seemed prosperous and peaceful, at least on the surface. Thanks to the railroad, Salisbury was a regional center of activity, and a small railroad junction located eleven miles west was booming with activity as well. Barber Junction was the gateway to Asheville— "The Land of the Sky" —and the healing springs of the Carolina mountains, which many tourists from the North frequented. In order for those traveling from Washington D.C. and points north to get to Asheville and other western destinations, either a change of trains or change of direction at Barber was required. Today, a tour of the North Carolina Transportation Museum, just north of Salisbury, begins at the old Barber Junction depot—restored, with its colored and white waiting rooms intact, and moved to its present place of honor in the 1980s. That little depot played a big role in the Lyerly murder story. And the story begins at Barber Junction. The Lyerly "plantation," as it was called, lay just off what is now Old U.S. Highway 70, about a mile east of the Barber depot. It was typical of North Carolina farms that had survived the Civil War and Reconstruction by replacing slaves with sharecroppers and hired hands. Surrounded by beautiful country, the site today inconspicuously blends into the rest of the rolling Piedmont hills of Rowan County, which are colored with rows of corn, cooled by wooded valleys, crisscrossed by streams. It's a section of the county where myths and legends were born and still thrive—the site of a mysterious subterranean wall in the Potneck section near the banks of Second Creek. It is said the area is sometimes visited by moving lights—a place from which strange sounds emanate—a "screech owl's heaven," where "bullfrogs dance in the water and croak." [7] Atop a knoll, near a dirt road curving amid these meandering streams, with their cacophonous choir, stood the Lyerly house—a large two-story frame dwelling with double-shouldered chimneys. This ancestral home had been there for a century, maybe longer; Isaac got it from his father, who had inherited it from his. And Augusta was the last of several Lyerly wives, the third of Isaac's, to preside as mistress of this humble mansion.

She had probably known Isaac all her life. He was already married when she was born in 1863 to Joseph Alexander and Selena Cranford Barringer, then living in the Unity Township—Isaac's neighborhood. Augusta's family moved away to an adjoining county when she was young and settled in the quaint village of Mt. Pleasant, where several more prominent Barringers had lived for decades. By the time she became reacquainted with Isaac, he had already lost two wives, and he needed another, who needed to be German. The Lyerlys had a history of exclusivity—Isaac's grandfather would have lost his inheritance had he married anyone *not* German. Anyway, Augusta made herself a good catch. Though the country had just come through a terrible depression, she'd married one of the richest men in Rowan County. And, in his day, Isaac was as sexy a man as any currently on the cover of *People Magazine*.

But in 1906 he was sixty-eight, old enough to have a son from a previous marriage as old as Augusta. Joseph now lived next door to his father and had a small family of his own. And though Augusta had given Isaac five more children—one every two to three years—none of these were much help to him around the farm. Their only son, John, was just eight years old, and the rest were girls. Mary, the oldest, was seventeen; then there was Addie, fourteen; Janie, eleven; and Alice, six. At his age, Isaac couldn't do too much in the way of hard labor, so Mary and Addie had to sometimes shoulder responsibilities usually borne by men.

For the three oldest girls, the survivors, it was as if time began on July 13, 1906. Addie's daughter can't say what the Lyerlys did earlier that day; Addie and Mary had talked mostly about the after, not the before. But we know this much. That evening the whole family was at home and in bed by nine, probably tired after a hard day's work. The youngest children were downstairs in the front bedroom with their parents: Augusta and Alice in one bed, Isaac and John in another. The bedroom of the three older girls was upstairs above the parlor, which was across the hall from their parents' bedroom. They were sleeping there that Friday until some time before midnight, when their dreams were interrupted by the smell of smoke. Addie, the first to be aroused, rushed downstairs and found her parents and younger siblings drenched in blood; one of the beds and her brother were on fire.

"*I* can tell you who did it," said a Barber octogenarian who's heard the story all his life, "It was old man Lyerly's sharecroppers, and they were lynched for it too." What he "knows" is the same story almost everyone's heard. Though possibly true, the belief has neither been proven nor properly probed.

Despite all that's been written and said, this case remains unsolved—which is not surprising, considering. There were no known eyewitnesses to the crime itself, though many saw the leftover carnage the next day. Among them was my grandfather, Sam Barringer, Addie's first cousin. They're dead now, all of those shell-shocked witnesses, and their descendants recall few and fuzzy details about the days following the murders. Sam had long passed before I knew anything about it, so I never heard his story, and my mother wasn't listening when he told it. The few available oral accounts passed down by other relatives contain conflicting and incomplete information. Newspaper articles—those that haven't been destroyed or lost—are just as bad. Politics was to blame for that. The Dixiecrats had their Jim Crow agenda back then, and they pretty much owned the press. They distorted the facts from the get-go and then left out some of the most important details—those that pointed to the possible innocence of the accused.

Clouding the picture further were other factors: the scarcity of bylines and the practice of plagiarism and other forms of conduct common among the day's reporters, practices considered unprofessional today. Though, at the turn of the twentieth century, "newspapers were the sole source of breaking news," the writing "was less objective and more personal" than is customary today. Reporters "often wrote sprawling accounts of an event, elaborating and exaggerating as they stretched the story, says Cate Kozak, a current reporter for *The Virginian Pilot*. [8] Called "yellow journalism," it was popularized in the 1890s by William Randolph Hearst to get Americans all hyped up about waging war against Spain, they say. Though a less well-known newsman from North Carolina, Josephus Daniels, may have taught Hearst a few of his tricks.

Nearly all of the surviving saga of the Lyerly murders comes from this politically-colored copy. And between its lines and lies, lie many missing components of the truth.

Biased and flawed as it was, the news coverage was nevertheless widespread. The horror that Addie and her sisters encountered when they descended the stairs that night was broadcast throughout the country. "The ghastly scene that met their gaze as they entered their parents' room beggars description," wrote the *Raleigh News & Observer* (*N&O*). [9] Greensboro's *Industrial News* and other prominent papers focused on the girls' heroism—the "story of their arousal, their fight with the fire, and their flight across the fields to neighbors...." [10] But the most vivid and emotional (and perhaps most accurate) account was written by John Charles McNeill, proably the first reporter to arrive the next day. "This is a horrible story to tell," he began, "but it is true so far as words can reproduce the scene, and its record should not be lost from the annals of crime. Along with the tragedy goes a story of wonderful heroism."

*So quickly and stealthily were the crimes committed that there was not enough noise to wake the three girls who were sleeping upstairs. Addie, 15 years old, was the first to wake. She smelt the burning cloth and ran downstairs. Her father's bed was in flames, and upon the body of her little brother a bureau drawer, full of combustibles and saturated with oil, was blazing.*

*She dragged the bodies off the bed, thereby burning her own feet and hands. Her mother's face was under her pillow, and little Alice was groaning. Addie did not go to the other bed, however, since it was not on fire, but ran back upstairs and waked her sisters, Mary and Janie, respectively 17 and 12 years old. "Papa and mamma are killed," she told them, "and the house is on fire."* [11]

# 2

# AN EERIE CALM

## SATURDAY MORNING, JULY 14

*When deep at night I wake with fear,*
*Peace steals into my heart at length,*
*When, calm amid the shout and shock,*
*I hear, Nic-noc, nic-noc.*

— John Charles McNeill

JOHN CHARLES MCNEILL

In 1906 newspaper bylines were about as rare as objective reporting. So newsmen in those days could easily conceal their subjectivity behind their anonymity—that is, if they wanted to. The three lead reporters of the Lyerly story must not have. By posting their initials at the end of their articles, they wore their biases on their sleeves, giving us a gauge for the accounts' accuracy and a glimpse into the goings-on underground, below the main plot.

They were John Charles McNeill and Henry Edward Cowan (H.E.C.) Bryant, with the *Charlotte Observer*, and John Moose Julian, editor and reporter for the *Salisbury Post*. Julian's is the version locals most often cite, while the *Observer's* coverage was most frequently reprinted in smaller papers throughout the state, as well as more prominent ones, including black papers, throughout the country. Years later, in 1974, *Post* reporter Joe Junod would base his recap primarily on Julian's coverage, a less detailed and even more subjective summary of what *Observer* newsmen had already embellished. Though Junod's story is the one locals most often point to as the truth of the matter, I found most unaware of the extreme circumstances that had originally colored this account. They hadn't heard about the media blitz of 1898 that had set out to ruin the reputations of all black, and some white, North Carolinians or the role the press played after it succeeded. They knew nothing about the original reporters of the Lyerly story or their agendas. Who told the story, however, had a lot to do with what was fact and what was fiction.

JOHN MOOSE
JULIAN

Other factors may have also been at play—like who was related to whom and whether or not either of them was a somebody—the ties between politics and the press, politics and family, and the knots that united them all. There were more than a few *among* Salisbury's leaders and newsmen and some *between* those in Salisbury and Charlotte.

Salisbury's most tangled line was probably the Julian family. John

Moose Julian, who had presided over Rowan County's Democratic Convention in 1902, was the son of Salisbury's Sheriff David R. Julian and brother of Deputy David W. Julian. The Julian brothers were city boys. Though their father had grown up on *his* father's farm, the future sheriff left the country life as a young man. In town, he started off as a store clerk, and by 1880 he'd moved up the ladder to merchant. Twenty years later, he was elected sheriff and thereafter hired his oldest son as deputy. John, on the other hand, had higher ambitions. While serving as chairman of the Democratic Party, he became the first editor of the *Post*, established on January 9, 1905. Before that, he edited and published the *Salisbury Evening World* he had founded in 1895, and he worked on both the *Truth-Index* and the *Salisbury Sun.* [1] But in spite of the influence John already wielded, he wanted more—he hoped to move beyond state politics in the upcoming election.

William Thomas (Tom or W. T.) Bost, who took over the Salisbury bureau of the *Observer* in 1905, didn't sign what he wrote, but other papers revealed that he played a key role in the story, nonetheless. First cousin to J. Frank Miller, Salisbury's Chief of Police, Bost was raised on a farm near the Lyerly place. With his ancestors among Rowan County's earliest, Bost may have also been related to the Lyerlys, like a lot of others living in the area. Along with Julian, Bost worked a few weeks for the short-lived *Truth-*

WILLIAM THOMAS
BOST

*Index* before it folded. Then he returned to the family farm until the *Post* needed him. He started off there as Julian's associate editor, and soon the two of them, together, tried to purchase the *Post* from its founders. But the deal fell through. While Bost was out of town rustling up his half of the payment, Julian found out he was broke; he'd been tricked into some worthless investments. Disappointed, Julian stayed on as editor, but Bost left to join the *Observer*. He witnessed the lynching in 1906 and would, in years to come, write about hundreds of legal "lynchings." [2]

Theo F. Kluttz, Jr., with the *Observer*, was definitely not a farm boy. His father, a former Democratic congressman and brother-in-law of *Observer* editor Joseph Pearson Caldwell, signed on as the Lyerly's attorney after the murders. As editorial writer in 1906, Kluttz, Jr. helped bring praise to the paper for its stand against mob violence, though he "...later become the cause of stormy dissension in the *Observer's* editorial office." [3]

JOSEPH PEARSON CALDWELL

Without the *Observer,* there wouldn't be much of a story to tell today. It's coverage was not perfect—it was far from it—but it left us the most complete and reliable reports available, thanks to Joseph Caldwell and the writers he hired.

Under Caldwell's management, the *Observer* thrived, even though it was plagued with tragedy. Caldwell had a knack for the news business and a gift for choosing talented writers, though bad luck when it came to keeping them. By the early 1890s, his *Observer* was an up-and-coming newspaper, and in 1906, it was printed by a modern 16-pager rotary press. However, as the *Observer* said years later, "men, not machines, make a newspaper, and Caldwell surrounded himself with some of the best newspapermen the state was to know." [4]

H.E.C. BRYANT

One was Henry Edward Cowan Bryant, but they called him "Red Buck," his red hair having something to do with it. Eventually celebrated as one of the "bright lights" of the Caldwell era, Bryant came to the *Observer* right after graduating from The University of North Carolina—offering to work for nothing, until Caldwell "thought he was worth something." Which didn't take long at all. He got the job after his first major assignment—an enthusiastic coverage of the white supremacist campaign rally in New Bern, North Carolina. [5] It was a lot like a Ku Klux Klan (KKK) rally, except with red-shirted, in place of white-capped marchers and the added touch of white women, adorned with white robes and garlands, riding on floats. Bryant was, after all, still a kid, and he got caught up in all the hoopla that his writing would continue to reflect.

A few years after Bryant signed on, Caldwell lost one of his brightest stars, Isaac Erwin Avery. Avery was widely acclaimed as the "best newspaper writer in the state," until one day in 1904, when he was found dead in his room, one floor above the *Observer* office. It was suicide. Caldwell was crushed by Avery's loss, which soon sent him looking for someone similar to fill his shoes. [6]

It wasn't long before Bryant, on Caldwell's behalf, found a suitable replacement in the poet lawyer John Charles McNeill. He tracked McNeill down in his Laurinburg law office, surrounded by his squirrels, 'possums and raccoons and offered him a job "without desk or deadline," to write whenever and whatever he wished. "McNeill had a poet's ear as well as a reporter's eye, and his verse caught the sounds of creeks and crickets, horses and hounds, and the soft sibilance of Negro dialect." After accepting Bryant's offer, McNeill would continue to write poetry as he worked as a reporter for the *Observer*. And his talent did not go unnoticed. For his *Songs Merry and Sad*, he received the Patterson Cup for the best contribution to literature in the state, an award presented to him in 1905 by President Theodore Roosevelt. [7]

With McNeill, Bost, Bryant, and Kluttz, Jr., Caldwell had a writing team that put most others to shame, at least as far as the Lyerly story was concerned. His dream team wouldn't last long—all four would be gone within the next two years—but in 1906, Caldwell was on a roll.

Even one of his weaknesses had worked to the *Observer's* advantage in the end. Though his drinking ran off a valuable editor, his resistance to the prohibition movement contributed to his falling out with another North Carolina editor. [8] And that was a good thing.

Josephus Daniels, editor and owner of the the *Raleigh News and Observer* (*N&O*), was a notoriously racist demagogue. His paper, boasting the largest circulation of any paper in the state, was the fourth major source of news on the Lyerly case. Besides reports by Bryant, McNeill, and Julian, it might have been the most influential, though least factual, of all. Daniels' reporters didn't identify themselves, but they didn't have to. Daniels' hand was in everything they wrote and, after 1898, in everything written by other Democratic papers in the state—with one clear exception—the *Charlotte Observer*.

Daniels lost his control over Caldwell and the *Observer* completely just a few years before 1906 when the two clashed over the endorsement of William Jennings Bryan as the national Democratic candidate. When Caldwell refused to favor Bryan's candidacy, Daniels pushed Caldwell too far. [9] Though still siding with the white supremacist sympathies of Daniels and other Dixiecrats, Caldwell, by 1906, was no longer Daniels' pal or his puppet. The rift over Bryan's endorsement had been the last of several straws that turned the *Observer* in a somewhat independent direction. This development, along with the survival of several Republican papers, served to blur the stark black and whiteness of the Lyerly story into something more like a softer gray.

On Saturday, July 14th, the day after the Lyerly murders, Bryant and McNeill were both on the scene to cover the story. Bryant focused his coverage on investigating possible suspects, while McNeill detailed the horrors of the crime scene, which, in this case, required little embellishment to produce an extraordinarily riveting account.

Even so, McNeill seemed in no hurry to delve into the gory details. Instead he lingered a bit in the peaceful setting outside the Lyerly home, before heading inside to a scene of hellish horror. Approaching the property, he made note of the groups of men gathered near their "buggies and saddle-horses in the grove," speaking in "low tones." Then he studied the "immense elms and sycamores in the front and the style of the house," and

concluded correctly that it was an "old home place." As he drew
nearer to the dwelling, he procrastinated further, taking time to
savor the smells of the "Zenias and hollyhocks...in bloom at the
gate and on either side of the walk." And even above all the
background noise, he could make out the sound of "chickadees
and catbirds...singing in the elms." [10]
But the music ceased even before he reached the door. Just
inside the gate, the facade of serenity crumbled with the
evidence of the slaughter. "On the steps and part of the yard
were scattered feathers and burnt pieces of cloth, and in the hall
singed feathers and straw were heaped in a corner and thrown
about the floor. There was a smell of scorched feathers and flesh.
In the rear entry the coroner was holding his inquest." [11]
Crossing the threshold into the front bedroom—the specific
site of the slaughter—McNeill first focused his eyes on the
condition of the room, averting them from the bodies lying
mutilated before him.

> *On the middle of the floor was a great pool of blood,
> not yet congealed. Pillows thrown into a corner were
> soaked with blood, as were the partly burned quilts and
> sheets that had been on the beds. At the head of Mr.
> Lyerly's bed, the floor and a heap of charred mattress
> straw were wet with kerosene oil. The side-rail and head
> of the bedstead were half burnt. Of course the room was
> in the utmost disorder.* [12]

Other reporters were arriving on the scene, and if McNeill
hadn't gotten graphic about the grisly details, another would
have. It was an event on which it was indeed difficult to speak
but impossible to remain silent. Yellow journalism
notwithstanding, the facts are indisputable: a young child was
murdered and burned.

> *The body of little John Lyerly lay on the floor, parts
> of it burnt black and below his knees the dry skin was
> loose and broken. His whole body was purple. Exactly in
> the top of his head, the blade of an axe had been driven,
> perpendicular to his forehead. From the look of the cut
> the axe must have sunk half-way to [his] eyes, and from*

*its position the boy must have been sitting up. The high head of the bed would have made such a stroke impossible while the child slept.* [13]

By now, however, the crime scene had been altered. The way things were when McNeill arrived is not how Addie and Mary had found them the night before. When Addie rushed downstairs to determine the source of all the smoke, she found her father and John together in the same bed—according to Bryant, who had gotten this information by questioning the girls the next day. Their story, or at least his version of it, was in the report that accompanied McNeill's in the July 15th issue. He wrote that Addie, upon entering her parents' room, "...saw that the bed on which her father and Johnnie slept was burning, and knowing in an instant that something terrible had happened, she rushed to her father and felt his brow and found it was cold. She passed her hand over Johnnie's face and that, too, was lifeless." [14]

By the time McNeill arrived, Isaac's body had been moved to the other bed—the bed that hadn't been burned. When he looked at Isaac, he saw that his face, "framed with gray hair and gray chin whiskers, was perfectly calm...."

*They say his eyes were shut when the first of the neighbors saw him. He must have been struck first and killed while he slept. There were two blows, however; one on the front, which seemed to have been made by the axe handle or a club; and the other behind his left ear. The latter was made by the butt of an axe, and crushed the skull completely in. It was blood, blood—on the floor, on the bedclothes and night clothes of the dead people; and while half a dozen neighbors moved silently amid the horror of it, cleaning it from the cold faces and dressing the bodies for the grave, the big clock on the mantel went on measuring time—nic-noc.* [15]

That still-ticking clock sat in the parlor—where Augusta's body now lay. Addie and Mary had found her in the bed now occupied by Isaac's body, where she had slept with Alice, and Alice, still alive, had lain "moaning at the side of her dead mother." But when McNeill learned that Mrs. Lyerly's body had been carried across the hall, where the neighborhood women were preparing it for burial, he entered the "neatly carpeted" and "tastefully furnished" parlor to examine and detail her wounds.

> *Here Mrs. Lyerly, who had been 40 years old, lay on the floor. Her white face wore a strange suggestion of a smile. Where her head lay on one side it showed plainly the broadside blow of an axe, the butt of which had cut off the lobe of her left ear, and the print of the body and blade of the weapon remained on her jaw and neck. The awfulest item of all the butchery was the other wound. The axe blade had been struck through her skull parallel with and about half an inch back from her forehead. Evidently she had been waked by the killing of her husband and was sitting up when the assassin dispatched her.* [16]

In contrast to this gory sight, earlier images of Isaac and his wife "...hung side by side on the wall, and looked from happy, young eyes at the whispering women who occupied the room." Isaac, with a goatee, was clad in his Confederate uniform and slightly smiling, McNeill noted, without sharing any details about Augusta. [17] Addie kept those portraits all her life and then passed them on to her children.

ISAAC AND AUGUSTA LYERLY

There had been four victims in all. But six-year-old Alice was no longer there. "Without ever regaining consciousness," Alice died that afternoon at the home of neighbor Filmore Cook, where the older sisters had carried her the night before. [18]

As McNeill continued his coverage, his judgment may have begun to falter. His description of the sisters' actions after they discovered the fire, shows some effects of disorientation. Unless other factors are at play.

> How they came down in their night-dresses, those three little girls, dragged the flaming mattresses and feather beds into the yard, drew and hauled water from the deep windlassed well in the back yard, and fought the fire for more than half an hour until they had conquered it; how they then scouted the premises, searched the numerous outhouses for the criminals or signs of them, this without waiting to dress; how they then set out for their nearest neighbor's, three-quarters of a mile away, Mary carrying little Alice in her arms, and Addie leading the other small sister, Janie, all this makes a story of heroism worthy never to die. [19]

First of all, the sisters were not all "little" girls. Eleven-year-old Janie could be described as a "little girl," but Addie was a teen, and Mary was a young woman, to become a bride in less than a year. A Richmond paper went so far as to refer to the girls as "tots," weeks after the story had broken, with plenty of time to get the facts straight, possibly basing its assumption on McNeill's description. All these distortions served to exaggerate the survivors' vulnerability and inflame the public against those who would soon be blamed for the crime.

And there are more problems with McNeill's portrayal. Addie's descendants were told that there was not much fire to put out and said there was possibly enough water in the house to extinguish it. Also, the older girls were later quoted as saying that they had brought some clothes from upstairs and dressed outside before heading off to Cook's house. And their closest relatives now insist that the idea of the sisters scouting the premises that night is absurd. This particular detail was, nonetheless, supported in a convincing anecdote later printed in the *Salisbury Post*.

McNeill's statement about the distance to the nearest neighbor is also iffy. The distance to Cook's house was correctly given as about three quarters of a mile, but Cook was *not* the girls' nearest neighbor. Census maps and locals' testimonies indicate that their half brother, Joseph, lived only about a quarter to half a mile away. Though all reports named the Cook home as the destination, why the girls chose it remains a mystery.

But the distance the story traveled is a matter of little dispute. The severity of the crime, the compelling plight of the three sisters, the racial aspects, and this family's standing within the community lured more than one *Observer* reporter to the scene, as well as newsmen from other locations. Though the *Observer* office, in downtown Charlotte, was about fifty miles south of Barber Junction, the trip was hardly an inconvenience. Throughout the day and evening, several passenger trains leaving Charlotte stopped at Barber, which was just down the road from the Lyerly place. And Barber was just as easily accessible from Asheville, Winston-Salem, Richmond, and D.C. Though few more distant papers sent reporters to the scene, Bryant's, McNeill's and others' accounts of the murders traveled as far as Fairbanks, Alaska, through telegraph wires, and elsewhere by word of mouth.

Eventually it would be Bryant's words that took the road most traveled. Bryant probably arrived on the scene by Saturday afternoon, July 14th, or perhaps he got there earlier and was squeamish about viewing the bodies—living up to the "Buck" part of his nickname. At any rate, he focused on interviewing the girls and bystanders and stirring up public passions. Well known by then as a political writer, Bryant didn't hesitate to weave the politics of white supremacy into his version of their testimonies, while McNeill revealed in his coverage of the case—as in his earlier writings and actions as a lawyer—an empathy with men of color, or at least an inclination toward Conservative, rather than Radical, Racism. Bryant had been involved in the political reporting that slandered blacks and Republicans holding office prior to November 1898. He had promoted the cause to re-enslave blacks, while McNeill, on the other hand, had tried to free at least one black man he felt had been falsely accused. [20]

It would be hard to accuse Bryant of exaggeration in his admiration of the "brave girls," but he did fudge on some of the details. He depicted the girls fearlessly fighting the fire for an hour and doing "...what they could to make their dying sister comfortable," adding that the "night was dark and not a soul did they have to comfort or assist them in their labor and sorrow." [21] With the moon in its first quarter, the night sky *was* definitely dark. And perhaps the girls *were* alone, but neither Bryant nor McNeill mentioned that a "Mr. John Henderson"—the use of "Mr" meaning he was a white man—had "worked at Mr. Lyerly's at the time of the murder." [22] So had a young man from Hildebran (near Hickory) named James Taylor, who Mary later said had stayed at Cook's house that night—and apparently *only* that night. But where was Henderson?

On the 68th anniversary of the tragedy, in an interview with *Salisbury Post* journalist Joe Junod, Addie shared details about that night that definitely don't jibe with reports of a lengthy fight with the fire. Junod quoted Addie's words, instead of paraphrasing them as Bryant had.

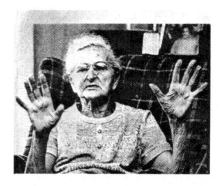

ADDIE LYERLY, 1974

*"I had asthma and the least smoke would wake me up. I ran downstairs and found Papa's bed on fire. John was lying at the end of the bed, Papa was at the head of the bed.... I got John out of the fire...his body was burning. There was so much blood that the fire didn't burn much. The murderers had doused the clothes and the bodies with kerosene...but it was mostly water and it smoked and woke me up... There was so much blood....*

*I think Mama must have woke up. She had one foot on the floor which I saw when I found Alice was living still. She lived until 3 o'clock the next day. Mama was dead. Her teeth were knocked out. The front of her head was split open. I put the bodies on the floor...but I was afraid the dogs would get them....*

*[Then] We put off across the woods to Mr. Filmore Cook's house. Mary was carrying Alice."* [23]

# 3

## WHEAT & CHAFF

### Or, The Usual Suspects

*"Her garments stained by the blood of her own sister, her heart bursting with unspeakable grief, made fatherless and motherless in a night, Miss Mary Lyerly told...a story of human butchery such as never before darkened the pages of Rowan County history. The bare recital of the facts freezes the blood, but the view of the room where four lives were sacrificed sickens and defies language...."*

— John Moose Julian [A]

Addie Lyerly, circa 1906

Close to midnight on July 13th, Addie, Janie, and Mary, the latter with Alice in her arms, fled through the woods near their father's farm to Cook's house. Afterward, several more journalists made note of the girls' heroic deeds and their presence of mind, and some further embellished the story and published errors of fact. But, for the most part, they agreed, essentially, with Bryant's and McNeill's accounts. The *Asheville Citizen* strayed a bit, saying it was the neighbors who put out the fire and saved the burning bodies from further destruction, but all other papers wrote, and Addie and Mary later testified, that it was they who extinguished the flames before fleeing to their neighbor's house. [1]

Bryant said once the girls realized their parents and brother "were beyond human aid," they turned their attention to Alice, laid her outside on the grass and attempted to revive her. Then, noticing that the fire "was making some headway in the feather beds," they left Alice unconscious on the lawn and focused on extinguishing the flames. "Water was drawn from the well, carried to the room, and poured upon the stubborn blaze. The remains of Mr. Lyerly and the boy were rescued from the flames and dragged from the bed to the floor." [B]

Most written and oral reports say that, on the way to Cook's house, the girls kept very quiet as they neared the home of one of Isaac's tenant farmers, Jack Dillingham. Fearing his involvement in the murders, "...they could not go by there. Leaving the trail at the little stream the children beat their way through the woods, briars and gullies to their destination." [B]

Which route the girls took is not clear in any of these reports. What's reasonably certain is that the Gillespie family lived west of the Lyerly home, and the Dillinghams rented the cottage that sat on a hill in the woods across the dirt highway, to the South. Cleared paths led in both directions, and both went through the woods and across a stream. The woods and streams are there today, but the cottages are long gone.

All accounts agree that Cook's home was the destination, but it's not certain where he was living in 1906. The 1900 census map and records show Cook owning his own home, located about a mile north of and directly behind the Lyerly house. The girls would have taken a path through their father's cornfields, through some woods, across a little stream, and across what is now Bob

Waller's property to get there—*if* that's where Cook lived in 1906. But the 1910 census records reveal Cook had moved at some point, within the prior ten years, to a rental home in the Steele Township, which begins just south of the Lyerly place. If Cook was in the latter location by 1906, that would put the Dillinghams between his and the Lyerly's home. Some reports say the girls fled through the cornfields to Cook's house, and others said they passed the Gillespies', the other tenants' house, on the way. If these reports are correct, they would not have gone South or past Dillingham's. Others left out the cornfields and the Gillespies altogether, saying only that they passed the Dillinghams.

In any event, no report explained why they didn't go east to their brother Joseph's place, about a half mile away. They could have walked up the main road to get there—not through the woods or across a stream or past any tenant house.

JANIE, LEFT, CIRCA 1906, AND MARY, YEARS EARLIER

John Moose Julian had to see for himself. And afterward he wrote that a "rugged" path had taken the girls "up and over a hill," and along that trail the next morning "were seen blood marks at almost every step." Julian had gone to Cook's house to interview the girls on Saturday and apparently asked Mary, though she must have been exhausted, to lead him on the route they had taken the night before. On the way, Julian found "A knot on the side of a small pine had caught a pink bow that had adorned the head of the baby" [a six-year-old, actually], and the bow "was spotted with blood drops." [A] Many years later, Addie told *Post* reporter Joe Junod that they crossed the stream and then "...saw the Dillingham house.... I could have touched it," Addie said. "I told Mary to be quiet. I thought maybe they had something to do with it." [C] If Addie remembered things properly when she told this, the girls had to have taken the southern route, because that was the way to the Dillingham's place. Even with all his detail, Julian never said where Cook lived.

Addie's concern about the Dillinghams deepens the confusion over the decision to go to Cook's in the first place. If the girls suspected Jack, why did they follow the route that passed his house, when they could have gone east and passed neither tenant? Why would they choose to cross a stream, go near the home of a suspected murderer, then continue on for nearly a mile in the dark on a hilly, rugged path, with a dying sister in their arms, when they had a blood relative living closer and just off the main road? Did they fear that the murderer or murderers could be travelers, still lurking on this road that ran to the train depot? Maybe this main road, traveled by strangers, was the only cleared path between the two Lyerly homes. Or maybe the girls' relationship with their half-brother was strained. Joseph later revealed his strong dislike for Augusta: "My father married a Barringer," he said, "and it's the biggest mistake he ever made." That's what Joseph's daughter told one of my aunts, a Barringer herself.

H.E.C. Bryant had his own way of telling things, which often degraded African Americans. His reports seemed to purposely cast suspicion on six living on or near the Lyerly farm, and he wasted no time at all incriminating the Dillinghams. The plight of the Lyerly girls presented the perfect scenario for the white supremacist press to exploit, and Bryant was just the man for the job.

> *One can easily imagine the picture of the flight of the Lyerly girls. When they had finished their work at the home, their thoughts turned to the brute or brutes who committed the foul deed. As they gathered their sister and started across the country they recalled that Jack Dillingham had had some words with their father the*

*day before. They were reminded also of the fact that their mother had been sauced by Dillingham's wife. Their courage had deserted them and they became a trio of innocent, unprotected young women, fleeing for shelter at a late hour of the night. As they moved along they were afraid lest Dillingham should hear them and come to carry out his plan of wholesale slaughter. But the trip was made in safety and Mr. Cook was notified.* [B]

The word "brute" in those days usually referred to a person of color. The term was used often by the North Carolina Democratic Party and the paper under its influence during that period of Radical Racism. The "brute caricature portrays Black men as innately savage, animalistic, destructive and criminal—deserving punishment, maybe death...," seen as "...hideous predators who target helpless victims—especially white women. [4] The "unprotected, innocent female imagery evoked by Bryant's report was a key element of the strategy used to arouse hatred against the black race, especially by North Carolinian Thomas Dixon, author of "The Clansman," prequel to the film *Birth of a Nation*, and by Josephus Daniels, author of the propaganda which facilitated the White Supremacist coup of 1898.

Since the investigation had barely begun, Bryant should not have excluded any suspect, including one or all of the girls. It was not his place to imply, especially at such an early stage in the investigation, the guilt or innocence of anyone. Just a few years earlier, the *Salisbury Sun* had reported a story about a seventeen-year-old girl who killed her sleeping father, apparently because he was an abusive alcoholic. She was said to have been "temporarily insane" at the time of the murder. Whites who committed murders back then were often judged to be insane. Two days before the Lyerly murders, in Colleton County, South Carolina, a prosperous farmer had axed to death his entire family, including his two-year-old daughter. Mr. Irnegan, a Swedish immigrant, was declared insane in the same report that first publicized the murders, with no hint of lynching in this or any account, all of which were brief. [5]

Papers were replete with murder and suicide reports back then, and more than a few murders were domestic, some committed by children. By 1906, many had heard of the famous

Lizzie Borden axe murder case. Despite the circumstances shedding serious doubt on Borden's innocence, the American public was generally unwilling to believe that a female could commit such a brutal crime. Such disbelief was part of "...a phenomenon that would mark virtually every 'trial of the century' for the next hundred years...." The female suspect was "championed" as a "'poor, stricken girl' who was 'innocent and blameless.'"[6] This doesn't mean Mary or Addie had anything to do with their parents' death, simply that Bryant didn't have enough information to know either way.

What happened after the girls made it to Cook's house is not clear at this point in the reporting. Certainly the Cook family was awakened, and Alice was put to bed and cared for while Mr. Cook set out to notify the neighbors and the authorities. Sheriff Julian was telegraphed from Barber Junction, and, with a posse of citizens, he left for the scene of the murder. But it wasn't explained why it took so long for the sheriff to get the message. Editor Julian wrote that his father was notified of the murders around 4 a.m. and "...immediately called out a half dozen deputies and drove at break-neck speed to Barber's Junction."[A] Addie recalled in 1974 that Mr. Cook went to the depot, and it "weren't long before hundreds and hundreds of people were there. There was such a mob of people."[C] According to Bryant's account, men and women began to assemble at the Lyerly home by 12:30. But testimony later quoted during the State's investigation put the first ones there at about 4:00 a.m. More likely, the first neighbors arrived right after midnight, followed later by officers and others from Salisbury, which was about ten miles west of the Lyerly home.

Around 6:00 a.m., Mr. R. A. Miliken, telegraph operator at Barber Junction, wired Colonel Arrington, Governor Glenn's secretary, to inform him of the murders. The governor was vacationing in New Jersey at the time. Miliken's telegram, containing several errors of fact, as well as some assumptions, was reprinted in the Raleigh *N&O* as follows:

> *An unknown man entered the house of Ike Lyerly, a most peaceful farmer at this place about three o'clock this morning, killing Lyerly, his wife and three children, ages raging from three to fourteen years, setting fire to*

*the house and is still at large. Two older daughters sleeping up stairs were awakened by the flames and smoke beneath and courageously extinguished the flames, saving the five dead bodies from being burned. There being no officer at law in this place and I being train dispatcher on duty, the neighbors have asked me to telegraph you to have bloodhounds sent here at once. I have made an effort to secure hounds at Charlotte and Salisbury but of no avail.* [D]

Colonel Arrington, acting in Governor Glenn's stead, reportedly took some immediate steps to help local authorities deal with the murders. Upon learning that the penitentiary's bloodhounds were only puppies, others were secured from Winston-Salem and dispatched instantly to the "scene of the horrible crime," said the *N&O*. Colonel Arrington was also informed that Sheriff Julian was already on the scene, "making every effort possible to discover the perpetrator of the crime." The "State offered a reward of $350 for the capture of the criminals." [D]

Greensboro's *Industrial News* said more about the dogs, which highlighted problems with the crime scene. It said Deputy Sheriff Hutchins of Winston-Salem "carried his bloodhounds to Barber Junction on a special train" and arrived there at about 8 a.m, and Sheriff Julian also arrived about the same time with bloodhounds from Salisbury. "The crowd gathered there, however, prevented the dogs from doing any effective work" — they "could do nothing toward finding the criminals, as many people had thronged around." [E] No report questioned why this contamination of the crime scene had been allowed. In fact, all except Greensboro's Republican paper ignored the issue altogether. One thing clarified by this report and others is that there were definitely a number of people at the Lyerly home before the sheriff arrived, though there were later attempts to cover up or downplay that scenario. Julian's paper said the victims, besides Alice, had been "beyond all mortal help and their bodies were not disturbed, pending the arrival of Coroner Dorsett." [A] This may have been the case where the bodies were concerned, but not so for the crime scene itself.

This type of negligence was not uncommon, nor was the problem exclusive to the rural South. A similar scenario occurred fourteen years earlier with the Lizzie Borden case, right in the town of Fall River, Massachusetts. Within an hour of that axe murder, "...friends, neighbors, physicians, policemen, and reporters tried to enter the house," and the "...sloppiness in protecting the crime scene would come back to haunt..." City Marshal Rufus Hilliard, the first officer on the scene. His mishandling of the situation would "...remain a stain on his reputation and that of the Fall River police." [6] If there was any such criticism of Salisbury or Rowan County officers, it was not in the papers.

An 1885 incident in Chatham County, North Carolina, made Salisbury seem like deja vu all over again, except for the way the cases were investigated. If you travel east, almost in a straight line, from Barber Junction to Salisbury, and then beyond through Pittsboro, North Carolina, you'll pass the site of another mass lynching of black Americans. It too followed a multiple axe murder. This one happened before the reign of Jim Crow, however, and considerable time, actually months, was taken to gather and analyze evidence before any arrests were made. Chatham's commissioners even authorized $1,000 to hire "the best detective agency in the South" to help solve the crime. In what seems like an extraordinary precaution for the time, a piece of clothing with questionable blood spots was sent to Philadelphia for analysis. [7] But two decades later, things were very different in North Carolina.

In the end, the contamination of the crime scene may have been the main reason the case was never solved, because it prevented the blood hounds from doing a job they were better at than one might imagine. Even in modern times, they're considered to be excellent trackers— "nature's finest detectives," they're called. There's even been a movement to bring back their use due to their unique ability to track airborne scents. One recent online story includes a photo with a caption that reads: "Ahead by a nose: bloodhounds follow scent left in the air and tracked one fugitive 13 days after he left a trail. A burglar was found even though he had driven home in a car." [8]

While the *Post* and the *Observer* seem to have ignored the bloodhound issue, a smaller Salisbury paper ran a brief follow-up to the *Industrial News'* story. The *Carolina Watchman,* noting that nothing more had been said in the papers about the hounds, claimed a resident on the scene that day had commented on the situation. It said George Anderson told the *Watchman* that "'A bunch was brought from Salisbury and a pair or more from Winston. The Rowan man did not turn his a-loose, but the Winston fellow released his and after an hour and a half of hard running, succeeded in collaring them; this he considered good fortune.'" [9] Anderson, a resident of neighboring Iredell County, was a member of Coroner Dorsett's jury during the inquest held at the Lyerly home later that day. Apparently none of the hounds led the officers to the homes of the accused sharecroppers, who lived within a few hundred feet of the murder scene.

In 1906, there appeared to be little else to go on—just bloodhounds, footprints or shoe prints, and eyewitness accounts. The science of fingerprinting was barely on the brink of being developed for use in criminal forensics. The technique had been used the previous year to clear up an identification mixup in a prison. The Army began using fingerprints in 1904, and by 1906, the Navy did too. In his book published ten years earlier, Mark Twain's Puddin' Head Wilson solved a crime using his own system of fingerprinting. The story, though fiction, detailed how anyone could have collected this evidence and used it to at least rule out suspects in 1906. If the technology had been used, and the evidence left untouched, it might have solved the crime, for there must have been fingerprints left on the axe handle—the bloody one they found lying under the porch. Though Salisbury officials proceeded like they knew nothing about the value of fingerprints, the *Salisbury Post*, incredibly, mentioned it in passing in a story it ran the following month. "A 'Jack the Ripper' murder was committed in the Bowery district early this morning," it said. "An easy clue to the murderer is a bloody thumb print on the sheet." [10]

Given the information about bloodhounds and the certain knowledge in 1906 of their tracking ability, it seems negligent that local authorities, constable E.A. Barber (Isaac's nephew) for one, didn't try harder to protect the crime scene until the dogs arrived, or that these dogs were not more readily accessible. Perhaps it was too easy to blame the nearest and most vulnerable suspects, with no real repercussions to officers who happened to arrest the wrong people, especially if they were people of color.

Nevertheless, one testimony in particular may have justified the arrests made. Henry Mayhew, Nease Gillespie's eleven-year-old stepson, implicated the families who had worked and lived on Isaac's farm, some his own kin, as well as George Ervin, who simply lived and worked at a sawmill nearby. McNeill paraphrased Henry's statement as follows:

> *He said that the elder Gillespie and his son John killed Mr. Lyerly, his wife and the little boy, Jonnie, and fatally injured the little girl, who died this evening, and that the other negroes arrested were implicated in the commission of the tragedy. He told the plain story as to how they entered the house at an early hour in the evening carrying with them two axes to do the bloody work with. After committing the deed they set fire to the bed clothing by pouring kerosene oil on the bed from a lamp and leaving the house to be burned with the dead parents and children. Their expectation was that the remaining three children who were asleep upstairs would be burned alive.* [B]

It was just one of several versions of what Henry supposedly told a neighbor, Mr. Walton, on the morning after the murders and then, later that evening, several officers who were investigating the crime. Other versions, also said to be Henry's words, say Nease killed the parents and Jack killed the children, and John, who was only fifteen, was implicated as an accessory to the crime along with three others.

And even more was said that day to vilify the suspects. As the neighbors gathered in the early hours of the morning, they discussed rumors of arguments Nease Gillespie and Jack Dillingham and his wife Della had supposedly had with Isaac and Augusta. Which is why, before the sheriff and his men even arrived, the crowd had convicted and tried its own suspects.

Bryant recorded his version of the conversations already spreading like wildfire throughout the crowd and beyond. Isaac's surviving children and several neighbors told Bryant what they had heard about Isaac's dispute with his tenants over the wheat crop.

According to Bryant, Matt Webb, Mary's beau, had worked with Nease Gillespie and overheard him say, "Old man Lyerly can cut that wheat and thrash it but he will never eat it or get the money for it." [B] One of Matt's living grandsons believes this

quote is an accurate representation of what Matt said, not the
twisted version later publicized—that Lyerly would not *live* to
enjoy the wheat. Joseph Lyerly said he'd heard his father discuss
the incident and shared his version of the conversation with
Bryant as well. Bryant paraphrased it.

> *Nease Gillespie, who is a saw mill hand for Mr.*
> *John Dellinger, moved into one of Mr. Isaac Lyerly's*
> *cabins last fall. He, his son and step-son agreed to work*
> *so much land if they took the house. A section for wheat*
> *was laid off. The Gillespies sowed part of this, but*
> *finding that they could get plenty of work at good wages*
> *[elsewhere] did not sow the entire lot. This, not being*
> *according to contract, worried Mr. Lyerly, who spoke to*
> *Nease and was, in turn, cursed. Finally, however, the*
> *matter was settled by Mr. Dellinger, the saw mill owner,*
> *agreeing to pay house rent for Gillespie. Nothing more*
> *was heard of the wheat until some time ago when it had*
> *been cut by Mr. Lyerly who was preparing to....* [B]

The rest is illegible, but other reports say Joseph told Bryant
that Isaac was preparing to thresh the wheat and keep the profits
for himself. Those same reports correct Bryant's misspelling of
the name of the sawmill owner, John Nelson Penninger.

PENNINGER'S SAWMILL

Bryant, like other white reporters in 1906, used "Mr." only when referring to white men. Gillespie's name was recorded as "Nease" or "Gillespie," but never preceded by "Mr." This systematic omission of "Mister" when referring to non-whites was customary during Jim Crow's rule. [11]

When Bryant continued his version of Joseph's story, he slipped in a few incriminating paraphrases along with the quotes.

> *"Monday Nease Gillespie went down to Mr. Lyerly's home and asked him what he was going to do with the wheat.*
> *'Why, I am going to thrash it and use it,' said Mr. Lyerly.*
> *"'You will not,' declared Nease."*
> *Hot words followed and Mr. Lyerly ordered the negro out of his yard. It was here Gillespie told his landlord that he would kill him or die in the attempt if he used the wheat without giving him a share of it.*
> *It was after this that Nease told Mr. Webb that Mr. Lyerly might cut the wheat, but he would never eat or sell it. Gillespie had been very insolent to Mr. Lyerly.* [B]

What was Mr. Gillespie thinking? That is, if he said what Bryant said he said. Maybe he *did* threaten Isaac, but that just sounds crazy. Why would he? Maybe Nease had a special relationship with these neighbors—they probably all knew his white daddy or granddaddy, who could have been Isaac's granddaddy as well. Maybe everybody knew Nease had a quick temper and that what he said when he was mad meant nothing. Or maybe he meant it, and he didn't care what happened to him after what "they" did to two young boys—both named Gillespie—a few years ago. Maybe he'd just learned that Isaac had something to do with that—what he'd suspected all along—and being cheated out of his hard work now was the last straw. Normally it would have been suicidal for any black, rich or poor, to threaten a white landlord—or white of any class. Maybe Bryant got carried away when he recorded Joseph's testimony, little of which was quoted. Surely had Nease said such things and meant it, some immediate action would have been taken by the law or the neighborhood, if anyone had believed he was serious.

Leon Litwick's *Trouble In Mind* documents race relations during the Jim Crow era and explains the fear white people had of the "Negro" in the South after Reconstruction, which was, roughly, the ten years following the end of the Civil War. Paramount was the panic over the misconception that whites were losing control and social status to people they believed to be inferior. Thus any form of "back talk" or "impudence" was perceived as an attack or exaggerated insult. Questioning, cursing, arguing, standing up to whites, or sometimes even looking a white person in the eye could mean death to a black citizen during those times. Litwack's book cites numerous testimonies and incidents of violence towards blacks for what whites deemed as uppityness. [12]  So the angry words of the sharecroppers, it seems, would have, more than likely, been seen as serious threats, whatever the men might have meant by their words—even if they'd just been blowing off steam due to the frustration most sharecroppers faced. This understanding of the status quo makes the reports of Nease's and Jack's alleged threats seem that much more bizarre.

The Lyerly girls told a story similar to Joseph's—but without Nease's alleged threats. Mary and Addie said they overheard an argument between their father and Nease's sons, Henry Lee and John. They said Isaac told the Gillespies they must sow the wheat or get off his land. Mary and Addie also recounted an argument they said they heard between their mother and Jack's wife, Della, concerning the use of a washtub. Recounting that incident, Bryant used his words, not theirs.

> *Friday Mrs. Lyerly had trouble with Dillingham's wife, who was taken to task for leaving dirty water in a wash tub, which had been loaned to her. The negress became mad and abusive.* [B]

Both Mary and Addie claimed they heard Della threaten their mother, swearing, "'If she says another word, I'll down her.'" [B] But it may have been the Lyerly family's clothes that dirtied the washtub in the first place. Wives of tenant farmers were often expected to take care of the landlord's laundry, among other things, including his sexual needs, in exchange for the privilege of living on his property or for food or some minor compensation.

According to Bryant, it was the Dillinghams, not the Gillespies, the girls suspected in the first place. Everything they said implicated them, much more so than the other suspects. Most reports named Dillingham's house as the one they had feared passing on their way to Cook's. They didn't mention the Gillespies at all at first, and though they later seemed to know about the disagreement over the crop, the only threat they recalled was Della's against their mother. Nobody, other than Henry Mayhew, expressed complaints about George Ervin, but he was blamed along with the others.

The neighbors who heard all this that morning were so riled they decided to take matters into their own hands and showed up early at Nease's house to sieze him. But he wasn't home. He'd gone to work at the sawmill about a mile away. However, Bryant said, Nease's wife, Fannie, ran to the home of farmer Dick File, who lived near the old Highway 801. He said Fannie got so scared, she went to File for protection, "...saying that she would be hanged for killing the Lyerlys when she had nothing to do with it." Bryant quoted Mrs. Gillespie as saying, "'I don't know nothing about it, but my husband does.'" [B] But he didn't clarify to whom she said this—whether he heard it himself or simply quoted hearsay. He described Mrs. Gillespie as "...hysterical and wild," and said "She talked two ways, but the officers believe that she gave her husband away to Mr. File." He also didn't identify who described her as "a fussy negro." [B] Bryant never made it clear where he got all of this information.

Now in his 80s, another Barber Junction resident remembers Dick File from his childhood. He says File lived about two miles from the Lyerly home, which means Fannie had to go some distance to get to his place, and it's assumed she traveled by foot. The resident recalls only that File was childless, and he had a horse named Old Bert. And another thing. "He would stare right at you, never batting an eye—said he did this so he'd know you when he saw you again." File would later tell the prosecutor that Fannie had indeed come to his house and said pretty much what Bryant reported on July 14th, but Bryant was the one who recorded *that* conversation as well.

Another paper agreed that Fannie had implicated her husband. The *Greensboro Industrial News* said Gillespie's wife claimed "...her husband and the other two negroes, who have formerly worked for Mr. Lyerly, 'plotted' at the well after bed time" for the past few nights. [F]

The *Industrial News'* version of the alleged dispute between Nease and Isaac was similar to other accounts, including another distorted version of Webb's statement. Using Nease Gillespie's alias, Graham, it said he "...made some agreement with Mr. Lyerly in the fall as regards a piece of land. Graham, failing to conform to some condition, was ousted and ordered to give up all his interest, and it was only a few days ago that this negro, it is stated, made the remark that 'Mr. Lyerly had cut his wheat, but would never live to enjoy any benefit therefrom.'" [F] Webb's original statement had again been exaggerated from a threat on Isaac's crop to a threat on his life.

Though the meaning of another testimony is unclear, Isaac must have insulted Jack. Bryant said Mary and Addie told the officers about a conversation they overheard or were told about. Their father, Bryant said, "had been after Dillingham about being trifling when the negro told him that he was going to leave and go to work at the saw mill." To this, Mr. Lyerly answered: "'Yes, if you go there and work five days right straight along I will set you up.' This seemed to rile Dillingham, for he told some one that, except for the reason that he lived on the old man's place, he would have given him a cursing." [B]

Cursing Isaac was one thing, killing him another. Nevertheless, after all of these stories circulated through the crowd, the people "who were looking for motives thought that Jack Dillingham and his wife should be arrested," along with the Gillespies. [B] And certainly, before noon, Nease Gillespie and his two teenaged sons, Henry Lee and John Gillespie, along with Jack and Della Dillingham and George Ervin, were in custody.

Josephus Daniels, who owned and edited Raleigh's *N&O* had his own way of reporting the news. Daniels' paper didn't bother with interviews—at least not until Caldwell's coverage of the story made his look pretty bad. The *N&O* came right out with blatant assumptions in its first report on the Lyerly murder case. Headlining the story as "Crimson Horror Shocks Carolina" in bold, one-inch type, it stated, unequivocally, that the tenant farmers "...had threatened the life of Mr. Lyerly because he harvested the wheat crop neglected by them." This writer, whoever he was, assumed the victims heads had been crushed by an axe, "the property of Mr. Lyerly." The unidentified reporter also predicted there was "...little prospect of a lynching, as Governor Glenn had instructed the sheriff to call out the Rowan Rifles in the event of trouble." [C]

The *Industrial News* offered several more interesting twists to the plot not mentioned in any other main reports. It ran an interview with Deputy Sheriff Hutchins, who, it said, arrived on the scene from Winston-Salem (Forsyth County) with his bloodhounds at about 8 a.m. According to this account, Hutchins said that as soon as he arrived at the Lyerly home "one of the negroes had been arrested." But the paper didn't say which one. Then it said Hutchins, in "...an interview with the wife of Mitchell Graham," received "...information which led to the arrest of another negro at whose house [was found] a pair of trousers on which was considerable blood [that had] apparently rubbed off of the man's hands." To this the paper added that Fannie Gillespie had implicated "...at least two of the parties under arrest." [F] Neither of these were named. As significant as all this may seem, it did not appear in most other papers in the state or elsewhere, besides Winston-Salem, where the story probably originated. Nor was this specific and incredibly damning "evidence" mentioned again anywhere, including accounts of testimonies later heard by the state solicitor. So it's likely this scenario was fabricated. I had eventually come to view the *Winston-Salem Journal* as one of the more sensational sources of information, though it filled in a few blanks from time to time.

The Hutchins interview, found only in the Greensboro and Winston-Salem papers, does conform to most other reports about the use of an axe. Hutchins allegedly told the *Industrial News* the axe "was taken from the wood pile and after the crime was thrown under the porch," which was basically the same story reported elsewhere. But this version also says the "negro woman further told Mr. Hutchins that after she retired last night she heard her husband, who was in the next room, get up and leave the house and that she never heard him come back; that she knew her husband, her son, and Dillingham were going to kill somebody, but did not know whom; that her son left home early this morning, and that the officers would not get him. In the meantime, her son was caught trying to board a freight train." [F]

The part about trying to catch the freight train turned out to be confirmed by other very brief reports that weren't highly publicized. And there may have been a reason for that. It would not seem logical for Fannie's sons to have waited until the next morning to try to catch a train out of town, *if* they had known about the murder earlier. This attempt to escape the next morning implies that they were innocent—that they had known nothing before anyone else had known it. The white press (which is the only press of any consequence left in the state after 1898), overall, did not highlight anything that implied any of the suspects' innocence.

The relationship among the Gillespies is confusing, to say the least. Editor Julian eventually cleared up the issue about Nease's name, which census records support, but the rest is still somewhat muddy. Mitchell Graham and Fannie Gillespie were both living in the Mt. Ulla Township of Rowan in 1870, and more than likely they grew up knowing each other. When they later married, Mitchell or Mich, now calling himself Nease, took Fannie's last name. But Fannie's name in the census records is listed as Mary, except when she was a child, that is if Fannie is the Mary that Nease was married to in 1880. The couple, Nease and Mary Gillespie, is almost certainly Mich Graham and Fannie Gillespie, because their household is listed right next to Fannie's parents, whose household Fannie was a part of ten years earlier (with her name listed as Fannie). Nease had apparently assumed a brother's first name at some point—the 1870 census records show he had a brother named Neaze Graham. But in the 1900 census, Nease is definitely using his original name, Mich Graham. This listing in Iredell County is the most reliable, because it shows the other members of Mich's household to be Mary, his wife; John, his nine-year-old son; and Henry, his four-year-old. Clearly, six years later, John and Henry are living with Nease and Fannie, and their ages correspond correctly. Also noteworthy is the listing for one of Mich's neighbors, just a couple of entries below Mich's on the same census page—a white man named Absalom Mayhew.

The Gillespie family relationships were further addressed later, during Fannie's testimony before the solicitor, which Bryant quoted.

> 'I have been married to Nease four years. We have lived together 20 years. Me and Nease and John and little Henry lived together. John is 15 years old. I am his grandma and Nease is his paw, by one of my girls.' [G]

According to Bryant, Fannie also said: "'I raised Henry Mayhew, the little boy,'" indicating he was he too was her grandson, but not related to Nease. [G] But later records show that Henry was Fannie's son. The "son" caught trying to board a train, referred to in Hutchins' testimony, was probably Henry Mayhew, which later testimony supports. And the other son referred to in this interview, the one who supposedly plotted the murder with Nease and Jack, is apparently meant to be John, though at this point, there's nothing printed to confirm this.

The alleged Hutchins testimony further conflicts with other reports of Henry Mayhew's statement, which says he learned about the murders *after* Nease, Jack, and John returned home and told everything they had done.

The Hutchins interview adds another very interesting piece to the puzzle, though Hutchins must have received it second hand, since he supposedly didn't arrive on the scene until 8 a.m. He told the paper that "When the officers arrived at Graham's [Nease Gillespie's] house about 6 o'clock this morning they found the woman washing, the clothing being in a pot, boiling. The clothes were taken out at once, but if there had been any blood stains on them they had been boiled out. All the apparel in the pot was men's underwear." [F] Hutchins' must not have done much laundry—his conclusion about the wash doesn't necessarily hold water. My mother taught me that blood stains are not removed by boiling—at least not without a good soaking in cold water first. Hot water will actually set the stain.

Jack was a murderer—someone supposedly told Hutchins. Jack, he said, "...told several negroes in the neighborhood that he killed a farmer near Roanoke [Virginia] some time ago." —a fact Julian's report corroborates, adding that Jack told Gillespie he had served time for this offence. Hutchins' source also said Jack

"...had been at Barber Junction for fifteen or twenty days, and Wednesday [two days before the murders] Mr. Lyerly discharged him for abusing a horse."[F] If Jack did indeed commit murder and pay for it with time, rather than his life, the victim must have been black. However, neither source included any documentation to support any of these assertions.

The Dillinghams *were* new to the area, apparently. This situation, if true, would carry some significance, since the Dillinghams could not have had the same neighborly ties as those who were born in Rowan County. Although one of Addie's living relatives insists her grandparents and their tenant farmers had all been on neighborly terms, she also believed, at least for many years, that all six of the accused were involved in the murder of her grandparents.

The *Industrial News* certainly sized up the situation correctly in concluding that "reports from the scene of the tragedy are conflicting."[F] Despite all the confusion, this much is certain: once Sheriff Julian and his deputies arrived at the site that morning, they wasted little time arresting five males and one woman for the crimes. Nease Gillespie and his sons, John and Henry Lee Gillespie (not Henry Mayhew), Jack and Della Dillingham, and George Ervin were taken into custody as murder suspects and transported to the Salisbury jail within hours of the officers' arrival. [13]

# 4

# THE INQUEST

## SATURDAY AFTERNOON, JULY 14

*This kind of inquisition violates the spirit of the Constitution.*
— Albert Einstein

SHERIFF DAVID R. JULIAN

While the crowd was gathered at the Lyerly home on the day after the attack, Coroner E. Rose Dorsett, from nearby Cleveland, held the inquest into the cause of the murders. The jurors, B.A. Knox, W.F. Thompson, M.F. Pyler, R.B. Harris, George R. Anderson (the one who had talked to the *Watchman* about the bloodhounds), and Arthur Thompson assisted Dorsett. They concluded that "...the Lyerlys were murdered with axes in the hands of Nease Gillespie, his son, John, Jack Dillingham and wife and George Ervin and Henry Lee." [A] Assuming the paper recorded the verdict correctly, those seven men decided that all six suspects were in that one bedroom, some swinging axes at about the same time. If so, they must have had the thing very well choreographed and practiced to not have killed each other in the process.

The verdict was as fast as it was illogical—really fast, considering the lack of eyewitnesses or conclusive evidence. But this was normal for the time, said Ronald Singer of The American Academy of Forensic Sciences. He said, in 1906, the inquest was usually a "done deal..., held only to legitimize what had already been decided." [1] What *was* decided at the Lyerly inquest left a lot of unanswered questions.

One question concerns the weapon or weapons used. The murder came to be known only as an axe murder, but several reports said a club or blunt instrument was used. McNeill's vivid description of the family's wounds definitely pointed to the use of both ends of an axe blade, as well as an axe handle. But he also wrote that one wound appeared to be made by a club. In the early reports about the murders, the weapon varied with the source. Even one version of Mary Lyerly's testimony, given under oath months later, said the murders were committed with blunt instruments. Fairbanks, Alaska's *Daily Times*, apparently getting its information from Winston-Salem, stated that the family members had been "clubbed to death." [B] But once Henry's story became widespread and established as "fact," the "blunt instrument" scenario was dropped until after the lynching.

Bryant had reported at some point, that on the day after the murders and after Henry's so-called confession, the boy led some officers to a place where Nease's axe lay, and that they said it looked bloody, though it was mostly just rusted. They assumed, however, it had rusted overnight after being rinsed off in the stream. So whether accurate or not, the murder scenario eventually came to be seen this way: It was committed by all six of the accused, with Nease using his own axe and Jack using Isaac's—one left in the woodpile. Della held the lamp, and God only knows what role the other three played, but, as the verdict declared, they had to have been involved—maybe just because they were black and lived nearby, or because they were related to Nease. Fannie somehow escaped criminal charges, perhaps because she was deemed more valuable as a witness than a suspect. Either way, she went to jail.

The most obvious question is "why?" The press explored the possibilities for the motive and decided on revenge by default. Those arriving at this verdict, however, were already aware of the rumored threats attached to Nease and Jack. "It was the general conclusion," McNeill said, "that the crime was committed in malice propense: that there was no other motive assignable for it. There was no robbery. A purse containing $2 or $3 was left on the mantel piece, and money in a bureau drawer and money in Mr. Lyerly's pocket was not taken." [A]  But his observation doesn't prove no money was stolen, because money could have been stored in other places in the house. And it doesn't take into account who really benefitted financially from these murders, which appears to have been Joseph Lyerly.

In Twain's story about the murder solved by fingerprinting, officials investigating that case also concluded, at first, that revenge was the motive, because they assumed money had not been stolen when it had been. So they went after a distinguished newcomer who was known to have been feuding with the victim. As it turned out in the fictional story, the killer had planned to take more money, but he heard someone stirring in the house and ran. [2]  Nevertheless, Bryant, who was surely familiar with Twain's work, also supported the general conclusion, the same as McNeill's: "Revenge seems to have been the motive for the bloody murder. There were more than $150 in house, and not a cent of it was taken." [C] Bryant also failed to explain why he was so sure of exactly how much money Isaac had in the house.

Interestingly, the Alaska paper, following Winston-Salem's lead, wrote that the murderers "robbed the house" before setting fire to it. [B]  Mississippi's *Laurel Ledger* ran the same story, ver batim, on July 20th. Though not very reliable on other details about the case, Richmond's *Times-Dispatch* also asserted that robbery was one motive, implying that Nease had known about $400 that Ike had earned on the recent sale of his crop. [3] Which seems to be supported by the other reports concerning Isaac's sale of the wheat crop. Whatever the reason, everyone in the press had prematurely decided, based on conflicting and circumstantial evidence, that the officials had the murderers in custody.

The most intriguing and suspicious "evidence" heard by the jurors, later in evening, was the testimony given by, taken from, or suggested to Henry Mayhew, who was said to have been among the crowd at the murder scene all day. That is, after he was apparently dragged back there from the train depot at Barber Junction. McNeill wrote that Henry, "...on being questioned this evening...became frightened and made a confession to constable E.A. Barber, Isaac Lyerly's nephew, and in the presence of W.A. Thompson and others." [A] The *Salisbury Post* (in an issue missing from the filmed archives) reveals that Henry had been "subjected to a severe examination" all afternoon before "confessing" what he knew about the crimes. [D] Perhaps it was the examination itself that had frightened Henry, though Deputy Goodman later reported that *he* had worried local blacks would harm Henry because of this testimony. It was not reported here or in any other paper until over a half year later that Constable Barber had gone to the Dillingham home and threatened to burn it down if the Dillinghams refused to go with him to the murder scene. Though it is not known what threat if any was made on eleven-year-old Henry's life before he gave his "confession" that night, evidence would later reveal that there was a lot not right about it.

The approximate time of the murder varies with reports, though all supposedly reflect Mayhew's words. McNeill's version says the suspects "...entered the house at an early hour in the evening," which is not specific, but definitely would not mean ten or eleven p.m. or later, as indicated in other accounts. If the testimony of the girls is accurate, making their arrival at Cook's home around midnight, then the killing must have occurred late, rather than early, in the evening.

And something else is off. Considering the threat to any black who committed a crime in those days, it's odd that none of these reporters asked why the accused, had they committed the murders, hadn't left the area, knowing they'd be the first blamed. Had they even known about the murders, guilty or not, they would likely have been long gone by morning, especially if Nease had made the threats he was said to have made and especially with railway lines so close by. The barely publicized report about John and Henry trying to catch the train the next day further supports suspicions about the scenario most prominently presented to the public.

Did the killer or killers spare the girls upstairs only because they expected them to perish when the house burned? As close as Jack and Nease lived to the Lyerly house, if they were involved and wanted the house and the remaining children destroyed, certainly they were watching and aware that it didn't catch fire as they expected. This would have alerted them to either return and finish the job or get out of town quickly. Henry Mayhew reportedly overheard Nease say after killing the Lyerlys, that, "Their expectation was that the remaining three children who were asleep upstairs would be burned alive." [A] This undermines the credibility of Henry's story, for if Nease *et al* had intended for the others to die in the flames, they could have easily accomplished that goal. Perhaps whoever committed the crimes either did not know the girls were upstairs or had fled the area and were unaware that the house had not burned. Or maybe the murderer was insane or someone who did not want the older girls harmed. It's even possible that the burning of the house was staged. Whatever the case, Nease, Jack, and Della lived so close to the Lyerly house, they would have known, by sight and by smell, if it had gone up in flames.

Former Rowan Deputy Sheriff, Eric Solomon, investigated the site of the Lyerly property in 2002 and 2003 and located the foundation of one of the tenant houses which he estimates to be between 300 and 500 yards from the Lyerly house. Solomon suggests the possibility that the murderers might have gotten drunk either before or after the killing and been oblivious to what happened afterward. But it's doubtful Nease got drunk enough to pass out and still arise at the crack of dawn and head off to work the next morning.

In the *Observer*'s film archives, an almost illegible article discusses these very issues. An unnamed lawyer, puzzling over the case, told the reporter it was the most intriguing he'd ever heard. He too wondered why the accused, if they were indeed the murderers, had not returned to finish the job. The *Statesville Landmark* was the only paper to venture a guess.

> *There are two theories as to why the girls sleeping up stairs were not killed when the others were killed; One is that they were supposed to be away from home: the other that it was expected they would be burned with the house while they slept.* [4]

Sometime late in the afternoon or past nightfall, right after Mayhew told his story, the eleven-year-old was taken into custody as a witness. Fannie was also taken for the same reason some time that day. The six suspects, however, had been arrested much earlier, *before* Mayhew's testimony implicated them. Later, at the Solicitor's investigation, it was reported that some of the white men took Nease over to examine tracks in the cornfield that morning, tracks they said matched one of his heel-less shoes perfectly. But the source didn't make the point that the cornfield was located near Nease's cabin, and he more than likely traveled through it regularly, perhaps on his way to work that morning.

Henry Mayhew had evidently told his story to several people at the scene. One was Deputy Charlie A. Goodman, who years later, at age 79, recalled what happened:

> *"I picked up a Negro youth, Henry Mahew who told me that his grandfather had come to his house late the night before and said: "Well, we killed them all!" Later, the boy told the same story to the coroner and others."* [5]

Goodman's great granddaughter, Susan Sides, in her essay on the Lyerly murders, told how her ancestor had hidden Mayhew "in the bottom of his carriage" and carried him to safety. Goodman was the deputy who said he feared some blacks in the community might try to kill Henry because of his testimony. [6]

Henry, Fannie, and the sextet of suspects were all taken to the Rowan County Jail at first, and all except Fannie and Della, and perhaps Mayhew, were removed later that evening by Sheriff D.R. Julian and his son, Deputy D.W. Julian (the editor's brother), to the Mecklenburg County Jail in Charlotte for safekeeping. It was the expected thing to do in those days, with lynchings so common all over the South. They boarded the No. 29 southbound passenger train from the off side at the Salisbury depot and were greeted in Charlotte by Deputy Sheriff Johnson who took all of the prisoners into custody, under the care of Sheriff Wallace. The move was kept secret by the Julians, who returned to Salisbury very late that same night to find that if they hadn't moved the prisoners, they might have all been lynched by the next morning. [A, D]

Some were concerned the prisoners wouldn't be safe, even in Charlotte. But Bryant, a long-time resident, said he believed "Charlotte people are generally law-abiding" and "...the negroes will be safe here." [A] Even so, others, a few days later, expressed more concern—one saying the mob had taken up a collection to finance the trip to Charlotte.

CR&O

Before he left the Lyerly property on July 14th, McNeill noted that the crowd had grown constantly throughout the day, and along with the numbers, grew the desire for evidence and revenge. "The men who went inside to see the situation came out with dark countenances," McNeill said, "and with the frequent remark that hanging is too good for the unspeakable brute who did this deed." As he left to head towards Salisbury, he "...met a dozen buggies" and said "parties of men" were "beating the neighborhood for evidence." [A]

Afterward, the press continued to add fuel to the already roaring fire. An unidentified *N&O* correspondent said the "four dead bodies, as they are being prepared for burial by a Salisbury undertaker, present a ghastly sight, sickening in the extreme." Oddly no other source mentioned an undertaker, and if there had been, would he have allowed the reporter to observe the procedure? The same reporter re-emphasized the horror saying, "hundreds of citizens from all over Rowan visited the scene of the terrible tragedy today, and many stout hearts were seen to fail when the ghastly sight was beheld." [7]

Of course, adding to the neighbors' outrage, was the dreadful victimization of the children and the emotional accounts of the three "little" girls who survived the horrors. Nevertheless, McNeill's final words that day were appropriately heart-rending, for no one should have to lose their loved ones in such a way. Mary and Addie "were at the inquest this afternoon," he said, "sweet-faced girls, with gentle voices. The fire was perhaps a fortunate circumstance for them," he surmised.

*...their fight with it seems to have averted the shock, which they must have sustained otherwise. They dictated their evidence and signed it quietly, and it was only when a friend came up to Mary and kissed her without a word that tears sprang into her eyes and she sobbed. Oh, it was pitiful.* A

Richmond's *Times-Dispatch,* however, played on the "stricken little girls" theme to the point of absurdity. In several early reports, the paper made the common and probably innocent errors of portraying the survivors as younger than their actual ages and characterizing Henry Mayhew's testimony as a "confession," from one of the *accused,* rather than an alleged witness. But the paper further misinformed readers, asserting that Henry's "confession" revealed a plan to "capture the surviving little girls and burn them alive." Recapping the story a month after the murders, when reporters had had plenty of time to get their facts straight, the *Times-Dispatch* recorded Mary and Addie's ages to be "about eight and six years" and went on to describe how the "little tots" had put out the fire, etc. These distortions must have had an explosive effect on those who believed them to be accurate. [8]

The reality of the tragedy was really bad enough without all the embellishment. What Mary, Addie, and Janie endured was more than most adults would ever have to, and John Julian's description of Alice and her wounds was enough to make anyone's blood boil, especially those looking for justification for a lynching.

*At the home of her dead father's neighbor she lay in her night clothes, a great mark extending from the right*

*side of the forehead over the eye to the temple, a great clot of blood covering the ghastly wound that drove away consciousness and meant certain death. She was a fair little thing and the heart of the most hardened melted and broke at the sight of her—the personification of innocence, a victim to the instinct of savagery.* [D]

Though not considered a hotbed for lynching, when compared to other southern states at the time, North Carolina was, nevertheless, no stranger to this torturous ritual. A white man, J.V. Johnson, had just been lynched in nearby Anson county two months earlier, and there were "unsubstantiated" reports of a recent lynching in Rowan of a man known as Snake. "Violence was in the air" on July 14, 1906, Joe Junod wrote years later, "as a huge crowd gathered at the Lyerly homestead.... Men grabbed their rifles and rope; women their children; preachers their Bibles; editors their pens. The murders would be avenged." [9]

Editor Julian's incriminating account certainly didn't have a calming effect. He summed up the situation, ironically, with imagery relating to blood hounds which, in this case, had failed to implicate the accused. Julian didn't distort the statement about the wheat, but he connected it with Jack instead of Nease, demonizing Jack in the process.

> *At the start there was little or no clue upon which to work. Certainly robbery was not the motive.... The first scent of a live trail was found when it became known that negroes who live near the Lyerly home had been at outs with Mr. Lyerly and that one of them—Jack Dillingham—a stout mulatto with a dare-devil countenance—had remarked when Mr. Lyerly cut his wheat that 'maybe he will thresh it but he'll never eat any of it.'* [D]

Most accounts after that either asserted or insinuated that talk of lynching was indeed on the lips of many. "Excitement is intense in the neighborhood," said an Asheville reporter, writing from Barber Junction the day after, "and there is talk of lynching if the criminals are caught." [10] But the *N&O* ignored the heated climate it had helped create and instead published a brief note by the *Associated Press,* stating there was "nothing to indicate a lynching at Salisbury," though Sheriff Julian took the prisoners to Charlotte anyway for "safe keeping." [11]

Though the concept of presumption of innocence got no publicity at all in the days that followed, at least one prominent white Salisbury citizen, John Steele Henderson, questioned the guilt of some of the suspects in a letter he wrote to his wife. The foregone conclusion made at the inquest, however, left an impression that stuck for over a hundred years.

# 5

# A GATHERING STORM

## SATURDAY NIGHT, JULY 14

*Word of the axe murders spread quickly, beginning 24 days of mob rule, injury, fear and more murder in the most spectacular of crimes in Rowan County's 220-year history.*

— Joe Junod, *Salisbury Post*, 1974

MAYOR ARCHIBALD HENDERSON BOYDEN

A fter leaving the Lyerly place on July 14th, where he had so vividly described the dreadful and heart-wrenching scene, McNeill traveled the ten or so miles east into Salisbury where he encountered yet another violent episode.

> *As I begin to write at 10:33 o'clock to-night there is a howling mob about the jail here. It began to form under the electric light at the crossing soon after nightfall.* [A]

Things hadn't started to heat up until right after dark. McNeill and a companion, Charles Mullen, had gone to the town square at Main and Innes Streets around 9:00 or 9:30 and found the street nearly full, with only about fifty men hanging around the jail yard. Someone tried to convince the crowd that the prisoners had been transported by train to Charlotte earlier that evening, but the majority didn't buy it. "'That is all a bluff,' one said. 'We have had the jail watched and nobody has left there. Those murderers are in the jail.' This talk was circulated until the [entire] mob believed it." [A]

McNeill couldn't figure out what exactly it was that finally set them off, but about fifteen minutes after he and his friend arrived at the square, a throng suddenly "broke through the gate and poured into the jail yard." [A] That's when the craziness began.

> *In a few moments it had changed from a sombre, silent, curious company to a mass of yelling, gesticulating men. In the hallway of the jail was a small congregation, not more perhaps than 12 or 15 men. They sprang to their feet as the mob struck the steps, joined hands, and barred the entrance.* [A]

A period photo of the Rowan County Jail shows just how easy it must have been to break through the gate and access the building. The "jail" was actually a house that had been converted into a jail. The structure, soon to be demolished, was then a three-story painted brick building, with six windows on each side and five on the front. The door was surrounded by what appears to be glass panels. The fence was composed of slender slats of wood that looked to rise no higher than three feet from the ground, and the gate appeared to be made of no stronger timber than that used for the fence. Obviously ornamental, the enclosure couldn't have blocked the entry of a child, much less a mob of maniacal men. It makes perfect sense that Sheriff and Deputy Julian smuggled the prisoners to Charlotte.

ROWAN COUNTY JAIL

While the two officers were away, the sheriff's other son tried to stand in for them. *Salisbury Post* editor John Moose Julian appeared on the steps of the jail and attempted to dissuade the mob from its purpose. But it was a futile display that did more harm than good. Julian's plea, instead of calming the mob, conjured up visions of the pitiful, slaughtered children, serving only to further inflame the crowd.

*It was a dastardly crime, he told them. He wept when he saw those little babies, with their heads crushed, and he agreed with the mob that no punishment would be too severe for such brutality.* [A]

At this the mob went wild with cheers and applause, and Julian's attempts to continue were drowned out completely. So in desperation, "He raised his voice to its capacity and proposed that the mob select six men to go through the jail and see if the prisoners they sought were there." But few heard him over all the howling. "Even while the [editor] was talking they cried, 'Crowd up, men, all together; they're in there and we must have them.'" The crowd, McNeill said, "...obeyed one voice as well as another, provided the voice counseled breaking into the jail." [A]

Then things really went nuts.

> *At this point there was a tremendous surge against the door-keepers who stood there as stubborn as iron and held the invaders at bay for ten minutes of strenuous struggle. Then the door guard was crowded in and a score or 25 of the mob got in.* [A]

Here, Julian stepped in and obstructed the flow. And seeing a "fellow with a mask" he declared, "We are taking the name of every man that comes in here." This threat seemed to stun the mob for a moment, and the masked man retreated. [A] They apparently could be identified, in spite of their masks.

Mayor Archibald Boyden took advantage of the brief calm and addressed the crowd, whose members he called his friends and fellow citizens. "'You have got the right men, he declared to them, but they are in Charlotte. I have never deceived you in war or in peace.'" Boyden must have been proud of his service in the Civil War, which he had joined at sixteen, though this crowd couldn't have cared less.

Again unconvinced, they screamed back, "'Bring them down.'" So Boyden tried to appeal to them as their "friend and mayor," explaining that all he wanted was the evidence. But, when someone blurted back, "Hanging is too good for them," Boyden concurred, "'I agree with you. But—(howl)—they are not here, they are in Charlotte.'" [A]

One might argue that the mayor was merely trying to appease the crowd with his encouragement of violence and premature conviction of the accused. But judging by his record, that's probably giving him too much credit. Neither the press nor the court again mentioned his endorsement of lynching that night. Nor was Boyden's association with an earlier lynching brought up when the mob violence was later investigated.

However, reference to these kinds of inflammatory implications by leaders and the press was later made in a Defense motion at the murder trial. That plea fell on deaf ears, as did Mayor Boyden's words that night.

All of the pleas that evening fell on deaf ears, actually, further silenced by the deafening cries from the mob. The crowd would not give in but continued shouting: "Throw them out the window," "Bring 'em," "We've got to have 'em." [A]

Finally, "after a second installment of the mob had broken in," Julian persuaded them to accept his plan to choose six men, a committee, to search the jail. While this was going on, McNeill moved back and "stood out amidst the crowd" and observed. He watched as the light of the searchers passed the windows inside the jail and recorded those next nerve-racking moments.

> They burst the glass from the panels and spattered its fragments over the people below. Every time they shattered a window the mob whooped. Meantime the street had filled with curious citizens, who were cautious and waited and watched in silence. "God dammit," cried a committee man from a corner top window, dark as hades, "we can't find him." "Well," shouted a voice from another window, "We'll have 'em before morning if hell don't freeze over." The jeers and whoopings kept going until the committee of six came down to report. Its mouthpiece was Mr. E.A. Barber. "I am," said he, "Ike Lyerly's nephew." (Cry—"A damned lie, you ain't no kin to him") "I came to lynch these men, with as much blood in my eye as anybody. But they are not here. And I'm sorry." (A voice--"Didn't you kill somebody yourself one time.") Hereupon the heterogenous cry arose, "Did you go everywhere?" "Did you look in the cells?" "Hell, they fooled 'em," "We are here to protect our women," "God damn 'em" [A]

It was becoming increasingly clear that no compromise would quench the mob's thirst for blood, nor evidence convince them of the prisoners' absence, but attempts at calm continued nevertheless. The crowd, McNeill said, "was not satisfied with the report of the first committee and demanded that another search of the jail be carried out by another six men. 'I have three daughters myself,' cried one. 'They have fooled these fellows. Here's a fellow they can't fool.'" Julian, who seemed willing to do anything to get the mob to disperse, consented to a second search and told them to name their men. So another group searched the jail and found nothing, and still another was sent, with the same result. "But the mob would not be convinced. It wanted more and more committees. But nothing seemed to transpire." [A]

Finally, around midnight, most in the crowd tired, and someone shouted, "'Let's go home.'" Then it looked as if the riot was over, when yet another would-be lyncher suggested they search the space beneath the jail. Apparently someone had gotten wind that Della Dillingham and Fannie Gillespie were still in town and being held in the basement.

*When the crush made toward the basement the advocates of law and order got the front door closed. By the back way and otherwise, what was left of the mob at midnight shook the scene, convinced that the prisoners had escaped them, and silence closed down on this most eventful news centre.* [B]

McNeill, who suffered from a chronic health condition, could finally get some rest. But it's doubtful he slept.

෬ಜ

The collection of reports printed the next day reveal that McNeill had been selective about what he disclosed in his report of the lynching attempt. He must have heard quite a few names that night, and though he lived in another city, it's possible he recognized some of the faces in the crowd. Referring to the man who had approached Julian, he said "He was the only masked man I saw," explaining that "The others made no pretense at concealment. They called one another's names clean across the crowd." [A] Despite all the name-calling, either McNeill failed to record any, or the *Observer's* editor, Caldwell, failed to print them.

McNeill *had* mentioned the name of one county resident, who lived near the Lyerly neighborhood and had admittedly come to lynch the prisoners. E.A. Barber was constable of Barber Junction and had participated in the Lyerly murder investigation. He was the man to whom eleven-year-old Henry Mayhew was said to have first "confessed" what he knew about the murders. Barber claimed he was Isaac's nephew, and Lyerly family records confirm it; his mother, Mary Magdelene Lyerly Barber, was Isaac's sister. It's not clear what the crowd accused Barber of that night, but he had gone before the Rowan County Court in 1904 and pled "no contest" to the charge of malfeasance in office. [1] The subsequent slap on the hand apparently had no effect on his later conduct, i.e. his threat to burn down the Dillingham's cottage or break down the door when he showed up there without a warrant the day after the Lyerlys were murdered. [2]

Though the rioters who came to lynch the prisoners finally tired and dispersed late that night, their appetites were left unsatisfied. And it wouldn't have taken much to whet them again. Reporting from Salisbury, an unnamed Greensboro journalist described the mob as a group of "nearly five hundred men and youths of this city," who surrounded the jail and demanded the prisoners be "delivered into their keeping that vengeance, sure and swift, might be wreaked." But when mob leaders learned the suspects had been transferred to Charlotte, "their rage knew no bounds." Though the crowd gave up on finding the prisoners in Salisbury, many left still believing them to be hidden somewhere in the Rowan County Jail. [B]

Either the same or another Greensboro correspondent reported the next day that the crowd had come from homes all over the county. "They were a disgusted, disappointed lot," he said, "and as they departed there was a popular sentiment that it made little difference how many whites were killed by the negroes." [B]

This same report revealed that editor Julian was injured during the commotion, saying the editor "played sheriff" in his father's absence and "pacificator" as well.

*Mr. Julian was in the thickest of the howl, and he
talked and shoved the crowd more than any man in it.
He bears the marks of a fist used upon him in the
general mix up.* [B]

Another Observer article carried more details, some very
telling, about Julian's confrontation. According to this version, a
"veiled coward," armed with a pistol, approached Julian who
"called him a coward and asked him to take off his cover. The
fellow replied:

*"John, I am your friend, if I wasn't I would smash
your face and I reckon I will have to hit you anyway."
He doubled up his fist and smote the editor on the head,
raising a few knots with his knuckles.* [C]

Either Julian didn't recognize the voice and other
characteristics of the man claiming to be his friend, or he knew
who he was and wouldn't tell. The paper claimed "Julian never
knew who did the work and had no way to get back at him." The
report also said Julian's "hidden-faced" attacker threatened to
shoot him, "but was cowed by Julian's sharp abuse of him." [B]
It's not clear what the reporter meant by Julian's "sharp abuse,"
unless he did something other than threaten to take names.

The same account elaborated on Boyden's and McNeill's
performances. It praised Mayor Boyden's wisdom in closing the
saloons "immediately upon the formation of the mob." And this
unidentified reporter revealed a heroic act his colleague had
apparently been too modest to call attention to himself. He said
McNeill, "did a wise thing."

*Leaving the door where the crowd was being stood
off, he went down into the plebeian ranks and after the
committee reported no negro there, McNeill left, saying
"Come on boys, there is nothing doing now. They have
taken the negroes away and fooled us." It had a good
effect for the mob wanted [lacked] another leader.* [C]

Describing the crowd as a "strange assembly" the same report trivialized the event by characterizing the rioters' conduct as "much like that of a few nice old ladies with brooms."

> *...the language was at an entirely inverse ratio to the actions. It was the ribald oath coupled with the simple life. A half-dozen good officers could easily have stood off the hesitating and captainless army.* [C]

It is perhaps this type of understatement that fed the denial that led to the successful attack later.

The same account included a few more details—ones McNeill neglected to mention and which also downplayed the seriousness of the threat. Apparently Salisbury resident and former congressman Theo F. Kluttz got involved in the effort to disband the would-be lynchers. "Kluttz was shoved up in the crowd and asked to make a speech," the report said. "He began it, but hasn't yet finished it."

> *The mob was just powerful enough to break up a speech, but not enough to break down a jail. When the howling crowd drowned him out, Kluttz walked off saying "Let me out of here, where is my umbrella? The mob jeered good-naturedly: "What are you doing there? You ain't got no umbrella."* [C]

The mob's words and actions, along with the paper's portrayal of them, made this serious threat to the lives of six people seem no more than a game.

Bryant may be the author of the report, though it doesn't bear his usual signature. Whoever wrote it didn't seem to mind the embarrassment it may have caused the former congressman. Theo Kluttz's son, who worked for the *Observer* in 1906, was also editor Joseph Caldwell's nephew. McNeill, who freelanced, may have had little contact with Kluttz Jr., but Bryant was said to have disliked him and later tried to get him demoted when Caldwell became too ill to run the paper. [3]

Whoever wrote it didn't conclude the story without condemning the accused, another indication that Bryant might be the author. Referring to Fannie and Della as the women "who will be important witnesses," the paper asserted, without adding, "allegedly," that "one of them held the lamp while Nease Gillespie and Jack Dillingham used the bludgeon." He said E.A. Barber had "told this" to the crowd, and after he did, "there was talk of going to the jail and lynching a woman who was on the ground floor of the county asylum." However, Barber was able to convince them "it would not do to kill the most important witness in the case." Fannie and Della were still in Salisbury that night, but Fannie may have been taken to Charlotte eventually, before the trial began. [C]

Addressing the "confession," the report disclosed what had become of Henry and said the mob had not come looking for him anyway. The statement is again presented as fact, rather than evidence to be examined in court.

> *The little boy of Gillespie, who heard the plot made, who was awake when the men returned from the slaughter and told of their work, who pointed out the spot where the second axe was to be found and where the blood was washed from it, was brought here and sent out in the country on the chain gang for safekeeping.* [C]

Not divulging the source of its next assertion, the account went on to slander one of the suspects.

> *The negro who says his name is Dillingham is a bad one. He has a habit of hiring for a day or two and leaving for a new home. In the spring he worked for Mr. R.L. Thomason a day, then got himself out by his impudence, went to several places in the same neighborhood and each time was driven away, finally going to Barber. He looks the criminal.* [C]

The location of Thomason's farm was not disclosed in the article, but census records show it was in Franklin Township, just east of Unity, Lyerly's neighborhood. The report implied the information on Dillingham came from Thomason, but didn't say so outright.

Even if true, the allegation doesn't necessarily incriminate Dillingham, when judged by today's understanding of the sharecropper scenario—where any black challenge to a white, even if justified, was seen as impudence. Also, if Dillingham had had trouble with several landlords, why would he choose to murder the Lyerlys, in particular, unless that confrontation, if real, had been the last straw or Isaac had been particularly unfair?

Landlord abuse in those days caused many sharecroppers to move frequently. Though some white landowners were kind and treated black tenants fairly, far too many exploited their workers and/or were notoriously cruel. Experiences of nonwhites living during Jim Crow rule were documented years later in sources such as *Remembering Jim Crow* and *Trouble in Mind*. Several men who survived some of the worst conditions later told how their wives had been at the landlord's disposal. Some landowners felt they owned the tenants, body and soul, simply because they lived in the landlord's house and worked his land. One former sharecropper told of a wealthy landowner known for his cheating tactics. He would solicit black families to come work on his farm, promising them good compensation. But when the crop was ready to harvest, he or his wife would pick a fight with the tenants so he could have an excuse to run them off his property without paying them. After that, he'd go out and recruit another family, lie to them to get the crop harvested and pull the same trick on them and on the next family after that, and so on. Some now living near Barber Junction say the Lyerlys had such a reputation. And the husband of one of Nease's descendants, who'd grown up in Granville county, told me a very similar story that his own family went through when he was a boy. Astoundingly, as he related the experience, I became aware that the cheating landlord he identified was a member of my husband's extended family.

Joseph Lyerly's testimony also indicated that Isaac had cheated his tenants. The dispute would have been a relatively minor issue for Isaac, but a major one for those whose very lives depended on the outcome. It was an issue that could have been settled in court—if the system had been a fair one. But the legal system and the entire social and political structure in North Carolina had just undergone a change that negatively affected people of color and, to a lesser degree, poor whites as well.

Whatever the case, in 1906 mostly one side of the story was portrayed by the press: Isaac Lyerly was an upstanding citizen, victimized by savage blacks and mulattos, whose acts were completely unjustified. When the black suspects later offered a conflicting characterization of the situation, they were branded as liars by the media or law enforcement officers.

One week after the angry mob at Salisbury conspired to lynch the alleged Lyerly murderers, another drama would begin in nearby Union County—the trial of the twenty-one suspected lynchers of John V. Johnson, who was victimized by mob violence at Wadesboro on May 28th, 1906. J.V. Johnson was a white man, accused of murdering his brother-in-law. What happened in the Johnson lynching trial would have some bearing on the events surrounding the Lyerly case—by setting yet another bad example.

# 6

# THE ROLE OF THE WHITE SUPREMACIST PRESS

1898 – Present

*The essence of propaganda consists in winning people over to an idea so sincerely, so vitally, that in the end they succumb to it utterly and can never escape from it.*

— Goebbels

The Vampire That Hovers Over North Carolina.

CARTOON BY NORMAN JENNETT,
PRINTED IN RALEIGH NEWS AND OBSERVER, SEPTEMBER, 1898

## INTRODUCTION

In December, 2006, CNN's Paula Zahn aired a two-hour special on race relations in America. Several hosts and celebrities gave their views, most agreeing that racism is still very much alive. A small town in Texas was highlighted during the program because of the prejudiced views of some of its citizens and its open display of racist signs, well into the 1970s. A hundred years after the Salisbury lynching, some from a black community in Texas still expressed a fear of driving through that town.

I know of two similar towns in North Carolina. They may have progressed recently, but they have an egregious racial history. And they both lie within 30 miles of Salisbury. Just about anyone over thirty, from the town of Faith, remembers a sign that warned: "Nigger, Don't Let the Sun Go Down on You" and held a prominent place in that town, also well into the late 70s. But when I showed up there to investigate a few years ago, no one I talked to could or would give me details about the lynching I'd heard had occurred there some time after 1906.

Then there's Denton. A couple of years after my trip to Faith, I was in my present home town on the coast, shopping at a local Food Lion grocery, when I overheard two young men talking as they set up a wine display. The familiarity of their dialect caught my ear, but I wasn't sure of its origin. "Where you from?" I had to ask.

"Salisbury," one said.

We struck up a conversation as soon as I revealed that Salisbury was my birthplace. One thing led to another, and I eventually brought up the Lyerly murders and the lynching. I wanted to know if either had oral history of their own. The other guy, from Denton, told me about a lynching tree there with a sign on it, identifying its purpose.

"Still standing?"

"Not sure," he said, "but it was there last time I was in town a few years ago."

Though I didn't reveal my opinions on the subject, the discussion naturally moved to "race." The guy from Denton said it was the Indians that really deserved "restorations," and he didn't like the idea of any black people getting part of his tax money. "I don't mind working with 'em," he added, "but I don't want any of 'em as friends."

Not too long after that conversation my cousin Marilyn and I headed to downtown Denton to look for that tree. When I asked the young woman working as cashier at a corner convenience store if she knew where it was, she lowered her voice before answering. "Well I don't know about the tree, but I do know people around here are real strict about those kinda things."

"What things?"

"You know, black people. I heard one was driving through town one time and had a flat tire. The boys came and took him away and beat him to death."

"When was that, in the 40s?"

"No...I think it was about ten years ago."

The Denton lynching tree had stood where the park is now. It was cut down not long ago, said a pair playing pinball in the same convenience store. As we walked the small area in the middle of town, now a pretty park, we figured the stump must have been dug up too, because we could find no trace of it. No physical trace, that is.

While my cousin was tracking down the tree site, I approached a lady having a smoke on a park bench, hoping to pick her brain about Denton's racial climate. She, herself, was not a native, she told me, but she'd been in town long enough to know those who *were*, were "strange." Not a black person was allowed to live in town until just recently, she claimed. One family of blacks had tried about ten years ago, and disappeared overnight— "never knew what happened to 'em."

She was also acquainted, she said, with an African American nurse who used to come to town to care for an elderly citizen, and this woman "would slump down in her car seat when she drove into town."

So where did all this blind hatred come from? I believe it had a lot to do with the rhetoric that ushered in Jim Crow rule in the South. And in North Carolina, specifically, it was the campaign of 1898, which also set the stage for the Lyerly murders and the lynching that followed.

This is a long chapter, quoting and paraphrasing academic research on North Carolina politics and economics. It may seem heavy with all the history, but it's essential to understanding the story. However, for those who don't want to delve into the details before moving on with the plot, I'll sum up how I came to see the situation after studying it for ten years.

After the Civil War, former plantation owners, the elite few who had pretty much owned the state and the South before, wanted that power back. Even though their wealth and status had died along with slavery, the South's growing industrial revolution, following the war, provided the salvation that led to their resurrection. To supply the demand for cheap labor now, they needed to lure or force lower class whites away from their rural lifestyles and into the cotton mills. But by the 1890s, elites faced a roadblock—a strengthening movement for social, economic, and agrarian reform, when whites and blacks cooperated, politically, to create an almost formidable coalition. These "Fusionist" goals conflicted with elites' plans, to say the least. They knew if the movement continued, labor unions and other reforms, cutting into their profits, would be next.

So the strategy in the late 1890s was to first break up cooperation between blacks and whites—a coalition that had elected a new party, one with democratic goals. Elites did this by diverting poorer whites' attention from what they really needed—making them *think* their greatest need was protection from blacks. This was done through indoctrination and rhetoric appealing to base emotions and instincts—with a lot of hoopla, references to religion, and especially using sex scares, laced with appeals to manhood. The press was a key player in this cause, and Josephus Daniels, of the *Raleigh News and Observer*, lead the crusade. The Dixiecrats' propaganda tactics leading up to the 1898 campaign were successful beyond their wildest dreams.

Once power was back in the hands of these white elites, they could now act as "protectors" from the "black brutes" they had conjured up. They kept the public focused on hating blacks by continuing to exaggerate and publicize black crimes and playing down black accomplishments. It became a whitewashed world.

Mill jobs and other employment opportunities, for the most part, were denied to blacks, leaving the majority of them stuck in the oppressive sharecropping system, picking cotton, and going nowhere, except back to a form of slavery.

On the other hand, cotton mill managers, exploiting the white supremacist climate, "...could dangle before poor white families something they lacked on the farm, giving them a glimpse of what increasingly defined white ladyhood: distance from all African Americans, with its implied protection from black men."[C] They kept whites satisfied with little—poor pay and poor working conditions—by keeping the example of much less fortunate blacks an ever-present reality.

"By 1900, more than 30,000 white North Carolinians labored in cotton and knitting mills, more operatives than in any state except Massachusetts. Most workers were women, and 31 percent were under sixteen."[C] Because labor unions in cotton mills were almost non-existent, the working conditions were often deplorable.

The majority of whites swallowed the white supremacists' bait—hook, line and sinker. But, to be fair, it was force fed to them. For the most part, they were not bad people; they were simply deceived.

But blacks knew what was going on, and some of them didn't sit back and take it, though most were blamed whether they fought back or not. Negative impressions of black folk created during the late 1890s carried over into the twentieth and twenty-first centuries. And we are all now paying for those sinful days, in so many ways.

Now the details.

ᏴᎵᎦᎣ

The Lyerly murders took place during the height of white supremacist tyranny. Unprecedented political events in North Carolina, just a few years prior to 1906, set the stage for growing racial violence, acted out by and against Americans of color.

After slavery was abolished and well into the twentieth century, the United States was at war. The War Between the States had been replaced by an uncivil war within the South—a war against black folk. Black leaders who had been previously hopeful about "race" relations after the Civil War and again in the mid 1890s, had understandably changed their attitudes by the turn of the twentieth century. With disfranchisement, segregation, and repeated, savage lynchings of many innocent blacks, some African American leaders and black newspaper editors had finally thrown up their hands and begun suggesting and even imploring members of the black community to arm themselves and fight back.

Ida Barnett Wells was one of these more outspoken leaders. Having worked hard to fit in and prosper in a white-dominated world, Wells changed her tune after three of her respected friends were lynched in Memphis, Tennessee only because they had fought back to defend their lives, attacked because they had prospered in a business that competed with whites. [A]

Certainly the political climate in North Carolina after 1898 led to a number of violent crimes by blacks, perhaps even the Lyerly murders. But what legal options did those like the Gillespies and Dillinghams have, once their rights to vote and hold office, and even sit on a jury, were taken away?

After Dixiecrats took over the state, they took over the press, muzzling the opposition and stifling North Carolina's black voice. "According to the state labor department, in 1900 the Democrats owned 145 of the state's newspapers, the Republicans 20, and the Populists 36 (and most of the latter would not last long)." [B] The only black publications left alive in North Carolina by 1906 were the conservative, AME *Star of Zion*, and two or three other small-town papers. The July and August archives of none of these has survived.

The 1898 campaign was treacherous. Modern historians have recently exposed the tactics used during that campaign in relationship with the political and social climate of the period before and after this election. The late 1800s had just brought back, for the first time since Reconstruction, a period of optimism and promise for blacks. It had also been good for poor whites in North Carolina, just recovering from a severe economic depression created by an elitist government. But this relief from oppressive elitist rule was even more short-lived than Reconstruction.

"Reconstruction's political leaders [had] created the basis of 'modern government'—public schools, public welfare institutions, property rights for women, tax exemptions for small homesteaders, and universal male suffrage. These accomplishments cost the old elites money and power and upset their aristocratic notions of hierarchy and privilege." And this "...trend toward more democratic government set off decades of struggle by white elites to turn back the clock." [B] Democrats had regained control of the state in 1876 through blatantly illegal, as well as less obvious means— "through violence, ballot tampering, and their control of the news media, which replaced economic issues" with a red herring: 'the Negro in politics.' [B] Right after the death of Reconstruction, the reinstated "Dixie" Democratic Party felt secure that it had permanently put things back the way they were before slavery had ended in the South.

However, in the years that followed, the party gradually began to lose some of its sway with the common man, who was badly in need of economic relief from the Dixiecrat's selfish policies. Hiding under a cloak of white supremacy, the party had used tax breaks and the fiscal power of the state to support their own interests, the interests of the landed, commercial, and entrepreneurial upper class. At the same time "...they undercut debtor support laws and adopted fence and stock laws that enclosed grazing lands and helped drive subsistence farmers off the land" and into the factories of textile, lumber mills, and tobacco owners—right where they wanted them—and working for extremely low wages.

As North Carolina joined the industrial revolution and became part of the "New South," things got even worse for whites. This period was characterized by "low wages, company towns, abusive foremen, peonage, underfunded public schools, high rates of illiteracy, and poverty...." [B] In other words, by helping Dixiecrats' regain power after Reconstruction, poor whites had cut their own throats.

But by the mid 1890s, the majority had had enough. "The economic depressions of the 1890s led more and more North Carolinians to contest Democratic rule," [B] and this time the old, intimidating tactics didn't fly. This time black voters, the majority of which were Republicans, along with whites hostile to corporate interests, some of these farmers supporting the Populist Party, joined together in a common cause, as Fusionists. By 1896 Populists and Republicans had taken over the state's legislature, senate, and governorship. [B] And, "For the first time in American political history issues of class took precedence over race...." [D]

The new Fusion legislature transferred power from the elites back into the hands of the people and opened a window of opportunity for blacks. Less restrictive voter registration requirements expanded the black electorate. [B] "Though men of color had held office during federally mandated Reconstruction (1867-1877), this time the election results were considered far more serious because it suggested a permanent shift in political and racial power." [D] Though really only a few black North Carolinians held important offices during this period, the Democrats twisted this positive progress for blacks into a negative phenomenon and used it as an excuse to inflame racial tensions, crying: "Negro domination."

This absurd insinuation "...had silenced reform movements in the past," but this time was different. This time Dixiecrats "...had to contend with the highest level of anger on the part of agrarian and working-class people the state had seen since the Civil War." [D] To divert attention away from reform now, the elites had to bring out the big guns. Cowardly murders in the dark of night and the blatant propaganda campaign to rally the masses of white men to defend their 'manhood' and white women were not enough. Winning the next election "...required the fantastic image of black men lusting for white women or hovering over the state like vampires and sucking away the lifeblood of the state." [B] Furnifold Simmons, the Karl Rove of 1898, "...chose as the central metaphorical figure of the upcoming campaign the incubus—a winged demon that has sexual intercourse with women while they sleep. The Democrats charged that while white men slumbered, the incubus of black power visited their beds. They summed up

JOSEPHUS DANIELS

their platform as 'safety of the home.'" [C]

The tactics are reminiscent of something even more familiar—those used in Hitler's regime. Months prior to the 1898 election, three of the most revered men in North Carolina history developed and carried out an illegal and multifaceted strategy to regain power of state government. Josephus Daniels, editor and owner of the *Raleigh News and Observer* (*N&O*), the most widely-read paper in the state, abused the power of the press, printing cartoons depicting blacks as devils or sexual deviants, while exaggerating reports of black attacks on white women. With their audience primed on this media misinformation, future governor Charles B. Aycock and Senator Furnifold Simmons traveled the state, spouting sexual-and-fear-inciting rhetoric, focusing on another fabricated threat of black domination and a need to bring the state back to their version of "lawfulness" based on white supremacist rule. "We don't know if Furnifold Simmons read Sigmund Freud, but we can be sure that Simmons read his audience perfectly. His barely concealed sexual reference—pent up volcanos, lava bursting forth, thrustings to the fore, federal bayonets, mongrel tickets, and pregnant issues—struck white men where they lived. Such language linked the most intimate issues of home and family to local politics and federal law in a bond that Southerners would take a century to uncouple." [C1] Daniels and other "...Democratic editors relentlessly sought to drive a racial wedge between black and white Carolinians." [B] "Simmons dispatched his agents everywhere. They founded White Government Leagues, embellished local accounts of African American 'outrages' for statewide broadcast, and reincarnated falsehoods in every Democratic rag." [B] Their short-term goal was to send blacks backward into a state of virtual slavery and to take away their recently hard-won right to vote. But their ultimate scheme was to secure control of the state's wealth and keep it in the hands of the minority. "Much like the McCarthyite witch hunts of the 1950s, the white supremacy campaign had its own kind of magic, which it worked through the media, campaign rallies, lynchings, and white race riots." [B]

NORMAN JENNETT CARTOON IN NOVEMBER, 1898
*NEWS AND OBSERVER*

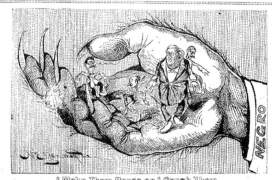

NORMAN JENNETT CARTOON IN OCTOBER, 1898
*NEWS AND OBSERVER*

NORMAN JENNETT CARTOON IN OCTOBER, 1898
NEWS AND OBSERVER

NORMAN JENNETT CARTOON IN OCTOBER, 1898
*NEWS AND OBSERVER*

DON'T BE TEMPTED BY THE DEVIL.

NORMAN JENNETT CARTOON IN OCTOBER, 1898
*NEWS AND OBSERVER*

The city that suffered the most obvious and immediate effects from this campaign from hell was Wilmington. "Wilmington provided the ideal setting in which to play out white fantasies of 'Negro domination.'" Wilmington's black population had outnumbered whites by more than two to one, and a significant number of Wilmington's blacks were educated, owned property and possessed skills that placed some in better economic circumstances than the average white citizen. Some of the city's blacks held important offices, and "..in this and other predominantly black areas of the state they actively contested white supremacy."

One black voice of protest, along with its many distortions, became the focus of the campaign's battle cry. Alex Manly, grandson of a former N.C. governor, yet still considered black by the "one drop" standard, ran the only black-owned daily newspaper in Wilmington and the entire state. (Several black-owned *weeklies* operated before 1898.) When Manly got wind of the revived publication of a Georgia woman's year-old speech characterizing black men as rapists who deserve to be lynched, he couldn't let the absurdity of her comments pass unchallenged. Manly's editorial response simply stated the truth—that white men were just as likely to take advantage of black women. He took it a step further, chastising white men and proclaiming that some white women were equally attracted to black men. The white supremacist press seized the opportunity to further inflame whites, making an example of Manly and of Wilmington's entire black population. "The white-owned *Wilmington Messenger*, along with The *Wilmington Morning Star*, reprinted the Manly editorial and their distortions of it every day from August to Election day, using it to goad white farmers and the poor to 'stand by the white race.'" [B] The Dixiecrats also used all the outrage exaggerations to chastise white Populists for voting with the blacks in the last election—as if their collusion with blacks had given blacks a sense of social equality to whites, thus resulting in their outrages on white women. [C] By diverting from the real issues to the focus on race, North Carolina Democrats in 1906, not unlike Republicans focusing on "family values" in 2004, "...blotted out nearly all consideration of other matters at stake in the election campaign, and allowed them to avoid discussing the economic goals of white supremacy, which ran counter to the interests of most white people." [B] Many whites fell for the race bait and denounced the former alliances that had brought progress to the poor. And so the Dixiecrats easily won the 1898 election.

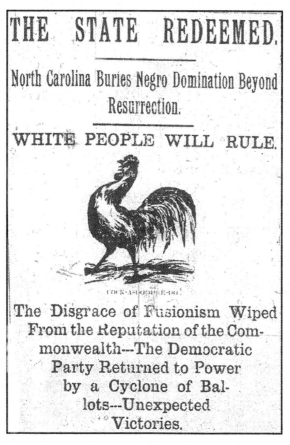

AD FOUND IN NEWSPAPERS ACROSS THE STATE
AFTER THE 1898 DIXIECRAT VICTORY

Now, the old Wilmington aristocracy, riding on the coattails of this victory, would not be satisfied until the prominent blacks were put back in their place or eliminated from the local population. A massacre ensued, and many blacks owning land or

holding prominent jobs or local government positions were
either murdered or run out of town, their property confiscated,
their jobs given to whites. With the state's largest city back
under control by the minority, and the state back in the hands of
the Dixiecrats, the elites, having accomplished their mission,
were then willing to resort back to their old paternalistic attitudes
towards subservient blacks. But the poorer whites had been
completely deceived—they believed blacks were out to get their
women, and they must continue to protect the "purity" of what
they were now convinced was a superior white race.

WILMINGTON RIOTERS, NOVEMBER, 1898

Effects of the White Supremacy victory of 1898 were
pronounced and far-reaching. In the short run, Republicans and
Populists recently elected on the Fusion ticket were removed
from office, while prominent blacks were removed from offices,
homes, and property as well. The situation in Wilmington did not
even allow some positions, Mayor for example, to run their
courses to the end of terms. Alex Manly fled town just before his
newspaper office was burned to the ground. Up in flames went
the state's black voice for decades. The repercussions of this
propaganda campaign would last for more than a century.
"...what happened in Wilmington was about more than party
politics or economic jealousy or even racism. It was about how
political rhetoric can license people to do evil in the name of

good. It reminds us that murder's best work is done after the fact, when terror lives on in memory." [C]

Within a few years, African Americans throughout North Carolina were to lose many of their constitutional rights. The first order of business for the new Democratic state legislature in 1899 was the passage of Jim Crow segregation laws followed by the disfranchisement of black men (and thus the political opposition), accomplished with the addition of an amendment to the state constitution. This amendment, supposedly restricting the vote to the literate, was clearly constructed to eliminate the vast majority of blacks from the process. A so-called "grandfather clause" was added to the amendment and allowed anyone, literate or not, to vote whose father or grandfather could vote prior to 1867. When the suffrage amendment was added to the ballot in 1900, the Democrats, Daniels and the *N&O* resorted back to their old propaganda tactics to guarantee its passage.

NORMAN JENNETT

Daniels' secret weapon would again be Norman Jennett's cartoons. In 1898 Jennett's degrading and demonic depictions of Fusionists and African-Americans had won him the praise and attention of leading Dixiecrats. He was considered a hero of the party at a young age— even before he was old enough to vote. After the Dixiecrats' success in 1898, Jennett left Raleigh to work and study in New York, but in 1900 he returned in response to Daniel's appeal: "'Your work two years ago helped us to carry the state, and the people of the state looked upon you and Aycock as the great leaders. They are going to make him governor and you will earn the lasting gratitude of the state if you can come back and help us carry the Amendment this year.'" [G] Jennett spent several weeks on the project, drawing cartoons "for passage of the suffrage amendment and election of Charles B Aycock."

Daniels' exploitation of Jennett's talents was a sinister stroke of genius. By displaying pictures along with type, Daniels was able to doubly influence a largely illiterate population. Though lacking the ability to read, this group would nevertheless understand the point the paper wished to convey. Furthermore, these who were the primary targets of this visual propaganda, were unable to read any facts printed elsewhere that contradicted the lies imbedded within the cartoons. For the literate, but non-discerning reader, the pictures served to reinforce and enhance the paper's written message. Later, in his 1941 autobiography, *Editor In Politics,* Josephus Daniels understated his role in this demagoguery. *"The News and Observer's* partisanship," he said, "was open, fierce, and sometimes vindictive, and was carried in news stories as well as in editorials." [H]

Though the *Charlotte Observer,* under Joseph Caldwell's editorship, figured prominently in the propaganda campaign, it participated without the cartoons and with less zeal than the *N&O.* In his book on the history of the *Observer,* Jack Claiborne wrote about its role in this uncivil war. "As the Spanish-American War was ending, a longer, uglier, more tragic war was beginning. But it was a war that Joseph Caldwell and the *Observer* expressed no reluctance about entering. It was the racial war that disfranchised blacks and restored white supremacy to North Carolina government. The goal was not only to eliminate blacks from politics, but also to raise an issue that would divert white farmers from Populism and reunite them behind the Democratic Party."[E]

As part of its involvement in the White Supremacy campaign, the *Observer* sent Red Buck Bryant to eastern North Carolina to write a series of reports on black officeholders. "His first story, from New Bern, was headlined 'Negro Rule: Shall It Last Longer in North Carolina?' The stories were later attacked by Populists as unfair exaggerations and 'Democratic lies.'" [E]

Perhaps Caldwell had been reluctantly lured into participating in the propaganda campaign by Daniels' coercive control. Daniels was known for his ability to make or destroy any man's career in the state. But Claiborne's claim that "Caldwell deplored the Wilmington violence and regretted that white 'wrath' was aimed at blacks instead of the white Populists who incited the blacks,' seems more than a bit naive, on Caldwell's part. [E] What did Caldwell and Daniels expect after inciting such hatred? It was ironic that Caldwell, himself, later became the target of Josephus Daniels' propaganda machine, and the two former friends did not speak again until Caldwell had a stroke that ended his newspaper career. [E]

Claiborne's description of Caldwell's and his business partner's vision exemplifies the duplicity displayed in the news media's reporting and editorials of the period.

> *Though Caldwell and Tompkins came from different backgrounds, they shared the same vision of southern progress.... Together they promoted manufacturing but opposed labor unions; supported education but opposed laws to limit the labor of women and children; urged a diverse agriculture but opposed the agrarian Populists; ...befriended blacks but endorsed white supremacy laws that denied blacks the right to vote and ultimately produced a harsh segregation.* [E]

Having conquered the 1898 campaign and having successfully introduced a bill disfranchising most African Americans by 1902, North Carolina Dixiecrats held a tight rein on their dynasty through continued control of the press—owning and running nearly every newspaper in the state. Though the media could now ease up on the intensity of its attacks on blacks, it did not cease publishing degrading letters or editorials depicting blacks as inferior brutes.

An editorial reflecting the changing role of the press in 1902 was printed in the Statesville *Landmark* in July of that year. The editorial was borrowed from Raleigh's *Progressive Farmer* and ran under the heading, "The Newspaper's Mission No Longer Entirely Political." The piece, which apparently addressed no one of color, began as follows: "The spirit of the new day in North Carolina calls imperatively for a change in the attitude of the press of the State. For thirty years the negro problem has harassed us; political feeling has run high, and the party spirit has dominated our newspaper offices. A change has come. The people are using a new wine and they cannot keep it in old bottles." Providing the background for his remarks, the writer explained that from the "days of reconstruction until now the North Carolina editor has regarded his mission as a political one. With changed conditions, it becomes his duty to make the development of the State's resources–its manhood, not less than its fields, forests and factories—paramount to party considerations." Though it didn't say outright what was meant by "changed conditions," the successful disfranchisement of blacks, earlier that year, was implied.

Despite this professed new focus of the press, Democrat-run North Carolina newspapers, in 1906, continued to print nostalgic commentaries about the good ole days of slavery and continued with subtle biases like omitting the titles of "Mr," "Miss" or "Mrs," when referring to blacks, omitting words like "alleged" or "suspected" when reporting crimes charged to blacks, and making a point to include the distinction of *colored*, while omitting the use of *white*, beside names of those accused of crimes. Blatantly biased commentaries continued as well.

One of the most self-serving and paternalistic examples of propaganda after 1902 was credited to the famous folk musician, Polk Miller, and printed in an August, 1906 edition of Daniels' *N&O*. Polk Miller, known for his banjo pickin' and storytelling, performed at opera houses along with his "Negro Quartette." Sometimes, as at the new Opera House in Albemarle in 1908, he was doubled billed with the racially-charged play, "The Clansman." [1]

Miller's letter is a tribute to the "Lost Cause" —a popular twentieth century perception about the Old South. His version of this fairy tale has him pining for the "good ole days of slavery," for nearly an entire newspaper page. It speaks volumes, not only of the times, but of the paper that printed it. The South, perhaps the North as well, is still recovering from the fallout of the contaminated, mythic view the letter perpetuates. Titled, "Christmas on De Ole Plantation Befo' the War," Miller's letter negatively contrasts the "Old" and "New Negro" and clearly exposes the aristocratic and paternalistic attitudes of white supremacy. It begins:

> *As the end of the year approaches I, like all other 'old timers' am reminded of the difference 'twixt de ole times and the new.' My boyhood was spent on the plantation, where all farm work was suspended at Christmas and the whole of the last week of the year was given up to pleasures of all sorts. The white folks and the*

*negroes came nearer to being on terms of equality than they have ever been since. By the crack of day the old negro men and women, with their children and grandchildren might be seen wending their way to the 'gret house' (old marster's house) to pay their respects to 'de white fokes,' a custom which had prevailed from time immemorial.*

*The outside world will never know how happy the negroes were on our southern plantations, and at Christmas especially, for that was one time in the year when every one on the place came to the Manor House, to shake hands with ole Master, ole Misses an' de Chil'un. They were dressed up in their very best clothes, and the expression of joy on their faces when the presents were given them, and the profound bows they would make in acknowledging their gratitude to their white owners for being remembered was worth a great deal in the way of compensation. As parents now find delight in giving their children presents at Christmas, my father and mother found great pleasure in giving to the negroes. And the old men and women were as happy as the children. The fact is, in those days, their happiness depended upon the good will and approbation of the white people, and they tried as hard then to see how much they could do, in the way of service, and from the love of pleasing, as they try now to see how little they can do, for the money they get.* [J]

Miller's letter blamed the Civil War for "breaking up thousands of happy homes" and bringing poverty to whites and blacks. It attacked carpetbaggers who "commenced to teach the poor, ignorant negroes all sorts of pernicious doctrines..." and took advantage of them and alienated them against their old white masters and led to their demise. "The once happy smile to be seen on the faces of the negroes at Christmas has given place to a look of discontent and misery, and in our cities the jails are full of negroes who commit petty crimes, in order that they may be sent to prison where they can be kept warm, and fed, for the winter." [J]

Miller must have convinced himself that freed blacks actually missed being slaves on the plantation, first because they were no longer able to celebrate Christmas with the master anymore or bow to him and kiss his hand, and second, because it had been an honor to take care of the master so he could be freed up to enjoy the finer things in life.

> *I have often thought that of the many good things which the old time negro misses by being set free, there is nothing which he misses so much as 'de Christmas of the good old times.' The conditions which prevailed in the old South made what was known as the 'typical Southern gentleman,' and the loyal and faithful negress made it possible for him to be one. The negroes, by their fidelity and loyalty, ...gave him the opportunity for study and the culture of his mind, while the over-seer and the faithful negroes furnished him the means which enabled him to enjoy the leisure to study the problems of government which made him not only the friend and adviser of his neighbors, but to wield a strong pen in shaping the politics of his section.* [J]

Miller's closing opinions reveal his true colors and exemplify and support the sentiments of the white supremacy agenda. Blacks were the object of the whites' affection and protection as long as they accepted their inferior status and supported what was best for the white elites at their own expense, otherwise they could get the hell out of the South, one way or another, dead or alive.

> *We of the South have no "Negro Problem" to solve. We stand where we have always stood on that question. This is a white man's country, (the South) always has been, and always will be, and if the negro stays here we are going to manage him, and in our way, too; and if he's not willing to stay under these circumstances, he can "git up an git."* [J]

Miller's story further exposes white elitists' true desire—the status of royalty in what was supposed to be a republic that had fought to end monarchism. The fact that many whites bought this fable must have been infuriatingly frustrating for blacks. The fact that many pioneers came to America to escape slavery in Europe, in the first place, makes this salute to servitude appear all the more pathetic.

As though the press wasn't obnoxious enough, the arts had to get in on the act, and it wasn't just the South enjoying the show. Further inflaming the already volatile racial situation, the entertainment media of the period produced the infamous "Clansman," which premiered in Norfolk Virginia's Academy of Music in September, 1905 and traveled to several other places, including New York's Liberty Theatre on January 8th, before showing in North Carolina and running throughout the South in 1906. The play was based on the book, *The Clansman – An Historic Romance of the Ku Klux Klan,* by Thomas Dixon, Jr., a native North Carolinian, born in the Piedmont town of Shelby, located not far from Rowan and Mecklenburg Counties. Dixon, who considered himself a defender of the Anglo-Saxon race, was quoted as saying that "the beginning of Negro equality is the beginning of the end of this nation's life." [K]

FRONTISPIECE FROM DIXON'S THE CLANSMAN

The work of Dixon, a Christian minister, is just one more example of the duplicitous nature of southern white supremacy. James Kinney of Virginia Commonwealth University wrote that "although Dixon personally condemned slavery and Klan activities after Reconstruction ended, he argued that blacks must be denied political equality because that leads to social equality and miscegenation [mixed marriages], thus to the destruction of both family and civilized society. Throughout his work, white southern women are the pillars of family and society, the repositories of all human idealism." [L]

For a while the play enjoyed enormous success, and then its influence finally went too far. It was of course praised by the Democratic press of North Carolina, but it wore out its welcome in several other places that said it helped incite the Atlanta Race Riot in late September, 1906, the month following the Salisbury lynching. The September 25, 1906 *Observer* printed two items on the banning of Dixon's play due to the recent riots in Atlanta. The city council of Montgomery, Alabama "unanimously passed an ordinance calling on the mayor to prohibit the production of Thomas Dixon's play, 'The Clansman,' Thursday next, on account of the excited condition of the public mind through the Atlanta disorders." And Macon, Georgia where the play was booked for the following Wednesday night, banned the production "by order of the mayor in view of the race riots in Atlanta."

The ban on the play didn't last long though, and by February, 1907, it was back in Norfolk, "its birthplace" and getting rave reviews. The *Observer* wrote on the night of February 19<sup>th</sup> that "the theatre was packed with the largest audience in its history, hundreds being turned away, unable to gain admittance." Because protests against the play "for political reasons" had been made, "Mayor Riddick attended the performance to judge for himself and said he saw nothing objectionable and in fact was much pleased." [M]

Daniels' *N&O* was not the only North Carolina paper that continued to promote propaganda after the success of the disfranchisement campaign in 1902. On July 15, 1906, less than two days after the Lyerly murders, the *Observer* printed an old letter it said was written by former South Carolina Governor Francis. W. Pickens in 1866 to a "Gentleman in New Orleans," which the paper characterized as providing "insight" into the "relation of the races in the South" and the "effects of emancipation." What prompted the paper to print this letter almost fifty years after it was written is not known, but certainly the intent is clear—to justify the continuation of white supremacy rule and attitudes.

About eighty percent of Pickens' letter deals with the "race issue," and the letter itself covers the equivalent of an entire newspaper page, enough 11-point type to fill nine 8 1/2 by 11 pages. Pickens cited verses from the *Bible* and provided unsubstantiated "evidence" of physical differences between African Americans and Anglo Saxons to back up his claim of white superiority, stating, in a nutshell, that the American South basically did the race a great favor by bringing it here and teaching its members how to become "tillers of the soil." [N]

Of course God had a hand in it—the way Pickens saw it. He quoted verses from Genesis, trying to substantiate his argument for Divine sanction of inequality between races. And here's how he explained it: God created the black race first, and then, as if improving upon his work, He created the white race, or "the other race." That "other race," was the one and only one "that God Almighty himself created especially to illustrate the dispensations of His Providence, the history of which is developed in the inspired pages of His Holy Book." [N]

As far as Pickens was concerned, to question this "Divine" plan was to be in cahoots with the devil himself. It was "simply wrong" to question the "God of Creation" in these matters; to do so would be following Lucifer's example. He warned that the "arrogant ones," wrapped in their "sanctimonious garbs of self-righteousness" and insisting that all men are equal, are doomed to the same fate that befell the Fallen Angel. [N] Pickens' interpretation of the Bible contained important implications for racial issues in the twentieth century. If one could prove that God intentionally created inferior and superior races, then God surely would sanction the white supremacist agenda.

In the midst of all his religious mumbo-jumbo, Pickens put his foot in his mouth. He apparently failed to realize the implications of his interpretation of Genesis. He declared that the black man and woman, the first race, were created in God's image, but gave no indication that the whites, the second race, received this divine trait. So a logical conclusion, if one is to follow Pickens' line of reasoning, would be that God is black.

As far as Pickens was concerned, not even Jefferson and Franklin were saved from damnation. They brought to America from France what Pickens saw as a misguided, evil concept of equality among men, which he said was influenced by doctrines of Voltaire and Rousseau. The founding fathers, through their great popularity and influence, then incorporated the idea into the belief system and institutions of America, and this, he added, "has been a canker worm, preying upon the vitals of our society ever since." [N]

Others just didn't get God like Pickens did. Not only does his letter attempt to justify slavery before the Civil War, but it encourages the continued enslavement of the race, characterizing it as an inevitable outcome of the interference by those misled idealists who evidently didn't understand the intentions of their Creator. Referring to those who fought to end slavery, Pickens said that they have "now forced upon the country emancipation of the black race, through carnage and fire such as has been seldom known in the bloodiest days of the world, all to enforce universal equality and under an idea that they have abolished slavery. But this has only changed the form of slavery. It will now take another form, will be wider-spread, and more cruel and crushing in the progress of time." [N]

Well he was right about that. It would be hard to argue that the Civil War effected little more progress than to change slavery from one form to another, but Pickens' evidently failed to see this new form of slavery as being fed by the propaganda he promoted, as well as the actions of people who believed as he did.

And it wasn't enough that Pickens had God on his side. He claimed that science, too, supported his bigotry. Citing no authority or source for his assertions, he went on for several paragraphs contrasting alleged anatomical and other physiological aspects of both "races," which science will today verify do not exist.

The letter ended with a misguided, but popular opinion. "The negro race seems destined to be forced to give way to a more vigorous and higher race, and the black man is doomed to perish here as did his predecessor, the red man. No doubt it is all for some wise and great purpose in the providence of Him whose policy is unknown to mortal man." [N]

A more common example of propaganda, titled, "The Negro and the Foreigner" printed in the *Observer* in September, 1906, was meant to be humorous. Its unidentified author defined it as a "story to illustrate" how "it requires some time for the latter to learn how to treat the former." The story consists of a dialog between a New England professor and a black servant, supposedly told to show that visitors from the North respect blacks only because they don't know them as southerners do. "'Whenever I see one at it," the "joke" began, "I think of something that happened at the State University a few years ago.'"

> "The university drew on Harvard or Yale for a young professor, who proved a first-class teacher, but he did not know much about Southern people. The negro was a new proposition to him. Eli Merritt, a typical, fat-bellied negro of the old school, looked after the apartment of the new comer. He would go in early and make a fire for him. The first morning the professor reared up in his bed and asked: "By what name may I address you, sir?"
>
> "The tone of the man's voice made Eli lift up his ears. He didn't quite understand it, but he answered: "Eli is mer name."
>
> "Is that your last name?"
>
> " No, sir, Merritt – Eli Merritt."
>
> "Yes, I see. Well, Mr. Merritt, is it very cold out this morning?"
>
> The "mister" non-plussed Eli. He was afraid to do more than answer questions.
>
> The next morning the professor got a little mad at Eli and left off the "mister" and called him Eli Merritt. I am telling you Eli's own story. He told it to the boys. The third morning the professor called Eli by his last name, just plain Merritt. The fourth day it was plain "Eli" and the fifth "You damned black rascal" and the sixth a little worse. In telling about his experience afterward, Eli declared: "I des knowed dat he wuz gittin' right when I heered him come down on dat d-d raskle proposition"

The piece is representative of Bryant's style and other "anecdotes," printed from time to time to denigrate blacks, in a seemingly harmless, though powerful way, depriving them of basic respect.

While the white press dominated the "news" in the South, good news about the black race was virtually unheard of South of the Mason-Dixon Line. And white supremacists went to great lengths to prevent any outside infiltration. The Chicago *Defender* was said to have been read extensively in the South, smuggled in and distributed by black Pullman porters and entertainers. "White distributors refused to circulate the *Defender,* and many groups such as the Ku Klux Klan tried to confiscate it or threatened its readers," noted one author. Despite the risks, "The *Defender* was passed from person to person and read aloud in barbershops and churches." However, the *Defender* was founded just a year before the 1906 lynching in Salisbury, and it is unlikely it had been distributed to the southern states before 1910, when editor/owner Robert S. Abbott could afford his first full-time employee. [O]

After editor Alex Manly was run out of Wilmington and his press destroyed, not another black-owned North Carolina paper remained in business by 1902 except the A.M.E. Zion Church's *Star of Zion*, Weldon's *North Carolina Republican And Civil Rights Advocate*, Littleton's *True Reformer*, and maybe one or two other small papers. But there are no surviving editions or archives for the latter publications. What remains of the 1906 archives of the *Star of Zion* contains no mention of the Salisbury lynchings, though they occurred not far from the campus of Livingston College, where the paper was printed at the time. It was rumored that the mob had planned to attack the college right after the lynching, so its very likely that this last remnant of the black voice in North Carolina dared not follow in Manly's footsteps. [C]

This absence of a black voice in North Carolina after 1898 was quite unique. Other southern states, even Georgia, had at least one black paper to give some balance to all the negative press that their African American citizens were being bombarded with. Even the white press's subtleties like never prefixing the names of African Americans with Mr. or Mrs. had an almost subliminal effect. Though many by 1906 had stopped using the "N" word or terms like "darky," there was something about the way they used the terms "Negro" and "mulatto" that in a way was worse, because they depersonalized the people whom these terms were used to describe. The white press of the day rarely used "Negro man" or "Negro woman." It was usually *the* Negro or *a* Negro—suggesting a thing, rather than a person. By contrast, African American editor John Mitchell, in his accomplished paper, the *Richmond Planet*, referred to this group of Americans as colored people, men, and women, or Negro businessmen. His paper would also use "white and colored people," as a group together in one sentence, respectful of both races, while the white southern press was normally only respectful of elite white people or white property owners. These subtle insults may have proved just as damaging to the image of people of color as the combined injury from omissions of good deeds and accomplishments and the focus on negative acts by black citizens.

In its reporting of the Lyerly murders and the lynching that followed, North Carolina's white supremacist press rarely considered the presumption of innocence and, more often than not, accused the suspects of the murder they were never convicted of. The following headlines publicizing the Salisbury lynching, show subtle and not so subtle differences in the spin used among different factions represented by the press—the radical Democrat, conservative Democrat, Republican, Independent, and Black press.

Radical Democrat:

*Atlanta Constitution* – "DOOM for Negroes at the Hands of Lynchers"
*Raleigh News & Observer* – "Infuriated Swarms Storm the Jail, Drag the Lyerly Murderers Out and Put Them to Death."

Conservative Democrat:

*Charlotte Observer* – "Mob Lynches Three: Avenges Murder of Lyerlys"

Republican white paper:

*Greensboro Industrial News* – "Mob Takes Three Negroes Accused of Lyerly Murder From Jail...,"

African American:

*Savannah Tribune* – "Victims Had Just Been Arraigned..."
*Richmond Planet* – "Barbarism Rampant in North Carolina: Three Colored Men Lynched."

Even New Orleans' *Times Picayune* used the word "alleged" in its subheading: "Three Alleged Murderers of the Lyerly Family Hanged and Shot at Salisbury, N.C." Baltimore's *Afro-American-Ledger* did more than headline the double standard—it spelled it out.

> *Whenever a Negro commits a crime against the virtue of a white person a howl will be heard which will echo from one end of the country to the other. Whenever a white man commits the same crime or even worse, it hardly attracts attention, and the publication of it seldom sees the light of day more than once.* [P]

North Carolina had no black papers like this one to tone down or balance the racial rhetoric that daily roared from the white press. So, more than likely, most living in Rowan County and communities throughout the United States in 1906 learned about the details of the Lyerly murders and the subsequent lynching through the skewed perception of the Dixiecrat press. This voice was duplicitous as well as distorted: inciting racial hatred, violence, and lynching. Then, it hypocritically condemned the violence—after it was too late.

# 7

# "SADDEST FUNERAL EVER"

## SUNDAY, JULY 15

*The cost of liberty is less than the price of repression.*
— William Edward Burghardt Du Bois

UNITY PRESBYTERIAN CHURCH

It was Sunday, the day following all the excitement and mob threats at the Salisbury jail and just less than two days after the murders. Things had settled down considerably, at least for a while, and some of the Saturday night crowd had left the city to face a much more somber scene. An estimated thousands gathered at Unity Presbyterian church near the Rowan County community of Woodleaf to attend the eleven a.m. funeral service for the Lyerly family.

Unity Presbyterian church was an old house of worship even in 1906. It still stands today, nestled among towering trees—white oak, elm, and sweet gum—on an expansive, grassy lawn, about two miles from the site that was once the Lyerly home. The Lyerly family had belonged to Unity for generations, and many of Isaac's ancestors share this final resting place with him.

It was an appropriately dreary day. Earlier that morning, hundreds had ignored the threatening weather and begun to assemble at the ancestral site, which, up until the night of the murders, had been the home of three generations of what an *Observer* reporter described as an "honorable family without blemish or stain." [A] People came from several counties, Rowan, Iredell and Forsyth, as well as the cities of Salisbury, Statesville, Winston, and Charlotte to pay their respects to the family.

The throng was overwhelming, the pews overflowing. "When the funeral reached the church, over two thousand people had fallen in the line, which was over one and a half miles long," and the procession arrived at the churchyard to find the building packed with people who had not been able to get inside the home, "there being room left only for the remaining little girls and near relatives." [A]

Both the Greensboro and Charlotte papers published the same word-for-word coverage of the funeral. Both reports commented on the composure and bravery of the bereaved "three remaining little girls." And both strayed from the solemn spirit that suited the occasion, using the opportunity to further accuse the suspects. "This pretty country place was the site of a death-stricken home, there being four caskets containing the remains of the Lyerly family, slain Saturday," they said, "by a band of negro brutes." [A, B]

Further fueling hatred toward the accused, the press understated the overall maturity of the survivors. "The three remaining little girls were calm and well composed, not realizing their cruel bereavement. No braver heroines ever lived than these three little girls, Mary, Addie and Janie." [A, B] Even if it was because of the girls' small stature, the reporting, nevertheless, left an inflammatory impression. Those at distances, unaware of the facts, continued to perceive the survivors as "tots" and "babies." The papers had apparently already eliminated all of the girls as possible suspects, whether Solicitor Hammer had or not. Nevertheless, assuming the girls' innocence, it would be hard to imagine how they had held up through what seemed to become a never-ending nightmare.

Details that were known about out-of-town family members were included in reports on the funeral. W.R. Lyerly of 39 Penland Street in Asheville, said to be a cousin of Isaac's, had sent several telegrams to Salisbury inquiring about the tragedy when he first heard the news, but it is not known if he attended the funeral. His wife and daughter, Mrs. W.R. Lyerly and Mrs. B.M. Marlow, however, apparently left Asheville immediately to join relatives in Salisbury. [C] Addie later attended school in Asheville and probably lived with these kin during that time, but initial reports said all the surviving children would reside temporarily with neighbor William Pleasant Barber and their uncle Alex Lyerly, "a merchant of considerable means," in nearby Cleveland.

WILLIAM PLEASANT (PLESS) AND
MARGARET WALTON BARBER

Barber's was the logical place for the girls' immediate accommodations. Barber's wife was Isaac's niece, and, according to a current resident, Barber owned a hotel at Barber Junction, in addition to a rather large house next to the Lyerly property. Now inhabited by Barber descendants, the house and property, distinguished by a beautiful red barn, still sit by the old highway. Barber was known by the nickname of Pless, a variation of his middle name, Pleasant. Fannie Gillespie's testimony, taken on July 20th during the Solicitor's questioning, said Pless was the one who informed her of the Lyerly murders. But it was constable E.A. Barber who was involved in the murder "investigation" on Saturday and among the crowd of would-be lynchers in Salisbury later that night. The exact relationship between the two Barbers is not known, though it's certain E.A.'s mother was Isaac's sister, so he had to have been related to Pless' wife, Margaret. Isaac was related to many in the county in one way or another.

Little more was said about the funeral. A local resident remembered only that Doc Webb had driven one of the four wagons that carried the coffins. It must have been a sad and shocking day for the entire county—similar in emotional impact to the Columbine and Virginia Tech murders today. Reports didn't discuss the impact on the community, they added only that Reverend Spence "preached a most beautiful sermon," and that all the murdered family members were laid to rest in a single grave. A large stone marks the spot today. Augusta's name on that stone, perhaps due to the haste of the arrangements, is misspelled, "Agusta."

Other than the prolificacy of the Lyerly family, the reason for such an immense crowd there that day isn't clear—whether it was because the family was locally well-known, or because of the high-profile status of the crime and news coverage, or both. The Lyerly and Barringer families were distinguished as being among the founding German pioneer families in Rowan and Mecklenburg counties of North Carolina—at one time like rural royalty, in a way. Isaac's great grandfather had gained local fame when he was chosen as one of two emissaries to Germany, sent to bring back a Lutheran minister and a teacher for the newly established churches in the area. On the way home his party stopped by England where they were received by King George and presented with a purse of gold, so the story goes. Augusta's more distant relatives were more recently renown. She was descended from a Barringer her people believed to be either the youngest brother or other close relative of the more famous pioneer, John Paul Barringer, whose descendants were generals, scientists, ambassadors, and one, a college president. One general's son co-owned the publishing house that had just printed a book of McNeill's poetry, *Poems Merry and Sad*, though he was probably better known as the first automobile owner in the area. "Only recently, Salisburians marveled that a man named Osmond Barringer had driven a horse-less carriage all the way from Charlotte. [D]

Before emancipation, both the Lyerlys and the Barringers had owned slaves, though by 1906 they were probably more land-rich than otherwise wealthy. Nevertheless, Augusta apparently still thought of herself as better than some of her neighbors. She did not approve of Mary's boyfriend, one of his descendants said, because his father had died, and his family was poor. To Augusta, Matt Webb was "poor white trash," not good enough for her daughter. And she had forbidden Mary to see him.

But the death of their parents changed all the girls' lives drastically. Before, they were expected to do a lot of work on the farm, including plowing the fields and milking the cows. Now Mary, almost eighteen, was free to live her life how and with whom she pleased. Not long after the funeral and the upcoming trials, within a year, she was enrolled in college, and her "unsuitable" beau, Matt Webb, became her husband. Addie and Janie would also continue their education. Janie would make it her career.

Continuing to educate the public, Daniels-style, the *N&O* included erroneous and condemning information about Coroner Dorsett's inquest within its report on the funeral. "Simultaneously with the verdict came a full confession of the terrible crime by Henry Gillespie and the seven negroes...," it said. Not surprisingly, the headline read: "Burial of the Four Victims of Negroes' Barbarous Hate." [E]

# 8

# THE PRISONERS SPEAK TO THE PRESS

## MONDAY, JULY 16

*I know not whether laws be right,*
*Or whether laws be wrong;*
*All that we know who lie in gaol*
*Is that the wall is strong;*
*And that each day is like a year,*
*A year whose days are long.*

— Oscar Wilde

PRISONERS WERE KEPT IN MOVABLE CAGES WHILE
WORKING ON STATE ROADS

*July 18, 1906.*
*Dear Mr. Henderson,*
    *I am receiving all of your letters—this one today*
*being dated the 17ᵗʰ. I am so glad to hear often of all the*
*details.... We were terribly horrified at the brutal*
*murders—How those poor girls stood all the shocks I*
*cannot imagine. I suppose being forced to exert*
*themselves over the fire or their little sister kept them*
*from losing their minds. I think it should have been so*
*much better for the mob to have lynched the negroes.*
*They will probably be acquitted or pardoned.... M----.* [1]

On Monday, July 16ᵗʰ, the *Washington Post* ran a front page story about the vandalism and violence directed at the Salisbury prisoners on the previous Saturday night, dispelling myths that the lynching crusade had been abandoned. Lynchers and others in the Invisible Empire [2] were like other terrorists; they were willing to bide their time and could strike unexpectedly. The report indicated that, after the failed attempt to find the prisoners in Rowan County's jail, the mob members transferred their mission to Charlotte on Sunday after the funeral. The *Post* said on the 15ᵗʰ that they were "coming into Charlotte to-night by every train. Many others have reached the city by private conveyance." So far, however, no attempt had been made to get at the prisoners, it said. "They are huddled together in one cell in the county jail and a detachment of policemen and armed citizens surrounds the building. In the several armories of the city the militia are resting on their arms awaiting the call of Sheriff Wallace, who says that he will uphold the law at any cost."

    Washington's report revealed a huge difference between Sheriff Julian's assessment of the mob's mind and that of Charlotte's sheriff. It said the Mecklenburg County sheriff had sized up the situation and was fully aware that the would-be lynchers were in the city. He did not doubt an effort might be "made during the night to get the negroes," said the *Washington Post*. And, "While he would regret to have to use violent methods to uphold the law," he said, he would remain "true to his oath as an officer of the law." [A] Sheriff Julian, on the other hand, would soon write Governor Glenn to say everything was hunky-dory—he wouldn't be needing any extra help on the day of the trial, which was now set for August 6th.

In addition, another or the same Washington reporter had concluded already that some of the suspects were not guilty. "A correspondent has just returned from the jail, where he saw and talked with all five of the prisoners," he said. There seems to be little doubt as to the innocence of at least three of the five." [A] John and Henry's alibis must have been convincing.

> *John    Gillespie,    Henry    Gillespie,    and    Jack Dillingham were all arrested on suspicion. The two first named claim they were plowing in a field two miles from the Lyerly home when the officer arrested them. The night of the murder they were both at home and this, they say, they can establish without the slightest trouble. But they are stepsons of Mitchell Graham [aka Nease Gillespie], who, it is believed, did the murderous act, and they are held as accomplices. The fifth man, George Irwin, has acted strangely since his arrest, and it is generally believed that he watched outside while Graham entered the house and dealt the death blows to the four victims.* [A]

Nease was described as being skittish, but eager to get his comments on the record. He apparently cooperated with the reporter and elaborated on the dispute many believed to be the motive for the killing. Unfortunately, his response was paraphrased, and no other papers quoted or even mentioned what he had to say that day. We can't be sure the reporter accurately represented his words, though they seem to jibe with later recorded interviews. This one began with Nease's "several difficulties" with Mr. Lyerly.

> *He admits this now. He says that the old man did not treat him right in the matter of a small settlement, but denies that he ever raised his hand against him.*
> *When asked to-night if he was not afraid he would be hanged for the crime, he said that every turn of the jail key frightened him almost into convulsions. He is*

*constantly on the lookout for a mob to enter the jail and*
*take him to his death.*
*    The fact that Graham [Nease Gillespie] is so much*
*more alarmed than the rest leads the officers to believe*
*in his guilt.* [A]

Imagine someone in Nease's situation not being alarmed.
The officers, like the reporter, seemed to expect men immersed
in stressful, life-threatening, and extraordinary circumstances to
act as if everything was life as usual, which for blacks in 1906,
was precarious enough. Nease was over fifty years old and had
been born into slavery. He'd lived through the horrors that ended
Reconstruction, and he must have known something about what
a lot of white people were capable of, when it came to matters of
"race." The press's comments reveal either denial or naivete
about this Jim Crow climate and disregard the significance of the
recent attack on the Salisbury jail. All of those prisoners had
every reason to be scared to death—guilty or not.

The *Washington Post's* attempt to present the prisoners' side
of the story might have done them a service, had it not otherwise
destroyed them. The same edition that indicated the innocence of
John and Henry also carried a catastrophic error. Either
following the *N&O's* lead or simply misinterpreting Henry
Mayhew's testimony, it said all six had confessed to the
murders! This lie, repeated and headlined by other papers, drove
at least one of the nails in the prisoners' coffins.

The *Salisbury Post's* filmed archive coverage of the Lyerly
murder story continues on July 17th. The evening edition had
followed up before that, with a weekly afterward, but these
issues are not accessible to the general public. The filmed edition
said little new had developed, except that Mayhew had repeated
his testimony to Tom Bost, the *Observer's* Salisbury
correspondent. But hardly insignificant was the additional
revelation that Fannie now "squarely contradicted the boy." [B] It's
known that the *Post* covered developments in the story before
the 17th because Joe Junod, in 1974, quoted passages from these
earlier editions. However, in 1974 Junod didn't mention the
violence at the jail on the evening following the murders, which
John Moose Julian had indeed covered in those unfilmed
editions, which I finally found in the *Post's* morgue. Also,

neither he nor Julian discussed the Washington paper's support of John and Henry's alibis.

The filmed report ended with only a brief summary of interviews between Charlotte reporters and the accused and witnesses. After finding some of the unfilmed originals, I learned that Julian had not conducted an extensive interview himself, though he *had* disclosed new information, not available elsewhere. Nease had taken Fannie's last name, the report said, and Henry Mayhew had been "subjected to a severe examination," before telling the officers his story on the evening after the murders. [C] For many years, few have had access to these reports shedding valuable light on the case, with suspects' declarations of innocence that contradict earlier, available and erroneous, reports of confessions. These originals are now deteriorating, with some parts illegible. So more clues to the mystery may have been lost forever, unless someone has some originals squirreled away in an attic somewhere.

The filmed *Salisbury Post* said Sheriff Julian received an executive order from Governor Glenn on the previous day, calling for a special term of Rowan Superior court to try the murder case. The order was accompanied by a letter complimenting the sheriff on his management of the matter so far, or so said the sheriff's son. When I searched for records stored in the basement of the present county courthouse, I didn't find an executive order addressed to the sheriff or a letter praising his performance. Instead I found one signed by Governor Glenn, addressed to Judge Benjamin Franklin Long, commissioning him to "open a special Term of said Court for the County aforesaid on Monday the 6th day of August 1906 and continue one week." And it seemed odd to me, at first, that the court was given only one week to dispense with this complicated murder case.

It was the county commissioners, Julian said, who set the date for the trial to commence, the earliest legal date a special term could be held. [B] So they were rushing the case *to* trial, as well as the trial itself. The *Post* included a list of jurors and their township residences, also said to be drawn by the county commissioners. None of those listed: "R.B. Brittain, Salisbury; Wm. M.L. Fesperman, Litaker; Daniel L. Eddleman, Litaker; S.C. Karriker, Atwell; J.S. Hall, Steele; T.A. Walton, Unity; Wm

G. Eagle, Morgan; D.A. Hodge, Gold Hill; R.L. Weddington, Atwell; Joseph Mesimer, Salisbury; J. Cowan Shaver, Morgan; Maxwell Holshouser, Gold Hill; J.P. Trexler, Salisbury; J.W. Rideoutte, Salisbury; W.C. Maupin, Salisbury; W.J. Allen, Franklin; C.M. Kimball, China Grove; W.A. Benson, Scotch Irish; S.H. Wiley, Salisbury; M. LaFayette Barger, Litaker; John R. Moose, Gold Hill; Charles A. Sloop, Litaker; R.A. Moose, China Grove; J.T. Barber, Cleveland; John D. Ketchey, China Grove; W.M. Irvin, Salisbury; J.C. Carroll, China Grove; D.H. Weaver, Atwell; C.A. Boyd, Salisbury; J.A. Carter, Salisbury; Wesley A. Frick, Morgan; M.P. Plummer, Mt. Ulla; C.D. Boger, Salisbury; W. Harris Boggs, Providence; J.M. Monroe, Jr., Salisbury; W.B. Hill, Salisbury" [B] —none, were designated as "colored." It was an all-white jury. And, W.A. Benson, among them, was the brother of the young woman murdered four years earlier, which led to the previous Salisbury lynching.

While the *Salisbury Post* only briefly summarized the content of the prisoners' interviews, in the most negative light, one *Observer* report dedicated an entire column to at least some of their side of the story. The coverage began with this conclusion:

> *Henry [Mayhew] is up against it and so is the State of North Carolina if it must rely upon him entirely for the evidence that will convict five men and one woman of the murder of Ike Lyerly's family Saturday morning.... Nease Gillespie's wife, whose testimony was regarded as important as any earthly witness's could be, goes squarely back upon the mulatto grandson. [D]*

Here we get the first indication that Henry was part white. "It is manifestly up to the boy," the *Observer* added, "to furnish the story that will land the quintette on the scaffold."

Though it's unclear who asked the questions in these next interviews, Bryant signed his initials to the report.

> *When The Observer's correspondent went to the country this afternoon to get his confession, the boy, just 11 years old, was in the most communicative mood. He gave the interview without the slightest persuasion and*

> *he shows all of the white blood that is in him. He does not appear to have any feeling in the matter, though freely expressing his belief that the crowd ought to be hanged.* [D]

Bryant emphasized Henry's "white blood," without addressing the question of who the father was. Did Bryant know? Apparently Mayhew's father or grandfather was white, as was Nease's and Jack's, for they were all described as mulattos. Bryant's reference to Henry's mixed ancestry called attention to white-on-black sex crimes, without addressing them directly. The Jim Crow press would not openly discuss or acknowledge *this* form of rape, even when the issue was staring everyone in the face.

The interviewer asked Henry to tell him what he knew about the murders "'...and who was in it.'" It's doubtful the response, printed in quotations, was all Henry's own words. And it includes at least one error the press might not have meant to publish—probably the name of Henry's real father.

> *"De was six uv 'em, Capt'n, five mens and one woman. Jack Dillingham, George Ervin, Uncle Henry, Ab Mayhew and paw and Jack's wife. Dey was talking dat night and went out about 11 o'clock. When dey come back it was near daylight. Maw begged dem not to go and paw (this is Nease Gillespie, the grandfather of the boy) told her, 'G---d d—n' her he would do as he pleased and it was none of her business. Dey said dey would get Jack to go long and paw and Uncle Henry went out. When dey come back, I heerd paw say dey done kill 'em an' he was glad. Paw said he kilt Miss Augusta and Mr. Lyerly and Nease de youngest ones. Dey use Mr. Ike's axe and paw taken his. He brung it back home and hid it."* [D]

Something is definitely not right about this so-called confession. Ab Mayhew, likely Henry's real father, was not a suspect, and his name wasn't mentioned again in any report, except in reprints of this one. There's also confusion about who "paw" is. If "paw" is Nease, as the paper indicated, then "paw," in the third from the last sentence, could not be Nease, because Nease is already mentioned in that sentence. Did Henry use the name of Ab Mayhew as another name for John Gillespie? If so, why would he do that? Later reports said Henry's father was definitely white, not mulatto or black. So did Henry actually implicate his real father? Or was it just a mistake on the reporter's part, confusing his real father's name with his stepfather's. It's likely Nease (Mich) worked for his neighbor, Ab Mayhew, while he was living in Iredell County, and that Ab (short for Absalom) had fathered Fannie's child.

There are other problems with this version. It's not a confession in the first place—Henry wasn't accused of anything. But by calling it a confession, the *Observer* continued to confuse the public and other members of the press who reprinted versions of Bryant's story. Another issue with this version of Henry's statement is that the previous one said John and Nease—not Henry Lee and Nease—left the house and went to meet up with the others.

According to all other accounts and the court records, the people incarcerated in the Mecklenburg jail awaiting trial were Nease Gillespie (aka Mitchell Graham), John Gillespie, Henry Gillespie (aka Henry Lee), Jack and Della Dillingham, and George Ervin. Since Henry Mayhew referred to an "Uncle Henry," he must have meant Henry Gillespie. So the only person left that the eleven-year-old didn't mention is fifteen-year-old John Gillespie, who was identified by Fannie as her grandson and Nease's son. Perhaps the inconsistency of Henry's story is one reason the case for the prosecution was deemed weak. Apparently there was little else to go on—the reports about finding blood-stained clothes and bloody axes in possession of the accused must have been unfounded. The *Observer* never corroborated or even acknowledged Winston-Salem's reports of alleged physical evidence linking the accused to the crime.

This account of Henry's testimony raises further questions. As reported, he said Nease and the others returned home after the killing "near daylight." But why would they hang around outside, when other reports said a whole crowd of people began gathering just yards away at the Lyerly home before daylight. What seems most puzzling is that Henry would make such damning comments about his kin, and that he would do so, so willingly. The possibility of duress must be considered. It did, after all, take him an entire day to come up with this "confession," which seemed tailor-made to justify the arrests made earlier. If Nease was abusive, as was later asserted, then perhaps this would explain Henry's willingness to condemn him. Though Nease may have raised Henry, he was not his blood relative, but what did Mayhew have against fifteen-year-old John?

Greensboro's *Industrial News,* a Republican paper, published the same interview and reporter commentary, almost verbatim, without crediting Bryant with writing it. The only changes made were the exclusion of the profanity and derogatory racial language. In the following paragraph, where Bryant uses the "n" word, the Greensboro paper chose to substitute "negro."

> *The little nigger's vernacular is all that marks him as illiterate. He talks brightly and was made to go slowly so every word could be taken. When asked how he knew that others went, he declared that he heard the people of his household say who was along. He told the story of the fuss between the old gentleman and Dillingham, "Jack was using one of Mr. Ike's horses and hit kicked him. Jack taken a board and knocked de hoss down and Mr. Ike fussed wid him. Uncle Henry got mad at Mr. Ike cause he wouldn't divide de wheat wid him. Uncle Henry is paw's son and told him what dey had had trouble about. Uncle Henry wouldn't help cut it and Mr. Ike said he shouldn't have any of it."*
>
> *The boy was then asked if he had ever had trouble with his grandfather.*
>
> *He said Nease was a very mean fellow who had beaten him many times. "He is a devil" he declared, "and cuts off maw's hair and paints her eyes wid hot pitch. He puts chloroform to her face and has not been wid her for a year. Me and maw was sleeping in another room when all ov 'em went over to Mr. Ike's and when Jack come back he said G-d d-m it he had killed 'em and he was glad and dat he didn't care if he was hung. Dey took Mr. Ike's life and dey ought to be hung. I specs to tell dis when dey has er trial. When is de gwine to have*

*it?" The little fellow was told and remarked that he was having a good time on the chain gang, where he is being well fed and treated well. He is allowed to move about with the guards and really seems happy.* ᴰ

If Nease had not been with Fannie for a year, as Mayhew claimed, why was Nease at the house that night talking about the murder he had just supposedly committed? Or, did Mayhew mean only that Fannie and Nease were not living together as a married couple even though they resided in the same home? Mayhew's earliest testimony said Nease (not Jack) had said, "G-d d-m it he had killed 'em and he was glad...." But in this last statement, Jack is the one who allegedly said he'd killed them and was glad about it, unless of course the writer confused the names. Whatever the reason, as reported, there are several holes in Mayhew's story. Interestingly, this version implicates Henry Lee, but doesn't mention John or George or explain what their roles were in this affair. If the reporters asked for clarification of any of these inconsistencies, they didn't report it.

Della Dillingham's interview was in same *Observer* report. The only female suspect, she, according to the paper, was kept in the same cell with Nease's wife, Fannie, who was held as a witness. Bryant described Della as "a coal black virago but excessively polite." Webster's defines virago as either a "loud, overbearing woman" or "a woman of great stature, strength, and courage," so apparently the latter definition was meant. Here's what else he said about her:

*The way she was known to be amazonian was learned incidentally. She told that Jack had once tried to beat her and he couldn't do it. That is evidently true, no man could. The Dillingham woman looked and acted very much more innocently than any one of the party going up to see her. She told of the story that she had fussed with the mother the day before. She declared that this was a story. Mrs. Lyerly and she had never been at outs and she loved them all. The wash tub episode, she declared to have taken place between Miss Mary Lyerly and Mrs. Lyerly. The young girl, having written her beau against the wish of the mother and denying it and refusing to help her mother wash, was severely whipped by Mrs. Lyerly. She said the girls had almost plowed the horses to death. The Dillingham woman was monstrously entertaining. She admitted that Jack and the old gentleman had fallen out about the horse because Jack could not work the one given him and the girls had worked the other to death.* [D]

Oral history corroborates that the girls did have to do farm work. And perhaps the little ones had their share of chores as well. Mary Lyerly's statement to the solicitor, as both the *Observer* and the *Post* recorded it, said that the youngest children had been out chopping wood on the night of the murder. These children were six and eight years old—the ones referred to repeatedly as "babies" by several papers. A living relative said this testimony about chopping wood has to be an error—that the children were too young to use an axe. This same relative agreed the girls worked very hard and probably did some plowing, but not as much as Della's testimony indicated. But these relatives, not living at the time, could only offer hand-me-down information they had gleaned from what Addie and Mary told them years after the murders.

Della's story suggests the possibility of another motive for the murder. Could Mary's forbidden "beau" have been involved? This theory would not likely account for the murder of the children or the fire, but these murders seem to defy all explanation. Numerous accounts of murders over forbidden love were reported in the early 1900s. One example, found in the May, 1902 *Savannah Tribune* and elsewhere, tells of a mass murder at a farm near St. Augustine Florida. It said a man named Austin, "crazed" by an infatuation for a girl of thirteen, killed the entire family of five when they opposed his desire to wed the girl. Then he killed himself. However, Matt's grandson says the Matt he knew was not capable of such a thing. "Matt was a very gentle person," Jim Webb told me and said his grandfather and Isaac had been on very good terms.

Fannie was questioned next, after "coming from the chain gang...in the cell with the Dillingham woman." The reference to the chain gang confuses Della's site of incarceration, later said to be in Salisbury. Rumors that spread years after the murders indicated that Della had been pregnant. Perhaps she was brought back to Salisbury and kept in a more isolated and less prison-like environment because of her condition, but nothing reported confirms this. In any event, the Greensboro paper reprinted Fannie's interview as well, and this time it didn't leave out the ugly language used by the *Observer*.

> "...*the conjured Nease Gillespie squaw was called out. Leaving off her story of Nease's cruelty, she was as dumb as a frog in dog days. She wears the pitched eyes and says: 'I an' Nease ain't spoke two pleasant words in three years. He sho' Gawd was mean to me. But I doan know anything about him going over to Mr. Ike's house, for I never has a thing to do with him and don't even live with him. He says he wouldn't stay with me, but he has to. He has been married before and has two or three wives.'*
> *This is all that could be wrung from her. The boy said she had begged Nease not to go over to Mr. Lyerly's and she goes squarely back upon him by denying that she said any such thing. Of the two, the boy is by far the more intelligent and appears to tell the straight tale.*" [D]

It's not clear what Henry or the reporter meant by "pitched eyes," and I found no one of any ancestry who could explain it. But the interview may clear up the mystery of the woman named Mary, who was listed as Nease's wife in 1880 and 1900. Perhaps Mary wasn't Fannie's other name or nickname after all. Maybe this was another woman altogether. But, if so, why would Henry Mayhew be listed with Nease and Mary in 1900 and then as Fannie's son in 1910?

Another report in the same edition of the *Observer* added a few more twists and contradictions. First it publicized a damning opinion, then punched holes in the very testimony that supported it.

> *It is now considered almost certain that four of the five negroes...are guilty.... One of the boys, George*

*Erwin, is believed to be innocent. Two axes were used
and a lamp was held by a woman.* [D]

However inappropriate the report began, it did elaborate on a
testimony mentioned only briefly in other papers. It revealed that
Nease had previously lived with and worked for a Mecklenburg
farmer, whom the reporter must have tracked down and
questioned. The man, who remained nameless, was quoted.

*In talking of the negro yesterday, his former
employer said: "Well, if he is guilty old Fannie, his wife,
fanned him on, for she was the meanest negro I ever
saw. Mich, or Nease, whatever you call him, was then a
good worker, but quick tempered. He would fly into a
passion, but was soon over it. Old Fannie never did get
over a mad spell"* [E]

Though the statement might legitimize Nease's alleged
threats against Isaac, it also explained why they weren't taken
seriously. Perhaps Nease was known to blow off steam once and
a while, without harming anyone. His former employer's
character assessment substantiates another's who testified at the
State's investigation held on July 20th. Continuing, the paper said
"Nease seemed eager to talk with his former master and denied
any connection with the crime." And Nease also wanted to
know, said the report, "'Where was the white man who had been
sleeping at the Lyerly home for a week. I saw him there Friday
afternoon when I passed by, in company with Mr. John
Penninger, my employer.'" [E] The reporter's use of the word
"master" is noteworthy, since slavery had supposedly been
abolished decades earlier.

This report didn't clarify whether or not Nease got a chance
to speak with his former employer. But the *Industrial News* said
he did, so the man must have thought enough of Nease to show
up on his behalf. "To this man," said the *News*, "he strongly
denied any connection whatever with the crime and implicated a
white man, whose name he did not know and who, he said, was
living at the Lyerly's when they were killed. This white man,
says Gillespie, had just come there to work for Mr. Lyerly." [F]

Nease had to have meant James Taylor who, for some reason, had spent the night at Cook's house on Friday the thirteenth.

This version agrees with the Charlotte report, and then carries the description of Fannie a step further, characterizing her as dangerous, not just ill-tempered. It said Gillespie's former employer "gives Gillespie a very good character, but says he was hot-tempered and would fight at the drop of a hat. Gillespie's wife, however, he represents as being a veritable virago. He heard her threaten a number of times to kill her husband." [F] This makes it sound more like *she* murdered the Lyerlys and tried, initially, to put the blame on Nease.

The same Greensboro paper noted that a Charlotte attorney "volunteered to defend the alleged murderers for the present, and consulted [with] them in the jail this afternoon." Perhaps this unnamed attorney was not Jake Newell, since it was reported later that Newell took the case around August 1st, having had very little time to consult with the accused prior to August 6th.

In addition to its version of the interviews, the *Industrial News* substantiated the rumor that the mob was planning to attack the Charlotte jail and said Sheriff Wallace had taken extra precautions to counteract any attempt to lynch the prisoners. Wallace, the paper reported, "will continue to keep the jail well guarded as there is still a possibility that a mob may come from Rowan and undertake to deal out summary justice to the alleged murderers." The *News'* use of the word, "alleged," by the way, set it apart from most of the others in this stage of the reporting. The word didn't even seem to be a part of Bryant's vocabulary, and Bryant was the one who did the most "talking" on the subject.

The same seemed true for the entire paper. The *Observer* continued to convict the suspects in its concluding remarks on the prison interviews, even as it appeared concerned about the impending threat of violence. Perhaps fearing its own words had been at fault, it now said that "...the good people of Rowan had decided to let the law take its course," that the "mob spirit had subsided" and that "Every effort will be made to give the murderers a fair trial," ironically using "fair trial" and "murderers" in the same breath. It indicated a fair trial could be had, ignoring the fact that an all-white jury would decide the fate of six blacks. For its grand finale, it said "...there is no reason why the criminals should not receive swift and proper punishment," [D] as if presumption of innocence was an alien concept.

But not every *Observer* reporter presumed guilt outright. On the day after the first visit to the Mecklenburg jail, the *Observer* ran a follow-up story, which did not help Nease at all, but at least presented itself as speculation rather than assumption of guilt. This one, said to be written by an "Observer man" who "went to the county jail yesterday and saw the five negro men," described their physical characteristics, without condemning them. He characterized Nease as "a tall, yellow negro, with muddy eyes and kinky hair," weighing about 175 pounds and "muscular, well-built and strong. His face wore a hunted, frightened appearance yesterday," said the writer, "and his nerve had deserted him; he seemed as meek as a lamb. His hands are horny and hard from labor." [G] The next statement at least used "alleged" in its condemnation. "Nease is the negro who, it is alleged, lead in the butchery at the Lyerly home."

Next the writer explored a hypothesis that Nease alone may have murdered all of the Lyerlys. Supporting the theory, he said, was "evidence of but six licks," and an analysis of the crime scene. The writer argued that the casual observer, upon viewing the "house, the dead bodies and the disorder generally" would probably conclude "that one man killed the four persons."

This explanation does make more sense than what the coroner's jury came up with—six people in one room with axes swinging, but it also assumes only a man could have done the job. [G] There was really no reason for that assumption, because several axe murders had been committed by women during that time, one by the wife of a well-known Arkansas farmer. The conviction said she killed her husband, her four-year-old, and then wounded two other children with the axe, before setting the house on fire. [3]

Ignoring such a scenario for this case, the report continued by speculating, in detail, how Nease, by himself, might have committed the act. The author's familiarity with the crime scene suggests he witnessed it himself on July 14th. Recounting it again here, in gruesome detail, could not have benefitted the accused.

*A powerful negro, like Nease, could have entered the first-floor sleeping room of the Lyerlys from the hall door, lifted his axe and dealt Mr. Isaac Lyerly the blow on the forehead; Mr. Lyerly, being a large, healthy man, could have risen after the lick, fallen forward to the foot of the bed on his face and received the second lick in the back of the head. From the way the body lay, the death-dealing weapon could have been used as described. In the meantime, little Johnnie, who was sleeping with his father, could have been getting up. One blow on the top of the head with the blade of the axe dispatched him. By this time Mrs. Lyerly was up and preparing to leave her bed, when the assassin wheeled almost in his tracks and drove his axe to the eye in her head. She fell back on her side, but was given a parting blow on the temple, just above the ear. Little Alice, who lay as if she had slept through it all, was struck a crushing blow with the pole of the axe. A half dozen licks, swift and certain, could have done the work.* [G]

The speculator, however, saw a problem with his own theory. "The night being dark, the murderer could not have seen without a lamp," he figured. "It was generally believed Saturday that Nease Gillespie used the axe, while a pal held the light."[G] Actually, no one was needed to hold a lamp that could easily have sat on the bureau or on the floor, but the reporter was right about the night being dark. On that date the moon was in its last quarter.

It was odd that this theory got any coverage at all, with Henry's version now being hyped as the official scenario. It made it clear, though, that there had been enough doubt to spark this kind of speculation. The writer did acknowledge the contradiction between the one-man theory and Mayhew's testimony, before turning his attention to the other prisoners.

These portrayals were not positive, but not overtly degrading either. Jack was said to be "a small, light colored negro, with bright eyes and a clean face," about 30 years old, the report adding that he "was very uneasy yesterday." George Erwin, John Gillespie, and Henry Lee, were described as "young negroes" and "the sort of darkies that wear wristbands of leather. None of them," it said, "seem to be of a high order of intelligence." The writer didn't identify his test for evaluating the intellects of these certainly exhausted and terrified young men.

The most irresponsible of all these reported interviews was John Moose Julian's. He didn't go to the jail and talk with the suspects himself; he summarized, in the worst way, the work done by other reporters. He left out the interview with Della entirely, and he made a point to quote the *Observer's* most damning statement, that it was "almost certain that four of the five negroes...are guilty of the murder...." Though Julian included the comments from Nease's former employer and those about Nease's suspicions of a white man's involvement, these hints at innocence were laced with his emotional condemnation: "To a man with a heart, such a crime as the Rowan negroes are charged with seems almost impossible." Julian did not mention Nease's explanations about the dispute with Isaac, and in the days that followed, he would continue to portray Nease as defiant and unconcerned, ignoring all other observations.

## "BOY CONFESSES: FIVE ARE MURDERERS: REVENGE WAS THE MOTIVE." [C]

This distortion screamed boldly from Julian's next issue— one hiding now in the *Post's* morgue—one of those that didn't get filmed. Then the *Asheville Gazette* headlined that same damning insinuation, as did others, across the state and beyond. [H]

# 9

# FORESHADOWS

## Monday through Friday, July 16-20

*There is no grievance that is a fit object of redress by mob law.*
— Abraham Lincoln

Central Prison in Raleigh

The media blitz over the outrageous murders in Salisbury must have displaced some attention from another serious trial that began in nearby Moore County just days after Isaac, Augusta, John, and Alice were killed. Though a separate case altogether, it would turn out to have some bearing on the Lyerly case. In the meantime, the accused and the county were probably grateful for the distraction.

Just two counties below Rowan, and almost directly in line with Salisbury, lies the town of Monroe in Union County. There, in July, twenty-one people faced charges for their part in a lynching in Wadesboro the previous May. Wadesboro, in Anson County, lies directly East of Monroe, and if one were to connect the dots on a map, from Barber Junction to Monroe, then make a right turn to Wadesboro, the capital letter "L" would be formed.

The *Charlotte Observer* covered the July 16th proceedings of Moore County's special term in Monroe, called to try the alleged lynchers of John V. Johnson, who had been awaiting his second trial after the first ended in a hung jury. A preliminary trial was held on June 1st in Wadesboro, the site of the lynching, but, according to the interpretation on that day, the lynching laws required that the trial be moved to an adjoining county. The original proposed location was Richmond County, but rumors of more mob activity altered that plan.

In a rare disclosure, the *Observer* said the accused were all from a "good section of the county, inhabited by some of the best people of the State." This was not something you'd normally hear about lynching suspects, especially not that they were "members of leading families," as these were said to be. Local lynching reports almost always tried to associate mob members with undesirables or outsiders and disassociate them from the "good" citizens. In this case, however, two members of the mob had turned State's evidence and identified those charged, making it impossible for the press to pretend they were all "bad citizens." The paper noted that, because of who was involved, this promised "to be a record-breaking case and the newspapers all over the country are watching the developments closely." [A]

Before hearing testimony, Judge T.J. Shaw questioned the jurors about outside influence, citing rumors "...that parties have been in this county seeking to mold public opinion, either for or against the defendants, and I want to know if any of you gentlemen have been approached on the subject." After questioning a couple of the jurors, Shaw released one from duty for saying the accused should be freed.

Concluding a long speech, strongly condemning the lynchers and others who would take the crime lightly, Shaw said those who participated in the mob were "'guilty of murder in the first degree.'" [B] And this misconception, legally speaking, would be echoed soon in Salisbury.

By the afternoon the grand jury had "returned true bills against four of the alleged lynchers," but it was still trying to decide the fates of the others. In the meantime, what remained of the day was spent arguing defense attorneys' motion that indictments against all should be thrown out on a technicality. The decision would remain with the judge, the day ending with no determination on the issue. [B]

The coverage of the second day's proceedings revealed that the decision on Defense's motion had been postponed "owing to the desire of the State to amend the bill of indictment." After eleven true bills were found on this revised indictment, the judge, who had been merely waiting on the formalities to finish, "quashed the indictments on the ground of improper venue." [C]

As it turned out, the technicality argued by Defense prevented the trial from continuing in Union County, so all were freed on bond that day, except one, Zeke Lewis, who would appear before the Supreme Court to settle the question of venue. While cases of the others were continued, it was speculated that they would never be tried. [C] And that prediction turned out to be correct.

What happened in the Anson/Union County lynching case would have a significant affect on the outcome of the trials in Salisbury the following month. The *Observer* summed up the situation:

> *The evening shadows lie across the great green of the court house square. Five carloads of Ansonians have left for home, including the 21 alleged lynchers. Frank Graham goes home for good: no true bill was found against him and he was discharged. Three of the 21 men*

*against whom true bills were found have not been taken,
namely Tom Johnson, Ben Holt and Battle Lewis. The
other score made their $5,000 bonds promptly to appear
here at the October term of court, and their cases stand
continued under a general order.* [D]

Continuing, the report described the scene inside the
courthouse as most of the prisoners were temporarily released
and one permanently freed.

*All the defendants made their appearance, except
three not taken, and lined up with their elbows on the
bar-rail. When the solicitor announced that Frank
Graham was discharged, Frank did not wait for his
fellows, but bowed and left the court room, smiling
delightedly. The others seemed happy, too. As they stood
there, waiting the approval of their bonds, 20 strapping,
sober, sunburnt men, it was hard to imagine them as a
mob crying, 'Damn the law!'*

*'You may go, gentlemen,' said the judge.*

*They made for the open door, followed by their
friends, and in a few minutes the room was all but
empty.*

*Such was the temporary collapse of the much-
discussed case..., and the newspaper men, the
stenographers and visiting lawyers found themselves set
down suddenly.* [D]

Afterward, the scene outside at the train depot played much
like a war hero's welcome. No one expected anything else to
come of the charges.

*In the court-yard the defendants stood to receive
congratulations. They, their lawyers and friends regard
the event as a great victory for them. The Supreme
Court, they anticipate, will affirm Judge Shaw's ruling,
and that will put the cases back to Anson, where, it is
said they will hardly get further than the grand jury. But
if the grand jury down there should find true bills, a
motion will then lie to remove the cases to another*

*county in the regular way on the ground that a fair trial cannot be had in Anson.* [D]

But the situation was not a triumph for everyone. "A very lonely, woeful figure this week had been Mr. Henry Kendall, who turned State's evidence. His old neighbors shunned him studiously. One of the defendants told me to-day that Mr. Kendall offered to shake hands with him this morning, and when he declined to shake, Mr. Kendall burst into tears. Most of the time he sat in the corridor, outside the grand jury room, waiting his call to testify and reading the newspapers."

The triumphant home-coming of the "many Ansonians who attended the trial of the alleged Anson county lynchers," was covered in the *Carolina Watchman.* "There were eager crowds at the stations between Monroe and Wadesboro to cheer the alleged lynchers as they passed through. They were also greeted by a large crowd on their return home." [E]

The handling or mishandling of the Anson/Monroe case was later blamed for the lynching of Nease, Jack, and John in Salisbury on August 6th. Pastor W.H. McLaurin of South Carolina made the connection in his commentary printed on August 9th. He said the "failure to bring those lynchers at Wadesboro to speedy justice, together with the many newspaper apologies, doubtless, is responsible for the terrible crime of Monday night at Salisbury." [F] Josephus Daniels also linked the two incidents in his August 8th editorial, in which he also blamed an error in the latest revision of the law for the suspects' release. Though, considering the source, it's just as likely the intent was to assure any future lynchers of impunity.

*The unfortunate omission in the Revisal by which the trial of the alleged Anson county lynchers came to an abrupt and farcical end at Monroe has in the Salisbury tragedy its direct reflection. The Anson situation has raised an unfortunate opinion that lynching is a safe pastime. It is spoken confidently that no jury will convict lynchers in the county in which they committed their crimes.* [G]

In effect, the entire affair was just another pretense of justice. What is most unusual about his case, though, is that the victim, John V. Johnson, was a white man.

∞

At least two forces were at work while the public awaited the Lyerly murder trial. Editor Julian was probably getting nervous about all the mob threats he had helped inflame with his unrestrained rhetoric and exaggerations. Then there was the ever-growing concern about what the North, specifically its business prospects, thought about Salisbury's and the state's stability. Anxious to get beyond the Civil War and a recent, devastating economic depression, Salisbury and much of the South was ready to ride the coattails of the growing new industrial revolution. It would not look good for Salisbury to appear as a lawless, redneck town.

Thus the duplicity deepened. Rather than face the threats head-on or attempt to correct inflammatory errors, John Moose Julian reverted to denial. His coverage of the Lyerly case from now until the trial was thus complemented by commentaries meant to reassure citizens that no mob violence could possibly occur in "good ole" Rowan. Its citizens were far too law-abiding and civilized to support such savagery, as he portrayed them. But he must have known that lynching was still very much on the minds the county's citizens. Or had that whack on the head made him forget the attempts made to lynch the prisoners just a few days earlier?

More than likely it was actually his acute awareness of the need to prevent another, more successful riot, that caused Julian to focus on the assurance of a speedy and efficient trial. He emphasized the certainty that the murders of "Isaac Lyerly, his wife and children will be avenged by the law..., and this should be enough to satisfy any and all who are either directly or indirectly interested in the case." [1]

This emphasis on a speedy trial was pretty much the universal cop-out in cases such as this. Knowing they wouldn't have the guts or heart to stand up to the mob or shoot their own friends if it meant saving a prisoner from lynching, officials sanctioned what amounted to many legal lynchings by rushing a case to trial without giving defense lawyers time for proper preparation. Or juries, themselves facing terror threats from the mob, would often ignore any evidence of innocence and push through an unjustified guilty verdict.

Others' predictions, however, were not as optimistic as Julian's. A back page article of the July 19th *Charlotte Observer* confirmed that the earlier lynching sentiments had not, in fact, been subdued. It said that, although the citizens of Charlotte who "reflect the better sentiment of the county" were glad that the prisoners were being held in the Mecklenburg Jail, there was nevertheless a "determined crowd," some good and some bad, remaining in the city "...for the purpose of finding out something." The report also revealed information discovered on the previous day—"that money almost to the amount of $1,000 had been raised for the purpose of sending down men enough to storm the Charlotte jail.... There is no calculating the possibility of evil to result from this attempt."[2] No mention of this plot was found in the *Post*.

Washington's correspondent, still reporting from Charlotte, wasn't playing Julian's game either. It noted again, a few days after it's first warning, that there was "some evidence that a mob will attempt to take the prisoners from the jail here." The D.C. paper also exposed an important sentiment among some of the locals, saying many of the "best-informed citizens think the authorities should have the five negroes sent to the penitentiary in Raleigh for safekeeping. It is pretty generally believed here that they are not safe in Charlotte."[3] That looked like a good idea on the surface. The state penitentiary, or Central Prison, still stands today in Raleigh like Dracula's castle looming darkly over the city. Anyone who's seen it knows it would have been a formidable obstacle to any lynching attempt. That is, unless its director was in favor of lynching himself, which was likely the case, judging by a letter from a future superintendent of the state's penitentiaries, J.J. Laughinghouse, written after an earlier lynching.

The Charlotte paper did conclude its comments on the subject in a more positive tone. It first suggested there was more than one reason why the mob should not attempt to take justice into its hands, one being that not all of the accused were considered to be guilty. The article said some of Lyerly's neighbors believed George Ervin was innocent. "His reputation has not been bad and nothing serious has been charged against him." Though others still believed all six were guilty, said the report, it nevertheless expressed optimism that eventually the "trouble will at last blow over, and that the men may be brought here for trial." [4] The implication that the accused might not be safe in Salisbury, conflicted with the *Post's* and Judge Long's later assumptions that they had nothing to fear there.

The closing statements of the report offered an opinion not to be echoed after the lynching. It "is certain," it said, "that all the men who would take part in this lynching are not hoodlums and they are not cowards. They have not the slightest fear that justice will be done. Charlotte needs to be apprized of these circumstances." [5]

Misinformation printed in the *Observer's* next headline was tempered a bit by the use of the word "alleged." The "alleged slayers," it said, "would be Given Preliminary Examination at Salisbury To-Day" and also predicted that "Sensational Evidence is Looked For." The article said District Attorney W.C. Hammer, more commonly known as Solicitor back then, would be in Salisbury to conduct an examination of the State's witnesses and added, in a backhanded sort of way, that essentially no evidence discussed thus far had amounted to much. "There will be some sensational developments if all the talk indulged in for the past few days crystalizes into something more substantial than hot air," the article added. "The little Gillespie negro is not the State's reliance only and there will be white people of character who will give evidence showing the wisdom of the arrests made Saturday." [6] The headline was wrong—the suspects were not examined that day at all. They remained in the Charlotte jail while testimony against them was heard and recorded only by the press.

Josephus Daniels' paper opted for the sensational as well. Referring to the upcoming trial, the *N&O* announced in a lengthy headline that "This Case Promises to be One of the Most Celebrated In the History of Rowan County." Earlier, the *N&O* had characterized the Lyerly murders as "the worst case of human butchery ever brought to light in North Carolina," but now it upgraded the murder to one of the most "diabolical in the history of the South." [7] Had Daniels forgotten about the massacre in Wilmington, just eight years earlier, that he, himself, was partially responsible for?

At least Daniels did not deny public hostility for the prisoners. His paper admitted the prisoners had had "some difficulty in securing counsel on account of the feeling against them in this section." Jake F. Newell of Charlotte and H.S. Williams of Concord had finally taken the case, less than a week before the trial was to begin. [8] The existence of this obvious "feeling against" the prisoners, which Daniels helped to create, would be denied on August 6th by Judge Long and Solicitor Hammer, when counsel for Defense tried to call attention to the problem.

An indictment of all six suspects was the most predictable thing of all—a sure thing. The grand jury would examine "evidence" against only the usual suspects, following the same old southern script. In his book about "Black Southerners in the Age of Jim Crow," Leon Litwack notes that the black suspect, if accused of a crime, "faced at the very outset the difficulty of securing competent legal counsel. Skilled white lawyers could find little time for black defendants unable to pay legal costs and, fearing the loss of their white clients, little reason to defend them at all. If assigned by the court to defend a black accused of a crime against a white person, even the most conscientious white lawyer faced formidable obstacles in his attempt to mount a serious defense. He had to think not only about his livelihood but in some instances about his life as well." [9] Litwack's findings and the Anson case fortell much of what was to come.

# 10

# THE STATE'S INVESTIGATION

## FRIDAY, JULY 20 AND SATURDAY, JULY 21

*Nease said he thought he could hold his wheat crop by law but thought he would let them have it.*

— John Nelson Penninger

JOHN NELSON PENNINGER

# INTRODUCTION

A week after the Lyerlys were murdered, a small room in the old Rowan County courthouse was crowded with lawyers, reporters, family members, and witnesses. But none of the accused was present, nor was there a lawyer there to represent them in their absence. It had been too dangerous to bring the prisoners back to Salisbury—and too risky for anyone, black or white, who might have tried to defend them. The witnesses had been summoned by Solicitor William Cicero Hammer for questioning. The *Salisbury Post's* "transcript" of this investigation was the first article I read after learning about the murders. Either Addie or my grandmother had saved it for years, and years later my aunt photocopied it. The copier missed a few small spots where the original was damaged and folded, but I could tell from what peeked out of those folds some important information had been covered up.

Finding those few hidden words was one of my biggest challenges in researching this story. At least one other source was needed to verify or clarify what Julian had reported and to fill in for the damaged parts of my copy. It also needed to be an equally comprehensive account of the solicitor's investigation, because that investigation would turn out to be the only thing even resembling a trial of the case.

As soon as I learned about the gaping hole in the *Post's* microfilm archives, I called the paper's office to see what they had in their collection and was assured everything available had been filmed and could be found in the Rowan Library. But that explanation didn't satisfy me, so I checked library collections throughout the state. Same story. Even after the North Carolina State Archives explained the situation—that they had filmed everything available, and every library's collection was the same—I couldn't believe I had the only record of the solicitor's investigation in existence or that the *Post* was the only paper to cover the inquiry in detail.

Sweet Meadows Café, I thought, ought to have some answers. It's the kind of place where you can get wild salmon on a salad, with a side of gossip—or Marilyn Harrison's famous crab cakes. So I hung around my cousin's restaurant for the next few days to see what I could find out about the mysterious missing articles. Marilyn's café (now under new ownership) is located in the center of downtown Salisbury, across from the newspaper office and just steps from the Confederate Memorial, Fame, from which Marilyn once snatched what she called a vile, racist flag. It was planted there, she told me, as part of a heated response to a peaceful demonstration led by attorney Michael King the day before.

There was always something going on at Sweet Meadows', and after being away from my home town for so long, having lunch there was like a family reunion. As a bonus, my illustrious and generous cousin Ralph was often around for interesting conversation and to pick up the tab. Anyway, some lunching there that day speculated that a fire at the *Post* building many years ago had probably led to the extermination of the now lost editions.

But I wasn't buying that explanation either. Though I later learned there had indeed been a fire in 1912, it didn't explain some of Joe Junod's quotes in his 1974 recap.

I finally tracked Junod down about a year later and spoke to him on the phone. He remembered the interview with Addie very clearly, he said. And no, she hadn't told him anything he didn't include in his 1974 story. The quotes he got from the *Post*, he said, were right there in the morgue; he didn't have to look any farther. His response helped me convince the *Post's* current editor that they were sitting on at least some of the unfilmed articles. The two I found in the morgue were badly deteriorated, but I was still able to make out most of the information not legible in my aunt's copy.

I now had everything the *Post* could offer, and yet I still sensed something important had been withheld from publication. I couldn't figure out what was up with Bryant—had he gone on vacation? And where was McNeill? Had his coverage of the riot on the previous Saturday night dampened his desire to be further involved? Given Charlotte's earlier reports, the prisoner interviews, and McNeill's detailed description of the murder scene, I couldn't figure out why the paper that had provided such extensive coverage and follow-up had ignored more than half of what the *Post* reported of this major development. Where were these guys when important details of the case were being revealed? Where were they when I needed them?

Over the past five or so years I had spent months in the Manteo and Kill Devil Hills libraries at the microfilm reader. I read for hours at a time, my eyes strained and aching from staring at the blurred and overexposed pages and my hands numb from pressing the forward and backward buttons. I painstakingly scanned all the *Observer's* microfilmed editions from June, 1906 through February of 1907. Everything remotely related to the subject that was copy-able was copied. Several sections of the film are so overexposed I had to hand-copy their reports, including McNeill's walk-through account of the murder scene. To be certain I'd missed nothing, I repeated the entire exercise. But there was one date missing in the *Observer's* archives—the day after the solicitor's investigation.

Looking for that missing report drove me to almost every county library in the state to see if any had reprinted it or covered the story themselves. The larger libraries have extra copies of their films to loan out, but many of the smaller ones don't, so the only way to view all the state's newspaper archives was to travel to every small-town library or pay someone to do it for me. I was borrowing to buy groceries, as it was, and I didn't trust anyone else to know what to look for anyway.

Frustrating and expensive as this delay was, what it taught me was worth it. The experience added to my understanding of just how ubiquitous the bias against black folk was during that period. As I reviewed these papers, I couldn't help but notice the many reports of lynchings and literal harping on black crimes and minor incidents. Most of the papers never published anything positive about blacks unless an "old-time darkey" was passing, and then not without expressing regret that few like him or her were to be found anymore. Never was a person of African descent pictured respectfully or well-dressed in any of these publications, but they *were* represented as unflattering cartoon characters of an advertised product, like the "Gold Dust Twins." Growing up in the South, I had become so used to this form of brainwashing via visual deprivation, that when I finally found black newspapers from other states, picturing distinguished-looking black citizens, dressed to the nines, some of them Harvard graduates, I realized I'd never before seen anything from that time period like it.

That discovery got me sidetracked on another quest—to see if there were any positive publications for black North Carolinians in 1906. After an exhaustive search, I didn't find one, at least not one that survived. Compared to African American voices in other southern states, like the *Richmond Planet*, the *Savannah Tribune*, the Baltimore *Afro-American*, the Chattanooga *Blade*, and the Atlanta *Independent*, North Carolina's silence was resounding. The only major black paper still operating in North Carolina after Alex Manly's office was burned in 1898, was the A.M.E. *Star of Zion*. But none of its issues for July or August, 1906 were in the filmed archives. Livingston College, one of the oldest African American colleges in the country, said it had nothing on the case at all in its files.

When I learned about *Planet* editor John Mitchell's activism, I was sure that he must have commented on or covered the case. For years prior to 1906, Mitchell had been a leading and outspoken voice for black Americans in the South, and he had gotten personally involved in preventing more than one lynching in Virginia. Surely he'd have a fresh perspective on the Lyerly case, I hoped, amazed to find most of the *Planet's* 1906 issues on film. But even Mitchell, I soon learned, had hedged in his coverage of the 1906 case. Jim Crow must have scared him off too. Furthermore, I never found out why Ida B. Wells, the very outspoken leader of the movement to stop lynchings, had not investigated this one. What exactly was going on in North Carolina? It indeed seemed to be the worst of times there for people of color.

After the disappointing results of that search, the lack of coverage of Hammer's investigation, even in the white press, still nagged at me. And extending the hunt another year hadn't helped. I remained perplexed as to why none but one of the leading reporters had adequately covered this important phase in a case that had been so sensationalized initially. The lure of the story must have faded with the failed attempts at lynching. After the initial feeding frenzy over the gruesome murders, most of the papers seemed to have lost interest in printing even inaccurate or biased details, which required some analytical thinking on the part of the reader, and, if scrutinized at all, would cast doubt on the suspects' guilt. With each passing day after the murders, fewer and fewer words were printed, and the ones that *were* published were usually those most damning to the accused, even more so taken out of context. By the time a week had passed, and the most detailed and reliable information had surfaced in this July 20th investigation, most publishers had reduced the two full newspaper pages of testimony found in Salisbury's paper into a one-to-two paragraph summary. These told the public, in essence, there was little left to say about the case that hadn't been said already—there were no surprises except that Fannie had gone back on her previous statements and contradicted Mayhew, whose testimony was usually described as "damning." The repeated portrayals of Fannie as old and crazy only served to strengthen the reliability of Henry's story. Josephus Daniels' *N&O* had gone so far as to headline one of its summaries with: "Weaving A Rope."

Just when I was about to give up, I found what I no longer thought existed. Bryant had, after all, written a much more comprehensive and relatively illuminating report, meant to be a transcript, of Solicitor Hammer's July 20th inquiry. I ran across it by mistake, while looking for something else, in a little library on the Old 64 route I often took to Salisbury. By then I had become more than weary of wasting time reading these small-town papers that, so far, had only rehashed the same information, often with multiple errors. But when I saw the town's name on the highway sign, it jogged my memory of the earlier axe murder and multiple lynching (in 1885) in Chatham County. I was told some time ago that the only copy of the research on that case was now missing, but such assertions had lost all meaning for me by now. I pulled off the highway as if drawn toward town—knowing the library had to be somewhere near Main Street. When I found it, the report that is, it felt like striking oil must feel to Texans. The Pittsboro *Chatham Record* carried the story I was looking for. And it was in Siler City, of all places. I'd driven from Manteo, Andy Griffith's hometown, to find the missing piece of the puzzle in Aunt Bea's.

It was obvious from the get-go that this paper carried more than just another recap. As I skimmed it, one line jumped off the screen. Solicitor Hammer had asked Henry Mayhew who his daddy was, and Henry "called out" the name of "a well-known white man." That was one hidden thing that had been bugging me all these years. Not having the original Salisbury report with me, I couldn't compare all the *Record's* information to it, but I was absolutely certain nobody had identified Henry's daddy before. I don't know how I had missed it in my search of the *Observer* archives, but this was Bryant's report, as the Chatham paper acknowledged at the start.[1]

So I had to go back to the Charlotte films again, to find the whole thing—to make sure nothing had been left out in this smaller paper's reprint. One thing for sure, this paper hadn't identified who that well-known white man was, and I was hoping Bryant had in his original report.

I thought Barbara Allen at the Kill Devil Hills library was going to get sick when I asked her to order the *Observer's* microfilm again. She had been more than a saint throughout this entire project, procuring newspaper microfilm through interlibrary loan from all over the country and as far away as Alaska—but I know she must have felt like strangling me at times. Now, five years later, I wanted to see Charlotte's again. She complained, only half kidding, that June, 1906 through February, 1907 were a set of dates she never wanted to see again. But she got me the film fast, this time from the Virginia State Library. And I learned the reason I hadn't found this report earlier. The "missing" section had been filmed out of sequence with the rest.

Finally, I was sure I had every published report of Hammer's July 20th investigation. I tried, without luck, to determine whether any of Hammer's descendants had kept his papers, as well as those of the other attorneys present at this inquiry, hoping one of these had passed on a personal transcript. This road led to a dead end. A lot of very prominent people, it seems, would like to forget about this case altogether, if they haven't already. However, I did learn that Hammer, in addition to holding the office of Solicitor, had also owned and edited the *Asheboro Courier*—a paper which carried the same white supremacist biases as most others in the state. It too reported nothing more than a summary of the questioning on July 20th.

Now that I had the information, I wondered how best to pass it on without coloring any of it with my own interpretations or biases. I decided that quoting Bryant's entire report might be the best way. Aside from his obvious biases, Bryant provided the most readable account of the investigation and also a good recap of the case up to that point.

What follows is Bryant's report, in full, as it was printed in the July 22$^{nd}$ *Observer*. Nothing is omitted or changed, except corrections of obvious misspellings. However, within brackets in the body of his quoted text, a few comments or other pertinent or omitted information from other sources are added. Julian's *Post* account might have provided the most information, had it been available in an undamaged form. So I included after or within Bryant's account any readable information in the *Post*, not already reported in the *Observer*. The reader is left to imagine the questions posed to the witnesses, as these are omitted in the original report. The price of this issue, by the way, was five cents in 1906, and Bryant's part was at least two cents of that total.

SOLICITOR WILLIAM CICERO HAMMER

THE LYERLY MURDER CASE: THE STATE HEARS
EVIDENCE: The Load That Rests on the Shoulders of a
Tiny Mulatto Boy, Henry Mayhew—A Most Interesting
Story—Old Fannie Gillespie Puzzles Lawyers,
Spectators and All—She Denies Having Made Certain
Statements Last Saturday—All of the Negroes Now in
Charlotte Jail Are Accused by Henry—Fannie Declares
That She Knows Nothing of the Murderers—Contradicts
Henry's Stories—The Lyerly Girls on the Stand.

Special to The Observer.

Salisbury, July 21.—One of the most interesting, as
well as most brutal murders ever committed in North
Carolina was the killing of the Lyerlys in Rowan county,
last Friday night, a week ago. As the days go by the
mystery that surrounds the horrible crime grows. Nease
Gillespie, his 15-year-old son, John, and his step-son,
Henry Lee, George Ervin and Jack Dillingham occupy
cells in the Mecklenburg county jail. Old Fannie,
Nease's wife, and Henry Mayhew, her mulatto grandson,
are held as witnesses. Della, Jack Dillingham's wife, is
in the Salisbury jail, charged with being an accomplice
in the crime. The principal witness up to this time is
Henry Mayhew, who is a boy in short pants. He tells a
plausible story, every word of which is damaging to his
step-grand father and others.

The readers of The Observer will recall that Mr. Ike
Lyerly, his wife, Mrs. Augusta Barringer Lyerly, and
two children, John and Alice, were murdered at their
home near Barber's on the night of the 13th. The
following day the negroes whose names are given in the
foregoing paragraphs were arrested. Last Saturday night
a mob broke into the Rowan Jail, but the prisoners had
been transferred to Charlotte. A special trial has been
ordered for the 6th of August.

## WITNESSES EXAMINED.

Yesterday, Solicitor Hammer, Attorneys T.F. Kluttz
and T.C. Linn met in a room in the court house here and
examined the witnesses for the State. This was not a

preliminary hearing, but simply an effort to get the evidence of the prosecution well in hand so that the case might be tried later. The proceedings were extraordinary, at times, but the case is an unusual one. The negroes who are interested have done well to escape the lynchman's noose, for a hot mob was on their trail when Sheriff Julian saved their lives. The evidence against the prisoners is very thin, but it is generally believed that they are guilty. Therefore, the hearing here had a good purpose. One side is trying to get up its evidence. The following detailed record of what happened here yesterday and to-day will read like a romance. A little negro, half white and half black, is the hero of the story. On him rests a great burden. An old lamp connects Jack Dillingham with the crime.

The hearing began at 10 o'clock. [2]

## STORY OF MURDERED MAN'S SON.

The first witness to make a statement was Mr. J.G. Lyerly, a son of the murdered man and a half brother of the children. He said: "Jim Taylor, the boy who had been working for my father told me of the murder about 4 o'clock in the morning. Taylor had spent the night at Mr. R.F. Cook's, with Sam. I went with Mr. Pless [W.P.] Barber to the old home. Ed [E.A.] Barber, Charlie Brown and Ed Carter were there when we arrived. I think Mr. Matt L. Webb was the first man on the premises after the girls left. He was accompanied by a Mr. Watson, a cattle dealer who occasionally stopped with my father. Watson was on his way there that morning to get breakfast." [3]

"Soon after I arrived there those who had assembled thought it best to arrest Jack Dillingham, as the girls had said something about a quarrel that father and Jack had had the day before. The negro had said something about cursing father.

"When we entered the house we found the front door open, just as the girls had left it, when they started for Mr. Cook's home. The bodies of father and John were on the floor. Dr. Chenault and myself hunted for and found the money, about $175, that father kept in the house. Some of it was upstairs, in a drawer, and the remainder in the little rear room, near the kitchen. [4]

"The house in which Nease Gillespie lived is located about a quarter of a mile west of the Lyerly home. Jack Dillingham lived southwest, about 300 yards.

"When we went up to father's home we saw a feather bed, a bureau drawer and a lamp in the front walk, where the girls had left them. The Lyerlys were all friendly. Father and his children were on the best of terms.

"Last Christmas I heard father say that he and Nease had had some words about their contract. Father had told Nease that he would have to work a crop, as he had promised to do, or get out of his house. Nease cursed him, and, in turn, was ordered out of the yard. Henry, old Fannie Gillespie's son, left and went to Mr. Leroy Powlas' to live. Nease continued to drive for Mr. John Penninger, a saw mill man." [5]

### MISS MARY LYERLY MAKES A STATEMENT.

The next witness to take the stand was Miss Mary Lyerly, the oldest daughter, of Mr. Isaac Lyerly. She was dressed in black. Miss Lyerly is 18 years old, has an attractive face, light chestnut hair and soft, attractive brown eyes. [Mary's correct age was 17.] Her lips are thin and sensitive. She seems intelligent and sprightly. After a most trying week she appeared fresh and composed yesterday. Her manner was that of a quiet, modest but plucky maiden. She is neither backward nor brazen, but willing and ready.

"I knew nothing after I retired about 9 o'clock," said Miss Lyerly, "until Addie called me, declaring that the house was on fire and that papa and mama were dead. I was nearly suffocated. The house was full of smoke.

"When I went down I found Addie at work. She had already dragged papa and John from the bed and was fighting the fire. I caught hold of papa and pulled him further out from the bed. We threw water on the bed and carried out the burning things.

"I went over and felt mama's face; it was cold. She was lying just as she lay when she went to sleep, except that her feet were hanging out. I saw blood all over the pillow. I picked Alice, who was still alive, up in my arms and carried her out into the yard, where we tried to bring her to. We could barely hear her breathe. Addie went back upstairs and brought us some clothes, which we put on in the yard. We then left for Mr. Cook's, Addie leading Janie and I carrying Alice.

## DOOR AND WINDOW OPEN.

"The front door and the window that opens into papa's room from the porch were open. The key was on the inside of the door. I always locked the door at night but after papa went out and, on returning, forgot to turn the key. Anyone could have gotten in through the window, without much effort. [6]

"Papa's axe lay at the woodpile, for I saw it there the afternoon before. John and Alice had been cutting wood. [7]

"When I went to bed papa was fast asleep, snoring. Mama was dozing off. That was a few minutes before 9 o'clock. Addie and I slept together. I heard no noise.

"The lamp, which had a porcelain bowl, was nearly full of oil. It had been filled the Saturday before. I know that it was sitting on the bureau and the burner was on. When we arose, the lamp was on the hearth.

"John Gillespie, and Henry Lee, son and step-son of Nease, started a crop. They lived in the house with Nease and his wife, old Fannie. One day Fannie came down home and got after papa for having Henry and his wife live in with them. She was mad because they slept on her beds. Saturday following, Nease came and asked father what was the trouble with him and the boys. They had some conversation and Nease cursed papa, who drove him out of the yard. George Cranford, who worked for us then, said that Nease declared that he would kill old man Ike Lyerly. Mr. Cranford told us about it the next morning. Nease was mad. Papa told him that he would have to sow the wheat or leave.

"Mr. Cranford went from here to his home at Hildebrand. [8]

"Nease was down there once or twice after that but I never heard any more until a few days before the tragedy. Nease came down and asked papa what he was going to do with the wheat. Papa told him 'thrash it.'

"Della, Jack's wife, and mama had trouble Friday morning about the soap suds in the tub. After mama left I went down to the spring and heard Della say: 'If she (meaning mamma) had said three more words I would have downed her.'

"Jack and papa did not get along together. Jack had been there just about a week. He told papa that he was going to work for Mr. Penninger. Papa said, 'Well, Jack, if you go there and work five days without laying off, I will treat.'

"I heard Jack say that he wouldn't go to work for no man before 7 o'clock.

"Mr. Jim Taylor, who had been working for us and sleeping in the house, spent last Friday night with Sam Cook. I was straining the milk when he left. Sam Cook had come over to our house to bring a grain cradle which his father had borrowed that morning. Jack was at the lot with Della who helped us to milk the cows. Jim Taylor, Sam Cook and Jack left together, going down the path toward the spring. [This would be across Old 70, going south, in front of Isaac's house, a few yards away.] That morning Jack had worked for Mr. Cook and then he went down to Mr. Penninger's to get a job. Jim Taylor had seen Mr. Penninger and secured work." [9]

On being questioned by the lawyers Miss Lyerly continued: "Papa kept most of his money in the bureau upstairs. Nothing in the house was disturbed. Even Alice's little pocket book, which contained 25 cents, was left on the bureau by her bed.

"We did not go by Jack Dillingham's house, which was close to the path that leads to Mr. Cook's, for we were afraid that Jack might hear us. We slipped by, fearing that they might want to kill us too. Sister Janie, who is 10, going on 11, said that she heard talking in

Jack's house as we passed. It was then about 11:30 o'clock. We arrived at Mr. Cook's at 11:55." [10]

### MISS ADDIE LYERLY ON THE STAND.

Miss Addie, the second Lyerly child, a blond haired girl of 15 years, told of her experience on the night of the murders in a very direct and interesting way. [Addie was 14.]

"That night," said Miss Addie, "after Mary and I had finished washing the dishes and doing our regular work I sat the lamp in papa's room, on the bureau, blew it out and went up to our room. Some time between 10 and 11 o'clock I waked up and felt the heat and smelt the smoke of a fire. Mama had been unwell and my first thought was that she had become worse. I went down to her room and, as I entered the door, I saw that the bed in which papa and John slept was on fire. Papa was on the foot of the bed, with his feet drawn up. His head was close to the wall, back wall. He lay on his right side. I felt him; he was not cold, but a little stiff.

"A fire was burning slowly but steadily in the middle of the bed. The bureau drawer lay inverted upon the breast of John, who lay on his stomach. The drawer was burning. John's feet extended over the edge of the bed.

"I pulled papa and John to the floor and called Mary. We worked in the dark.

"After we had put out the fire I ran upstairs and got some clothes for us. I did not see any light or hear any talk as we passed Jack's house." [11]

Miss Addie corroborated other statements made by her sister. On being interrogated she made the following additional declarations: "When I went down mama's face was covered with a pillow. One of her feet was on the floor. Little sister lay beside her on her back, just as she had slept.

"When papa turned off the Gillespie boys, Nease came down and asked him why he had done it. Papa told him that they would not work the land, and they had to get out. Nease was ordered away and as he went he muttered something but I could not understand what he said. Mr. Cranford told us that Nease was saying that he would kill 'old Ike Lyerly.'

"Jack's wife said that if mama had uttered three more words she would have downed her.

"Della, that is Jack's wife, knew how we all slept."

Mr. Matt L. Webb, an illiterate white man who drove a wagon for Mr. Penninger, stated that he and Nease had worked together. In part he said: "Three weeks before the tragedy, in conversation with me, while loading lumber at Mr. Powlas', Nease brought up the subject of wheat. He declared that he thought the crop would be pretty good this year. I told him 'yes.' Then he said: 'Well, old man Ike Lyerly can cut mine but he won't eat it, or get the money for it.' I told Jones Thompson what Nease had said and he declared that Nease wasn't dangerous." [12]

### LITTLE HENRY TELLS HIS STORY.

After the foregoing persons had had their say a small, bright faced, curly haired boy, with blue eyes, and pretty features came in. He carried a little white, soiled hat in his hand. His lips twitched nervously, and he seemed uneasy. He looks more like his Anglo-Saxon father than he does his African mother. When asked who his father was he called the name of a well-known white man. [13]

"Do you like Nease Gillespie?" some one asked.

"No, he has been mean to me," was the quick reply.

Solicitor Hammer took Henry between his legs, pulled off his hat and patted him on the shoulders, saying: "boy, we're not going to hurt you. Nobody wants to harm you. Now you must tell us all you know."

[The *Observer* mentioned in a later article that Hammer weighed about 400 pounds.]

"Nease Gillespie beats me. He's my grandpa. He whipped me last Friday. Pa (meaning Nease) and John met Henry Lee and Jack at the branch, this side of Mr.

Ike's, Friday night [the night of the murders]. That's what pa and John said when they came back. Pa said that he didn't care what they did with him after he had done what he wanted to do. Maw, old Fannie, asked paw where he was going and he said 'It's none of your business, but you'll know when I come back.' She said no more. Paw and John came back before day. I was in bed with maw.

"When paw and John came in they set down by the fire and maw asked paw where he had been and he said: 'God damn it, I've been down to old Ike Lyerly's. By God, I went down there and killed them. I told you I was going to kill them, and so, by god, I did.' [14]

"It skeered maw nearly to death when paw said that. John didn't say nothing. Jack and paw done it. Paw said that Jack's wife held the lamp. All met at the branch. Paw took his axe with him. I saw him get it. He washed it off at the branch but there was some left on the pole. He and John said they washed it. We saw the axe the next morning and there was a speck of blood on it. Paw said he killed Mr. Ike and Miss Gussie (Mrs. Lyerly) and Jack killed John and Alice.

"Maw never asked no more, for she was skeered.

"Jack used Mr. Ike's axe. He and Mr. Ike fell out about a horse. Paw and John said they set the bed afire.

"Before day paw put his old overalls with John's, in a bed tick of straw and burned them. He burned his shirts too. We saw them burning them. They burned them because they had blood on them. Blood was all over the shirts and the overalls.

"I left home early that morning and told Mr. Mann Walton that paw had killed Mr. Ike and Miss Gussie."

"Do you know where you would go if you were to tell a story, Henry?" asked Solicitor Hammer.

"Yes, sir, to the bad place," answered Henry.

"Who made you?"

"The Lord," was the ready reply.

"Paw said they threw the lamp in the brier patch. I saw a church lamp at Jack's house the day Ma and me went down there."

The boy started when Mr. Hammer called to some one in a loud voice, and said: "They're not going to hurt me, are they?"

He was assured by a number of his country acquaintances that he would be all right if he told the truth.

"I saw the lamp on the mantel piece. Paw said that they threw it in a brier thicket.

This little negro tells a most interesting story. His words are full of meaning and the State must rely largely on what he says to convict the negroes who are now imprisoned in the Charlotte jail. Henry is disposed to tell too much but his story yesterday tallies, in the main, with the one he told the day after the murder at the coroner's inquest. He is smart and very bright. If his story is true, Nease Gillespie, John, Henry, George Ervin and Jack and his wife will hang. No half-grown boy ever had more responsibility resting upon him. It is a question of life or death.

## NEASE'S WIFE TELLS DIFFERENT TALE.

If the blackest old hag in darkest Africa were brought here and put side by side with Fannie Gillespie, the wife of Nease, it would require an expert student of negro faces to tell which was the native of America. I have never, in all of my experience with negroes, seen Fannie Gillespie's equal. She is black, dirty, mean and stubborn. For two inches back the hair has been clipped from her forehead, and the remaining kinks are done in thread. For several inches around her eyes the skin of her lean face is dark colored, as if she had applied tar to her face until it had come to be a part of her. She wore a filthy, short dress, and nothing more. Her feet were naked, wrinkled and scaly.

"Fannie Gillespie," she said, "is my name." This is an instance where the man took the name of his wife. Nease, who had been known as Mich Graham, became a Gillespie after he married Fannie. The children in neighborhoods where Fannie has lived, fear her. They say that she is crazy and likes to run people.

She is not formidable looking, but when her foot falls it does so without making a sound or leaving a track. She glides swiftly, but silently. One thinks of the missing link as she approaches him. The night of the murder she and little Henry were in the same room. Their stories do not tally.

"I raised Henry Mayhew, the little boy," said Fannie.

"What is the matter with your face and eyes and head old woman?" asked a lawyer.

"Nease put pitch on me and cut my hair while I was asleep. He has been doing that for a long time. I guess he does it for it happens while I am asleep. He has whipped me many a time.

"I have been married to Nease four years. We have lived together 20 years. Me and Nease and John and little Henry lived together. John is 15 years old. I am his grandma and Nease is his paw, by one of my girls.

"The first I knew about the death of Mr. Ike was before it came light when Mr. Pless Barber came along and called Nease and asked him if he knew that some one had killed Mr. Ike, Miss Gussie and the children. I called to Henry, waked him up and told him about it.

"Nease got up, and left for his work. He didn't stay for no breakfast. I told him if the Lyerlys were dead to come back and tell me but he didn't do it. I was in one room that night and Nease was in another. John didn't come to my house that night. He went away at dinner time Thursday and didn't come back. He was at Mr. Mann Walton's. Nease come home about sundown. [15]

"No, sir, I didn't see no crowd at the well. If I told the sheriff that I have forgotten it. I did not say that Nease knew about the murder."

Old Fannie had declared, on the morning after the crime that she had seen a crowd of men at her well Friday night. This, Sheriff Julian said, was true.

Fannie contradicted the sheriff. Mr. Dick Files said that Fannie had told him that Nease knew about the murder. This, Fannie denied, also. She did not know anything about Nease's axe or overalls. She explained the fire in the yard, which she said had been built on

Thursday, by saying that Nease had told her to burn up the bed bugs that were literally eating him up.

"Nease had a pair of old overalls and a good pair," continued Fannie, "John had two pair. Saturday is my wash day. I put three pairs of drawers and one shirt in the pot that morning, when they came after me."

Here Dr. Dorsett produced two wet shirts which had been taken from the pot in question.

### AFRAID OF NEASE.

Fannie had made the error that she would admit. She saw that she had left off one shirt.

"No, I never saw Nease, Jack and John talking together," declared Fannie. "Nease did say that Mr. Lyerly could cut the wheat, but he couldn't eat it. I was afraid of Nease. I ran because Nease had told me that white folks would do you whether they had anything against you or not. When little Henry said 'Lord, look at the people' I left, but I didn't run. I went to the home of a negro named Brooks.

"Henry is truthful. He is a very good boy."

Old Fannie had not seen Henry since the morning after the tragedy. She had no idea what he was saying.

"Nease didn't eat anything that morning. Me and the boy ate what cold things we had. Nease drank coffee."

Earlier Fannie had declared that Nease did not as much as take coffee.

"No, I don't know what Henry says."

She was told that Henry had said that she was frightened when Nease told her what he had done.

"Well, if Henry heard that I didn't."

### HENRY WAS BROUGHT IN.

A most interesting thing occurred here. Little Henry was brought in. The boy saw his grandmother and tears welled in his eyes and his mouth puckered.

"Come here, Henry," said Mr. Hammer, "and teach your grandmother how to tell the truth."

The boy told his story over again. Old Fannie turned her head away and beat a gentle tattoo upon the floor with a pitiful looking big toe.

"Didn't paw say he killed them, mama?" asked Henry, with tears in his eyes, as he looked his grandmother in the face, after she had turned around.

"I never heard him," answered Fannie.

"Well, he said," declared Henry with spirit.

Henry was returned to the jail.

Old Fannie wilted a little but screwed her lips into a funnel and made up her mind to tell nothing. She told those about her to take her out and hang her or do anything else they wanted to do. Sheriff Julian and Solicitor Hammer tried to explain to her that no one wanted to harm her.

"Henry Lee told his daddy," said the old negress, "that old man Ike Lyerly should be killed.

"Yes, I told Mr. Roseman (a constable) that white folks stuck together but negroes wouldn't do it. I said the negroes would be some account if they would stand together. Mr. Dave Alexander of Mecklenburg said to me once that negroes would not be any good until they learned to stick to each other." [16]

"Is that why you are sticking to Nease?" was asked.

"If a negro won't stick to me do you reckon I'm going to stick to him? Me and Nease hain't got along together in several years."

Mr. Dick File came in the room at this juncture and told the solicitor what Fannie had said to him the morning she was running from the officers.

"'You reckon they will kill me?' she asked as she came up," said Mr. File.

"Have you done anything?" I asked. "Did you have any hand in the Lyerly affair?"

"'No,' she said, 'but my husband did.'"

Here old Fannie broke out again and said: "Hang me when you get ready."

Everybody had become convinced that Fannie was lying and that she had made up her mind to continue to do so. She had been trapped in a dozen or more instances. In a way she was defiant. If a rope had been placed about her neck she would not have flinched. She had been treated kindly by Mr. Hammer.[17]

Mr. Hammer sent a parting shot after old Fannie: "Now, old woman, are we to believe you or the boy?"

"Believe him—(and a long pause) if you want to," said the negress.

Henry had stuck to his story, but it was very evident that he feared his grandmother.

Fannie Gillespie is a wonderful woman. She looks like a savage, but she thinks well. It was plain to one and all that she lied yesterday, but there was no way to correct her. Henry told someone after he left her presence that she was afraid of Nease. That, he declared, was the reason she would not tell the truth. It was suggested that Fannie was a believer in the ancient practice of conjuring. When asked concerning this she half-way admitted that she feared the tricks of a conjurer. She said that Nease was called a conjurer. Her stories of Nease's cruelty to her, his burning her with pitch, cutting her hair and trimming her finger nails to the quick, while she slept, are pitiful to hear. Little Henry has been led to believe that what Fannie says about Nease's cruel treatment is true. Old Fannie is cunning. She knows what to say and what not to say. She has a certain sort of nerve. Although she was coaxed here, the effect would have been the same had she been threatened. Half a savage and half a wizard, she is an interesting character. One moment, those who watched her as she fenced with Mr. Hammer, Mr. Kluttz or Mr. Linn were almost sorry for her, but the next they felt for the lawyers. For two hours they tried her, but she told nothing. Boldly and doggedly she disowned declarations that she was said to have made last Saturday. Good men, men who would not see a hair on the head of an innocent negro harmed, were as good as charged with lying by her.

## JACK WOULD FIX MR. LYERLY.

John Henderson, a tall, black negro, wearing overalls, took the stand after Fannie had been ushered out. He said that he and Nease and Jack were going to Barber's one night. On the way Jack said: "me and old man Ike Lyerly had a fuss."

Nease declared: "Yes, if you fool with old man Ike he'll have you on the chain gang."

"That's no more than I have been," said Jack. "But if old man Lyerly don't mind I'll fix him."

## THE TROUBLE BETWEEN MR. LYERLY AND JACK.

Mr. Sam Cook, the young man who walked away from the Lyerly home Friday evening late, with Jim Taylor and Jack Dillingham, said: "I left the Lyerlys at 6:30 and started home. Jim Taylor went with me. Jack came on at the same time. As Jack started away Mr. Lyerly said: 'Well, Jack if you work over at the saw mill five days I will treat you.' 'Yes,' Mrs. Lyerly said, 'and I'll give you something good to eat, Jack.'

"After we had left the house Jack said: 'If I wasn't on the old man's place I would curse him out.'

"Taylor and myself went to bed at 9-o'clock that night. We were in a back room. Taylor is at his home at Bridgewater now." [18]

## THE FIRST TO SEE THE AXE.

Mr. Charles Brown, of Cleveland [small town just west of Barber Junction], made the following statement: "Mr. W.U. Carter and myself went to the Lyerly home. We got there about 3:30 o'clock. As we passed Nease's house we noticed a light. Mr. Pless Barber and Will Barber soon came.

"About 5 o'clock we arrested Jack Dillingham. We knocked at the door. Ed Barber told Jack to get up. Jack's wife told us to not come in. She did all the talking. Jack said nothing. He was a long time making his appearance.

[The Barbers are either not present to corroborate any of the several testimonies that include their names, or all the reporters have omitted their testimony.]

"Nease came by the house about daylight. He asked if all were dead. He seemed at a loss to know what to say. He wanted to say something but could not form his sentences.

"I saw the axe at the Lyerly house. It lay beneath the porch, two steps east of the front entrance. There was blood on the handle as well as the axe.

"I know that Henry told his story after 4 o'clock. There had been one or more fires about the yard. There was evidence that clothes of some description had been burned. One of the party picked up a rock and announced that it was still warm.

In a cooking pot in the house we found two shirts and three pairs of drawers."

## JOHN PENNINGER TALKS.

Mr. John Penninger, the lumber man, said: "Nease and George Ervin worked for me. Nease left before supper but George remained there.

"I had heard nothing about the wheat since February. Nease told me that he thought he could hold his part by law but would not do that: he would let Mr. Lyerly have it. Nease came Saturday morning, curried his horses, watered them and started to gear them, but he changed his mind and told me that he believed that he would not work that day. That was before the Sheriff came. A man by the name of Gray and Jim Taylor told me of the crime. I went down and asked Nease about it. He said nothing until I spoke to him, but he had hardly had time to do so.

"Friday afternoon, at the mill, I made a trade with Jim Taylor. I hired him and asked if he would stay that night. He said no, he would go to Mr. Lyerly's. He left my place between sundown and dark.

"Nease was arrested at the Lyerly place." [19]

## ANOTHER THREAT MADE.

Mr. R.F. Cook, declared that Jim Taylor left for his old home, at Bridgewater, last Tuesday. He said that Nease had told him that if he did not get his wheat he would get old man Lyerly.

Chief of Police J. Frank Miller, of Salisbury, said that he saw the Lyerly axe and that it was bloody. [20]

Mr. Arthur Thompson said that little Henry showed him where to find Nease's axe and that, when he picked it up in the yard at 5 o'clock in the afternoon [about 17 hours after the murders occurred], it had blood on the eye and the handle. In pointing the axe out Henry had declared: "That is the axe paw killed Mr. Lyerly with. He washed the blood off of it at the branch."

The examination of witnesses did not amount to much to-day. Solicitor Hammer and Mr. Kluttz will go to Barber's this week and study the topography of the country and examine a few persons who have not been to Salisbury. Several men collaborated Henry Mayhew's story about the place the lamp would be found. More light was thrown upon the character of Jack Dillingham. Tom Giles, a well-known negro from Franklin township [just east of Unity Township], was in town today and he testified to the vicious disposition of Jack. He said that Jack had once "killed" his wife for a while. Jack threatened Mr. R.A. Rainey, for whom he worked a short while in Franklin. The investigation will continue. H.E.C. Bryant.

[Bryant's account of Hammer's investigation ends here.]

I don't know why Bryant didn't mention Deputy Goodman's or Sheriff Julian's testimony and a few others that the *Post* carried exclusively. He must not have followed up with all of the next day's developments in the investigation. His report was written and filed a few days before Julian's ran in his weekly edition. Julian's provides important statements by Henry Lee Gillespie's wife, Emma, and other testimony that adds to or clarifies what Bryant reported. It also includes documentation that brings both news sources under suspicion of withholding information—information that might have further weakened Henry Mayhew's testimony.

The following testimonies were those omitted from Bryant's report.

Deputy Sheriff Charles A. Goodman said: When I went for Henry Mayhew [probably means he picked Henry up at Barber Junction Depot] he at first refused to go. He also denied his identity at first. After admitting his name he asked me where his father and mother were. I told him in jail. He asked me if they were going to kill them and him. I told him he was only wanted as a witness. He said at first that Jack and his wife committed the murders and then said his father, his brother John, George Irvin and Uncle Henry were in the party. He said his father took his axe and they used this and Mr. Lyerly's. He told me that Nease had washed the blood off his axe and threw it down in the yard. He said that Nease had burned the clothes, a part of them in the fireplace in the house and burned the straw out of a bed tick and that some bloody straws were in the yard.

"I scratched in the ashes and towards the well near Nease's house. Saturday afternoon about 2 o'clock I found a white shirt button and also a lump of blood. I gave these to Dr. Dorsett. A bluish shirt was found in a briar patch. It looked like some one had tried to wash it. When we started up to look for the axe Henry said 'them people will swear on a stack of Bibles as high as the sky that they didn't do it.' The boy said the lamp was taken from a negro church and thrown in a briar patch after the killing." [B]

"John Brown said:

I found the lamp just as it now is with a little oil in it. We found the lamp 15 or 20 feet from the road when we stopped to pick some blackberries. The lamp had been placed there fresh. Mr. Sanders, who was with me, carried the lamp. He asked Addie Lyerly whose it was. Miss Mary was sitting there and said it was not their lamp. [B]

E.J. Roseman, of Salisbury, was an important witness. He said:

"When I got to the Lyerly home at 8:30 Saturday morning Shoaf Poteat, Ben Cauble and a Winston officer were with me. We took Nease Gillespie out in a cornfield 25 yards from the house to some tracks beyond all tracks made that morning, except where one man had walked. We had Nease to make tracks by the side of these and they corresponded exactly. The right heel was worn off up to the shoe and did not make an impression of a heel. I said, 'Old man, that track fits you mighty well.' He made no reply. Ed Poteat and myself went down to Henry's and arrested him and John. Henry and John were sitting down in front of the house. Barber and Poteat went in to search the house and left me with them. John asked, 'Have they got Jack yet?' I asked him Jack who. He said the Jack that worked for Mr. Lyerly. I told him they had some negroes but I did not know any except his father. Coming up the road I asked him why he inquired about Jack and he said Jack had made threats. He said that Jack had told him he was going to fix Mr. Ike and Miss Gus before he left there. He said Jack had knocked a horse down and Mr. Ike had got after him about it." [B]

Neither Barber's nor Poteat's testimony is included in any report. Poteat is among the thirty witnesses listed in the court records, but E.A. Barber is not.

Sheriff Julian's testimony, which his son said was the first one taken that day, was recorded as follows:

He said he saw Dillingham who said he knew nothing of the tragedy. Heard a man go by his house about 11 o'clock. [I think he means p.m. here.] Said he (Dillingham) passed Lyerly's house that morning about 11 o'clock but didn't stop. Asked him if he went up to the gate and he said no. Said he remained in the big road and didn't go up where the white men were. When Ed Barber went over to Dillingham's house they had to threaten to tear the door down before they would admit him.

They said that when Fannie (the negro woman) went up to Mr. Lyerly's next morning she was excited and when Mr. File asked her if she had anything to do with the murder she replied in the negative but said her husband did. At the Lyerly home saw Isaac Lyerly on the floor near the bed and his son right behind him. Mrs. Lyerly was lying on her bed with one foot and part of the limb outside the bed. Mr. Lyerly's head seemed to be mashed to pieces and the little boy's head appeared to be beaten into a jelly. It looked like an axe had gone into the side of the face and head.

"The little boy's legs were burned into a crisp and it was the most horrible sight I ever saw. Mrs. Lyerly's head was cut. Some material had been thrown on the little boy and a bureau drawer over it to hold it down. A lamp was there with burner off and the lamp empty, sitting on the floor." [B]

The copy of Julian's original report, the one I got from my Aunt Nellie, was the most badly damaged where Penninger's testimony was printed. By going into the *Post's* morgue and unfolding some of the damaged pieces on their original, I was able to make out the rest of what the *Post* said Penninger told the solicitor that day—something Bryant failed to mention:

*"Taylor was at my house Friday evening when Nease came home with team. Taylor told me he would go back to Lyerly's and stay there that night and come over the next morning. I don't know whether Nease was close enough to hear this or not. The next day Taylor told me he could not work until Monday. All of my hands left and I told him I could not give him work until the middle of the following week."* [B]

So maybe Nease thought Taylor would be at the Lyerlys the night of the murders, and maybe he didn't. But if he did, it's doubtful he would have gone over there and tried to kill anybody, unless, of course, Taylor was involved.

Charles Brown's testimony is another in the damaged part of Julian's report. The readable part includes more information left out of Bryant's. Julian's said Brown told the solicitor that "Nease walked up and asked, if all were dead, and if anyone had been in the house to see about it. He seemed to want to say something and did not know what to say." [B]

*"I think Frank Miller found the axe, about two steps east of the door step, under the edge of the porch. The axe had blood on the handle, it was all smeared with blood. Do not remember seeing blood on the axe, I think Beaver found lamp and R.M. Saunders took it to the coroner's inquest."* [B]

Saunders is listed in court records with other witnesses. He is probably the same person as the Sanders mentioned earlier in another testimony Bryant recorded. Police chief Frank Miller is not listed in the court records as a witness.

The *Post* was the only paper, out of the hundreds I reviewed, to print or even mention Emma Gillespie's testimony. It was very brief and also in the damaged section. Most of it is still readable, though, and it supports her husband's alibi. She said she was Henry's wife and claimed he was at home with her on the night of the murders, that he rarely left her alone.

What's most unforgivable about this news coverage is its sins of omission. One very important piece of information was mentioned only briefly and *only* in the *Asheville Gazette*. It said Hammer's inquiry had adjourned at some point on the first day, waiting on a witness expected to confirm John Gillespie's alibi. "John Graham, an important witness,...will tell where John Gillespie, one of the murderers, was Friday night," the paper said. [C] Ironically, the *Gazette* called John a murderer, while offering the only substantial indication, so far, that he might be innocent. Though it didn't follow up on the expected testimony, what it did print appears to be valid. The man in question must have been Richard, not John, Graham, listed in the witness section of the official court documents as "colored." Perhaps if a more locally-based, prominent paper like the *Observer* or the *Post* had investigated, or simply acknowledged, this witness, a young teen would have been spared torture and death.

Julian acknowledged and even halfway explained one of his omissions. He included a *reference* to E.B. Walton's testimony, but didn't print what Walton said. Walton is the Mann Walton mentioned in Bryant's report—the one Henry Mayhew allegedly visited on the morning of the murder and told that his "paw" and the others had killed the Lyerlys. Mann was a nickname for Emanuel, which is the "E" in E.B., the only Walton listed as a witness in the court records. He was Isaac Lyerly's nephew and a bachelor, with whom his mother, Isaac's sister Catherine, lived in the neighborhood just south of Isaac's. He was also Pless Barber's brother-in-law. Julian disclosed only that **"E.B. Walton was examined but for reasons that will appear later his testimony is not published today."** [B] If Walton's testimony in any way corroborated Henry Mayhew's, I cannot imagine any of these reporters or officials keeping it from the public.

So, did Walton confirm Henry's alleged story or not? Did Henry go to him on the morning after the murders and say Nease and the others had killed the Lyerlys? And was Fannie telling the truth when she said that John stayed at Walton's house on the night of the murders? Walton must have been asked all of these questions, and the case against the accused and Henry's credibility revolved around his answers. If Walton's testimony did not confirm Henry's story and *did* corroborate Fannie's, publishing it would have discredited almost every assumption the press had made about the guilt of those in custody. And it would have taken a lot of the spice out of their cooking. It would have, at the very least, supported John's alibi and put Henry Mayhew's entire testimony into question.

Despite the racial biases of most of the responsible papers reporting or summarizing this investigation, there was agreement among several about one thing, once the investigation was over. The *Observer* and the *Greensboro Industrial News* both put it this way: "the great mass of testimony is, of course, worthless" [D] The *Weekly Post* flip-flopped a bit, but it still indicated doubt about the guilt of some of the prisoners. It stated with certainty that "the murderers are in custody," while otherwise admitting it was "violating no confidence to say there is doubt in the minds of many who have followed the testimony from the beginning as to the guilt of all the parties under arrest."

Those who did not read these views or examine either Julian's or Bryant's lengthy accounts, were left with a much more damning impression of the suspects, if they accepted the more hyped impressions left by other papers' headlines. The *Richmond Times Dispatch,* the one that described Mary, Addie and Janie as "tots," headlined its brief in one-inch bold letters: **"NEGRO BOASTS OF KILLING A FAMILY."** Even the *Gazette*, which hinted at John's innocence, printed a headline that damned two of the others: **"Evidence Indicates Guilt of Gillespie and Dillingham,"** and since John was also a Gillespie, this paper didn't help him much after all. [C] Daniels' *N&O* omitted any comments about the overall weakness of the testimony and used one-inch bold type to continue to damn the suspects: **"NEASE THE CHIEF: Belief Points to Him as the leading Butcher."** This same report asserted, with no modification, that "Two of the negro men did the killing while others held lighted lamps...," [E] as if that's what the investigation had concluded.

Another *Observer* report summarized and misrepresented some of the testimony Bryant had recorded. For one thing, it represented part of Henry Mayhew's testimony as entirely accurate. Another distortion evaluated Penninger's testimony as "damaging to Nease," [F] when it had actually indicated that Nease was not upset about the crop after all, that he thought "he'd let Lyerly have it." [B] Unless Penninger said something Bryant or Julian didn't record, there was nothing damaging in his statement at all; at worst it was neutral.

This same article also included another curiosity. It indicated there was more to Hammer's exchange with Henry that Bryant didn't relate, though it appears to be an embellishment, the writer having some fun at the expense of the black community. The "quote" of that conversation is prefaced with this remark: "If Henry is ever accused of going to Sunday school, he can prove a thousand alibis." The rest follows.

> *"Do you know what will become of you if you be good, tell the truth and behave yourself?" the solicitor asked.*
>
> *"Yes Sir: I'll go ter hebben," the kid readily answered and he was just as well informed about the other place.*
>
> *"Well, who made you?" was the next theological interrogation.*
>
> *"De Lawd," was the response, as glib as if it had happened yesterday.*

> *"Now do you know what Christ Jesus came into the world for little man?"*
>
> *"Naw, sir, I never heerd of him," he said, and all queries pertinent to the creation of the world, the age of Methuselah, the first man and the well-known things of the child's catechism were passed up. Henry knew only what became of the wicked folks who violate the Sabbath and don't have a chance to go to Coney Island, and pleaded his ignorance to all else.* [F]

This account does its best to humiliate Fannie. Noting she had first said her age was 45, but today "she says she is 53," the writer said she looked "every bit the difference." If the 1900 census records are correct, and Fannie's name is also Mary, then 53 would be her correct age in 1906.

The report continued:

> *She worried the lawyers nearly silly and when Solicitor Hammer said, "You are the worst nigger I ever saw," he came nearer the truth than all lawyers do. She was asked repeatedly if she had not been hoodooed and she knew nothing of such terms. When Mr. Bryant whispered to an attorney that she might understand the word conjured better, her black face beamed and broke into a laugh that was audible.* [F]

The rest of this account repeats what Bryant reported about her fears that she might be hanged, adding that "nobody knew where she gained the idea that she was going to be punished." [F] I still couldn't figure out why she had not been considered a suspect.

# 11

# THE FLIP SIDE

*It is easier to be callous or rude toward dehumanized "objects,"
to ignore their demands and pleas, to use them for your
purposes, even to destroy them if they are irritating.*
— Philip Zimbardo, *The Lucifer Effect*

Volume II.    OCTOBER, 1903.    Number 4.

The

## South Atlantic Quarterly.

### Stirring Up the Fires of Race Antipathy

Whatever be his view of the negro problem the average American knows that in the last few years there has been a notable increase in the general ...... . This development has occurred in both ...... In the South it has manifested itself ma...... North. We see it there in restricti...... ssage of laws for "Jim Crow" car...... ching, and in a general augment...... on the part of Southerners to...... trage." In the North it is seen...... South, and it is especially no...... was supposed formerly not t...... occasional acts of violence, as th...... in a growing opinion which an...... nd in private conversation wit...... in the North is most strongly hel...... oteworthy that in most of the large...... rapid increase of the negro populatio....
The causes of this de...... ps numerous. But there are three facts w...... ottom and which are worthy of special consider...... are; inherent race antipathy, the progress of the negro himself, and the fact that the negro problem is, and has been for a long time, a political matter.
Race antipathy is as old as the negro's residence in America.

JOHN SPENSER BASSETT

Examples of biases and shortcomings in these 1906 reports, so far, have not given a complete picture of just how vicious Josephus Daniels could be and had been in the past. After serving as the equivalent to a propaganda minister during the 1898 campaign, he continued for years to control much of what was printed in North Carolina—and so much more. And it took a lot of guts for anyone to challenge him or his agenda.

In 1903 Daniels revealed the lengths he would continue to go to preserve the myth of white supremacy. This time his target was a white man—John Spenser Bassett, a popular history professor at Trinity College (now Duke University). A few years earlier, Bassett had founded the *South Atlantic Quarterly,* which embodied Trinity president Kilgo's ideals of scholarship and social involvement. The *Quarterly* had, for some time, criticized the Democratic Party's race baiting in the 1898 campaign and the promotion of white supremacy by the local press. But since nobody seemed to be paying much attention, Bassett finally pushed the envelope to stir things up a bit. And, being born and bred in the South, he thought he could get away with it. Bassett had the unmitigated gall (as Daniels saw it) to put Booker T. Washington right up there with General Robert E. Lee in his list of greatest men born in the South! [A]

Daniels was rabid. He launched a torrent of attacks against Bassett and the college, specifically targeting Bassett's criticism of lynching. "Far from feeling abashed at the increase in the lynching of blacks in the South, Daniels vigorously and proudfully defended the practice," history professor Joel Williamson wrote years later in his analysis of the situation. What Bassett saw as evidence of growing hostility of whites against blacks, Daniels spun as "'the growing glory of Southern manhood and Southern chivalry'...." "For a month, Daniels kept up a ferocious barrage of invective, including, for example, a yellow journalistic trick of repeatedly printing Bassett's name as 'bASSett'." [B] And he did his best to get him fired. Bassett, in turn, felt obligated to explain that he was not promoting the mixing of races just because he admired Washington's accomplishments, and he published a response to that effect. Then he offered to resign. In an incredibly gutsy move for the times, Trinity's board of trustees, facing a threat of possible

financial devastation from decreased enrollment, stood up to
Daniels and stood behind Bassett. [A]

Unfortunately Trinity's action in this case was the exception.
Racist rhetoric found in thousands of copies of original 1906
newspaper pages, from across the state, prove it. The propaganda
machine Daniels set into motion in 1898 was still pumping out
almost exclusively negative impressions of blacks in North
Carolina. Throughout Daniels' coverage of the Lyerly murder
case, it's very likely he used codes within the pages of the *N&O*
to send messages to the mob. One noted already is the report
headlined, "Weaving a Rope."

But there is some evidence that Daniels' influence may have
been waning by 1906. On July 25th, the *Greensboro Industrial
News* printed a letter by T.T. Hicks that blasted Daniels and his
tactics. Speaking of him, Hicks said:

> *This distinguished citizen has been supposed by
> many in North Carolina, for several years last past, to
> possess the power almost "to kill and to make alive." It
> was said and admitted that the governor hesitated to
> determine important matters of state until Mr. Daniels
> was consulted.*
>
> *It is believed that fear of being held up to ridicule
> and criticism by him in his paper of the "largest
> circulation in North Carolina," has prevented many a
> man from espousing the cause and pursuing the course
> his conscience dictated. Certain it is that his spirit of
> intolerance, harsh criticism and denunciation, have been
> felt very severely by all those who dare to differ with him
> in matters of state policy; and in many cases judges and
> juries whose decision did not conform to his views have
> been censured and condemned.* [C]

Hicks went on to illustrate what he saw as evidence that
Daniels was losing his sway. It was a situation in which Daniels'
tactics had finally failed him—one in which he had attacked a
member of his own party. "For several months," Daniels
informed his 10,000 subscribers that John C. Drewry "had arisen
in Raleigh to enslave the state," exhausting the language "to
supply words of denunciation" of "Drewry, A DEMOCRAT,

because Mr. Josephus Daniels wanted some one else to be senator from Wake." Despite these attacks, Drewry received the nomination by a large majority. Hicks reasoned that if Daniels could be beaten on his own turf, Wake County, "all other good citizens [should] take courage. Josephus Daniels may still bark but he has lost his power to bite." [C]

Even so, when it came to issues regarding blacks in 1906, Daniels' bite still carried venom. In several reports leading up to the day of the trial on August 6th, the *N&O* characterized Nease as the "ringleader," the "chief" "one of the two killers," "a master of the art of concealing his guilt," "and leader of the murderers...in this worst case of human butchery." Nease was not just presented as a murderer over and over again, but as the worst, most savage one in North Carolina history. The *N&O* did make available new developments that might have highlighted the human side of the murder suspects, had it not been for the overwhelmingly negative assumptions coupled with them. In most cases the negative canceled out the positive altogether.

Also an organ for the Democratic Party, the *Charlotte Observer* was no friend to African Americans either. However, it was much more conservative in its bias than the *N&O*. As mentioned before, the *Observer's* editor, Caldwell, eventually had a falling out with Daniels over the candidacy of William Jennings Bryan, which led to that paper's break from Daniels' influence. Because of this rebellion, Caldwell also became the target of Daniels' vicious attacks. During his tenure as editor, it was rare to find a politically independent newspaper, but Caldwell's "example set a pattern for political independence" and resulted in his "being hailed as 'the emancipator of the North Carolina press.'" Caldwell was also one of the first editors to hire women writers, one he later married. [D]

As with Hammer's inquiry, without the local press, we'd have little clue at all about the defendants' side of the story. They were not present at the hearing to respond to the statements made against them, nor was their lawyer. So there's no official record of any cross-examination or scrutiny of the testimonies recorded that day.

Only a couple of papers, one the *Richmond Times-Dispatch,* explained why the prisoners were not brought back for the investigation: "because it is feared that their presence might cause renewed excitement and might be the means of more trouble." This same report further supported that view, saying, "There are now in Salisbury several former neighbors and friends of the Lyerlys, and they are intent upon having the lives of the negroes in the Charlotte jail." [E] Sheriff Julian couldn't allow his son to print anything like this, though, because he was doing his best to convince Governor Glenn and the public of a different reality.

Or maybe it was all part of a plan. Perhaps Daniels told Governor Glenn to stay out of it and let the prisoners be lynched. Maybe Sheriff Julian's role was to respond to Glenn's offers for help by falsely assuring the governor that he had the situation under control. Perhaps the powers that be had orders from a higher power, the Invisible Empire, better known before 1906 and now as the KKK. A closing note in one of Bryant's reports, filed a day after the Richmond paper's statement came out, contradicted the threat printed in the Richmond paper, saying that "The kinsmen of the Lyerlys are behaving very well. They are civil gentle peaceful citizens." [E] But the point of this story seemed lost on Bryant and others. Most of the people who committed crimes against blacks *were* good people—like all people who can be influenced, especially by powerful forces and propaganda, to do bad, even horrendous things. Truth is, there's a Hitler hiding inside us all.

Despite all the hostilities they faced, the defendants somehow got themselves an exceptional lawyer. Jake F. Newell, a prominent Republican, nicknamed the "silver-haired orator," was known for his successful defense of stubborn cases. But, as he later revealed, Newell's investigation faced exceptional roadblocks. He had been told to stay out of Salisbury, for one, and if he ever got a chance to speak to the prisoners in Charlotte, which one would assume he did when he took the case, any information he obtained from them was not made public. The prisoner's side of the story was being lost in the testimony against them and the way it was summarized by most of the press. And it at first appeared they would get no chance at all to respond to the allegations.

Maybe it was just to sell papers, like a Pulitzer-Hearst war, but the lead reporters again rose to the occasion. Whether they did the suspects any good, though, is debatable. John Moose

Julian, John Charles McNeill, H.E.C. Bryant, and even someone from Josephus Daniels' paper went back to the jail and gave the accused a chance to respond to at least some of the testimony brought out in Solicitor Hammer's investigation. It was the least they could do, especially Daniels, after openly and repeatedly condemning them in his early reports. Though we'll never know if these interviews were accurately recorded, we at least have an alternate perspective to consider.

But first, another jolt in the story hit the papers. Editor Julian said his father got a letter in the mail on the morning of July 25th from two inmates in the Charlotte prison. Alexander Massey and W.N. Mitchell, the *Post* said, had overheard Jack Dillingham make a confession. Charlotte's Sheriff Wallace reportedly sent along a note with the letter, stating that one of the prisoners had handed it directly to his deputy, Mr. Johnston, who noted on the back that he received it himself on July 22nd. It said:

> *County Jail, Mecklenburg. Known by all concerned to the Sheriff of Rowan County.*
> *This comes to let you know that Jack Dillingham has confessed that he and a white man Did the killing of that family. But Jack Did Not give the name of the white man. Jack also stated that the killing and threats made was on account of a quarrel with the family and his wife—and says the other men don't know anything about it. \*\*\* Jack says he was not afraid to tell it to us as we was in jail and [would] not do him no harm.*
> *The confession was made to the Below names and we thought it just and right to tell it.*
> *Your Servant*
> *Alexander Massey*
> *W.N. Mitchell* [G]

The *N&O* repeated the story, adding that all attempts to ascertain the name of the white man referred to in the letter had been unsuccessful. It didn't say who made these attempts, but they must have been pretty lame ones, because everyone else knew the white man in question was James Taylor. Agreeing with the *Post*, the *N&O* also said the officers didn't believe the story. The *Post* obviously knew who the white man was, and the

*N&O* probably knew too. Taylor, the young man who had been working at the Lyerlys up until the night of the murders, had already been implicated by Nease and his sons. The *Post* indicated it knew when it first responded to the accusation: "...the slightest clue connecting [the crime to] the white man, to whom it is certain he refers, has never been found."

So, was Taylor questioned? We learn from Hammer's investigation that Taylor was said to have gone home to Bridgewater on the Tuesday following the murders. From the court records, we learn Taylor was listed among the witnesses. Hammer's Asheboro paper finally addressed the matter, briefly, in a very small paragraph at the bottom of a back page. Reiterating what the note said about the "confession," the *Courier* added that "The matter as to Jim Taylor has been thoroughly investigated, and there are not the slightest grounds for belief that he was connected in any way with the murder." [H] But there were no substantial grounds for connecting any of the accused to the murder either, other than a now suspect confession by Henry Mayhew. This report shows Hammer knew, not assumed, Jack had made the confession, he just didn't believe what he said. Did Hammer know something else, that, whether true or false, the confession itself was valid? The *Post* also assumed or knew Jack made the confession and also concluded he was lying: "...it's certain that he does not tell the truth when he says that none of the other negroes arrested with him had anything to do with the crime. If he does," the *Post* continued, "the whole structure upon which the State has built its case, relying to a great extent upon the story of little Henry goes to smash."

It's strange that any would see a need to support Henry's story now. It was evident to many that at least George Ervin was likely innocent. Also likely was that the reporters and Hammer and others knew Walton's testimony didn't corroborate Henry's story, even if they were keeping that secret to themselves. If any one part of Henry's story lost its credibility, the rest had to be suspect as well.

In the meantime, during all the uproar, Bryant had gone over to the Salisbury jail to talk to Della again. And the *N&O* sent someone to Charlotte to talk to Nease and John. Bryant's interview came out in the *Observer's* July 22nd issue, and the *N&O* report ran the same day.

The *N&O* reporter wanted to know what Nease had to say about the damaging "evidence" Fannie Gillespie had given and also asked about his religion. Regarding Fannie, the paper said Nease "Quickly...replied that she had been 'sorter goin' on funny for about two years, and you can't tell much what she is meanin'." When asked about church membership, the "quickness with which Gillespie grabbed at the question" was "worthy of notice." Nease said he was indeed a member and had been in the Methodist Church for twelve years. [1]

The *N&O* also included a possible explanation for Mayhew's behavior. Nease said Henry, "who had been living with him since he was a very small boy, will get scared if you point your finger at him." [1] This aspect of Henry is consistent with how he was portrayed at Hammer's investigation, his needing repeated assurance that no one would harm him.

Nease outright denied the truth of Fannie's alleged accusation. According to the *N&O*, Nease said "if confronted on the witness stand by his wife and she should say that he had told her he knew something about the murders, he would say that it was not so." "The only thing Gillespie will admit," said the report, "is that he had rented a piece of land from Mr. Isaac Lyerly for his son and his step-son to raise a crop on...." [1]

This interview ends on a surprisingly supportive note—at least for the *N&O*. Its tone is only benignly negative as compared to the earlier harshly incriminating reports in Daniels' paper. It ends with John, Nease, and Jack insisting on their innocence, which this reporter evidently considered a possibility. "Gillespie, if guilty is a master of the art of concealing his guilt and comes to the prison bars almost at a trot to talk to reporters and others, but it is all in his own favor. The only noticeable thing about him is his constantly being in motion." [1] One thing this description does for Nease, if nothing else, is make him seem more human and vulnerable, compared to Julian's insistence that Nease retained a defiant demeanor throughout his incarceration and afterward. Nease was said to have reiterated that he was home all night on Friday the 13th of July. John, who the interviewer also acknowledged, said "he spent that night at the home of Ella Chambers, who lives a mile and a half from the

Lyerly home." And Jack also, according to this report, continued to deny his guilt.[I]

But the *N&O* could have and should have done more. The Graham witness, which only the Asheville paper mentioned, was not brought up, nor was there a word of any effort to find and question Ella Chambers. No one with the name of Chambers is listed among witnesses in the court records, but there are others named in the records that were also ignored by the press. They include: Phil Lyerly, Robb Gray, M.C. Torrence, and W.D. Templeton. Julian had stated at the end of his report of the State's investigation that Hammer and Roseman had gone back to Barber Junction on Sunday (the 22$^{nd}$) and, along with another inspection of the grounds and cottages on the Lyerly property, had questioned "a number of persons who will probably be made witnesses in the trial...."[J] The press, it seems, could have interviewed some of these witnesses, since it had given considerable space to those implicating the prisoners.

While the *N&O* was at the Charlotte jail, Bryant asked Hodge Krider in Salisbury for permission to speak to Della. She was detained in the Rowan County "prison," the same old house that had been attacked on the 14$^{th}$. Bryant's tone also seemed different now. Perhaps the general weakness of the evidence against the accused, which he had just heard and laid out for print, had caused him to further question Della's guilt. Maybe he knew something else he didn't print. This time, he portrayed Della more as a human being than a criminal, and his portrayal of her physical characteristics, this time, made *him* seem more human. She was "hefty and muscular," but not an "amazon," as he had labeled her earlier. He noticed also that her face wore "a troubled look." He said she didn't want to say much,[K] though it's doubtful he related everything she did say.

He said Della had very little to add in regard to the murders. "She would say nothing except that she and Jack were at home Friday night," Bryant reported. "She said that old Fannie thought that Nease and George Ervin committed the crime at the Lyerlys' but she did not know that they did. She said that George Ervin came by and told her that he was going away." Della was apparently referring to Taylor, not Ervin, as Jack's interview later indicates. Della also elaborated on the comment she had made earlier about Mary's relationship with her mother,

Augusta. Bryant didn't quote her but said what she told him was
"to the effect that Mrs. Lyerly had whipped Miss Mary with the
stick used to stir the clothes, because she had written a letter to a
young man, whom she did not like. Miss Mary had told Della
that she did not think that her mother should treat her thus after
she had plowed so hard all summer and made a regular field
hand." [K] The Greensboro paper had responded to Della's earlier
statement about the incident, calling the story "untrue." It's not
clear whether the *News* interviewed Mary or whether Hammer
questioned her about Della's statement, but the information was
printed along with the paper's summary of Hammer's
investigation and omitted from both Bryant's and Julian's
accounts of it. "Miss Lyerly declares that no such circumstances
ever existed...," the *News* said. After recording this last interview
with Della, Bryant said the same about Mary's response, but in a
nicer way—i.e. "that Della was mistaken." Mary's word was of
course taken to be more reliable than Della's.

Also from Bryant, we learn a little about Della's
background. Della said she was raised in Burnsville—a small
town just north of Asheville—and her maiden name was Young.
Jack was raised in Madison County, Virginia, she said, and the
couple came to Rowan County from Rocky Mountain, Virginia.
[K]

This ended the last recorded conversation with Della.

But her husband Jack was interviewed again, at least twice.
When he spoke to Jack on July 24th at the Charlotte jail, an *N&O*
reporter said he denied the alleged confession the two other
prisoners said he made. Jack also told this unnamed newsman
that Jim Taylor had said he was going back to Isaac's house on
the night of the murders and "he had told Dillingham that he
needed about ten dollars very much to get home on." [L] This is
also what Penninger (the sawmill operator) told the Solicitor
during his investigation—that is, the part about Taylor saying he
was going back to Isaac's house that night. If Dillingham was
unaware that Taylor did not, after all, sleep at the Lyerly home
on the night of the murders, then he must have been innocent,
unless, of course, he committed the murders, as alleged, along
with Taylor. Whatever the reporter believed, he didn't add any
derogatory remarks about Jack to this report.

He did disclose more details about the "confession," after interviewing Mitchell. The report said it was *Reverend* Mitchell who actually heard Jack confess, Mitchell explaining "...that he and Dillingham were sleeping in the same cell and that for some time Dillingham has been crying out in his sleep: 'If you tell on me I will kill you, and you will be like a baby on the ground.' or words to that effect." Mitchell was very afraid that Jack might "attack him some night during one of these spells," said the report. [L] Concluding, it said Mitchell was believed to be the one who wrote the note and Alex Massey had merely passed it on to the deputy, and that the incident would be fully investigated. Interestingly, Massey, not Mitchell, is the only one court records show as a grand jury witness.

Finally, Julian, himself, went to Charlotte to interview the prisoners—on the 26th, after the other reporters ran their stories. Julian mostly summarized what they said, though surely he must have guessed this might be their last chance to speak.

Sheriff Wallace had allowed him the use of a remote room, Julian explained, which prevented any others in the jail from overhearing the conversation. Reverend Mitchell, who he described as "a colored preacher...awaiting trial for a fraudulent transaction," was brought in first.

> *The parson writes a splendid hand and talks intelligently. He declared that Dillingham with whom he is confined, voluntarily and without any solicitation, had unburdened himself. Dillingham, says Mitchell, told him that he with a white man to whom he referred to as Jim, had killed Mr. and Mrs. Lyerly and the two children and that the other negroes under arrest were guiltless. Mitchell was emphatic and reported Dillingham's confession in the latter's own language.* [M]

Mitchell was then returned to his cell, or "cage" as Julian called it, and Nease was brought in. Again portraying Nease differently than others had, Julian said he was "Apparently...as unconcerned as on the day of his arrest when he appeared utterly indifferent to what had happened or might occur." In response to the first question, Julian continued, "...Gillespie protected his innocence."

"Why did you tell your wife it was none of her d- business where you were going on the night of the tragedy?" Julian asked, [M] assuming Nease had said it.

"'I didn't tell her that,' he answered. Continuing, he said: 'I didn't leave home that night. I stayed right there and didn't know anything about the killing until the next morning.'" [M]

> *Gillespie did not give an inch. When told what Henry, his 11-year-old stepson had said, he was not in the least bit disturbed but protested his innocence. He even went a bow shot beyond a declaration of ignorance of the crime and said when asked if he had borne Mr. Lyerly or any member of his family enmity that he liked all of them. Told of his wife's statement that he had said that "old man Ike might cut his wheat but he'd never live to eat it" he repudiated the utterance. Sheriff Wallace took a hand in the interview but without budging Gillespie.* [M]

Next out of his "cage" came Jack.

> *Unlike Gillespie he was nervous and answered all questions excitedly, volunteering to make oath to every word he uttered. Like the older man he professed the highest regard for the Lyerly family. He is a willing talker, in fact he appears anxious to explain at length every circumstance that is against him. To illustrate: "Did you ever have any trouble with or feeling against Mr. Lyerly?" I inquired.*
> *"No sir, no sir," he hastily replied, "I always got along with them."*
> *"How about you knocking down one of Mr. Lyerly's horses, his reproaches and your back words?"*
> *Then Dillingham entered into a lengthy explanation in which he proposed to show that while the incident alluded to was real, there had been no feeling on his part. He admitted that his wife and Mrs. Lyerly had had heated words about a wash tub on Wednesday or Thursday preceding the murder but insisted that he knew nothing about it until after his arrest.*

*Dillingham emphatically denies that he ever made any confession to his cell mate.*

Last to be interviewed, George Ervin had nothing more to say than he knew nothing about the crime. And Julian added that George had "heretofore borne a splendid reputation" in his community. [M]

Julian's summary of the interviews and interviewees is typical of his other conclusions. The Reverend Mitchell, in Julian's opinion, was a "buncoer" (swindler) and Nease was "a study" of "stolid indifference." If Jack continued to persist in his denials, as Julian saw it, "the tragedy in its fulness" might never be known. Julian said that the experienced Salisbury and Charlotte officers believed that at least "one of the guilty party will squeal when confronted with the chain of circumstantial evidence that seems strong enough to send as many as three of the defendants to the gallows." Julian surmised that it was "fairly certain that that person would not be Nease Gillespie, assuming that he is guilty." [M]

Though Hammer's investigation had dominated the *Post's* July 25th weekly issue, there was an interesting brief item almost invisible on the second page of that report. It said a Mr. John Graham from China Grove (just South of Barber Junction), had "escaped from the Morganton hospital for the insane ten days ago." Deputy J.H. Krider was said to have caught the man near his China Grove home "after a hard race" and returned him to the asylum. "Mr. Graham says that after making escape he avoided public highways and it required six days for him to make the trip from Morganton to his old home." Since the report is not dated, it's possible Graham was in Barber Junction in time to commit the murders. Several trains ran daily from Morganton directly to Barber Junction. Since many whites who committed murder in those days were deemed to be insane rather than guilty, it seems that a certified insane man like Graham might have at least been considered a suspect. And we know this Graham is "white" because there's a "Mr." in front of his name. The report about the Swedish immigrant who had axed his entire family had appeared in several local papers on July 12th and 13th. The idea of copycat murders may not have been discussed much in 1906, but the possibility should not be ruled out, especially with an "insane" man on the loose.

One other item of interest, directly related to the Lyerly murders, came from the *Winston-Salem Sentinel*. It was printed in the *Post's* July 20th evening edition and again in its next weekly issue. It said a "citizen" and "gentleman" told the *Sentinel* that Mary and Addie gave him a detailed description of what they did right after their family members were murdered, and that it brought tears to his eyes. He "said" he followed the girls, as they retraced the route they had taken to the Cook home, saying "'the girls had first visited the woodshed and other outhouses, including the barn, to see if they could find the murderers.'" "'This,'" he said, "' was more nerve than most men could exhibit.'" [G] Addie's and Mary's descendants told me they thought this whole thing about checking the outhouses was nonsense. But the story was also reported by the *Observer* on the day after the murders, and its implications, if any, perhaps should be considered.

# 12

# ASSUMPTION OF GUILT

*Injustice anywhere is a threat to justice everywhere.*
— Martin Luther King, Jr.

JOHN STEELE HENDERSON

On July 14, 1906, prominent Salisbury attorney John S. Henderson wrote to his wife, vacationing in Asheville. His letter begins:

> *My Darling Wife: A horrible murder occurred last night about nine miles from here on the Statesville Road. Mr. & Mrs. Isaac Lyerly & two children, a boy and a girl, were brutally murdered about 10 or 11 o'clock. They were killed with an axe, and the murderers then set fire to the house—but two daughters upstairs put out the fire and then gave the alarm. Three negroes have been arrested and are now in jail—but I don't know what the evidence against them is. This is the worst and most awful murder in the history of the county. I hope the perpetrators will be brought to justice. The Town is in an uproar on account of it.* [A]

Writing on the day after the murders, Henderson had very little information to go on. After nearly eight years of examining hundreds of reports on the case, I still don't know what, if any, real evidence there was against the suspects. Assuming the press's case represents the State's, all Hammer had so far was circumstantial, which, even though weak, was highly publicized and distorted. Defense Attorney Jake Newell did, we later learn, gather some evidence, but none of it made the headlines. If Newell's arguments had been heard, perhaps they would have included some of the following questions or scenarios.

Surely Newell would have challenged the logic in some of the State's case, starting with the contention that Nease and John were out in the open, near the well, burning clothes after setting the Lyerly house on fire. If they were outside that close by, they would have known for sure that the house did not burn, and that the older girls would be aware of the murders before long. Also other neighbors might have smelled the smoke and would be there soon to see what was going on. It would make no sense to call attention to themselves by burning their clothes so near to the crime scene. The situation was more likely just as Fannie had described it, ie: Nease had asked her the day before to burn the stuffing in the mattresses to kill the bedbugs. Furthermore, no one returned to the house to kill the older girls, though we are told by the press and Mayhew that it was the suspects' intention to have them perish in the fire.

There were more than a few sketchy "facts" for Newell to question. For instance, why the discrepancy in the times given for Matt's arrival, and why wouldn't some of the neighbors, and especially Joseph, have gone over to see about the murders immediately? Who was at the crime scene first, and who among these might have tampered with the "evidence." Newell might have found out when Matt Webb really got there and also tracked down Watson, the cattleman, to see what he knew. And certainly he would have investigated the story about the girls checking the out buildings looking for the murderers.

And what about the physical evidence, the bloody axes, the shirts, the lamp, and the ring? If axes were used to commit the murders, then it's no surprise a bloody axe was found on the premises. However, the so-called rusty, bloody axe found at Nease's, hours after throngs of people walked all over the property, is suspicious—not only because it could have been planted, but also because only one person testified to its existence, and it appears to have been more rusty than bloody. Where were these axes during the Solicitor's investigation—why was there no reference to anyone identifying them as they testified about finding them? Two "wet" shirts were reportedly presented at the investigation as evidence, so why couldn't two bloody axes have been identified? Furthermore, testimony at Hammer's investigation didn't indicate the shirts were bloody, only that they "seemed" to have been recently washed. Was it a crime to wash clothes? Does finding a lamp in the bushes mean it was put there by any of the accused? And what happened to Augusta's ring the *Post* said was lying next to the axe found under the porch? Even though only one report out of hundreds mentioned it, the ring was indeed found there, say descendants. So did this mean anything, or had the murderer simply stolen it and accidentally dropped it when he or she threw down the weapon? McNeill had described Augusta's wounds as the "awfulest" of all. Had she been the main target?

The story involving Walton is a bigger mystery. Fannie said John was staying at Emanuel Walton's on the night of the murders. The next morning, Henry Mayhew allegedly went to Walton's and told him his "paw" had killed the Lyerlys with the help of all the other accused. But then it was said he went with John to the train depot. Had he instead gone to Walton's to find John to inform him of what he just learned himself, and to convince him it would be best for both of them to get out of town as quickly as possible? If the press wouldn't print Walton's testimony with the others', could it possibly have corroborated how reporters had spun the story so far?

Several other questions were never publicly explored. One was why Joseph Lyerly was not considered a suspect. Joseph had something to gain, financially, from this murder, and he did end up profiting from it. Had he been badly in debt? According to the *Post*, he was in town on the day after the murders taking care of some financial matters, perhaps depositing in the bank the money he took from the house. We know he disliked Augusta, and she may have been in the way of his inheritance, because she was about his age and, having already made it through her child-bearing years, would have likely outlived him. Isaac had not recorded a will, but court records did reveal that Joseph took the surviving girls to court in 1907 and forced the sale of the land they had all inherited after Isaac's death.

Nease remained consistent in his denial of any guilt in the matter. He insisted he was home that night. He had a former employer attest to his character. Implicating Fannie, instead, as the most likely to commit a crime, the man acknowledged Nease's temper but said he was not dangerous. Nease got up the morning after the murders to go to work, as if nothing had happened. Then it was said he went by the crime scene, facing a crowd of upset whites, to try to find out who was killed and who wasn't. If guilty, why would he still be in the county by then?

Jack's involvement seems possible, and his reputation wasn't good. It was he the girls pointed to as the one they suspected from the beginning. The press stated at least once that Henry Mayhew had accused only the Dillinghams the first time he was questioned. And then there was Jack's alleged confession to his cell mate. But he denied it all, the "confession" and his involvement, and he said he thought James Taylor would be sleeping at the Lyerly home that night as he usually did. He, too, stayed put, when he could have easily gotten away, long before anyone considered him to be a suspect. This indicates he also knew nothing about the murders before anyone else did.

Most important were the problems with Henry's "confession," —the holes in it and how it was obtained. On July 15th, after the first riot at the jail, John Henderson, now having read that "confession," wrote again to his wife.

> *I was at home last night and knew nothing about the vast crowd, which had assembled to lynch the negroes in jail for the horrible murder of the Lyerly family. I did not know a word about it until this morning. Before you receive this you will read all about the matter in the Charlotte Observer. The negroes had been sent to Charlotte, so the mob could [illegible] their vengeance. The probability is that all the negroes would have been killed, some of whom are probably innocent.* [A]

Already, Attorney Henderson must have suspected problems with Henry's testimony and Coroner Dorsett's verdict as well. The July 15th edition of the *Charlotte Observer* he referred his wife to carries reports of both.

Among the specific problems with Henry's testimony are the logistics of how the axes were used, George Ervin's assumed innocence, and how it changed with each report. As already mentioned, it seems illogical and improbable that Nease would have killed Ike and Augusta at the same time Jack was wielding an axe in both directions in order to attack both children, sleeping in opposite beds with their parents. More than one source expressed a general belief in George Ervin's innocence, even though Henry lumped him in with the rest of the group. Indeed, there seems to be nothing whatsoever, not even hearsay, linking George to this crime, other than one statement Della allegedly made, when she probably meant to say Jim Taylor's name instead of George's. Reporters said George offered no response to the accusations, but then there was nothing specific for him to respond to. He was evidently arrested before Henry gave his "confession," which puts the whole thing under further suspicion. And there were several different versions of Henry's story, though all were supposed to have been Henry's words, one even implicating a man that may have been his real father—a man that hadn't been arrested and whose name wasn't mentioned again, at least not in print.

There seems to be no conclusive evidence at all linking any of the accused to the murder. And much of the testimony is hearsay. There appears to have been no search for evidence implicating anyone in the white community and not even a discussion of any other possible suspects, except for Fred Taylor's quiet arrest in Statesville, which was mentioned only once, only in the Greensboro paper. Henry's testimony, taken after the arrests, seems custom-made and was possibly acquired by duress.

Perhaps all of these inconsistencies and questions would have been resolved if the presumption of innocence had been at all considered.

# BOOK TWO

## TRIALS AND TRIBULATION

I cannot see, if you were dead,
Mr. Nigger,
How orators could earn their bread,
Mr. Nigger;
For they could never hold the crowd
Save they abused you long and loud
As being a dark and threatening cloud,
Mr. Nigger.

— John Charles McNeill,
*Lyrics From the Cotton Land*

# 13

# RED SKY AT MORN

## Monday, August 6

*Herein lies the tragedy of the age; not that men are poor—all men know something of poverty; not that men are wicked—who is good? Not that men are ignorant—what is truth? Nay, but that men know so little of men.*

— W.E.B. Du Bois

Suspects, Left to Right: Seated, Jack Dillingham, George Ervin, Nease Gillespie. Standing, Henry Lee Gillespie, John Gillespie

# INTRODUCTION

The second phase of the Lyerly murder story begins with the arraignment of the six suspects on August 6th. When that day in court ended, most of the newspapers covering the proceedings had little time to publish the details before a much more sensational story developed and dominated the front pages of their next issues.

Up to this point in my research, the *Observer's* coverage stood out as the most reliable and detailed published source for the rest of the story. The *Post* did a reasonably thorough job as well, especially considering its smaller size and circulation. It includes much of the same information found in the *Observer*, plus a bit extra, but its overall tone is more biased, and some of its issues remain "lost." The remainder of my account, beginning with the arraignment, will come from these two sources, unless noted otherwise.

☙❧

August 6th was the hottest day of the year—so hot that several in New York City died from exposure. And if northern cities were sizzling, the temperature inside southern jails must have been unbearable. The suspects got a hiatus from *their* cells early that morning when they boarded a train in Charlotte and headed to Salisbury to face the charges against them and more. The break from the heat was brief, though. The atmosphere inside the packed second-floor court room had to have been stifling, and the tempers of some sitting in the spectator seats were hotter than the sweltering air. So, as it turned out, the prisoners were taken from the pen and thrown into the fire.

But the sheriff's climate report said things were much cooler than they really were. His decline of the Governor's offer to send troops for extra protection of the prisoners belied the threat of a lynching. Despite all signs of an impending storm, he maintained a facade that the general feeling among the public, now that things had cooled down, was that the law should prevail.

John Moose Julian's editorial prediction that morning, however, was less rosy than the view his father had painted. Its focus on discouraging violence, alone, negated what the sheriff had told the governor. Despite his obvious racial biases, as one of Salisbury's "better element," Julian would have been opposed to lynching, at least publicly. The more conservative white supremacist Dixiecrats had taken this stand after missions were accomplished in 1898 and 1900. Once blacks were stripped of their rights and back in their "place," these of the "better element" adopted a sort of nobles oblige or paternalistic role in race relations. Julian maybe naively believed his editorial on August 6th would convince any would-be lynchers that the law had the matter well in hand, and there was no need for extralegal judgement or violence. But he and his party had underestimated the power of the monster they'd created.

Though the intent of the editorial seemed aimed at dissuading mob violence, its harping on the horror of the crime was counter productive. Emphasizing the competency of Hammer and his assistants, Julian said the officers had "visited the scene of the tragedy and left no stone unturned to make certain the avengement of the most atrocious crime in Rowan county's history." And his next comment would have been fine, if it hadn't been for his prior repeated attacks on the suspects. "...interested persons, however hot their blood may be with indignation, do well to restrain their passions and prove to the world that any man, though he be guilty of the most heinous crime, will be given the right guaranteed every individual by the constitution." [1] It's also pretty ironic, coming from a state legislator whose party just took from black citizens *several* rights supposed to be guaranteed by the Constitution. By now, it's clear Julian meant "conviction" in place of "justice" when he said: "There has never been any reason to fear that justice would fail in these cases," and the same when he concluded his editorial with "speedy justice is assured." Here he had one last chance to call attention to evidence that challenged the prisoners' guilt, and yet his readers heard not a peep about presumption of innocence.

That editorial was on a back page. On the front page was something rarely seen in the *Post*—a photograph—this one of the five male prisoners. Taking up over a tenth of the page, it sat dead center on it. It was the same photo that had been displayed on the unfilmed front page of the weekly edition of the *Post* carrying Hammer's investigation, and it's the only known photo of the accused. In it, George Ervin, seated in the middle, is shoeless and looks resigned, even meek if not just incredibly tired or sad. Henry looks scared, and John, standing beside him with slumped shoulders, appears depressed or shy. Sitting upright, with his fingers locked and clutching just below his knees, Nease shows only a hint of fear, and a reluctance to reveal even that. Whatever Jack was feeling, he seems the most relaxed, sitting with his arms loosely crossed and resting on his bent knees. His hair and skin are quite light-colored. All except Jack and Henry are wearing overalls. Della is not in the photograph at all.

And her absence may be significant. There was neither a photo nor even a mention yet of her small child. Exposing this information, depicting one of the so-called "savages" as a young mother, might have caused a softening of public sentiment. One thing for sure; the photo helped the would-be lynchers identify their targets. It might as well have said in the caption: "Here they are boys, come and get 'em." When the alleged lynchers were later arrested and tried, not one newspaper published either group or single photos of those suspects for its front page adornment, unless perhaps the missing issues of Salisbury's papers carried a picture of them, which is doubtful.

Another item on the front page, near the photo of the suspects, caught my attention. Just to the right and one column over, is a one-paragraph story about another axe murder. It said that a sixty-year-old white woman had "split her husband's head open with an axe, killing him instantly," proving, to all who believed the report, that a female, even an older one, was capable of fatally wielding an axe. The woman was arrested, the article said, but there was no talk of lynching. [2]

Again, it's hard to know all that went on in Salisbury on August 6, 1906, but the following account includes what the *Post* (probably John Moose Julian) and the *Observer* (presumed to be Bryant) and a few others reported.

This chapter in the story began with the sheriff taking considerable pains to divert any early attempts at lynching, despite all his contradictory denials about danger. First, he set aside plenty of time to transfer the prisoners from Charlotte, leaving Salisbury with his deputies Shoaf Poteat, D.W. Julian (the sheriff's other son), and officer Frank Cauble, in the afternoon of August 5th. Then, very early the next morning, they all got off the train before it reached Salisbury's station—at the Dixonville crossing—from whence they proceeded up Horah (Hoo-rah) Street to Church, then to Innes. The prisoners were detained briefly on Innes Street in Harper Brothers' stables, where they were all met by Solicitor Hammer.

After hiding in the stable for a while, they finally headed to the jail, sitting just north of the courthouse on Main Street. About 75 men were gathered near the square, the intersection of Innes and Main, by the time they got there. "All of the negroes, the two witnesses as well as the accused men," one reporter observed, "were badly frightened." [A]

Not long after that, downtown Salisbury was packed, the streets full of people by midmorning. Julian didn't say how he figured out that three thousand visitors from a half dozen counties were there, but that's what he reported.

And he seemed to know even *more* about this crowd, that is *before* the lynching occurred. "Most of them were steady, substantial agriculturists, possibly as many as 500 of them hailing from the immediate section and neighborhood where the crime was committed. There was no bluster or boast and ninety-nine out of a hundred of those who discussed the matter expressed the opinion that the law should be upheld and that violence would be extremely dangerous." [A] The largest group of visitors, Julian said, was from Cleveland, which he mistook for the Lyerly's neighborhood, which is several miles east of Cleveland.

Cleveland *was* close enough that many of Lyerly's friends and relatives resided there. I assume my grandfather, his brothers, and my great-grandparents, all Augusta's family from another nearby township, were there as well, but no one in my family has said for sure. Editor Julian predicted that "in the almost impossible event of trouble" this group of lawful people, some likely his own relatives, would "be able to show clean hands." [A] But that doesn't exactly explain how my great grandfather ended up with a piece of the rope and some of the victims' fingernails in *his* hands. Again the possibility of trouble is presented as an almost impossibility. And surely everyone knew by now that this was a lie. Even the *Mooresville Enterprise*, a weekly in a small town just southwest of Salisbury, said "some of the very best" of "that good old county...favor an onslaught of the jail" and "dosing out to them full measure of the heinous lynch law." [3]

It was all starting to sound like a game—one with serious consequences. Both Julians went through the motions to try to prevent what they insisted couldn't happen. Whether in denial or political paralysis, the sheriff continued with the mixed messages. Julian reasserted that his father "did not anticipate any violence," but just to take the side of caution he would see that the jail was "guarded day and night." [A] The next day's *New York Times*, commented on the sheriff's over-confidant attitude, noting that the prisoners "were brought to Salisbury from Charlotte on Sunday night without military guard, the authorities seeming not to fear that any violence would be done them," [4]

With the courtroom packed to capacity by 10 a.m., the proceedings began. Even that early in the day, the heat prompted the judge to clear the doorway and windows to allow air to come in and circulate. Presiding over this smoking volcano was Benjamin Franklin Long from Statesville, a town just west of Cleveland and about thirty miles from Salisbury. Solicitor Hammer, T.F. Kluttz, and T.C. Linn appeared for the State, and Jake Newell, with H.S. Williams, on behalf of the defendants.

All those called to serve on the grand jury showed up. Among them, J.M. Monroe had been Julian's predecessor as sheriff. Monroe's ninety-nine year old grandson told me, just days before his death, how Sheriff Monroe had quashed an illegal lynching a few years before the Lyerly murders. But the public execution turned out to be such a spectacle, Monroe had regretted having allowed it. Soon after that fiasco, the county banned public executions. That ban, which was meant to make executions more civilized, if such an oxymoron is possible, probably contributed to the support of future lynchings. There were those who sought revenge for the Lyerly murders and wanted to see someone suffer. Just days after the arrests, weeks before the trial began, a group of Rowan citizens signed a petition, demanding the executions be made public. Even that early in the game, innocence was not even considered, much less presumed.

Not everyone in Rowan was eligible to decide that desired conviction. There were restrictions, some on the books and others understood. After Clerk J.F. McCubbins administered the oath to the grand jury, Judge Long explained the legal conditions under which the State would excuse a juror, which included: having a pending lawsuit, residing outside of Rowan County, or having failed to pay the poll tax for 1905. This last stipulation excluded a lot of blacks from serving, as it excluded them from voting, due to the recent law passed by Dixiecrats, disfranchising many who *had* voted in the previous election. Women were also excluded, not having yet won the right to suffrage.

In other southern states, the poll tax was being used for the same purpose. George Stoney, in his "Suffrage in the South," writes that "most of these restrictive measures date, not from Reconstruction days in the 1870s, but from the white supremacy conventions that came in the late 1890s and early 1900s. During the preceding ten years Negroes and white farmers, combined in the People's Party, all but broke the Democratic political hold in the South; and the openly avowed object of many legislators at these conventions was to keep the vote from all except white Democrats." [5] In North Carolina, the poll tax was combined with a literary test and a grandfather clause, which all worked together to insure the virtual exclusion of blacks from the political and legal processes.

As one might expect, there were no blacks among those in Rowan County's grand jury on August 6th. As for the white men who were called, "No one chosen offered an excuse as to why he should not serve on the grand jury," but W.J. Allen was excused due to illness, and J.S. Hall took his place and was appointed foreman. [A] A couple of potential problems remained, nevertheless, that none of the news reports addressed. W.A. Benson, from the neighborhood just north of the Lyerlys, was not excused, despite his connection to a previous lynching. Judge Long, who hailed from Iredell County, may not have known this detail, but Mayor Boyden and Sheriff Julian were aware of this possible prejudicial situation. One of Benson's relatives still uses strong words, including the "N word," when discussing the 1902 case.

The other issue had to do with a 1902 State Supreme Court decision. Apparently Jim Crow had not succeeded in *legally* excluding blacks as jurors after all. In *State v. Peoples* (141 N.C. 784), "...the court ruled that the exclusion of Negroes from a grand jury, which found an indictment against a Negro, where they were excluded solely on account of race or color, denied equal protection of the laws and was a violation of the Constitution of the United States." Not that this decision, had the defense lawyers known about it, would have made any difference in this case. They'd have had some trouble proving the reason for exclusion, even if everybody knew why. And, it was not until 1913 that "the legislature undertook to assure fairer jury trials by providing for the summons of jurors from adjoining counties, or from counties in the same judicial district, in important criminal trials." [6] As many know, there were few if any black jurors selected for North Carolina cases or in other southern courts until decades later, much less black judges presiding over these cases.

Even with the multitudes crammed into the court room that day, Bryant noticed a gaping hole. A "feature of the crowd was the absence of local attorneys. There were six out of 30 present." [B] Perhaps some of these feared if they showed up they'd be appointed to assist in defending the accused, an assignment that could mean the end of a white lawyer's practice in the South and even his life.

After the jurors were sworn in, Judge Long asked Sheriff Julian to call special deputies to assist in keeping order in the courtroom. Those summoned were H.C. Lentz, Shoaf Poteet, J.D. Shoe, W.P. Sloop, and W.A. Steele. The judge informed those present that the court would grant as much privilege to the spectators as possible, but there was to be absolutely no crowding around the jury box. To ensure this order, the five special deputies were sworn in and "stationed in various parts of the court house." [B] Judge Long might have been aware of what had happened at a highly publicized Chattanooga trial just five months earlier, when things got out of hand in the courtroom.

Long began his opening statement by expressing his affection for Rowan County, then he got down to business. He said he loved it almost as much as his home county of Iredell, and though he preferred to be in Salisbury under different circumstances, he would not shun his duty. Then he explained the circumstances leading to the calling of the special term of court and instructed the jury as follows:

> *Should the evidence laid before you be such that you believe the petit jury could return a verdict of guilty you should report a true bill; should the evidence which you will investigate satisfy you that the jury to try the case could not bring in a verdict against those accused you will ignore the bill.* [A]

Next came his lengthy address, and despite the judge's repeated assurance that the prisoners were safe in Salisbury, the concern over mob violence, ironically, monopolized it. Though no complete record of this speech could be found, Julian's paraphrase of it follows. And it acknowledges threats of lynching from the get-go.

> *Judge Long said he had been told before he came there were those who would constitute themselves a court and dispose of the case before he arrived. He hoped it was not the case in good old Rowan, whose people were law-abiding. He recognized, although a judge upon the bench, that there were circumstances where good citizens excused those who were guilty of mob violence. The court referred to those who take a sober second thought and let the laws which they themselves put in operation take its course, and of those who lost their heads and gathered others for the purpose of taking the laws in their own hands. He spoke of the sentiment in North Carolina against mob violence. He told of the laws on the statute books in regard to lynchings and said that under the laws of North Carolina those participating in such a crime were guilty of murder in the first degree. The moral tone of the people of Rowan was complimented and His Honor expressed the greatest confidence in the citizenship of the county.* [A]

Julian didn't elaborate on the "circumstances where good citizens excused those who were guilty of mob violence," because everyone knew what the judge meant. Had rape or "outrage" been connected with the crime, even the judge might not have condemned a lynching, if he didn't outright condone it. Long later used the argument to censure the lynching in Salisbury, specifically because it had not involved rape and because enough time had elapsed between the murders to give the mob time to cool off. But this hint that Long might have empathized with mob violence under any circumstance served to weaken his preliminary protests against it. It's hard to see how the crowd could have taken him too seriously once he revealed this lack of respect, no matter how subtle, for the majesty of the law.

There are also some problems with Long's reliance on the law to protect the prisoners. First, the state statute addressing lynching did not, and still does not, carry the death penalty, as Long erroneously asserted. Second, this "anti-lynching" statute was so poorly constructed, perhaps by design, that it was almost impossible to convict or even try anyone for the act of lynching itself. [9] The attempt to try the suspects of the Anson County lynching had simply fizzled out because of a technicality. Furthermore, how could Long be so certain that an all-white jury would pass fair judgement on six black suspects? Surely the judge could see that not one man of color sat on that jury, which, in itself, as much as eliminated the chance of a fair trial. And it makes no sense for him to have expressed such confidence, considering the violence that took place at the jail just weeks earlier.

Even so, Long's lecture on lynching wasn't finished yet. And as he continued it, he also continued to misinterpret the law.

*A man cannot fight a duel in North Carolina and kill his antagonist without being guilty of murder, neither can a man smut or mask his face, or without such concealment, deliberately take a person out and hang him without being a murderer. The law says so, the laws which you made and which I made. It is not the words of a judge.* [A]

Finally, after a vague allusion to the looting that went on after the recent San Francisco earthquake, Long wrapped up his opening address. He charged the jury to keep their "eyes and ears open and should any plot or attempt at violence come to your attention investigate the same and we will set this case aside for the present and dispose of any such attempt if it takes all summer." [A] He explicitly warned that "any person who attempts to interfere with the jury's duties or shows any hostility toward a witness which may appear before the jury should be reported, and the person or persons will be summarily dealt with." [A]

By now, this display began to border on the ridiculous. The judge didn't need anyone else to tell him there was talk of lynching. He had admitted to his awareness of such "vaporings" from the beginning. The whole long speech was well represented by Bryant's brief summary. Long, he wrote, "...made light of the rumors of mob violence and said that the good men of Rowan would not lynch a man except in hot blood." [B]

Maybe Long thought he was doing the right thing. Maybe he hoped, by appealing to the better natures of the citizens, he could somehow avert any further violence. Bryant seemed to think the spectators took Long's words to heart. "The men who stood in the back part of the hall leaned forward so that they could catch every word. The charge seemed to make a good impression." Bryant guessed this response was due to their current state of sobriety. "At that hour in the day the people were in a receptive, docile frame of mind," he added. [B] But Julian saw a different influence at work. He said the judge's words caused no apprehension among the listeners "because the moral forces of Rowan county were much stronger than the mob sentiment." [A] Long's last words on the subject in his opening address more closely echo Julian's. Long said he was certain the mob could not "triumph amongst a Christian people, and of Anglo-Saxon descent." [B]

Before proceeding with the case, Long repeated the criteria for finding or ignoring a true bill, and then H.G. Cranford was sworn in as special officer in charge of the jury. By then it was 11:45, so the court adjourned until 2:30 for lunch and also so the grand jury could examine the witnesses.

As the spectators filed out the door of the Courthouse in "throngs of 25 or more," the scene reminded Bryant of "the strenuous campaigns of 1896 and 1898, when thousands of people assembled to hear Aycock [previous governor], Glenn and others speak." [B] Bryant had covered that campaign himself and strongly favored the white supremacist cause.

Bryant had also noted that there "was not a drunk man in the court room." But, an hour after the adjournment, "the streets were literally alive with men," he said, and the "barrooms were doing a thriving business." So much so that "many conservative people" were beginning to worry that "too much whiskey would make a mob." The growing uneasiness among "the better element" prompted one of the officers to approach Long about closing the saloons. Even so, the only report of an early closing of the bars said it didn't happen until sundown. [B]

The Grand Jury was to hear only seven witnesses that morning. Court documents found in the basement of the present Rowan County Courthouse list the following, sworn by J.S. Hall, foreman: Mary Lyerly, Addie Lyerly, Janie Lyerly, Alex Massey, Matt Webb, Sam Cook, and Henry Mayhew. [7] The only person who could have substantiated Massey's story about Jack Dillingham's alleged confession in the jail, and the one said to have actually heard it, Reverend Mitchell, was not listed among these witnesses. Several papers had previously reported that Mitchell would be brought to Salisbury to testify, but his omission from the grand jury witnesses that day was not reported or discussed.

Henry Mayhew was the first to be called before the jury, and he was understandably scared to death. "As Deputy Pat Sloop escorted Henry from the jail to the court house, the boy was weeping bitterly" and said to be afraid that some harm would befall him. But Sloop "assured the little fellow that no one cared to hurt him and this seemed to be a relief to the boy. It was 1:45 o'clock when he went before the grand jury." [B] Apparently all of the witnesses told jurors what the press had already reported, because they concluded that a true bill was justified. We don't know what was said in that room, because the press was not allowed there, and descendants of those involved, the few who could be located, say they know nothing about it.

Official evidence of this day in court was found in a huge, hard-bound book with a dusty and decaying cover, containing the minute dockets for the case of the State versus the accused. The handwritten records for the special term of August 6th begin

with the following declaration of demon-seduced guilt, signed by
Solicitor Hammer.

> *The grand jury came into court in a body and*
> *returned the following, true bill,*
> *State of North Carolina Rowan county, Superior*
> *Court, Aug. Special Term 1906.*
> *The jurors for the State upon their oaths, Present,*
> *that Nease Gillespie alias Mich Graham, Henry*
> *Gillespie, John Gillespie, George Irvin, Jack Dillingham*
> *and Della Dillingham late of the county of Rowan on the*
> *13 day of July in the year of our Lord A.D., 1906 with*
> *force and arms, at, and in the County aforesaid, did*
> *unlawfully and feloniously wilfully and of their malice*
> *aforethought, not having the fear of God before their*
> *eyes but being moved and seduced by the instigation of*
> *the Devil did Kill and murder Isaac Lyerly, Augusta*
> *Lyerly, Alice Lyerly and John Lyerly Jr, against the form*
> *of the statute in such case made and provided, and*
> *against the peace and dignity of the State.* [7]

Names of witnesses for the prosecution and the defense are
also included in these court records. Listed are: "John Bean,
Charles Goodman, E.B. Walton, W.M. Saunders, Richard File,
Matt Lee Webb, Mary Lyerly, Addie Lyerly, Sam Cook, Filmore
Cook, John Henderson, E.A. Brown, Emma Gillespie, Fannie
Brook, "colored," Mrs. J.D. Cline, Ben Cauble, W.P. Barber,
J.G. [Joseph] Lyerly, J.N. Penninger, James Thompson, Charles
Mowery or Lowery [last name unclear], S.M. [Shoaf] Poteat,
Richard Graham, "colored," Henry Mayhew, Walter Cauble, a
small boy, Jim Taylor, Phil Lyerly, Robb Gray, M.C. Torrence,
W.D. Templeton." [7]

This list raises new questions. First, what was up with
Fannie's last name, and second were any new witnesses there on
behalf of the suspects?  "Fannie Brook" has to be Fannie
Gillespie, but it's not known why Brook was written as her last
name. Perhaps she had married someone named Brook in the
past and never officially changed her name. There had been one
mention of her visit to the home of a Brook some time after the
murders, but without elaboration. These court records also

include witnesses who were either not questioned at Hammer's investigation or their answers weren't recorded by Julian's or Bryant's accounts. Some on the list may have been present on July 20th & 21st to testify for the defense, but we already know that very little of what the defense had to say was ever recorded—only Emma Gillespie's brief testimony was found and only in the *Weekly Post*, the one that wasn't filmed. The Richard Graham listed must have been the John Graham the Asheville *Gazette* said was supposed to testify on John Gillespie's behalf. The *Observer* had very briefly indicated, right after the prisoners were interviewed, that some witnesses for the defense might have existed. Furthermore, reports said Henry and John Gillespie claimed they could prove their alibis, so it's very likely some of the witnesses were in court on August 6th to do just that. Jim Taylor, Sam Cook, and John Henderson, all said to be Isaac Lyerly's former employees, were more than likely there to testify for the State, and apparently none of these three were seriously considered as suspects, though all had worked at the Lyerly place, and Jim Taylor is the white man Dillingham's "confession" implicated—the man all of the Gillespies asked about with suspicion, either at the time they were apprehended or later, when they were interviewed in jail.

The most notable omission from the witness list is that of constable E.A. (Ed) Barber, Isaac Lyerly's nephew, to whom Henry Mayhew supposedly originally "confessed." Given the iffy legality of Barber's methods of interrogation, Henry's testimony should come under suspicion, if for no other reason than the questionable character of the one who procured it. But Barber would evidently not be called to explain these circumstances. And, as will be shown later, defense attorney Newell probably never got a chance to question either Henry or Barber.

Even if all of the accused had someone in court that day to substantiate alibis, they would likely have been found guilty anyway. During Jim Crow rule, a black man's word in support of another black would rarely carry much weight unless a white man also supported the claim. A black's testimony, when given against another black was readily accepted, however, while rarely taken seriously when it implicated a white man. [c] As Andre Siegfried put it in the 1920s, after his observation of conditions in the South, "...the two races are by no means on an equal footing in the courts. The statements of the whites are always accepted until they are proved to be false, but a coloured man must produce ten times as much evidence." [D]

When court reconvened at 2:30, the grand jury had not yet completed its investigation of the witnesses, so some minor matters were disposed of during the delay. Then finally at 3:40 the grand jury filed in, and foreman John S. Hall "handed the judge a true bill against Nease and John Gillespie, Jack Dillingham, Henry Lee, George Ervin, and Della Dillingham." [B]

Hall was then asked to wait in the jury room "...so that he and his associates might be called in on another matter. It was generally understood," said the *Observer*, "that the court had in mind certain threats of lynchings that had been made. Court officers had heard rumors concerning the formation of unlawful mobs." [B] Long probably gave some kind of immediate attention to the threats, but on the day after the lynching, he denied there had been any hint of trouble at all.

The grand jury's decision was followed by the climax of the day. As the clock struck four, the prisoners were brought into the courtroom. This time Della was with them.

*Della entered carrying her baby, a boy of about a year. As the accused negroes marched down the aisle, in charge of the officers, the spectators made considerable noise trying to get a better view of the procession. Once more the officers cleared the aisles and windows.* [B]

Once they entered, Jake Newell escorted them all out again, into a private room for a consultation. This apparently didn't last long, and the prisoners were returned and seated at the bar. After the bill of indictments was read to them, all pled not guilty to the charges.

It was now time for the "Silver-haired Orator" to live up to his name. And he did, though the press recorded only the briefest summary of his address. The *Observer* noted only that Newell asked for a continuance, "reading affidavits from his clients, saying that they could not get a fair trial. The act of the mob in breaking in the jail here the night after he prisoners were carried to Charlotte was cited to show that an inflamed public sentiment prevailed." [B] A lot more than that was cited, but neither the *Observer* or any other paper, out of dozens I reviewed, printed it.

The actual and complete wording of the prisoners' request for a change of venue could not be found in the present courthouse with other records. But the original transcript *was* sitting in North Carolina's State Archives collection, and it paints a more powerful and realistic picture of the circumstances leading up to the trial than did the press. It tells what the court and the judge actually heard that day and how reasonable the request was, one that Judge Long should *not* have ignored.

> *Nease Gillespie, John Gillespie, Henry Lee, Geo. Irvin and Jack Dillingam [sic] and Della Dillingham being each duly sworn say each for himself:*
>
> *That a most foul and brutal murder was committed on the 13th day of July 1906, in this, Rowan County of which the affiants stand charged, which has naturally and irresistibly inflamed the passions of the people of the entire county of Rowan to such an extent that it has been impossible for us to have a preliminary hearing to this time, the people of this Rowan County being so unreasoning that the officers of the law were unable to afford us the protection necessary for such hearing.*
>
> *That we are informed and believe that after we were arrested and placed in the common jail of this Rowan County, the anger of the people of said County became so great that as we are informed and believe our lives were not considered safe in the county of Rowan and we were removed to the County Jail of Mecklenburg County where we have remained until being removed on yesterday.*
>
> *That on the night after the commission of the felony, with which we stand charged a mob of more than a thousand people assembled in the yard of the jail, of Rowan County and demanded that we be released to the end that we be then and there most foully murdered by the infuriated crowd assembled in the yard without any pretense of a trial and investigation of the murder that had been committed and that the jail was searched by different committees appointed by the mob on the night*

*aforesaid, and it is a common occurrence to hear threats
of violence to our lives to this time. That various and
sundry articles have appeared in the news papers
published in Rowan County, to-wit: the Evening Post,
Salisbury Semi-Weekly Post, Carolina Watchman, as we
are informed and believe all expressing the conclusion
that we are guilty of said murder, and referring to us in
the most loathsome terms as "Black Brutes,"
"Murderers" and such other terms as are calculated to
arouse the indignation of the entire community and
County of Rowan.* [8]

And so it *was* acknowledged that the press had convicted
these people from day one. And the press, of course, didn't
report it—at least not when it counted. It never published this
entire address, or anything close to what was delivered in court
that day. After the lynching, the *Watchman* and the *Post*
mentioned, briefly, the concern over derogatory statements in the
press, but they also published Hammer's denial that any such
conditions had existed, even though Hammer, himself, had just
demonized the defendants.

The next part of the motion reveals there were witnesses for
the defense whom counsel had little, if any, opportunity to
interview. Furthermore, it seems to say that some of these
witnesses were being held in custody, in some undisclosed place,
by parties unknown to the defendants or their counsel. It's not
clear exactly when Newell took the case, but it was stated more
than once that the prisoners were having difficulty finding a
lawyer, especially from Rowan, to represent them. Newell very
likely had only been on the case a few days, and it was totally
reasonable for him and the accused to request more time, which
they argued expressly and substantively in this last half of the
motion.

*That material witnesses to the defense in this case
have been kept under guard by the order and authority
of persons to affiants unknown and that the attorneys
who have been endeavoring to prepare our case have
been unable to this time to see and confer with them as
to what they know as to the innocence of the affiants of*

*the commission of the crime with which they stand charged.*

*That this is a special term of Rowan Superior Court and that it is not due process of law to require that affiants go to trial of this case in so short a time after the commission of such a crime and before convening of the regular term of Rowan Superior Court as provided by law for the trial of criminal causes, and that ample time has not been given affiants to properly prepare our defense for the crime with which we stand charged;*

*Wherefore your affiants and each of them for himself pray that this cause be continued to the convening of the regular term of Rowan Superior Court for a trial on its merits as your affiants are advised, informed and believe that no proper defense of the action can be made at this time and that by reason of the inflamed condition of the public sentiment that a fair and impartial trial cannot be had in Rowan County at this time.* [8]

The motion was signed by all the defendants and sworn before John B. Manly, Deputy C.S.C. The records available in the Courthouse noted only that the "Motion to continue for reasons aforesaid [was] denied," with the Defendants excepting. [7, 8]

Long seemed so concerned with getting the defendants tried before they could be illegally lynched, he contributed to the lynching himself. Or perhaps this was all about politics and the disdain for the Republican party, in which counselor Jake F. Newell held a high position of leadership. Whatever the reason for Long's denial of Newell's motion, justice, in this case, was more deaf and dumb than blind.

Leon Litwack's *Trouble in Mind* reveals how Judge Long's unwillingness to delay the trial was typical in these kinds of cases.

*To forestall lynch mobs, courts often speeded the conviction and execution of black defendants, distorting whatever semblance of constitutional protection remained for them. The ordinary legal procedures designed to ensure a fair trial found little toleration when an offense was deemed serious enough to justify mob action.* [C]

After Newell presented his request, Solicitor Hammer argued against delay, and Judge Long agreed. Since the press didn't publish the details of Newell's motion, it was easy to get away with what it did report, farcical as it was, considering all the threats made while court was in session, alone. The *Observer* said only that "Hammer denied that there is now any bitter feeling here against the defendants. He said that no decent element wanted to harm the negroes." [B] There was no discussion about any "indecent" element that may have had other designs or how even "the decent element" was capable, at times, of indecency. Was Hammer totally oblivious to what was just reported—that the proceedings had been put on hold momentarily to deal with rumors of lynching?

Judge Long seemed all too willing to play along. Whatever he realized or was willing to admit, he said he saw no advantage to delaying the trial three weeks. "He realized that there is interest here as well as in the adjoining counties." [B] Then he went back into his warning mode, further addressing threats of lynching, how it would be punished, and yadda, yadda, yadda. And then he overruled Newell's motion, and the fate of three of the defendants, at that moment, was sealed.

Newell, with nothing left in his bag of tricks, then requested a special venire of 200. Hammer wanted to argue against *that* request as well, "but in his desire to be fair he would make no objection." So Sheriff Julian was ordered to "have the special venire here by 10 o'clock tomorrow morning." [B] That was quite some task to ask the sheriff to fulfill in such a short time, but perhaps he already knew it wouldn't be necessary anyway.

Before adjourning for the day, Judge Long revealed some important, and probably little-known information about the statute that "discourages" lynching. [9] "'I want to read to you a little law on this subject,' said the court. The statute giving relatives of the victims of unlawful mobs the right to sue a county for damages was read. Judge Long declared that this act had done much to stop vagabonds from breaking in jails." Then he commended the author or supporter of that law, Cyrus B.

Watson, along with Sheriff Julian "for taking his prisoners to Mecklenburg when he thought they were in danger." [B]

Despite his repeated implication that there *was* no danger, the judge, yet again, reminded the grand jury of its responsibility to "investigate any threats or rumors of lynching. The law giving the jury power to summons anybody to testify about such things was cited." And finally, before adjourning at 5:30, Long instructed the sheriff to turn a searchlight on the jail, he reminded the officers of their oath, and he instructed them all to "keep every man away from the jail yard. This, it was declared, was done because of what the court called 'vaporings.'" [B]

Then the *Observer's* report concluded with a few words about the prisoners and the audience.

> *The negro prisoners were composed but frightened. Henry Lee was the saddest looking person that I ever saw. The perspiration poured off him. Nease Gillespie showed no signs of fear. He seemed very much interested in the proceedings of the court. Jack Dillingham is the brightest and most intelligent negro in the bunch. His wife is a jet black African with too much white in her eyes.*
>
> *The audience here to-day...was composed of about 800 white persons, 700 men and 100 women and 200 negroes. Everybody wanted to see the prisoners.* [B]

Some believe that Long, in his denial of a continuance, did only what he felt would decrease the possibility of a lynching—speeding up the legal process. Indeed, many praised him, even some in the black community, for his resolve to afterward punish the lynchers. After learning what went on in Chattanooga, Tennessee just five months earlier, though, made me wonder why Long hadn't done things differently. He must have known about the Chattanooga case, first of all, because it was highly publicized, and also because North Carolina's governor, Glenn, must have also known about it, as he and Tennessee's Governor Cox communicated and cooperated with one another on at least one other issue—immigration. Furthermore, the Chattanooga case had culminated in what post bellum southerners hated more than racial equality, maybe even more than interracial marriage—interference of the Federal Government in their state affairs.

In many ways, by comparison, the Salisbury scenario was eerily similar to the one in Chattanooga—and very specifically so. Chattanooga involved charges against a black man named Ed Johnson, who was accused of sexually assaulting a white woman in the city's St. Elmo section in February, 1906. Though Johnson protested his innocence, officers tried everything in the book to get him to confess, as the evidence was weak, and the victim of the assault could not definitely identify Johnson as her attacker. When Johnson refused to admit guilt,

> *the sheriff tried one of the oldest tricks in the law enforcement how-to book, a tactic that has long since been banned as unconstitutional: the sheriff had Broaden, the other black man who had been arrested in the case, put into the same cell as Johnson.... In doing so, Sheriff Shipp turned the other inmate into an agent for the state. The sheriff hoped the future preacher would have some sway over Johnson.*
>
> *"You should not go to your death with a lie upon your lips," Broaden told Johnson. "You should pray with me and confess your sins to God and to man."*
>
> *In the next cell, the sheriff planted an undercover deputy who could hear if Johnson did confess. Despite many tries, however, they were frustrated. Johnson stuck to his story of innocence.* [E]

Had it been a similar set-up that led to the so-called confession Jack Dillingham made? And had the officers ignored the results because the sought-after confession was not what they wanted to hear and/or because it implicated a white man?

There were too many common details leading up to the lynchings for Judge Long to ignore. Before Johnson's trial could commence, a mob of men had attacked the county jail in Chattanooga, not knowing that Johnson and the other suspect had been taken to Nashville. When the Chattanooga mob refused to believe the prisoners had been moved, the judge suggested that a small group of men accompany officers in a tour of the jail to convince them. "Even though the leaders of the mob went home disappointed that Thursday night, they had put Sheriff Shipp and Judge McReynolds on notice: convict and punish this Negro quickly or they would be back." [E] Had Long been put under similar pressure? Johnson's trial and conviction did come quickly after that. Just two days later, the grand jury in Chattanooga was addressed by the judge in much the same way that the local press and Judge Long, collectively, addressed the Salisbury grand jury. "Such outrages as this," Judge McReynolds began, "must have the immediate attention of the law, that the law may be preserved. It's the 'law's delay' that brings about mob spirit." He went on to warn that "...if in the investigation of this most dreadful crime there is any attempt to interfere with the due process of law, the law shall and will be preserved at any cost of treasure or human life. These are not idle words, but after deliberate thought and full determination." The grand jury, after just two hours, returned with a true bill against Ed Johnson. [E]

There is not nearly the information available on the Salisbury case as there is on this one in Chattanooga, even though the two developed within months of each other. It could be that the outcome in Chattanooga led to the secrecy that still surrounds Salisbury. Though there is no way to know if what went on behind the scenes in Chattanooga also occurred in Salisbury, I had suspected something similar, even before I read about the Ed Johnson case. Little if anything about Chattanooga was unique, except that the corruption was documented and verified by witnesses.

Here's what went on behind the scenes there. Later in the afternoon of the Saturday on which the true bill was handed to Judge McReynolds, prosecutor Whitaker and Sheriff Shipp met privately at the judge's home to discuss the case. The judge reminded the others that "...it was an election year and the people demanded swift and certain justice. Second, he had promised the mob the trial would take place quickly, and he would not go back on his word." So they all agreed to begin the trial quickly, but the date that Johnson was to be returned to Chattanooga would be kept secret. [E]

Authors of this account of the Ed Johnson case explain that such a clandestine meeting as this would be considered "highly unethical" today. But 1906 was "long before the American Bar

Association had issued their 'code for professional conduct,' which prohibited ex parte, or private, communications between judges and prosecutors in a case. Indeed it was commonplace in 1906 for the judge and the prosecutor to map out the strategy for the trial together." [E]

I would not be at all surprised if Hammer, Sheriff Julian, and even Governor Glenn met with Judge Long to discuss the Salisbury case. If the latter two did consult together on it, it would not be the first time the two worked together on a case that involved a lynching, though at that time, Long was the solicitor and Glenn, the prosecutor. Whatever happened, both should have known, even as the plans were being made to try the Lyerly murder suspects, that the Ed Johnson trial and lynching was under investigation by the U.S. Supreme Court—and in part because of the very circumstances that Long had allowed in his court room.

The points of contention in Johnson's trial his lawyer took to Washington for the Supreme Court to consider dealt with the very same infringements of Constitutional rights Judge Long repeated just months later. Surely he was aware of the High Court's intervention in the Chattanooga case and its justification for that intervention. The story was covered in the *Charlotte Observer,* and the Statesville paper (Long's hometown paper) had originally been owned by the same men who now owned the Charlotte paper, so surely the story was reprinted there.

When asked by Justice Harlan "...why the United States Supreme Court should care about the Chattanooga case," these are the arguments Johnson's attorney, Noah Parden (a black man), presented:

1. His client had "never been afforded the presumption of innocence."

2. "...there were specific violations of the Fourth, Fifth, Sixth, and Fourteenth Amendments."

3. The defense lawyers "were denied enough time to investigate adequately and research properly the case against their client."

4. The defendant was "...denied his right to be tried by a jury of his peers. Not one person in the jury pool was black..."

5. The defense was not granted the requested change of venue. It "...should have been moved to another jurisdiction,

because the Chattanooga community was contaminated by overwhelming anger and a thirst for revenge in this case. Such feelings were evident, if not encouraged, by newspaper reports detailing the brutality of the crime and the desire for swift and severe punishment. Just days before the trial, thousands of citizens had formed a lynch mob and stormed the county jail in an unsuccessful attempt to kill Johnson."

6. "There was so much pressure on the sheriff, the district attorney, and the judge to act quickly and punish severely that the basic rights of the defendant were ignored. The elected officials were trying to preserve the rule of law and quell the bloodthirsty appetites of the mob by proving to the public that the court system would provide the justice, or at least the result, it wanted, Parden said. Instead, the case became a race to see which would kill Ed Johnson first—the court officials or the lynch mob." [E]

"In essence, Parden was asking the Court to intervene directly in a state-court criminal trial for the first time in the nation's history." [E] And intervene it did. The headlines were all over the nation's newspapers, and certainly the South was outraged. Though Ed Johnson had been convicted of the charge of rape and his death sentence set to be meted out within days, the Supreme Court, on March 18th, issued a temporary stay of execution. Justice Harlan had convinced the other members, including Chief Justice Fuller and Associate Justice Oliver Wendell Holmes, of the merit of reviewing this case. All were reluctant to intervene in state-court criminal cases, noted the authors, "But this time was different." [E] In asking for his fellow colleagues' support, Harlan had told them "...there was little doubt that Johnson had been denied a fair trial, and told them about the lynching attempt and the prejudices that permeated the Chattanooga community.... This was the time for the U.S. Supreme Court to send a message to law-enforcement and court officials throughout the country that they were expected to obey the spirit as well as the letter of the law." [E] Judge Long and Sheriff Julian, apparently, didn't get that message.

With the Supreme Court's stay of execution, Johnson's status changed immediately to that of a federal prisoner. But the South, in general, cared little about what the Supreme Court had to say. The South resented the North's interference in what was universally known as their "Negro Problem," and southerners sure as hell didn't care for people in Washington D.C. telling them how to run their courts. In contempt of the High Court's order, Ed Johnson was lynched by a mob the following night, and even the governor blamed it on the Supreme Court's intervention. Then, less than five months later, Salisbury played the same damned game, almost move for move. Long, with Chattanooga's example behind him, was far more at fault for repeating McReynolds mistakes, than McReynolds was for committing them in the first place. And he did so, even as the Supreme Court was investigating McReynold's mishandling of the trial, the lynching of Ed Johnson, and specifically Sheriff Shipp's role in that crime.

Though Long spent a good portion of the day discussing threats of mob violence, he remained in denial—or maybe in cahoots with other officials, the mob, or both—insisting that Salisbury was a safe place for incarceration of the prisoners until court reconvened.

# 14

# EYE OF THE STORM

## MONDAY NIGHT, AUGUST 6

*We thought we were done with these things but we were wrong.*
*We thought, because we had power, we had wisdom.*
— Stephen Vincent Benet

ROWAN COUNTY COURTHOUSE AND JAIL

When court adjourned for the day on August 6th it was 5:30, giving the crowd about a half hour more to drink up before the bars were closed by Mayor Boyden. No doubt, plenty took advantage of the opportunity. Salisbury was famous for its liquor, and Rowan was said to be the wettest county in the state. For that and other reasons, it was foolish for the solicitor and the judge to insist the trial be held in Salisbury.

The other reasons weren't trivial ones. Despite denials by the local press, racial tensions were high, and the mob spirit was as strong as ever. Julian hadn't reported the strike of black workers at the Spenser railroad shops on the day before the Lyerly murders. But that didn't mean it didn't happen. Both the *Observer* and the *Industrial News* reported that U.R. Pratt, a white blacksmith, knocked down and badly beat one of his black helpers before firing him. That behavior crossed the line as far as nineteen other black workers were concerned. They rallied together and demanded the beaten man be reinstated and Pratt discharged. Had the mob's attention not been diverted by the axe murders, it might well have gone after this group of protestors. Instead it turned all of its pent-up passion toward the murder suspects on the night of July 14th, and it was left unsatisfied. Then, just a week or so later, another mob or part of the same met train No. 30 at Barber Junction, intending to lynch a "colored" man named John Black. When they learned it was a case of mistaken identity, they left that situation even further "disappointed." Only an eastern paper reported that story, but the Invisible Empire had its own means of communication, and so did the rest of Rowan and the surrounding counties, so certainly the story had circulated. Still in the air during *all* of this unrest, was a persistent rumor that would "not die down" —that Tom Uzra of Rowan County had been lynched in May for shooting a superintendent at Granite Quarry, just south of Salisbury. The victim, J.A. Roach, lived, but it's doubtful Uzra did. There were "unconfirmed reports to the effect that his body was found dangling from a tree in a pasture near Rockwell," or so said a paper in a neighboring county. [2] Topping it all off was the recent and highly publicized failure of the lynching trials in Monroe, along with the heroes' welcome the suspects got after their release. That, in itself, pretty much put a stamp of approval on mob "justice."

**DEFENSE ATTORNEY
JAKE F. NEWELL**

Maybe the Julians needed a weatherman to know which way the wind blew, but Jake Newell had his own anemometer, one on loan from the Klan. He feared the worst that morning, despite all the claims to the contrary. He told the *Observer* on August 7th he had written Governor Glenn the previous week about his worries. But Glenn, Newell said, had denied any cause for worry. "He replied that the authorities there had assured him that there would be no danger and that he had ordered them to take whatever steps they deemed necessary in maintaining order." [A]

Newell had another concern. He was certain of the innocence of at least one of his clients, John Gillespie, and he especially wanted to protect him, considering his age. Newell must have been reasonably certain the others were innocent as well, for the case against them seemed weak. No matter how slim the evidence or how good his reputation, Newell knew what he was up against. He needed more time. And he needed a safe place in which to consult with his clients and the witnesses. [A]

But the situation he found upon his arrival in town that day confirmed his worst fears—he could tell right away there'd be a scene of some sort that night. "I reached Salisbury and saw the crowd at the court house and heard it talk; I knew that trouble was brewing. Every movement of the great mass of people assured me that I had had the correct opinion." [A] It wasn't just Newell being paranoid either. Even in the midst of all his denials, Sheriff Julian told Newell that very morning it "wouldn't be advisable" for him or his associate to "appear on the streets" of Salisbury. Julian told Newell this, but he told Governor Glenn and Judge Long an entirely different story, that is, if the governor can be believed. Newell said it was his realization of the "seriousness of the situation," that led him to request a continuance. And his interview with the *Observer* reveals he had told the judge even more than what the press or the court records disclosed in their coverage of the indictment proceedings. "I called Judge Long's attention to the fact that my clients were not only in danger of being dealt with violently, but we, as counsel, had also been threatened. I laid special stress on the point that a fair and impartial trial could not possibly be held." [A]

But the sane and just approach was not taken by those in charge. The trial was not removed from Salisbury. Long decided it would begin there the next morning, without further postponement. The prisoners were not returned to Charlotte that night. Doing so would have messed with the myth the officers had tried to create, and it would have caused more delay and expense to the county. The suspects, instead, were walked across the street from the courthouse to the old jail, the same building damaged just weeks earlier, during the first attempt to murder the prisoners. By now town commissioners had decided a new jail was needed, and an architect was already in the process of drawing the plans. The July 23rd *Observer* had noted that all who looked on the old structure were "convinced" of "the frailty of the cage holding the murderers of the Lyerly family." They must have known it would take little effort to break into it now.

Denied the continuance he sought in court that day, Newell now desperately needed to confer with his clients. And he would have to risk his life to do so. He told reporters the next day he had gained permission to examine the State's witnesses in the Rowan County Jail that evening after court adjourned, so he "went down shortly after eight o'clock...."

> *Already a crowd had gathered, but there was practically no demonstration. When I talked to the guards, they informed me that they were afraid for me to go into the jail, as it would create a suspicion of the removal of the prisoners. The guards at this time were thoroughly rattled and totally inadequate and incompetent.* [A]

But didn't Judge Long, just hours earlier, order the officers to "keep every man away from the jail yard?" Maybe they didn't understand the orders, but Newell apparently did. According to his version of the story, he went straight to Judge Long, who was staying across the street in the Vanderford Hotel, room 36, and "informed him of the conditions." [A]

That was around 8 p.m. But Long didn't call the Governor for help right away. Instead he decided to confer with the officers about what action to take. The plan finally chosen was for the sheriff, the solicitor, and the mayor to try to talk some sense into what was quickly becoming a drunken, blood-thirsty crowd.

At 9 p.m., a full hour after Newell reported to Judge Long, Bryant assessed the situation which, by then, he too considered a threat to the lives of the prisoners, even though he hadn't thought so earlier. Judge Long had "knocked the mob spirit out of the crowd" that afternoon, Bryant claimed, but by evening things had changed drastically.

> *...this time things look blue for the negroes. Swarms of people are congregating in the streets, and all they lack is a real plucky leader. At this very minute 500 men have congregated in front of the jail, where a dozen or more deputies sit with their guns across their knees. A few keen yells would set the crowd on fire and it would storm the jail. If the deputies do their duty they may have to kill some of their fellow men.* [C]

SALISBURY TRAIN DEPOT IN 1906

Salisbury, being how it was at the time, made it easy for the mob members to congregate there. Today it's considered a rather small city, but it was once the largest in the western half of North Carolina, and a booming one at that. In 1906 it was a major railroad stop between Washington D.C. and Atlanta, a corridor businessmen called the "Golden Avenue." [E] During its heyday in the early 1900s, at least 44 trains passed through the station daily. By 1906, Salisbury had electric lights and streetcars. The streetcar operation had been constructed the year before, mostly for a new working class created by the recent industrial revolution in the South. It carried workers into town and to their jobs at the Spencer Railroad Shops from the newly developed suburbs built to house them. And on that August night in 1906, it and the trains carried multitudes to the scene of the action. From the train station on Depot Street, travelers could walk down Liberty Street just a short distance to the Courthouse on Main. And the streetcars ran right by there.

STREETCAR PASSING VANDERFORD HOTEL ON
MAIN STREET

With each car and train that arrived, and by other means, the crowd multiplied by hundreds or more. "Every street car that passed emptied its load in front of the court house, which is but a short distance from the jail," Bryant said. They were said to have come from several of the surrounding counties: Davidson,

Cabarrus, Iredell, Stanly, and Mecklenburg. [C] One current Rowan County resident recalled his father saying that some traveled to town from as far away as North Wilkesboro and farther yet from Boone, in the northern mountains. He saw them, himself, riding by his farm. There were far more that day than usual, driving their hacks down a well-known trading route used by many to bring their goods to the Salisbury market or for processing in the town's plants. Though it wasn't business they came for that day.

And it wasn't until around 9 p.m. that the jail guards got down to their business. That's when editor Julian said he noticed a group of men beginning to fill "the alleyway to the northeast side of the jail and a bold one in the party cleared the fence and landed in the yard." [B] Apparently the officers had interpreted the Judge's orders to the letter or ignored them as long as possible—someone had to actually step foot on the premises before they'd react. Then when they arrested the trespasser, his buddies demanded his release, threatening violence to the officer who had restrained him. Further encouraged by this defiance of the law, the party next tore down portions of the "weak" fence surrounding the jail at the north side. [B]

By then, the leader Bryant thought was lacking showed up and took control. A "fine looking fellow with a determined face" yelled out at the mob, "'Come on boys: Are we going to let our white women die and not fix the niggers that killed 'em.'" [B, C]

The suggestion must have knocked the wind out of them. Everyone had been thinking and whispering it, but yelling it out like that made it a dare—a challenge to their "manhood." Even so, they didn't react immediately. They paused just long enough to give the officers a chance to consult with each other about what to do next. But no longer. As soon as they caught their breath, the rioters quickly picked up "...the enthusiasm of the speaker and swept the resisting officers before them." [B] As the deputies took their stand at the rear door and began closing it, the mob leaders brought out previously concealed weapons and started shooting, with many bullets striking the door and "...one clipping the hair from the left side of Deputy Pat Sloop's head." [B]

Maybe it was the heat instead of stupidity that had kept that door open so long, but now it was closed. The out-numbered officers had somehow resisted the first attack. That gave Sheriff Julian a chance to cross over to the Vanderford Hotel, where he conferred with Judge Long and Solicitor Hammer in the latter's room. It apparently wasn't until then that Long called in the Rowan Rifles. The judge was "preparing to do the best he can," Bryant said. "If the negroes are lynched it will be over his strenuous protests." [C]

U.S. SENATOR
LEE SLATER OVERMAN

So much for strenuous protests. While waiting on the local militia to show up, Long and one of Salisbury's most distinguished citizens, Senator Lee S. Overman, went over to the rear of the jail and addressed the mob, pleading with them to observe the law. Many sources said several others, including Sheriff Julian, Solicitor Hammer, Thomas Vanderford, John M. Julian, Mayor Boyden and many other "good citizens" begged the multitude to disperse at one point or another, before things got completely out of hand. The Judge who had just so confidently warned against such violence, was now pleading with the perpetrators to cease and desist.

The independent or Republican Mooresville *Enterprise* exploited that golden opportunity, reprinting a Richmond paper's next-day satire about the scene.

*Here was the sovereign state of North Carolina through the mouths of her sworn and selected officials and representatives abjectly begging and pleading with a mob of law-breakers to be merciful and respect her laws and leave her prisoners in her custody. No wonder President Roosevelt with instances of this kind before him, is disposed sometimes to sneer at the whole doctrine of state sovereignty and is unable to conceal his impatient contempt of state governments and their machinery.*[3]

The mayor's presence during this appeal presented another opportunity for ridicule. Though his past should have brought his present loyalties into question, nary a news source touched that topic. Mayor Archibald Henderson Boyden was one of the original members of the first organization of the Ku Klux Klan in North Carolina, which held its first meeting in the law offices of Kerr Craige in Salisbury. Though the nature of Boyden's involvement in the Klan in 1906 is not known, he'd been, by his own admission, an active member in the past, according to Leslie Black's article on the Boyden family. A.H. or "Baldy" as he was called, "sometimes" remained "'on duty' doing Klan work for weeks at a time.... Boyden often recalled those days immediately after the Civil War, relating his activities in 'curbing the uprisings of disturbers of the peace.'" Not only was he a Klan member, but on the night after the Lyerly murders, Boyden reportedly agreed with the mob that the prisoners were guilty and deserved to be lynched. [4]

By the time Boyden, Long, and the others started pleading with the present crowd to disperse, three of the rioters had already broken into the jail with sledge hammers and were headed up the back stairs toward the cells when they were discovered and arrested. They were now being held in custody in a bedroom inside the building.

"'Let our men out and we will leave!' shouted a tall man of 40 or a few years more who seemed to speak with authority." He was responding to the officers, who had, perhaps as a last resort, sought his assistance. Bryant would later label him "the man wearing the Panama hat," and according to other reports, this was the same man who had instigated the attack in the first place.

The officers, surprisingly, honored his request. Or more specifically, "Senator Overman advised the officers to turn out the three fellows who had been captured, and that was done." [C] They released the men they had detained, apparently not bothering to identify them first, and, as he had promised, the leader instructed the crowd to leave. The officers must have known this man, because they appealed to him and took him at his word. Bryant and the *Industrial News* both said Solicitor Hammer told the man "that he could disperse the crowd with a wave of his hand." [C] And the *News* added that "The fellow promised to use his influence to that end and said if the guards would release the men caught while breaking into the jail he would call his men off." [J]

As chancy as this approach appeared, there seemed to be some wisdom in it. After the detained men were released and the crowd ordered by their leader to cease the attack, things quieted down for a while. "For a time good order prevailed. Many of the would-be leaders moved back off." [C]

Through this entire ordeal, neither John Moose Julian, Mayor Boyden, Senator Overman, nor the Sheriff seemed to know the name of even one person in this crowd, for only descriptions were used to distinguish those mentioned in the news accounts. Maybe Bryant and Julian were behind the coverup, failing to print names they knew or even those yelled out loud. But the *Industrial News* said "The mob appeared to be strangers to one [an]other, never calling any names and referring always to each other as 'gentlemen.'" [K] Whatever the case, they were all standing in the midst of that mob in a well-lighted area and should have been able to identify more than a few of the culprits then or later, so they might be charged with conspiracy, especially those who had just been taken into custody. The editor's own reputation should have told on him. It was rumored, said Mark Wineka in his recent book about the *Post*, that Julian "...knew every Rowan Countian by name." [E]

Apparently, though, not the three detainees. By the time they were released, it was about 10 p.m., and it looked like the worst was over. Bryant could now see no leaders in the crowd, now that "the good-looking man in the panama hat" had left. And the "officers had about concluded that the multitude bore no ill will to any one, but had assembled to see what some other fellows were going to do," he said. "Hosts of beardless youths and collarless laboring men sat on the alley fences, the curbstones and adjacent doorsteps." [D]

But "the dangerous men had not yet arrived." [D] After the "good-looking" man's demands were met, the "mass of two hundred or more men dissolved" but only "for the instant," and then they "soon gathered again in knots." [B] It was only later that a man named George Hall was revealed to be one of the three who had been let go. As the group was beginning to disperse upon his and the others' release, Hall mounted the steps to speak.

He cursed his cohorts saying, "'You would not follow me and I want to say to you that you are all a set of cowardly sons of bitches.' He then shook hands with Mr. Hammer, much against the latter's will, and joined the retiring crowd." [D]

It took something out of the ordinary to get the crowd riled up again. Hall's speech didn't seem to have much effect. After he finished it, most were convinced, so the papers said, that the crowd was benign and peace was about to be restored. It was then that the Rowan Rifles finally showed up and formed in a single file at the north end of the jail. It was incredibly bad timing. "The presence of the military," Julian said, "seemed to enrage the mob and confusion indescribable followed. Stones and other missiles were hurled from the two sides and over the jail at the uniformed men and the mob openly dared them to shoot." [B]

While this was going on, the Rifles' commander, Max Barker, was somehow able to maneuver his men into the jail through the rear entrance and into the hallway. But the closing of the door, as the last soldier entered, set off yet another wave of violence. The militia's firing of blank cartridges "inflamed and infuriated the countrymen who took charge of the mob, organized it and made a determined effort to enter the jail. As the rifles cracked the leaders of the lynchers gritted their teeth and moved closer to the jail, putting out the lights as they went. Then it became a question of shoot to hurt or retire and let the mob take the negroes." [C]

But suddenly, something scared the mob straight once again. Two men among them were hit by bullets. "Here there was a cessation of hostilities on account of two accidents.... Mr. McLendon, a railroad engineer from Charlotte, and Will Troutman, a drayman of this city were shot. McLendon was wounded in the thigh, Troutman in the stomach, both balls coming from weapons of the mob." [C] It was later reported that no one knew where the shots came from. Perhaps Bryant wanted to make it look like the officers were doing their job.

This lull in the commotion brought the Solicitor out in the open again. He got back on the steps at the rear of the jail and again addressed the "increasing throng." And once more Bryant became optimistic about the outcome. "Although many in the crowd were whooping," he said, "it otherwise seemed lifeless and, overall, indistinguishable from a crowd at any event or celebration, "as a county fair crowd waiting for the balloon to go up." He felt secure that peace had been restored, enough to go out among the multitude to take a "tour," as he called it, "among the would-be lynchers." Returning to wherever he was when he began the tour, he surmised that, unless more arrived from the county, "the mob will never have the nerve to make the dash on the jail that it will require to get the prisoners." [C]

Hammer's reappearance seemed to have a restraining effect, after all. The mob, yet again, began to disperse, and it seemed for certain this time no further violence would ensue. Most everyone let out a sigh of relief.

Here, Bryant took advantage of the calm to wax philosophical. It gave him the opportunity to discuss his favorite subjects—hunting and hounds. "The mob is not like a lot of bear hounds trying to close in on their quarry," he wrote, "but like a bunch of dogs that had run for an hour or more to find that they had been following a skin instead of the real thing." Bryant again concluded that the mob was ineffective because it lacked a leader. "Unless some daring fellow takes charge," he surmised, "Solicitor Hammer, with his powerful voice and mighty fist, can keep back the hosts." [C]

The response to this last absurd assumption was another explosion of violence, which sent the Rowan Rifles out of the jail, seeking their own safety. Who knows what ignited it this time, but "Pistols cracked and heavy timber crashed against the door. One soldier fired through a panel of the door but the discharge of his weapon produced no effect and the door was gradually giving away. Capt. Barker had no authority to shoot and realizing the uselessness of remaining at the jail without power to employ his guns took his men to Main street near the corner of Council." [B] Bryant said that the militia moved "up the street double quick...," [C] but Max Barker later denied it. "We did no such thing," he told the *Post*. [5]

With this departure, however quickly it occurred, the mob was at last triumphant and the jail guard was powerless. "By shooting down a hundred or more men on the outside," Julian said of his father, "he could have saved the prisoners but it was not a part of Sheriff Julian's program to take action that would result in butchery." [B] Evidently it was not a part of Sheriff

Julian's program to prevent butchery either. The *Observer* later reported that "Sheriff Julian had instructed the soldiers not to fire until he ordered them to do so," and when they did fire they were using blank cartridges. [D] Barker later denied the latter part of that statement as well—but not the former. [5]

All their methods of defense were pointless anyway. Instead of shooting to protect the prisoners, afraid to injure these "unknown" and lawless citizens "from other counties," the Sheriff and his men "...fought valiantly with their hands." Jailer Hodge Krider, Bryant said, "was the last man to give way. He argued in vain." [C] But apparently he didn't shoot, despite the fact that there could not have been too many on the narrow stairs leading to the top floor or even in the building at one time. Not surprisingly, this hand and mouth defense against the weapons of madmen was unsuccessful.

From about 8 p.m. to 11 p.m—three hours—the Salisbury and State officials had time to take the action needed to turn this thing around. But, basically, they did little but talk, even though by 9:30, it was "evident to Mayor Boyden and Sheriff Julian, who know their people, that heroic efforts must be made to save the prisoners."

Looking back from the twenty-first century, idiomatically speaking, it looked like this: Long threw the officers to the lions, went back to the Vanderford Hotel to fiddle while Rome burned, and literally and figuratively waited until the eleventh hour to call for help.

By that time, the mob already controlled the jail. And its members were moving from cell to cell, looking for the prisoners. "The silence that fell on the crowd that remained outside while the leaders went in was appalling," Bryant said. "Instead of being merry and noisy the throng had become serious and solemn." [D] They could hear the "treaders," tripping "like ghosts about the jail," stopping at every cell and "crying out 'Here is one.'" Except for this sound, all was "quiet as death." [C,] [D] Then suddenly, the silence was pierced by a command from within the jail:

"Bring a rope.... We have the negroes, fetch the ropes."
The crowd remained hushed.

*The main street of the town was almost as calm and as quiet as a death chamber. Many men, who love law and order, stood on the side-walks and shook their heads. Many brave men wept to see a few negro brutes taken out of the jail in a civilized community and slain like sheep-killing dogs.* [D]

In the process of looking for their victims, the jail-breakers opened the cells of other prisoners and invited them to go free. Tom Brown, confined in a cell with John Fraley, who was awaiting trial for robbery, left immediately, but Fraley remained, proclaiming his innocence and desire to be tried. [6]

Then finally the mob leaders got their men. "Exultant shouts greeted the five thousand spectators below when the mob arrived at the cells where the defendants charged with the murders were confined." [B] The hunters, "with their game came running, tumbling down the steep steps. The negroes were jerked, cuffed and kicked until they landed on the ground." [D] They were dragged to the rear of the jail where they were questioned by members of the lynching party.

The mob designated itself judge, solicitor, and jury. E.A. Barber was consulted, and he insisted George Ervin was innocent of any connection with the crime. Then, one source said, George was taken a few blocks away and questioned by "some conservative members of the party," who decided to let him go. He was about to be turned loose when someone expressed concern that he might be in danger from others in the crowd. So he was taken back to the jail and placed in the custody of the sheriff, who by now had been left behind, unable or unwilling to try to stop the lynching. Other accounts say George was taken to the lynching site along with the others and made to witness the atrocities before being returned to the custody of the officers. Another said that the mob gave Barber "... respectful attention and decided to leave Ervin and Henry Gillespie in the jail" and that "No attempt was made to take the Gillespie or Dillingham woman." [B] Either way, Barber's defense of Ervin, at the very least, proves he knew something was not right about Mayhew's story.

Though Della Dillingham wasn't lynched, she *was* attacked. She was being detained in an outbuilding on the jail grounds, and at some point, "Several strong fellows forced the door and entered and beat her with their fists. She carried a number of bruises from the effect of blows received. But she was not removed from the room." [D]

Then the mob reached its verdict. Three were convicted and sentenced to execution by lynching. And so the death march began, heading down Main Street, north, towards Spencer. "The negroes were walked along in the middle of the streets, each one between two strong men. There were about 2,000 people in the crowd that followed the lynchers," and the "crowd grew as the procession marched." [C] According to the *Post*, as well as leading publications in Raleigh, New York, Richmond, and other cities, the sheriff shouted at the crowd as the leaders of the mob carried the prisoners away. "'They have got the prisoners and you men of property in Salisbury will suffer for it.'" [7]

The march proceeded slowly. The arms of the prisoners were bound with heavy rope, and according to Julian, "there was no attempt to lay violent hands upon the negroes as they were led from the jail yard." [B] If so, that soon changed. The August 7th *Washington Post* and other papers reported that "On the way to the hanging the negroes were cuffed and slashed with knives by their captors." [H] Evidence from Coroner Dorsett later confirmed that the victims were indeed tortured.

And that torture was prolonged. Current Salisbury resident, Jackie Graham, has heard the story of the lynching all her life, from both sides of her family. Her great grandparents, the Penningers, lived in a house still standing today on 14th Street, which Jackie says the mob passed on its way to the lynching tree. Despite the *N&O's* claim that the crowd was quiet and orderly, the Penningers told Graham the commotion could be heard blocks away, and they were petrified as it moved near their home. To do that, the procession would had to have moved in a somewhat semi-circular pattern before reaching its final destination. The papers reported only that the procession turned onto Lee Street from Main, ending up in Henderson Park. Part of Lee runs past the site of the lynching *and* near the Penninger's old home. So it appears that this testimony gives a reliable picture of the route taken.

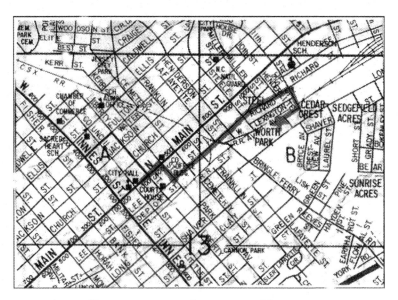

ROUTE OF THE LYNCHING MARCH

Putting together all accounts, this is the probable route: the mob marched north from the courthouse and then took a right on Kerr St. From Kerr it went north again on Lee. Next, instead of turning right on what is now Henderson/Bringle Ferry, the more direct route to the destination, it kept straight, going north until it came to Eleventh Street beside the old Vance (later named Cartex) Cotton Mill. By turning right on Eleventh, the crowd would have passed by the south end of the mill and in view of the Penninger house. The route would then take the procession across the railroad tracks and right again onto a dirt road that ran back south, alongside the railroad tracks, toward Henderson Street and into the wooded park. About halfway between Eleventh and Henderson Streets, very close to the railroad tracks, stands an old oak tree covered with vines. It is to this tree that a current black resident led me when I asked a group in the nearby convenience store if anyone knew where the lynching tree stood. Taking the route described, that tree stands exactly one mile from the courthouse. If the mob had gone the most direct way, the trip and the torture would have been shortened significantly. After all the talk about these victims and other blacks being savages, brutes, and animals, it was, after all, the whites in the mob who acted like animals—like cats, prolonging the kill for sport.

This blood-thirsty throng proceeded without pausing until it reached its destination. It stopped near the residence of Attorney John Steele Henderson. And "Just at midnight the mob halted beneath a large oak tree...." ᶜ The *Raleigh N&O* and the *Lexington Dispatch* noted that the tree had been the site of several lynchings.⁸

J.M. Julian, who followed the procession to its end, said Nease Gillespie made no plea for mercy during the long march and "doggedly professed his innocence in answer to every question." Dillingham, "though terror stricken," also "denied any knowledge of the murder of the Lyerly family." And fifteen-year-old John Gillespie "begged piteously and repeatedly declared his innocence." Since the press often claimed lynching victims confessed, Julian's statement is significant. These three victims maintained their innocence, even while being tortured. ⁹

At least one spectator was brave enough to intervene, Mr. W.J. McMahon, of Pittsburg, Pennsylvania. He "...was at the scene of the death," and "He did all that he could to stay the mob...." "His words of counsel were heard, but not heeded. Little John clung to his arm and begged him to save his life." ᴰ But there was nothing more McMahon could do. The mob would have its way.

The three were not hung immediately. "Instead of killing the men at once the leaders tried to make the prisoners confess to the murder. They were told to get on their knees and pray, as one of the lynchers climbed a big tree and was sitting on a limb smoking a cigarette, waiting for a rope." ᴱ This "'young fellow' smoked a cigarette and blew out rings of smoke while the negroes were having their last say on earth." ᴰ However, neither Dillingham nor Nease Gillespie confessed to or denied the crime they were accused of, and "John Gillespie, in tears, maintained his innocence to the end."

Finally tiring of efforts to wring confessions out of the victims, the mob began the executions. "Each negro's feet were tied to his head, and he was drawn up to the timber...." ᴳ The limb had been too low to hang them in the usual manner.

The *N&O* gave the most detailed and chilling account, including on its front page a huge picture to accompany the description.

> *...one of the doomed men, a rope having been adjusted about his neck, shot up into the air. Snap! went the rope, and the victim fell to the earth in a convulsed heap. Instantly he was seized and again strung up. This time the cord stood the strain and the negro hung from the gallows of Judge Lynch, struggling a moment, then slowly growing still.*
>
> *A second and a third man then darted into the air and hung by the side of the first, turning with a slow and horrible movement in the calm air of the night.*
>
> *A crash of guns rang out, followed by another and another. The mob were pouring volley after volley into the dangling bodies. Then the firing ceased. The work of blood was done.* [10]

It was later said and confirmed that when the rope broke and the body fell, it landed on one of the reporters.

"At midnight, less than an hour after the final attack on the jail, the three bodies were swinging in the moonlight from the limbs of a big oak." [C]

Judge Long had not called Governor Glenn until after 11 p.m. And Glenn later swore he reacted as soon as he got the call, wiring orders to the military commanders at Charlotte, Greensboro, and Statesville to proceed at once by special train to Salisbury. But the governor had scarcely gotten word that the Charlotte troops were ready to be dispatched when he received a second long distance call from Judge Long, reporting that it was too late—Nease, John, and Jack were dead.

LYNCHING TREE TODAY

Earlier that evening, at the first word of violence, a crowd had gathered at the *Observer* office to follow the progression of events. Throughout the evening, "News of the awful affair spread like wild fire over the streets and within five or ten minutes the bulletin board was surrounded by a great mass of people, all eager to devour every word in the specials."

Then when they heard the news of Governor Glenn's order to send out the Charlotte Artillery on the first train, "...the crowd surged toward the soldiers' headquarters and a number volunteered their services to go along and assist in quelling the riot." [F] The soldiers, it was reported, were ready to depart within thirty minutes, "But, just as they were preparing to leave, a telephone message came instructing the troops not to come."

"Of course," continued the report, "the only topic of conversation was the horrors of the tragedy. Almost without exception the opinion was expressed that it was a very bad blunder to take the negroes back to Salisbury for trial. 'I think,' one gentleman remarked, 'that the State authorities might have at least taken the precaution to bring the negroes back to Charlotte to-night and allowed them the protection of the Mecklenburg jail. They could have been returned to Salisbury to-morrow morning." [F] The defense of course had attempted to do just that—that is, get the prisoners out of Salisbury. But Long and Hammer had blocked this preventive measure.

Even a dissenting opinion expressed at the *Observer* office that night agreed with the notion that the prisoners had no chance of safety in Salisbury. "People in this section will not stand for any such crimes and the mob did right," was the opinion, which added "there is no doubt in anybody's mind from the circumstances of the killing, that every one of the negroes is guilty. The mob did the right thing and the State authorities might have known what to expect." [F]

Then and later, no matter who criticized the lynching or when they expressed it, the concern was almost never for the victims. It was the law that had been wronged, a blight on the county and the fair name of Salisbury—a sin against civilization. And the majority of people at the *Observer* office that night shared that sentiment. They "deplored the awful crime committed. It was pronounced by nearly every one a crime against civilization," said the report. [F]

Current residents I interviewed early on held the belief that the lynching served to settle what the law would have taken care of anyway. Maybe they weren't familiar with the difference between a lynching and a legal execution by hanging, and then maybe they were. The latter is meant to cause death quickly by breaking the neck, while the intent of the former is to effect a prolonged death, including torture and humiliation. Greensboro's Republican paper made sure its readers knew that these murders in no way resembled a legal hanging. "The process of death was very slow. The men were drawn up and as the man walked out from them the rope broke. They were drawn up singly again and when all were disposed of the crowd of five thousand was ordered to sit down while the leaders shot. An incalculable number of shots were fired into the bodies of the wretches and one rope was cut in two." [11]

About two weeks later, the *Observer* published another correspondent's perspective on the lynching titled, "That Fearful Night in Rowan." Nothing new was revealed in this recap, but it does tell us that more than one *Observer* reporter was on the scene that night, and perhaps it was he on whom one of the bodies fell when the rope broke. He identified himself only as "an *Observer* man," telling the "boys about what he saw at Salisbury Monday night." He said, before beginning his account, that if he lived to be "three score and ten" he hoped that "such a scene" would not befall him again. [H]

In 2003, almost a century after this mass lynching, a Rowan resident from the black community named James, whose father was a friend of my grandfather's, recalled what his dad had said about one of the mob's victims. James' father told him Gillespie had been strong and had fought off the men before being overpowered by their numbers. He also said that Nease's ears had been cut off and his tongue cut out.

Some of Nease's own descendants say he was innocent. He told a family member so that night before his death. "God knows I'm innocent," Nease said, "but they're going to lynch me anyway. And I just want to see the sun go down one more time before I die."

☙

Though nearly every major paper in America and perhaps some in Europe covered this disgraceful event, most reports are repeats of the *Observer's* story or divulge little or no new information. The details here are taken primarily from John Moose Julian's and Bryant's eyewitness accounts. As far as knowing what actually happened that night, we are left, once more, at the mercy of the Democratic press. Its reporters were probably the only ones who felt safe among a crowd of Klansmen. Undoubtedly, no black reporters were on the scene to give their perspective, and no eyewitnesses are still alive. Most of their descendants, at least the ones I talked to, remain tightlipped about that night, if they know anything at all. At least two of these are said to continue to this day to display pictures of the lynching on their walls.

Two days after its initial report on the lynching, Josephus Daniels' *N&O* displayed on its cover a five by seven photo of the victims hanging from the tree, with onlookers smiling at the camera, some of them children, some of them said to be the lynchers themselves. [9] And on the inside of its first issue after the lynching, the *N&O* ran the biggest newspaper ad published in any of the hundreds I reviewed. In this 16 X 20 inch, full-page "ad," the word, "LYNCHBURG," spreads across the top and the bottom of the page in letters wrapped around a center circle. The letters gradually grow smaller toward the center and larger at both ends of the word. The "L" alone is ten inches long, and the "H" is about two inches high. And one more thing. Four arrow-like shapes, with points meeting in the center, form a large tilted cross inside the circle, with another lined cross in the center of that one. [12] The KKK's official symbol is a cross inside a circle. Was this "ad" Daniels' not-so-subtle seal of approval for the Salisbury lynching?

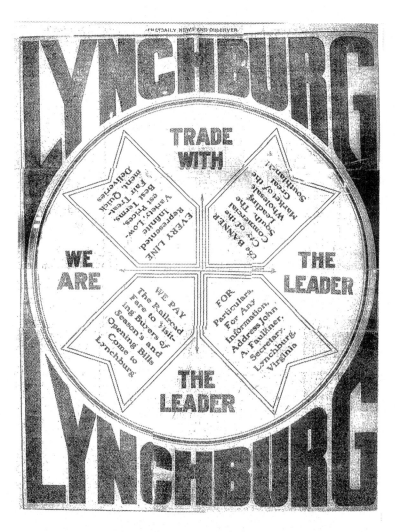

ADVERTISEMENT IN AUGUST 7, 1906
*NEWS AND OBSERVER*

# 15

# THE MORNING AFTER

## Tuesday, August 7

*We said we wouldn't look. But in the end we went. And I think it has always been the same with people. They protest. They shudder. And they say they will not go. But in the end they always have their look.... And we were sick with nausea and fear, for something had come into our lives we could not understand.*

— Thomas Wolfe, *The Child by Tiger*

Murdered by a Mob, Nease Gillespie: center,
Jack Dillingham: right, John Gillespie: left

# INTRODUCTION

W hen I first started researching the Lyerly story, a man
visiting the Okey Dokey shop in downtown Salisbury told
me there had been a lynching in the nearby town of Faith, just
south of Salisbury. A male who looked to be in his 40s, he said
his name was Lowery—that one of his ancestors had participated
in the Salisbury lynching and the one in Faith, as well. I
wondered if he was the Lowery listed as a witness in the court
records. But when I tried to get details, he clammed up.
Afterward, he and Clyde Overcash had some fun at my expense,
neither of them cooperating with my attempts to investigate. So I
decided to drive down to Faith to check out this lynching rumor
and also the more substantial witness accounts of the racial
billboard that had stood in the town until the 1970s—the one that
said "Nigger Don't Let the Sun Go Down On You." Adding to
my interest in Faith, was the impression I'd gotten from a T.V.
special that aired a few years ago. It said the 1979 Greensboro
massacre of members of the Communist Workers Party had been
committed by a group of Klan members who rallied in Faith the
night before to view the racially inflammatory film, *Birth of a
Nation*.

I found what I was looking for in the middle of town—a
local eatery on Faith's Main Street. After scanning the seating
area for a middle-aged or elderly customer, I asked one of the
waitresses if she knew any long-time residents who might be
able to share some of Faith's history with me. She introduced me
to one of her customers at a nearby table, and he invited me to
sit.

"Don't know anything about any lynching in Faith," he
responded to my first inquiry, though he said he'd lived there all
his life. He wasn't too keen on talking about the billboard either,
but he did seem to know a lot about the nearby quarry.

As it turns out, his story on the quarry was pretty
fascinating—enough to make me want to check it out. So I got
directions to the quarry and ended the conversation headed
nowhere else, thanking him for the information. Before leaving

Main Street altogether, though, I checked with a couple of shopkeepers and passers-by, who all knew about the billboard. Some had heard about the lynching too, but could give me no details. I realized I was wasting my time interviewing the white people in Faith, and I didn't see any dark-skinned people out on the streets to ask. The absence of color in the town that day reminded me of a report I'd come across in one of Salisbury's 1906 newspapers. The section on Faith news boasted of having no "negro" residents at all.

Anyway, I headed in the direction I was told I'd find the quarry and got sidetracked again. Just down the road on the right, I ran into Barringer Street. Now Barringer Road, lying west of Salisbury near the old Lyerly place, is named after my great grandfather, Augusta's brother. But here on the south side of Salisbury was a Barringer Street I'd never heard of, so I had to wonder how it got its name. Forgetting about the quarry and the billboard, I made the turn and looked for someone to ask. Halfway down the road, in the middle of a dog-legged bend, I stopped and called out from my window to some young people sitting on a porch. "Hey, know of any Barringers living on this street?"

"No, don't know of any."

"How about any older neighbors, anyone who's lived here a while."

"Uh...Yeah...there's an old guy living right up there on the right," one answered, pointing out the house. "He might know."

The man was within sight, standing out in front of his house, raking leaves. As I got closer, I thought he looked kinda like a Barringer, so I pulled into the driveway, got halfway out of my Volkswagen and asked.

"No. I'm a Lyerly."

I almost fell out of the car. Bobby Ford Lyerly was Isaac Lyerly's great grandson and Joseph's grandson. He said most people hadn't believed him when he told about the murder of his great grandfather, and so he'd pretty much shut up about it. I think he was glad to find someone who did believe. Except for something about Janie, though—the youngest surviving sister— he could tell me little not already printed in the papers. Janie had been so afraid that night, Ford told me, she hid under the stairs while her older sisters were putting out the fire and tending to Alice. Seems like all the papers had ignored Janie. Ford recalled one other thing that day as we spoke. He knew someone who was there at the lynching that night in Salisbury. That man told him it was the worst thing he ever saw in his life, and he never, ever, wanted to witness anything like it again.

*Salisbury, N.C. Aug. 7, 1906.*
*My Darling Wife: I shall be very glad to see you and Mama next Saturday – but I doubt whether you ought to come home so soon. Stay longer if you wish. Mary has told you all about the mob last night. So may have more such scenes. Judge Long is determined to arrest some of the lynchers, if he can find them. One of them is in jail now and it is feared the mob may endeavor to release him to-night. The military will be sent here from Greensboro and elsewhere to maintain order. Our Rowan Rifles last night – commanded by Max Barker – had no orders to fire and were told not to do so. Officers of the law are helpless if they will not resist a mob. I dislike the idea of having a company of troops to come here from abroad. I don't know whether anything more will be attempted. Engineer McClendon, a member of the mob was shot and killed. Another man, named Hannah, who lives in one of our houses in Spencer was also shot and badly wounded – I think he will live. I hope we'll have no more trouble – but I don't know what a large, angry, drunken crowd may do to-night.... I have just dined with Baldy. Mr. Bryant of the Charlotte Observer & Mr. Williamson were also there. I am glad you and Mama & Bessie were not at home last night. Mary stood the ordeal splendidly, but I am sorry she was at home.... Your devoted husband, John S. Henderson.* [1]

At the bottom of another of Henderson's letters, the following is noted: "J.S.H advised the Judge to take stronger measures, but without success." [2] Perhaps a family member, before donating Henderson's letters to the university archives, wanted to explain or justify Henderson's role, as a prominent citizen, in trying to prevent the lynching.

On Tuesday, August 7th, Salisbury and the governor definitely had some explaining to do. The day had hardly begun before Governer Robert B. Glenn reacted in his own defense. Sometime early that morning, Sheriff Julian received a telegram from Glenn: "Make every effort to identify and arrest the mob that lynched prisoners. If needed wire me and I will come to, Salisbury." [A] Judge Long got a similar telegram. "Spare neither time nor expense in trying to bring the mob to justice. If needed I will go to Salisbury." [A] Also, as soon as he possibly could that morning, Glenn gave a statement to the press.

> *"When I returned from Morehead City the 2nd inst. I wrote Sheriff Julian at Salisbury that, if necessary, I would put the military under his order. On the 4th a letter came from him saying that he did not think there was any necessity to order out the military as it seemed that the people were desirous to have a fair trial and that it was better not to order out the troops as that would only serve to incense the people. I made no order therefore for the troops and I was very much surprised to be awakened last night after 11 o'clock by a telephone message from Judge Long, asking that the military be ordered out. This I promptly did and also called out troops from Greensboro, Charlotte and Statesville. The Statesville office could not be reached, but the captains of the companies of Charlotte and Greensboro answered the call promptly and had their men ready when another message came from the judge stating that the mob had done its work and the orders to the troops were then countermanded."* [A]

This first attempt at damage control was just the beginning. And it didn't explain why Glenn had accepted the sheriff's assessment of the situation and ignored all other signs, including Jake Newell's concerns. Much more was to come. But first Salisbury made an even bigger spectacle of itself.

The jail and courtyard were a mess. That could not be remedied right away. But there was no excuse for leaving the three mutilated bodies, Salisbury's strange fruit, hanging on the tree near the train tracks for residents, visitors, and passers-by alike to see. Hundreds of people were at the gruesome lynching scene collecting souvenirs. [D] While some were cutting off body parts, others were having their pictures made with the victims—creating mementoes to mail to friends and relatives living out of the county or out of state. Both the *Washington Post* and the *Richmond Planet* verified that thousands visited the scene of the lynching and "some of them cut off fingers, ears and other parts from the dead bodies and carried away the gruesome souvenirs." [4] The Greensboro paper said "The mob was not the only collector of these things," and reports that a "respectable," but unnamed, white woman had cut off an ear or finger and put it in her purse were so embarrassing the Mayor and Senator soon felt it necessary to renounce the story as false. [5]

Even children weren't spared the gruesome scene. Whosever idea it was to take Addie and Mary to view the spectacle, it was Pless Barber who drove them there in his surry, Addie said years later. [3] Perhaps they had asked to go because they believed those people had murdered their parents and siblings. Several today say this was beyond unacceptable. But Scotland Neck's *Commentator* and the *New York Times* were among the few to say so in 1906, both considering it yet another aspect of the multifaceted tragedy.

When Addie told *Post* reporter Joe Junod about it in 1974, she said the mob "punished them in every way."

*"Oh, my goodness. There were thousands of people. We drove up beside the bodies. They were shot up and cut up.... They made them climb up that tree and then made them jump off and break their necks."* [3]

Maybe it's a good thing Addie believed the three had died this way. By now she had more than enough memories of brutality to deal with, without adding more. As bad as Addie's description sounds, the death of these three was worse than she was led to believe. Having only had their necks broken would have been a picnic compared to what they suffered.

It's doubtful any one in Salisbury got much sleep the night before, especially editor Julian, who was, nevertheless, back on the scene early in the morning to record what he saw—or some of what he saw. He didn't say a word about the mutilation.

*Their bodies hung suspended from a limb of the massive oak that shades the east end of the park near the corner of Long and Henderson streets and at the break of day hundreds of men, women and even children were looking upon them. The three corpses touched. The left side of the forehead and face of Nease Gillespie, the most conspicuous of the trio both in life and death, was stained by blood that coursed down the face from a hole in the forehead made by a bullet that made certain the death strangulation had already produced. The same indifferent, defiant look that has marked him as a man of physical courage and cunning, unknown to fear and indifferent to fate, told the character of the man.* [C]

It wasn't enough that Nease Gillespie had been tortured, mutilated, and lynched, on top of being denied his constitutional rights. Without having taken the time to know the man or properly expose the facts of his case, John Moose Julian finished him off. After the vicious assaults on his body, Nease Gillespie was left defenseless, again, to endure the indictment of a newsman and white supremacist legislator.

Though Bryant had also failed to expose evidence that would possibly have prevented the lynching, he didn't mince words about the mutilation that went on afterward.

*At 2 o'clock to-day the bodies of the negroes were still hanging on the tree. Thousands of people have seen them. The heads are earless, the hands fingerless and the feet toeless.... The red tape of the law kept the gruesome things there for women and children, as well as men, to gaze upon.* [B]

Whatever Bryant meant by "the red tape of the law," it sounds like an excuse. And to Bryant, the desecrated human beings were no more than "gruesome things." Though the "negro" label, alone, had made it easy enough for many to feel nothing for them at all.

Leaving the bodies hanging to be picked at by these human "vultures," certainly made Salisbury look worse than it already did. Albert Monroe, the former sheriff's grandson, said a woman traveling from New York to Florida could see the bodies from her window as her train passed Henderson Park. Upon reaching her destination, she wrote a letter to the editor of one of the local papers outraged, asking what kind of town would allow such a thing.

Exactly how long this perversion continued wasn't specified. We know it was at least as late as Bryant revealed—past 2 p.m.[B] The *Carolina Watchman* said only that the bodies were removed sometime during the day and "taken to the county home and buried." [D]

The county home, on the Old Concord Road, is now a home for the elderly. When I went there looking for the graves of Nease, John, and Jack, a staff member named Jackie directed me to an incredibly small burial ground, just north of the home, and right beside a busy street. I found only one marker, a cross with no inscription, among several sunken areas that must have been graves. It looked large enough for only a few common graves, dug there in the past to bury Salisbury's poor or executed. A "poor house" or "workhouse," Brookside Home, operating in Salisbury at the time, was in the news the same week of the murders—its inmates were striking because of starvation. [6]

As if the mutilation wasn't spectacle enough, some of the alleged lynchers were still in town, hanging out in the streets and bragging. How they'd helped string up the "negroes." How they'd helped break down the jail door. But why should they worry? Nothing had happened to those who tore up the place on July 14th.

Della, Henry Lee, and George were now back in Charlotte at the Mecklenburg County jail. Della, who'd by then been incarcerated three weeks, had a one-year-old child. No one ever explained what became of this child, likely still nursing at the time of Della's arrest. Della had just witnessed or heard her husband being dragged from his cell and carried away by a maniacal, gun-toting, mob. She suffered the horror of a brutal beating, left fearing for her own life. Not allowed to hold her husband or say goodbye to him before he was dragged away and murdered, she, along with the other two survivors, was carried to the scene of the lynching to view the massacre. In recounting this last scene, the media downplayed the emotional impact of the tragedy, referring to Della's husband only as her "cell mate." She must have known he and the others were left hanging on that tree to be mutilated, humiliated, and scorned. She had reason to fear some remaining mob members or another group altogether, their lust for revenge still unsatisfied, would come after her next. She was returned to Charlotte and not allowed to attend a funeral for her husband. At the moment, her only substantiated "crimes" were failing to clean a washtub she'd borrowed and speaking a few angry words after Augusta scolded her about it.

Della's fears were not unfounded. Further supporting the Charlotte paper's report that Della had been beaten and had good reason to fear even worse violence, was *Industrial News'* assertion later that the "...mob was much put out because it did not hang at least two more." And, though it didn't elaborate on the circumstances, it said Della's condition was "...such as to make it doubtful she can be brought here..." —meaning Salisbury—for the trial to be held at the regular term, beginning August 28th. [7] No one would be arrested or tried for the assault on Della.

Furthermore, she now had a right to legal recourse against Rowan County for failing to properly protect her and her husband from the mob. But the chances of her taking advantage of this law were slim to none. Long didn't bring up the statute's remedies after the need for them became relevant.

Henry Lee Gillespie had just lost his younger half brother and his father (or stepfather), and he'd also been in jail since July 14th. He, too, may have had rights to legal recourse for the lynching of his relatives. And he, too, had good reason to fear being victimized by a mob. Likewise, he was not free to attend the burial of his relatives—or free at all, though any charges against him were now based only on hearsay.

The *Salisbury Post* was the only paper anywhere to report that Henry Lee made a confession that morning, a very convenient one. The Tuesday evening edition claimed:

> *Henry Lee Gillespie, before leaving for Charlotte that morning, told a Post interviewer, in the presence of the officers, that he heard Jack Dillingham make a confession to the negro preacher Massey.... Gillespie says that Dillingham stated that he, Nease and John*

*Gillespie murdered the Lyerlys and that Nease had told Massey to say nothing about the confession.* [C]

Julian must have printed this for his father's sake; it was hearsay not mentioned later in court or documented in any other way. Used by towns that had hosted lynchings in the past, it was a common tactic, that is, to claim a confession of guilt had been made. Since they didn't get one from the victims, they had to come up with something. The statement was safe for Julian to print, since Nease was no longer alive to defend himself against it, and Massey was back in jail, not around to deny or confirm it. However, Massey and Mitchell, *both,* had been brought to Salisbury the night before to testify in the upcoming trial, Bryant said, even though the official court records do not show Mitchell among the witnesses for this case. He said Mecklenburg jailer E.O. Johnston had shown up that night, worried these prisoners in his charge might be lynched along with the others. "He would have been willing to take them home by private conveyance," he told the press. [B] Judging by what they reportedly said earlier, both men must have been ready and willing to testify to what they had written in their note to Sheriff Julian in July—that they overheard Dillingham confess that he and Taylor murdered the Lyerlys. Both testimonies, at the very least, would have been needed to give any validity to the claim, given that the word of a black man was rarely deemed credible unless something else, usually the testimony of a white man, backed it up. It makes sense that Massey, alone, testified before the grand jury, only if Hammer wanted it that way. And he got what he wanted after all—the jury ignored Massy's testimony and indicted the defendants.

If Henry Lee did make a confession that morning, and if it was indeed made "in the presence of officers," the use of coercion must be considered. It could be the truth, the product of duress or fear, or a complete fabrication concocted by the Sheriff and his two sons, the deputy and the editor, in an attempt to at least partially justify the lynching. Or possibly, Henry went along with the scenario, since it would have cleared him and the other two prisoners and could no longer harm the ones already lynched, other than their reputations, which he was powerless to amend anyway. Nevertheless, Julian failed to note that this alleged new confession contradicted Massey's original version. It also contradicted Henry Mayhew's testimony, which was supposed to have been the basis for the case against the accused in the first place. The fact that not even the *N&O* repeated what should have been a highly-publicized story makes its validity all the more doubtful.

None of the reports discussed where Henry Mayhew and Fannie were on Monday night while the jail was being stormed. They must have been somewhere in Salisbury, because they were among the State's witnesses expected to testify on Tuesday. These two, charged with no crime, were nevertheless sent back to the Mecklenburg jail. Solicitor Hammer had explained earlier, in response to Newell's request for a continuance, that the witnesses were incarcerated because they could not post bond to ensure their presence in court. When court reconvened on Tuesday morning, Judge Long dismissed the other witnesses until re-subpoenaed, but Fannie and Henry were not freed. The special venire of 200 that Newell had requested for the Lyerly case was also discharged.

George Erwin, also spared by the mob, was now back in Charlotte with the rest. The only known case against George was also now classified as hearsay evidence.

It would have been totally insane to put any of them back in the Rowan County Jail. That jail may have been in bad shape before, but it was now barely fit for *anyone's* confinement. A Raleigh correspondent, there that day to assess the damage, said the jail was a "veritable wreck." "Not only had every window pane been broken, but the blinds and sashes had been literally thrashed to splinters by the fury of last night's mob members which used bricks and stones with telling effect." [8] A current resident's old photo of the jail must have been taken right after the lynching. Some damage to the fence and the windows can be seen in the front view, but most of the damage, which occurred at the back of the building, is not detectable. Clearly visible, though, is a soldier on guard, pacing, on the front lawn. Tents are lined up along the sides of the building inside the fence, and another appears to have been pitched, concealing a Gatling gun, right at the steps leading up to the front doorway.

Soldiers were sent to guard the jail that day for one reason—to keep George Hall from being released by another mob attack.

By now, Hall's arrest earlier that morning was no secret. He was said to have been the first who broke into the jail, so maybe it was only appropriate that he, if no one else, sat in it now. Earlier that morning, Bryant said, Hall had shown up in the streets, boasting of his exploits. He told someone "he tied one of the ropes and helped to hang one of the negroes." Soon afterward, "the man was pointed out to the solicitor, who recognized him as the fellow who first forced a way into the jail...." The man who pointed Hall out told the solicitor his name. [9]

> *Then it all came back to Mr. Hammer, who had been instrumental in sending Hall to the roads for three months. Hall is a whiskey distiller, an ex-convict and a bad man. His arrest was ordered and he was locked in a cell. Here the court scored. The imprisonment of Hall had a good effect. Others, who had been recognized last night, soon disappeared from the streets. The well-to-do young farmer who led the first attack on the jail was seen a number of times this morning but no one here knew his name. It is believed that he belongs in Montgomery or Stanly.* [B]

The "well-to-do" farmer would continue to show up in reports. He was also called the "man in the panama hat." It may seem odd that reporters could know so much about this man and others they described, without knowing their names, but the phenomenon is common in lynching accounts. In this case, it might have been assumed the man was well-to-do simply because he wore a panama hat. These hats, made famous in 1906 by Teddy Roosevelt and later worn by celebrities, were hand woven in Equador. They were quite expensive and may have been uncommon, thus making this particular leader stand out in the crowd. But it doesn't explain why Hammer seemed to know him well enough to trust him, without knowing his name. [J]

Somehow Julian or one of his reporters got the scoop on Hall before the *Post's* August 7th evening edition went to press. In addition to its front page account of the lynching that ended in the wee hours that same morning, this issue contained the following report, subtitled "Hall's Record." Though Julian, as usual, didn't attribute the source of this information, he implied that he got it from Hammer.

> *George Hall is a man who has been lawless and violent for many years. He has been indicted for distilling liquor in Stanly and Montgomery counties since Mr. Hammer has been solicitor: he has been indicted in several cases for retailing around Troy and in other parts of Montgomery county. He was engaged in running a distillery with a man named Thos. Hall and Isaac Phillips and others. The revenue officers did not go into that country; it is a mountainous, hilly section along the Uwharrie river where it flows in[to] the Yadkin.*
>
> *For twelve months the sheriff was unable to locate him; they knew he was in the county, but could not get him. Finally the sheriff took six or eight deputies and stayed in that community three or four days. They finally located him at his barn about 2 o'clock at night. He was down several feet below the top of a shuck pen with the shucks several feet deep over him. He had his head through the rails of the pen so he could breathe. They got in on top of him with their guns, and threw the shucks out, and told him they had repeating rifles and shot guns, and if he moved or resisted in any way, they would kill him.*
>
> *He gave bond and forfeited it. It has been collected and turned over to the school fund of Montgomery county. He was arrested again and sentenced to three months on the chain gang. After he got off the gang he left the country with a young woman; in three or four weeks he abandoned her and returned to his family—a wife and several small children. He was arrested again by the vigilance of the officers of the county, and was tried and sentenced to the road for nine months. While he was on the chain gang a letter came to him that his wife was dead, and that his little children were homeless at Spencer. An appeal was made to Mr. Hammer by his counsel, to ask for his pardon. The solicitor told his lawyers to verify the statement that his wife was dead*

*and get a proof of her death, and after that was done, he would consider that question. His counsel made a partial investigation, but failed to get any information as to the death of his wife; in fact, Mr. Hammer's recollection is that his counsel ascertained that his wife was not dead.*

*He served his term out, and has not been heard from until last night, when the solicitor saw him in the crowd and recognized his face but did not recollect his name.*

*Hall would go to protracted meetings in the lower part of Davidson and Montgomery, with a one-horse wagon, and sell liquor out in the woods on Sundays.* <sup>C</sup>

Since that was long before computers were in common use, Julian's research seems astounding. Hammer must have been able to recall it all, without the records before him for reference. In any event, Hall's reported actions reveal a history of lawlessness, but there's nothing in the *Post's* account indicating he was violent, as the paper depicted him from the beginning.

The strategy now was to make Hall look as bad as possible—and as foreign as possible. A fall guy was needed, and it needed *not* to be one of Rowan County's leading citizens. The press tried to make it look like Hall wasn't a resident of Rowan at all, even though more than one source said he and his family were living in Spencer, which was definitely in Rowan. They tried to focus on where he was *from*, but no county wanted to claim him. A paper from one county claimed another was Hall's home, and that county said he hailed from a different one altogether, and one after another denounced him. It was as if he'd dropped from the sky.

> *Montgomery citizens declare that he was born in Randolph, not in their county, but it now develops that the prisoner is a native of Cabarrus. But most of his days were spent in the Uwharrie mountains, of Montgomery county, where he led a gay and wild career, distilling gambling and evading the law.* <sup>K</sup>

The military was brought in from several locations and Gatling guns as well, now that Hall was in jail. The *Watchman*, unlike other local papers, discussed the obvious irony in the situation—the extra effort put forth to protect Hall from freedom, not used to save the lives of the Lyerly murder suspects.

> *It has been a matter of some conjecture among people of the community why all these precautions were not taken to protect the prisoners when they were first brought here from Charlotte. Had this been done—and conditions certainly justified it, the men who were lynched would be in jail now, and no one would have been hurt. All that was needed Monday night was a strong armed force with a determined, nervy man at the head of it, and there would have been no lynching. There was plenty of time to secure this, the situation demanded it, and why it was not done is a problem past understanding.* [D]

A day later, after more suspects were arrested, the *N&O* justified the extra precaution taken on Hall's account, without acknowledging that the previous prisoners had needed it as well. There would be strong motivation to spring Hall from jail, it explained— "men who participated in Monday night's crime are afraid to allow their colleagues to remain in jail for the reason that some one might turn State's evidence and implicate all." [E]

Even though so much could be recalled about Hall, "Few of the lynchers were known even by sight to the Salisburians who scrutinized and had to do with them," Julian's paper said, after it pretty much destroyed Hall's chance of getting a fair trial. [C] His report about Hall exposed the extensive efforts authorities were willing to expend to catch a bootlegger, and by contrast highlighted just how helpless they seemed when it came to apprehending mob members—particularly those who had been recognized, but had "disappeared from the streets" after Hall was arrested. And authorities seemed in awe of the "man with the panama hat," apparently failing to question him—one who certainly knew the names of several men in the mob—even though, according to Bryant, "...he was seen a number of times," on the streets of Salisbury that same morning. [B]

From that day and for weeks afterward, followed an almost unceasing discussion about who the lynchers were and where

they came from. Bryant at first said the bulk of the mob was
thought to have come from a community of outsiders brought in
to work on the nearby Whitney Dam project. [B] And the press,
overall, eventually fell in line with the official position on the
matter, one even the Greensboro paper echoed. "It appears," it
said, "that the actual instigators were men of bad records from
other counties. It has been found that the conservative element in
the mob, the men who saved the necks of a woman, and Henry
Lee and George Ervin, came from the neighborhood of the
Lyerly home." [L]

McNeill, who hadn't been heard from since July 14th, was
back on the beat on August 7th and had a few things to say on the
subject and more. He found that day, after speaking to "all sorts
of people," agreement among them that the "lynching was an
outrage against the good name of Rowan county; and that the
mob which did it was composed of a crowd of hoodlums, the
scum of several counties, floating population from Whitney, and
such like, who, not representing Rowan, yet have brought shame
upon her." [F]

"Whoever the men were," McNeill said,

> *there were giants among them. Some of the rocks
> which they threw into the jail through windows were as
> big as a peck-measure. Almost all the side and back
> windows of the three-story jail were beaten in by thrown
> rocks and coal. The panels of the back door were
> hammered in, and what is left of it is full of shot-marks.
> Inside the rear hallway the plastering is ploughed up
> with scattering bullets. There would seem to have been
> more shooting here than at Wadesboro.* [F]

While talking to people on the streets that day, McNeill
picked up on a "sympathy...against the lynchers," that some said
was just "...temporary talk, inspired by the current investigation,
and that when things cool off the people will be right glad that
the negroes are dead and out of the way." [F] The *N&O* agreed,
noting a "strong sentiment in favor of the lynchers" and,
furthermore, that the women of the area "are thoroughly aroused
and many approve of the lynching." [G]

Already that morning Bryant began working on damage control. His remarks seem insensitive, considering the mutilations still going on, even as he wrote. "Had a stranger entered this thriving little city this morning without having read the papers, he would not have dreamed or imagined that three dead negroes dangled from lynchmen's ropes within two miles of the Rowan county court house. All was quiet save the marching of a few pedestrians and the monotonous call of the soap seller" [H]

Despite Bryant's attempts to persuade his readers that things had gotten back to normal, things were not at all calm. The same day's paper reported that a "colored" man named Caldwell Barber of the Cleveland area, was thrown into jail by Deputy W.A. Thompson for nothing more than making remarks about the present feelings among blacks in that area. Some in the black community were understandably angry and upset about the lynching. And Caldwell may have had more reason than most. Census records show he worked as a servant for Mann Walton in 1900. If Caldwell was living there in 1906, the place Henry Mayhew allegedly went after the murders, then he may have known what was said at Walton's that morning had nothing to do with a confession about the Gillespies' guilt—what the papers avoided printing. The paper attempted at first to overstate Mr. Barber's "crime" but then corrected itself, though not without creating a negative effect. "This negro made threats, or rather remarks, to the effect that 'there would be more families left in a worse condition than the Lyerly family.'" [10] There was no follow-up on Caldwell's arrest in 1906, but he is listed in the 1910 census records, this time with a wife and family, and living in Isaac's township. He survived.

The arrest of Mr. Barber for speaking his mind supports statements from several sources that indicate it was not uncommon for blacks to be punished for talking about a lynching. It also perhaps explains why no non-white investigation of the murders or lynching can be found in print. It's likely no one of African descent dared ask questions, much less criticize the lynching. Even defense attorney Jake Newell was unable do much in the way of a normal investigation. These types of repercussions to blacks speaking out against or even talking about lynchings illustrate that more than the Fifteenth Amendment had been denied to people of color.

Much of Salisbury's own observations of this day's events—the day after the lynching—may never be known. All August 8th issues—those of the *Salisbury Sun*, the *Salisbury Weekly Post*, and the *Salisbury Evening Post*—are missing from all archives. Likely one or more of these carried a photo of the victims, hanging from the tree in Henderson Park, with perhaps more than one of Salisbury's "best citizens" captured smiling at the camera and standing beside the corpses like fishermen or hunters proud of their trophies. The *Post* has just such a photo in its files now.

The one in Daniels' *N&O* shows two children standing near the bodies in the foreground, and a man, seen in other photos as well, staring into the lens of the camera. One man is wearing what looks just like a Panama hat. The *Carolina Watchman* published another view of the lynching, the same view found on a copy of the postcard now in the Rowan County Library's archives, in which at least six white faces are clearly recognizable, some children. [1]

All the photos were likely shot the morning after the lynching, in which case those posing with the dead bodies were not necessarily associated with the murders. Current Mooresville resident, Lois Work, born in 1906, has a copy of yet another view of the lynching, reprinted in her local paper in 1949. The caption explained they "were merely the curious who had come to see the awful aftermath of the dead." The young boy staring at the camera was identified as Mooresville resident, Bully Leonard. A man wearing a Derby hat, leaning against the tree with his hand on Dillingham's shoulder, looks like he had been personally proud of the accomplishment.

It seems all the adults clearly recognizable in those published photos should have been arrested on some charge. And Monroe, the town that just got blasted for its lynching trial fiasco, wasn't about to let them or Judge Long off the hook.

*In his charge to the grand jury before the mob assembled, Judge Long made a blustering speech against lynchers, and told what things he would do to the men who were so much as caught making threats.*

>After that the mob assembled and the officers allowed the militia to sneak off without protecting the prisoners.
>
>Now let the judge who made so much smoke do some firing.
>
>The names and faces of many of the lynchers must be known. Judge Long can arrest and put every known one of them in jail for contempt of court. Will he do it? [11]

# 16

# REACTIONS

*Lumberton, August 8, 1906. To the Editor of The Observer:*
*The writer, a private citizen who loves his State, and deprecates whatever would stain her good name, begs to express to you unqualified approval and endorsement of your editorial of this date on the lynching in Salisbury. Brutal murder and outrage of at least one innocent man, though a negro, richly merits the severe yet dignified condemnation of your editorial and of all good people.*

— J. A. McAllister [1]

JUDGE BENJAMIN FRANKLIN LONG

**"I**t was all over," wrote the *New York Times*, on the day after the lynching. But it wasn't—not by a long shot. The gasps of the men and the boy as they were asphyxiated and the bullets fired into their bodies on the night of August 6th were sounds that echoed round the world. If Salisbury thought it had dealt with an ordeal that horrible night, it was in for another shock—it hadn't seen nothing like the attack on its way—from just about everywhere. The *Industrial News* said August 9th that "The unfortunate lynching at Salisbury has for the past few days held public attention to the exclusion of almost every other question." [2] If this happened in 2006, Larry King, Jon Stewart, Wolf Blitzer, and others would be talking about it for weeks. Months. Maybe years afterward.

Things were nowhere *near* normal in Salisbury. And they wouldn't even appear to be so until a scapegoat was found and convicted. With the Anson County fiasco still fresh in the public's mind, criticism of the Rowan lynching was overwhelming.

Salisbury was under siege again, and this time the onslaught was wielded with the power of the pen, rather than the sledgehammer. The press was like a mob itself. Once the first shot was fired, the rest joined in, riddling Salisbury with its bullets of criticism. The comments published after the lynching, alone, are enough to fill a book. Criticism was so widespread the *N&O* published a note of thanks for the *Baltimore Sun's* forbearance. "It is one of the few papers in the nation which has not yet joined the chorus of painful advertisement." [3]

North Carolina's press, now dealing with another sensational story, was back in full force as well. And though the *Charlotte Observer* had at first sided with the local papers in Salisbury's defense, it, too, soon joined in with the majority of critics from around the country, who not only condemned the lynching, but questioned the actions of those charged with protecting the prisoners.

The northern press had a field day, especially those "damned Yankees" in New York. None of the local papers acknowledged that the U.S. Supreme Court was in the process of investigating just such a lynching as the one in Salisbury, but the *New York Times* hinted at it. Though it got the number wrong, its first headline about the Salisbury lynching read: "Mob, Defying Court, Lynches Five Negroes." Following this report, which certainly reached a wide audience, the *Times* made scathingly condemning statements about Salisbury officials and depicted Salisbury citizens as ignorant rednecks, in so many words, which must have been a particularly hard pill for the town to swallow. It said "the authorities of Salisbury...showed that they lacked both the knowledge and the feeling," to properly handle the situation, and "The lynching instinct seems to have been particularly well developed in the town of Salisbury."

> *Not only did they hang and shoot men who, if guilty, would certainly have received prompt punishment, but having done that, they resented the apprehension of anybody who took part in the lynching, and, gathering in howling crowds, threatened the jail guards with death if they insisted on vindicating the law.* [4]

The *Times* attack got even more personal, as it expressed outrage at the added insult of leaving the bodies hanging after the lynching, something the local press pointed out only matter-of-factly, failing to condemn it.

> *It is perhaps characteristic of such a community that, the day after the negroes were hanged, thousands visited the tree where the bodies had been allowed to remain and in cold blood many secured 'souvenirs' of the episode in the shape of conveniently detachable fragments like fingers and ears. As if this were not enough, the two girls who were the only survivors of the Lyerly family were taken to the place and allowed to inspect the work of the mob. Of course, one must keep in mind the fact that the crime of which these negroes were accused, apparently with justice, was of more than ordinary atrocity, but they were immediately apprehended, there had been no delay in bringing them to trial, their conviction, if guilty, was sure, and if convicted they would have paid the*

*statutory penalty which the people of North Carolina have seen fit to exact. The Governor has the assistance of a courageous and determined Judge, and of course if the militia stands firm the mob will not effect its intended jail delivery. It is not likely that the local authorities will be any more efficient now than they were when they let the first mob work its will, but they will hardly venture any open opposition to the State officials and their agents.* [4]

And, while it was at it, New York took a jab at South Carolina. Responding to a recent lynching of its own, a Charleston paper had displayed the usual duplicitous white supremacist attitude. And the *Times* had this to say about that:

> *In discussing another lynching recently, The Charleston News and Courier condemned such acts and even denied that they lessened the frequency of the crimes they avenge, but it...also said: 'With our peculiar racial conditions, the time is far off when our people will await the ordinary process of law to punish atrocities practically unknown in countries which white races inhabit alone. It is as much as the better sentiment of the South can do to discourage lynchings and so make them as few as possible and hold in check the passions which, when some such incident as this in Atlanta taken place, may one day be unloosed, and the maddened multitude will go forth to kill hundreds, innocent as well as guilty in order to overawe the whole race from which the felon comes."* [4]

Pointing out the hypocrisy in that editorial, the *Times* said it sounded "...as much like a threat as like a condemnation and is not likely to do much toward ending the lynching madness." [4]

As it turned out, both the *Times* and the *News and Courier* had been prophetic. The Charleston paper's threat was not an empty one. And a little over a month later, Atlanta was indeed the scene of a "maddened multitude unloosed," just as the *News and Courier* predicted it. France's *Le Petit Journal* portrayed that scene on the cover of its October 7<sup>th</sup> issue. The *Afro-American Ledger* described it in words.

LES « LYNCHAGES » AUX ÉTATS-UNIS

SEPTEMBER, 1906 MASSACRE OF BLACKS IN ATLANTA, *LE PETIT JOURNAL*, OCTOBER, 1906

*A surging mob of 10,000 howling demons thronged the streets and shot, beat and cut to death every Negro they could get their hands upon. Peaceful men returning to their homes after a day's work, on the street cars, were taken from the cars and shot and beaten to death without any provocation save that they were black.*

The *Ledger* said it was the "wildest night ever seen" in Atlanta and believed it to be instigated by the passing of a trolley car "on which were Negro men sitting not far from white women." The *Observer's* subheading spun it differently, as far as the cause went, but it didn't mince words about the violence, calling it "a race war of alarming proportions."

*Four Attempted Criminal Assaults on Women... Following a Long List of Similar Crimes Recently Infuriate Citizens to the Point of Indiscriminately Attacking Negroes and Beating Them to Death in Many Cases—Many Dragged From Street Cars and Negro Barber Shops Wrecked—Women Also Beaten—Number of Dead is Given by Atlanta Constitution as at Least 15 and Late Rumors Say 25 or 30 More Have Been Killed in Various Parts of the City....* [5]

One of the most surprising criticisms of Salisbury came from the *Chattanooga Times*. Even though Chattanooga had been the site of a lynching that defied the highest court in the land, its paper had the gall to condemn Salisbury. The *Chattanooga Times* echoed others' criticism in pointing out that Nease, Jack, and John had been lynched with no direct proof of guilt. And it contrasted Salisbury's with Chattanooga's lynching, arguing that the mob in Salisbury "had no such incentive as was afforded the mob" in Chattanooga—meaning that the Lyerly case did not involve rape. Even though the validity of the Ed Johnson trial was under investigation, the *Times* pointed out that Johnson had a least been convicted. The editorial mirrored the general sentiment throughout the South that a sexual attack on a white woman by a black man not *just* justified lynching—it mandated it, while any other accusation or charge merited a trial by jury. [6]

Comments from the *Raleigh N&O*, the *Charlotte Observer*, and the *Salisbury Post* at first defended the officers and Salisbury in general. Bryant protested against several suggestions that the guards should have used their guns, insisting that "many on-lookers would have been killed." [A] The *N&O* said the "officers are not to be blamed." They "made a brave and noble effort, but were outnumbered by the angry crowd." In regard to the Rowan Rifles' failure to shoot, the same editorial surprisingly put the responsibility on the Governor rather than the sheriff. [B] And Julian's "condemnation" of the lynching looked more like a justification of it, focusing on the atrocity of the Lyerly murders and a certainty of the suspects' guilt. [C]

But almost everyone else refused to let the lynching pass without condemnation. The local papers were inundated with commentary from the public as well as the press, and most were critical of the officers and the militia. One author whose letter was published in the *Observer*, suggested that, in the future, Glenn should take a tip from Napoleon's action against the mob in Paris in 1795—he had "planted his artillery and swept with grape shot the street through which the mob approached." The same author noted that Glenn's administration had been "punctuated with instances of mob violence," though he felt it wasn't Glenn's fault. In at least one other lynching case on which Glenn and Long had worked together, twenty-three defendants were acquitted of any involvement in that lynching. None were convicted. [7]

One piece of public advice was eventually taken to heart. It suggested that the governor "should promptly direct every sheriff in the State to give him warning of the first authentic whisper of the formation of a mob, and hurry troops to him, by special train if necessary, with instructions to them to shoot to kill." [8] On August 14th, Glenn issued an executive order to all county sheriffs and militia captains, which in essence, said just that.

The majority of the criticism focused on the blot on the state and the "fair name of Rowan," the trampling upon the courts and the law, and the violation of peace and order. Most suggested that the only way to stop mob violence was to shoot into the crowd. While one said it was important *not* to shoot— to keep mob members alive to testify against others. Very few seemed to care at all about the victims.

The *Observer* printed one that stood out in its attitude toward the suspects and fairness concerning the facts of the case. It began by calling the "negroes" suspects instead of murderers and insisted that all "right-minded men" must consider the possibility that all of them may not be guilty. "There are wise men who have followed every step in the progress of this case and weighed every word of the State's evidence thus far adduced, who entertain the most serious doubt of the guilt of all, but who believed that there are facts and circumstances, not yet brought out, bearing upon the case, which would be developed in its trial and put a different face upon it." [9]

One of Salisbury's oldest papers, the *Carolina Watchman,* must have had either a Republican or independent leaning. It made several rather astonishing revelations in its August 8th editorial, critical of the party in power. Noting that crime had "been on the increase...for the last six years," it included lynchings among those that had "come and gone so rapidly that it has become a common occurrence to read of such events."

And that assessment was followed by a startling accusation. "Some of these have occurred under the eyes of officers of the law and in several cases they have taken part." Defending his position, *Watchman* editor William H. Stewart said: "We have published these things as they have occurred and not belonging to the county cliques we had nothing to hide and hid nothing. Let us hope this latest crime is the climax, let us hope the destruction of the jail, the lynching of good men, and massacres are not yet to follow." [10] Even so, the *Watchman* was just as quick to refer to the suspects as "murderers" as any of the other papers. Its editor seemed more concerned about what might happen in the future, if the trend continued, than what had just been done to three still legally innocent blacks.

Greensboro was, at the moment, dealing with its own threat of mob violence. Its Republican paper and the *Observer*, as well, publicized its own sheriff's tough stand against lynching as a contrast to Salisbury's. Part of Sheriff Jordan's comments—the part about "too much talking and too little business"—seemed to speak specifically to Judge Long's rhetoric. "I don't intend to have anything of the kind here," Jordan said. He used the press to warn the public that he meant business—either his deputies or Captain Hobgood's men would shoot down anyone who dared cross the line.

Hobgood issued his own warning. "'Each one of my men is armed with twenty rounds of ammunition. Look at these shells; they are of the riot variety and each one contains two buck shots, and you can bet that everyone of my men knows how, and will shoot at the command, 'fire.'" [E] This must have really rubbed salt in Salisbury's wounds.

The state Republicans certainly didn't pass up the opportunity to blame this example of lawlessness on the Dixiecrats, who had pledged a "return to law and order" even as they were raping the state in 1898. The *Raleigh Enterprise* and *Durham Caucasian* said the tactics used during that campaign led to just this kind of violence in 1906, pointing to Dixiecrat red shirt terrorism as setting the example. The state Republican Party's 1906 Hand-Book said the same and more.

> *...the Democratic party put a premium upon one sort of crime, when a Legislature of that party's choosing voted State money in defence [sic] of ballot*

*box thieves. Nor did the Red Shirt campaign of 1900 pass without its aftermath of easy defiance of constituted authority and the successful triumph of lawlessness as applied to things political. How easy the step to crimes social and racial!*

And this,

> *Under 'democratic auspices' the Lyerly family was killed in cold blood at Barber Junction; under 'democratic auspices' the three alleged murderers were lynched at Salisbury. Under 'democratic auspices' the militia was called out with orders not to shoot—for fear that some good white citizen might be injured. A few hot bullets scattered through that mob of hoodlums might have saved the state the terrible disgrace of that shocking event—a few bullets might have shown that under 'democratic auspices' 'God Almighty reigns and the law is still supreme.'* [11]

This minority voice of reason, blaming the logical source for the problem, would soon be drowned out by the Dixiecrats' booming praises for Governor Glenn's response, or what *Richmond Planet's* John Mitchell called "mawkish sentimentality."

The criticism from the North and the Republicans was brutal, but comments from the deeper South, specifically South Carolina, cut the deepest. "We are confident that such a lynching as this that occurred at Salisbury could not have taken place in this State," said a South Carolina paper the *Observer* didn't identify. That criticism, the *Observer* said, was "the most biting and most humiliating of all." If the deeper southern states were critical of North Carolina, then the whole world must be, and "We await the reproof of Georgia and Mississippi," next, it lamented. "Other sections of the country will view the affair with contempt which will be all the more bitter for us to bear because we cannot avoid the feeling that it is deserved." [E] North Carolina could stomach criticism from its own state and even the North, but not from one of the lynching capitals of the world.

By this point, the *Observer* was not so quick to jump to Salisbury's defense. And it took specific offense at the *New York Post's* mistake of confusing Charlotte with Salisbury, misplacing the site of the lynching. Even so, when the *Spartanburg Journal* suggested that Governor Glenn disband the Rowan Rifles and court-martial its officers, the *Observer* asked for fairness. "The Rowan Rifles had no right to fire to any purpose, except by order of the civil authorities and they had no such order," it insisted. A week or so later, Captain Max Barker, himself, requested that the governor investigate his actions, and Glenn agreed to do so. The *Industrial News* said Barker wanted to "...show that he acted with as much authority as was given him and he objects to the impressions having gone abroad that he hit the turnpike the moment the danger point was reached."

He also told the *Post* and the *Salisbury Sun* "...that the Rowan Rifles were not issued blank cartridges but regulation riot ammunition, multi-ball cartridges. There is no blank ammunition in the possession of my company, never was except at maneuvers, and blanks are not issued to companies."
12

Even praise from the *Atlanta News*, strongly supporting the lynching, couldn't have eased Salisbury's pain. It was way over the top. The August 10<sup>th</sup> *Observer* quoted only two brief phrases from it when it denounced it as "a disgrace to journalism." But the *Washington Post* printed quite a bit if not all of it.

> *Aroused to a frenzy of fury and vengeance, 3,000 men, representing the patriotic citizenship of Salisbury and surrounding country, assembled at the county jail and took therefrom three brutal negro murderers, who had shamefully assassinated the Lyerly family, on July 13, and promptly dispatched them to their doom.*
>
> *Nothing short of the stake would have meted proper punishment to them for their awful crime, but the North Carolina patriots who handled that case had mercy upon them, and simply took them out and hanged them to trees and shot them to death.*

*One by one the Southern communities are falling in
line in the determination to mete out swift justice and
proper punishment to murderers, assassins, and to the
heinous criminals who assault and kill the helpless
women and young girls of the South.* [13]

Others may have printed it too, but the North Carolina
press didn't dare, even though the piece's editor was said to be
chief of staff to Georgia's governor. Unlike Georgia, the ruling
Dixiecrats in North Carolina could now hide under their veil of
civility and wouldn't publicly condone lynching outright or
agree with anyone who did—not anymore—not now that things
were pretty much the way they wanted them. They now
preferred to keep blacks in their place by more *outwardly*
"civil" means. Modern historians Timothy Tyson and Glenda
Gilmore wrote about North Carolina's facade of civility that
followed the 1898 Dixiecrat takeover. Tyson said a "stone wall
of coercion" stood "Beneath the green ivy of civility." Now
that elitist rulers had stripped blacks of nearly all their rights
and had taken almost complete control of the state, they didn't
want to be seen as radical when radical tactics were no longer
needed. [14] And so Atlanta's comments only added to
Salisbury's disgrace.

And it's no wonder Atlanta went to hell just a month
later—its bloodbath was one of the most violent and
unprovoked race massacres in U.S. history—and no way could
they blame this on Salisbury. Georgia had its own issues.

At least a few people from Salisbury and the rest of the
Western part of North Carolina didn't want to look like a bunch
of backward yahoos. Local businessmen were trying to woo
northern and foreign investors to the area, and Glenn wanted a
sufficient supply of cheap labor to work in these northern-
supported industries. Both feared the lynching might scare
them all off. Glenn had just a few months earlier spoken in
favor of another Tennessee meeting of the Southern
Immigration and Quarantine conference. Quite concerned about
luring immigrants to North Carolina, he told the *Chattanooga
Times* "'I am most heartily in favor of having another
conference of the governors of the southern states to secure
concert of action and a better labor supply for the south. The

South is now having greater prosperity than ever before in the history of the country, and the most serious trouble confronting it is the labor supply.'" [15]

Glenn expressed his concerns about the lynching's effect on these plans for the New South in a letter to Long on the morning after. "The amount of damage to the State cannot be estimated in dollars and cents for it shows a lawless spirit amongst certain of our people which may deter enterprise and immigration into our midst." [F] Any concerns he may have expressed about the effect of that lynching on those who endured it or their families, was done so in private. On the same page as his continued coverage of "Last Night's Lynching," Julian printed an optimistic view of northern interests in the area: "Mr. J.B. Walker, of New York, who has valuable real estate interests in and around Salisbury, spent Saturday in the city. Mr. Walker is enthusiastic over the splendid progress of the city and is one of those who believe that Salisbury has a future." [C] Did Walker feel the same a couple of days later?

What Hickory's Republican *Times Mercury* had to say about this particular affair may be lost forever. Except for one issue in June, the entire year is missing from the filmed archives. Later issues, however, reveal that its editor, J.F. Click, didn't mind speaking out against Dixiecrat hypocrisy. Even though it went overboard at times, his voice was refreshing. Click, in 1908, even chanced a lawsuit, calling Charles B. Aycock, the revered "education governor," a drunk.

He also made fun of radical racist Josephus Daniels for schmoozing with the black population in the North, seeking votes for his favored presidential candidate, William Jennings Bryan, after publicly abusing southern African Americans in his 1898 and 1900 campaigns. The paper teased Daniels about serving some black people fried chicken on Bryan's lawn, pointing out the hypocrisy from a man who preached separation of races in *all* social situations in the South. Though Click's motivation was probably as political as Daniels'and his sense of humor crude, he must be commended for having the guts to take on Daniels and not let him get away with using and abusing black Americans as it suited him. Click also regularly pointed out atrocities committed by the "Night Riders," a spinoff of the original KKK. Even into 1908, Click continued to criticize the Wilmington massacre and the Red Shirts tactics, as had Raleigh's *Enterprise* and Durham's *Caucasian* in 1906, attributing the violence then, to what Daniels, Simmons, and Aycock started in 1898. And Click *really* had it out for Daniels' paper, summing up its duplicity in a nutshell.

> The *[News and] Observer*, in its own estimation, is the biggest little thing out of hades. It is as inconsistent as it is short sighted and truthful. There is nothing its editor has not stood for and then stood against. He will believe anything and do and sanction anything he thinks will put and keep his party in power. [16]

The Republicans were also, of course, using blacks for their own political purposes. John Mitchell said in his *Richmond Planet* that they were becoming more and more like Democrats every day. The Democratic *Chatham Record* was among others, besides Mitchell, who criticized Republicans in 1906 for suggesting extension of the law that had recently disfranchised most black citizens—a law they fought against in 1900. [17]

Self-serving or not, it was J.F. Click's political bias that made his voice so unique. Amid all the same old, same old, he must have had a few unique, choice words for what went on in Salisbury and the involvement of all the well-known Democrats in the fiasco, including Senator Lee Overman, Julian, Glenn, Hammer, and Long. It's a shame those editorials are lost.

Though we don't have Hickory's comments, we do have the next best thing—opinions from even farther west—Asheville. The *Citizen* was one of the few in the state that satirized the rhetoric.

> *"Spare no effort or expense to arrest and identify the mob,"* wired Governor Glenn yesterday in reference to the Salisbury lynching. Were it not so serious a matter we would feel tempted to wax 'yumorous' on the foregoing. It's the same old yarn, this official zealousness when harm is done, this talk of 'vigorous prosecution' after mob law has had its fling.

*Were the marvelous display of executive zeal, which invariably follows lynchings in every section, devoted beforehand to the proper equipment of the militia, which every now and then is made a spectacle of to such an extent as to approach the point of absurdity, there would be less outbreaks of the kind which disgraced the state last Monday night. Can you imagine anything more droll than the trotting out of the state soldiery armed with blank cartridges? Was it a nursery game of 'soldiers' with which the authorities hoped to awe a mob of five thousand men bent on obtaining vengeance? Wasn't it a real naughty mob not to go home when the soldiers drew up in imposing file with empty rifles?*

*As to Governor Glenn's telegram, while his after zeal is commendable, its import is almost as big a joke as the blank cartridge incident. "Arrest and identify the mob!" Considering that the said mob numbered at one time five thousand men, it can be easily determined what a task the governor has set Sheriff Julian. Some wise authority has said that you cannot hang the public, and a mob of five thousand in a city the size of Salisbury comes pretty near being the public. Any community is in itself the public, and when the community rises up and takes concerted action, what is going to stand against it unless a greater force overshadows it?* [18]

The Asheville paper, however, had to bite its tongue a few months later. A wanted black man was gunned down by a mob near Asheville in November. Growing up in Asheville at the time, future writer Thomas Wolfe was struck by the incident and later based a short story on his memory of it. "The Child By Tiger" was about a black man who had been a sharp-shooter in the army. After returning to the South, he had not been able to readadjust to the Jim Crow codes, and eventually, after a humiliating incident, he snapped and went on a shooting spree.

Judge Long might have missed much of the criticism that morning because he had business to attend to at court. A Greensboro paper said Long might as well have not bothered for all that got accomplished that day, but Long opened the session at about 10:40 anyway. Julian's paper said the "horrible tragedy of last night almost made Judge Long ill. But this morning, he was all right and ready to proceed against the lynchers." [C]

If he got any sleep at all that night, he woke up to face yet another attack. I can imagine him sitting down for a peaceful moment with a cup of coffee, before heading across the street to the courthouse. Then opening the *Salisbury Post* or the *Charlotte Observer*, or God help him, the *New York Times*, he is forced to again face the fiasco of the previous night, including a not so flattering view of his involvement in it. The reports and editorials portray him and the city's distinguished leaders pleading with the mob to obey the law. And his delay in calling the governor for help looks woefully inadequate all spelled out in print. Was Long corrupt, bowing to demands of mob leaders, purposely ignoring Jake Newell's early warning and the writings on the wall? Did he honestly believe he was doing the right thing? Or had he let politics interfere with his judgement? But how could anyone who knew the law, more so one in charge of upholding it, think that rushing a murder trial, denying defendants their rights, could be doing the right thing? Either way, he knew the outcome had been disastrous. Maybe he, more than anyone, had some explaining to do.

He entered the courtroom that day and the next on the defensive. The session began about 10:45, understandably later than usual. The *Industrial News* saw "...noticeable suffering written on the face of Judge Long. His attitude was yet determined but it was changed completely." He must have been upset, though he didn't really vent until the following day. He was probably still too shaken to say much. Bryant said the officers and spectators in the courtroom "were as mournful and as sad as if they were attending a funeral. Sheriff Julian and his deputies looked sad. Some of those who tried to beat back the mob wore bruised heads." [D, A]

Before addressing the assembly, Long ordered the jury back into the courtroom, and Solicitor Hammer moved for a day-to-day continuance of the trial of the remaining defendants, now back in Charlotte. His request was quickly granted this time. Defense Council could not be in court that day to make the request on their clients' behalf, because a threat on their lives was still out there. Several sources noted both Newell and Williams were warned not to show themselves on Salisbury's streets that day.

Long then told the grand jury he had work for it to do, and the *Industrial News* had this to say about that:

> *And there appears to be. The mob spirit is far from dead and a portion of its work has been the notice served upon Newell and Williams, attorneys for the negroes, not to come down town this morning. They have not and were not in the courtroom when Hammer made the motion for cessation.* [D]

First on the agenda was the case against George Hall. But before that got underway, Long addressed the spectators. He began, as if it had all been a surprise, saying "he had been informed that a band of men had broken into the jail last night and committed murder." [A] He then went over all the reasons why this outrage, in his opinion, should not have happened.

> *"There was a venire called here to try this case this morning at 10 o'clock. The grand jury had found a true bill and the court had made an order that 200 veniremen appear at the court house that the case might be investigated and tried according to law. But last night, when the court had become satisfied shortly before that the best sentiment in this county would uphold the laws of the land and stand by the courts in the administration of the law, a band of men broke into the jail, took three prisoners out and lynched them as the court is informed."*

Long's defense of his actions, his view that the "best sentiment" was somehow the majority, or having "best citizens" within a community would somehow prevent others or even those very citizens from creating or participating in a lawless mob, seems flawed to modern readers. Some, including at least one descendant, sees his views and actions as a product of his times, though that doesn't explain why some of his contemporaries, leaders also charged with upholding the law, like the judge that followed him, saw things differently. Even as Long spoke, the three victims were still hanging, mutilated, within view of railroad passengers traveling through town. Long was apparently not outraged enough to put an end to that outrage.

In spite of the presence of that scene from hell and the appalling acts that created it, Long declared, in closing, "God Almighty reigns and the law is still supreme." And he announced that the court would not adjourn until the matter of the lynching had been investigated. Then he finally instructed the grand jurors to retire to their room and proceed with their "deliberations and investigations." [A]

During the recess, there were again rumors of mob action, that efforts would be made to release Hall from jail that night. "Some of his associates were still in town," Bryant noted, but didn't say how he knew who they were or why they had not been arrested as well. He did say that as soon as the Judge got wind of the rumors, he immediately rang the court house bell and called the court to order. [A]

"I feel that it is incumbent upon the court to make public announcement pending the investigations of the grand jury. The probability is that the court cannot make an investigation this afternoon and I desire to say a few words before the adjournment of that body to-day." [A]

> *"That jail (pointing in the direction of the prison) was invaded last night by a mob and it has gone out on the wings of electricity that Rowan county has allowed the mob to do this. It has gone out that the citizens of this county have permitted this outrage. I think this is a mistake. The representative citizens did not do it, and they are not responsible. But they will be responsible if such a thing is allowed to occur again.*
>
> *"The court hears that idlers going about on the streets have threatened that processes of the court will be further interfered with. I therefore deem it proper to make proclamation that the square next to the jail be cleared and no one but the sheriff and his officers shall be allowed to occupy that place. I give warning to all*

*persons to keep their children and themselves from the*
*square next to the jail.*
*"That jail will be protected at all hazards and its*
*prisoners shall have full protection of the law. This*
*town is under municipal government and if the mayor is*
*present I hope he will take note again of what I say. I*
*shall instruct him to keep the streets clear about this*
*enclosure and men in groups or by themselves shall be*
*kept out. This order shall be in force during the sitting*
*of this court and there shall be no excuse for anybody's*
*going there. If he does, he goes at his own peril.*
*"I have felt it my duty to clear my skirts so that no*
*man may say he was taken by surprise. I saw last night*
*a number of young boys hooting and hollering at that*
*jail. There may have been good citizens in the crowd*
*and if there were, I do not want them to get hurt. The*
*sheriff is instructed to put a force of deputies armed for*
*the protection of the jail and the prisoners in it. If it be*
*necessary, he has the power to summon any man in the*
*county to his aid and if that man fails to serve, he is*
*guilty of a crime. He is instructed to use force if*
*necessary and to repel force with force if any attempt is*
*made to come into the precincts of his men."* A

That said, court was adjourned until 10 a.m. the following
day. With the Lyerly murder case now truncated by the
lynching, there was no longer any need for the subpoenaed
witnesses. They and the special venire of 200 summoned on the
previous day were dismissed just before court adjourned.

The prisoners on the previous night surely would have
appreciated the care now taken to prevent Hall from being
freed, had it been offered to keep them from being tortured and
lynched. Everything the Judge ordered on the day after, for
example: "to use force if necessary and to repel force with
force if any attempt is made to come into the precincts of his
men," was just as much a part of the legal duties of the sheriff
and his deputies the night before, whether the judge had
expressly ordered it or not. Ending his report on that day's
court session, Bryant said Mayor Boyden and Sheriff Julian
conferred, agreeing to keep the area free of crowds, and that

"no one anticipates trouble." [A] But when it came down to it, these were just more hollow words. What really kept Hall in jail that night was a pair of Gatling Guns, one at the entrance to the jail, another in the square, facing the jail. And the fact that he was white.

Sheriff Julian had finally come to his senses and requested reinforcements. Glenn responded by sending "...two additional military companies to aid the Rowan Rifles in protecting the prisoners," said the *N&O.* [B] Mitchell's *Planet* was one of the few pointing out the obvious—the precautions taken to protect Hall were "not done in order to keep anyone from lynching him, but to prevent a mob from releasing him." [G] But then this was an out of state voice and one of a different color—one that had been silenced altogether in North Carolina after the 1898.

J.C. McNeill remained in town that night to observe and write about how things were going. His observation of the scene around the jail now holding Hall began at 10 p.m. By then soldiers were everywhere. General J.F. Armfield's Iredell Blues, with Major R.L. Flanigan and Captain J.E. Deitz; the Hornets Nest Riflemen, under command of Captain W.S. Charles; and the First Battery Field Artillery of Charlotte, under Captain Mark W. Williams, all guarded the jail.

*The place is brilliantly lighted. Soldiers are breaking down the high board fence which separates the front from the back yard. Those not on other duty are pitching tents, their rifles stacked opposite each tent. There is very little liquor in evidence in the crowd. It is composed, or seems to be, of mere curious spectators, awed into silence.*

*A number of special police officers are on duty outside the jail fence, and 12 or 15 special deputies are sitting on the steps. I asked a policeman, as a test, to let me cross the fence. He replied that if I did he would shoot me. But he wouldn't have done so, for a few minutes later a young drunk man came shouldering his way through the crowd, loudly and profanely announcing that he was boozy and that he would say what he pleased, go where he pleased and do as he pleased, and that the first man who laid hands on him he would shoot him dead. This with his hand on his hip pocket. He vaulted the fence and went boldly up to the sentry line and a shiver went through the ranks of onlookers lest the police or the soldiers should fire on him. Chief J.F. Miller arrested him, however, and sent him away. How tremulous things are is illustrated when the passing cars run over torpedoes, placed on the track by mischievous boys. At every explosion the crowd starts and shakes.*

*There was a rumor that a mob would meet No. 12 at the depot and prevent the Charlotte Artillery from leaving the train. Capt. Williams had taken the precaution to set one of his Gatling guns at the door of the baggage car and, if the mob had materialized, what he would have done for it would have been a caution.*

*At 11 o'clock there is not a mouse stirring. The streets are almost deserted, there being scarcely more than a dozen people on the sidewalk between the court house and the jail.*

*Guests of the Vanderford Hotel have drawn their chairs out to the street, where they are sitting quietly, enjoying their cigars and watching the sentries on their beats. One Gatling gun now stands in the court house square, commanding a broad-side of the front of the jail yard, and the other has been placed in the back yard. They are putting electric lights on the rear of the jail. The soldiers are taking it easy, eating good ham sandwiches and making merry. It is plain to foretell that there will be no mob here to-night.* [A]

Governor Glenn arrived in Salisbury some time that evening and met with Judge Long, Solicitor Hammer, and Sheriff Julian until midnight. The trial of the alleged lynchers was to follow the next day, and the Governor said he would do anything in his power to see that the lynchers were brought to justice, including remaining in town until the end of the trial if necessary. [H] After testifying the next day, he left town.

# 17

# CONSPIRACY

## WEDNESDAY & THURSDAY, AUGUST 8 & 9

*Laws are like cobwebs, which may catch small flies, but let wasps and hornets break through.*

— Jonathan Swift

ROWAN COUNTY JAIL WITH MILITARY GUARD

## PART ONE

*Salisbury, August 8, 2 a.m.—Two military companies—infantry and artillery, both from Charlotte— are guarding the jail and preserving order; but according to appearances throughout the night their presence is not needed. Acting upon orders from Governor Glenn, telegraphed from Raleigh, Judge Long today began an investigation of the lynching Monday night. Although there were not less than two thousand people in the mob, and although a considerable number of men broke into the jail and had a hand in taking the prisoners out, there has been but one person identified.* [1]

That person was George Hall. His day in court had arrived already—just two days after the lynching. The state was embarrassed, and Governor Glenn had come under considerable attack. A fall guy was needed—and fast. The state had to show it would uphold the law, punish the mob, and keep its business prospects interested. A lot more was to come.

It may have been Hall's earlier "sins" that got him into trouble in this case. Making and selling liquor illegally was perhaps a less forgivable sin in Salisbury than in any other place in the state.

*"Really and actually," wrote a contemporary of the 1880 Salisbury scene, "the thing that maintained and supported Salisbury at the time was wholesale and retail whisky," With a dozen open saloons, half a dozen distilleries, and two wholesale whiskey warehouses, Salisbury held the title of being "the wettest and wickedest town in the state;" and the production and sale of the ardent spirits comprised the chief industry. This was so well understood that when a little kitten was presented by a Salisburian to a friend in Charlotte, the pet was promptly named "Boozy" to indicate its birthplace.* [2]

"Salisbury was the home of several major distilleries, J.B. Lanier's operation described as 'one of the largest in the South.'" And "Retail sale by the drink was legal in Salisbury long after it had been voted out in other cities in the state." [2] McNeill's depiction of the "boozy" man testing those guarding Hall on Tuesday night served to further substantiate Salisbury's reputation.

McNeill probably stayed in Salisbury Tuesday night. After reporting conditions in the streets outside the jail and around the square on the day after the lynching, he showed up at the courthouse Wednesday morning on behalf of the *Observer*. Bryant had caught a train to Greensboro anticipating a lynching story there.

Little had been accomplished in court on Tuesday. Things didn't get going until 11 a.m., and Judge Long spoke for most of the remaining session, before and after the lunch recess. Still defending his position on Wednesday, he talked most of that morning too.

The preliminary business was handled quickly. McNeill noted first that Solicitor Hammer had requested to be excused from court that morning and local counsel would appear in his stead. "He stated that he had business out of the city some two miles, in connection with the case against the lynchers" [A] Then Long called in the grand jury and "proceeded to charge it."

He began by recapping the circumstances leading to the special term of court. Not to insinuate that it was improperly called, he said it was, nevertheless, a duty he had neither anticipated nor requested. He had, in fact, not been feeling all that well when he was asked to cut short a vacation to meet the Governor's demands.

> *"For myself, gentlemen, I will say that I was beyond the bounds of the State, 300 miles from here, recuperating: I was not due to ride this district at this time, but I was assigned by the Governor of North Carolina to hold this court, and I came."* [A]

Governor Glenn, by now, had given yet another statement to the press. It disclosed more specifics about his conversation with

Long on the night of the lynching and made Long look even worse. Here's Daniels' version of it:

> "...I was startled when Judge Long called me up about half-past eleven o'clock on Monday night. I got up from bed to talk to him and immediately ordered him to use the military which he informed me was already out. I had felt no uneasiness during the day as Sheriff Julian had not notified me of any pending trouble, and there was a good judge and a good solicitor on the scene. The first intimation of trouble was in the message at 11:30, when Judge Long said the military was already out and that he wanted my sanction. I told him to use not alone the military but also to call out a posse of good men and to give orders to the soldiers to shoot if necessary. The talk of my having ordered that blank cartridges be used is folly. I see by the papers that the mob was gathering at nine o'clock Monday night and if I had been informed at that time, in place of after eleven o'clock I would have been able to order companies from Charlotte and Statesville to Salisbury to repel a mob attack, but until Judge Long called me up I was not uneasy and knew of no danger or trouble in Salisbury." [3]

Daniels may have just been spinning the event in favor of the man he put in office, shifting blame to Long, but the part about not hearing from Long until after 11 p.m. agrees with what all the papers reported and what Jake Newell said as well. Even so, it was disingenuous for Glenn to simply accept the Sheriff's denial of danger. He read the papers and knew the jail had been attacked once already. Furthermore, no action was taken against anyone involved in that criminal act, so those men were still on the loose and had already plotted other attempts. His close relationship with Governor Cox of Tennessee, who now blamed the Supreme Court for Chattanooga's lynching, certainly kept Glenn current on the developments in that case, as well as the corruption and errors that led to it in the first place. Even if Glenn could not have predicted the lynching, the possibility of it couldn't have been more obvious.

Long may have been put in the middle of that situation. Nevertheless, his duty was not to politics, but to the law, and in that respect, alone, he failed. The pecking order had him on the defensive on this next day in court. And George Hall was now at the bottom of that order.

Before getting to the business at hand, though, Long made yet another long speech condemning the lynching, this time, openly defending his actions and those of the court. He reiterated that there was no need for the violence due to the speed at which the trial had proceeded, indicting himself in the process. "'A motion was made by counsel for the defendants to postpone the trial,'" Long declared, "'and the motion was not allowed: nobody had a right to complain but the defendants themselves'" [A] Long seemed to imply that defendants would have had justification for an appeal or even a mistrial—if they had been convicted—if they had gotten a trial. It was the very denial of this motion that ensured no complaints would be heard.

What must have seemed incredible to anyone in court on August 6th or who read Bryant's report of those proceedings, Long next made statements that contradict that report. "'During the entire day there was not a suggestion made to me that the law and the court would not be respected," he said. [A]

> On the contrary, your good citizens expressed the opinion to me that a fair and impartial trial would immediately be had. The only opposite suggestion was made to me by a special deputy, who said that if the barrooms were not closed at a certain hour, men might get in drink and beside themselves. You remember that I said to you that if there were any signs of an outbreak here, known to you, I wanted you to inform me of it. I therefore presumed that you had no such information, since you did not communicate it to me. I thought that the prosecuting officers had taken every necessary precaution. I had no power to order out the military, but I appointed double the number of deputies the sheriff wanted. [A]

Recall the *Observer's* record of the murder trial for comparison. One part of the report said grand jury foreman J.S. Hall was asked to wait in the jury room "...so that he and his associates might be called in on another matter. It was generally understood that the court had in mind certain threats of lynchings that had been made. Court officers had heard rumors concerning the formation of unlawful mobs." [B] In fact, Long's reported response to Newell's request for a change of venue was that "the talk of lynching was not all being done by citizens of Rowan." [B]

If these reports were incorrect, Long would certainly have corrected them in his address this day, but instead he acted as if the threat of mob violence had not existed. And after court on August 6th adjourned, when an attack was obvious, he ignored it again, until it was too late.

Even Solicitor Hammer's newspaper said the trial had been attended by "a large and threatening crowd." And, though it claimed "Long's charge to the grand jury had calmed the threat during the day...," it admitted to "...a strong undercurrent of determination visible in the crowd as the night grew darker." [1]

The *Lexington Dispatch* confirmed what must have been obvious to all—that trouble was brewing from the get-go, and the threat didn't end with Long's warnings to the court. It said Long "spoke hopefully that the people would not attempt a lynching." But "Even while he was talking, the trouble was forming." [4]

The *Carolina Watchman* implied that officials knew help would be needed early on, even before the escalation.

> *The mob began to gather early in the evening, and any one who circulated among them could have no difficulty in coming to a clear understanding of what they were there for. They made no secret of their intentions, talked openly and above board of what they were going to do—and as the sequel proved, they did it.* [5]

The *Watchman* also confirmed that Long waited until "after eleven o'clock" to inform Glenn of conditions at the jail.

Continuing his address, Long, once again, referred to the events on the night of the lynching as if they might actually have been rumors—as if he'd been out of town and gotten his information elsewhere. "'Gentleman, it has been said that, in the early hours of the night, there was an unlawful assembly over there,' pointing to the jail, 'and that the court and others went and tried to dissuade the members of it from further crime and to disperse them.'"

McNeill recorded his next words under the subheading, "His Position Misunderstood." "'...there has been a misconception of my position...,'" Long began,

*"Not while I am judge will I ever go and beg a criminal not to do an unlawful act. But I did as a judicial officer go to that jail and warn that mob and tell them that they and their people would suffer for their deed, not through me, but through the law, and I told them to disperse. They made as if to disperse, but this was only for the purpose of reinforcement. And, even after that jail yard had been lighted with electricity, so that it was almost as bright as day, a band of ruffians, lawless men, warned as they had been by my charge to you on Monday morning and evening and my words to themselves at the jail, overpowered the officers and took three prisoners in the jail—these very brave men!—and carried them over here near the town of Salisbury—after they had put out the lights, thereby disclosing the fact that they were unwilling to be seen—and hanged and shot and mutilated these prisoners. It is reported that a near kinsman of the people whose lives had been taken pleaded with the mob to let the investigation go on."* [A]

It looks like Long would have sympathized with the lynchers more if they'd been successful the first time, on the night of July 14th.

*"If immediately after the Lyerly murder had been committed a mob had lynched the murderers, some allowance must have been made for the passions of the moment and the judgment of the country would not have been harsh. But no such allowance can be made in this case."* [A]

Pressure from the Governor and elsewhere may have been the only reason the trial was held at all. Or maybe Long took the assault on the jail personally, or he wanted to amend the mistakes he'd made, whether he admitted them or not. Whatever his reasons for pursuing the case, the hanging bodies were now his own personal albatross.

Long's verbal outrage continued, denouncing the mob as "a band of cut-throats and murderers...guilty of murder in the first degree: that every man who aided and abetted that mob, by his presence, his acts or his words is guilty of murder in the first degree." [A] Again, though this charge was morally correct, there was no law to back it. The emptiness of these words would soon be revealed, but with less press coverage than Long was getting this day.

> *"Are you for the mob, or for the court? Take your stand, gentlemen. "If you sift this thing to the bottom, as I demand of you, you will find that the men who participated in this mob and led it are not men of good reputation or of any standing in Rowan county, but men who ought to be behind bars. I bring you face to face with your duty, gentlemen. I am going to do mine, before God and man, without fear or favor." [A]*

With three military companies present, Long would, understandably, now feel confident about doing his duty without fear. No one could fault him for leaving the mob scene and returning to his hotel room that night when things got out of hand. But why didn't he call for reinforcements then?

Long wasn't the only one who had found the heat too hot in the kitchen. A current Rowan resident recalled a story about Dick File, the Lyerly neighbor reports said Fannie ran to when she'd gotten scared the day after the murders. File, he said, was in Salisbury on the night of the lynching, and when the mob went crazy, File broke a nearby store window, leaped inside, and hid under a counter until things cooled down.

Next, addressing the law related to lynching, Long brought up the Anson County case. The "...attorneys for the State and the court must have overlooked section 3233 of the 1905 Revisal," he said, [A] referring to the technicality that acquitted the accused in that case. The problem occurred when the revisal of the original 1893 law against lynching failed to clarify the definition of lynching in the section relating to change of venue, leaving a loophole for offenders. In the end, the statute supposed to discourage lynching, made it impossible to convict a lyncher of murder or anything else.

Nevertheless, Long made it clear to this jury that he expected an indictment.

*"Before I will take this investigation into my own hands, as this statute empowers me to do, I am first going to put you on your mettle, gentlemen. I will not admit that Rowan county will not punish men guilty of crime. The law will live longer than the mob. The mills of the gods grind slowly, but they grind exceeding fine. When I shall have retired from the bench, there will be another judge to occupy it. "* [A]

After this last charge, the grand jury adjourned, and the court proceeded with less important cases while awaiting the verdict. Not much later, in the afternoon session, the jurors "filed in and returned a true bill for murder in the first degree against George Hall...." [A]

Long had gotten what he wanted—a murder indictment. That was no small accomplishment, coming from an all-white jury in a Southern lynching case.

He also got a moment of fame. His words about the mills grinding slowly and fine were quoted, usually admiringly (though sometimes satirically), in papers nearly everywhere, including the *Afro-American Ledger* of Baltimore. [6]

Before adjourning the morning session, Long re-emphasized "his assertion that the mob comprised ruffians, and that when the truth is discovered it will appear that the virtuous and intelligent citizenship of this county is not fixed with the ignominy of this crime." McNeill said afterward that Long asked him to add to his report something he'd failed to say in court, "...that the deputies were duly armed and the reason they did not fire into the mob was that there were a great many good citizens among it, trying to induce it to disperse." [A]

For the judge to have eliminated the "virtuous and intelligent" from the actual act of savage, blood-thirsty murder wasn't much of a stretch. But there were other ways for the "virtuous and intelligent" to participate. And we do have to consider that several newspapers, including the one edited by the sheriff's son, said Sheriff Julian scolded the "men of property" as they headed out of town with the prisoners. Having property may not mean they were virtuous and intelligent, but they apparently weren't riffraff either. And, if Julian knew they were "men of property," he must have known who they were and where to find them.

Future reports and letters laid considerable blame on the sheriff and implicated the "better" citizens. However, that Wednesday after court recessed, Hammer also made excuses for the officers' failure to shoot. He, too, asked McNeill to add a comment for the record: "...the people who are criticizing the local authorities do not know what they are talking about; ...the development of the facts will exonerate them from any kind of blame." [A]

By now, others beside Hall had been identified as mob participants, but that may have been for show. They already had their goat. McNeill reported the arrests of Francis Cress and Bud Bullyboy, saying the solicitor was "...sending against each defendant four different bills of indictment; for murder in the first degree, for conspiracy, for assault with a deadly weapon with intent to kill, and for resisting an officer." [A] The *N&O* said Cress was "a well-known citizen of Salisbury," and census records show he worked as a lumber yard driver. "Bullyboy" or Bill McConeyhead, whose name would later be printed a number of different ways, was thought to be the one who climbed the tree and tied the ropes. "With each arrest the interest in the prosecution of the lynchers increases," said the report, adding that a posse was headed to Faith in search of more "men wanted for the crime." [D]

Another Raleigh correspondent had more names to report later on in the day. "Up to nine o'clock tonight the following had been arrested" on murder and other related charges: George Hall of Montgomery County; G.H. (George) Gentle, of Rowan; John Cauble; Henry Goodman; Bud Bullabough (alias Bullyboy or McConeyhead); and F.M. (Francis) Cress. It didn't say right away where the last four were from, probably because they were from Salisbury. Deputy Goodman, the one who said he protected Henry Mayhew in his carriage on the way to Salisbury after the murders, had a brother named Henry, but not necessarily the Henry Goodman arrested. Census records show two Henry Goodman's, both about the same age, living in the deputy's neighborhood, though there were more than two living in the county at the time. Likewise, not enough information about John Cauble was given to distinguish him from several others in

Rowan County with the same name. Both Bullyboy and Gentle were from my family's neighborhood, just east of the Lyerly place, and Gentle, the *Statesville Ledger* said, was living there at the time of the lynching. George Hall's current residence was recorded wrong, perhaps on purpose. The report finally said the last four were Salisbury residents and all "were sent to jail without bail" to "be tried for their lives." [D]

Though only these few were arrested so far, "it was rumored that one hundred citizens will be indicted for aiding in the crime Monday night." Each prisoner would be tried separately, and trials for Hall and Gentle were expected to take nearly a week. [C] Certainly at least a hundred citizens participating that night were known by name, but no more than seven were ever arrested. And one of those names was kept very quiet.

Before filing his report on Wednesday's court proceedings, McNeill commented on the scene outside the jail and around the square.

> *...all night long last night and all day long to-day the sentries have been pacing their beats until the paths they have made are as smooth as an ancient lane. Gen. Armfield says he slept two minutes last night. And his subordinates report that they slept not at all. The air was swarming with mosquitoes where their little tents were pitched. It is no wonder that, when a false alarm was given before day, the boys were in position and ready to meet a charge in less than five minutes."* [A]

As for the artillery stationed at the court house square, "cushioned with fair green grass and deeply shaded with elm and maple," the soldiers lay sleeping on blankets— "so sound asleep that if you stirred them with your foot they would only mutter and sigh and succumb again. The riflemen, however, fully uniformed and stationed in the sunlight, either doing their beats or sweltering in the thin shade of their tents," looked over to the artillerymen with "envious eyes." [A]

The following day, the *N&O* said Long's prediction that the military would remain in Salisbury all summer to try the lynching suspects was unlikely. "This would be a difficult task," it said, since "strong sentiment in favor of the lynchers" prevailed." [D]

Both the *Post* and the *Observer* covered the lynching trials. Both printed detailed witness testimonies, some paraphrased, some quoted. This time Bryant represented the *Observer*, and Julian presumably reported for the *Post,* and each filled in details omitted by the other. Judging by their coverage of the Lyerly case, it's likely they omitted or distorted important facts. At any event, except for bits and pieces from other papers, it's all we have. The *N&O* printed one relevant item on the first day. Hall had confessed to using a sledge hammer to break down the jail doors but denied any involvement in the actual lynching. It said the maximum sentence for these crimes was 20 years imprisonment, exaggerating it by five. It also said that "All the prisoners" would be "tried for their lives." [D] Another error.

Before delving into the proceedings on Thursday, Bryant rewrote a bit of the lynching history and addressed other points. He confirmed George Gentle's arrest and two others, but not all of those listed in the *N&O*. He pounced on the "penny-a-liner correspondents," as he called them, for sending out sensational stories appearing in the northern papers. They "are calculated to do much harm," he said. Those fabricating these stories, using Salisbury headlines, would be located and exposed, he warned. The "sin" committed was representing the lynchers as "reputable citizens," backed by the community. "He is not only hurting Salisbury," Bryan said of one, "but the entire state."

Then he presented his revised version, or the establishment's version, of the lynching.

> *The lawless element for many miles around had come to Salisbury for the purpose of having a little fun. Feeling encouraged by a noble throng of respectable on-lookers Hall and his kind went to work to force an entrance to the county jail.... Hall had beaten out a window of the jail and gone inside, followed by two companions. The officers arrested the intruders, but when the Panama hat fellow outside began to clamor for the release of them, Senator Overman said: "Turn them loose!"*
> *Solicitor Hammer protested against this.*

*The newly made prisoners were given their liberty,
with the understanding that the mob would disperse.
Hall is the man who went in the window. He came out
and cursed his followers for not sticking to him, shook
hands with Mr. Hammer and left.
The mob retired for a time, but soon returned and
stormed the jail with lead and rock. Hall tied one of the
ropes that hung the negroes. These acts make him a
leader if not the real active leader....
Had the good people here known that the mob was
composed of such cattle as Hall, Bully Boy, Cress and
Gentle, they would have singled them out and shot them
down like mad dogs, but when 3,000 men, women and
children surged about with the members of the lynching
party no one could tell who was guilty or who innocent.
The people had not been warned to stay away from the
jail and it was late in the evening before the wisest
spectators really anticipated any trouble. The first
thousand of people, who assembled in the streets, were
out to see the great imaginary mob, which was supposed
to be somewhere forming, for a sudden onslaught, come
in sight in a rush. The officers of the law contemplated
no trouble and laughed at the growing crowd. Seeing
things here as they were Monday night is quite different
from seeing them from afar off, and hindsight is always
better than foresight.* ᴱ

This version certainly covers for the judge, the sheriff, and
Hammer. It's hard to say what was going on with the portrayal
of Overman, but he would soon publicly protest it.

Bryant's report settled the official public record of the
lynching and also established a negative impression of the
lynching suspects. His account of the trial includes his
subjective, usually unflattering, characterization and physical
descriptions of the accused, along with what he chose to disclose
about the proceedings.

Attendance was low that day, he said. The public had not
known what to expect, because "It was not certain when any of
the men charged would be arraigned." But Hammer got to that as
soon as court was called to order.

Hall, "small and muscular," was sitting in the prisoner's box. Bryant said he looked to be about 35 years old, with a "sunburned, beardless face and light clay-colored hair. He was clad in "a cheap suit of clothes, a collarless shirt, and a large gray slouch hat." As he stood up to respond to the charges against him, his grayish eyes "wandered about the room."

> *If Hall is a man of courage his looks do not indicate it. His general appearance would make him a little sand-hill farmer and distiller. Ignorance and recklessness would appear to be the fellow's strongest points.... His courage would not fill a thimble if it were a material thing.* [E]

"Do you have a lawyer," asked the court?

"'I could not get nary one to come to the jail to see me,'" Hall responded.

Judge Long appointed former congressman, Theo F. Kluttz to represent him, and Kluttz consented. Then Hammer read the bill of indictment charging Hall with "unlawfully killing Nease and John Gillespie and Jack Dillingham." And Hall pleaded "not guilty" to the charge. [E]

When asked how he would be tried, Hall replied, "By God and my country."

"May God send you deliverance," was Hammer's response.

When the surviving black prisoners later stated their intent to be tried "By God and country," the paper reported no response from Hammer at all. On August 6th he had announced that all six black prisoners had committed murder by instigation of the devil, but he connected no such deviltry to Hall's motivation.

Bryant said Hall had no reason to "complain of his treatment in court. If he had plenty of money he could not employ better attorneys than the court has given him." [E]

Kluttz conferred with Hall briefly, then asked the court, just as Jake Newell had, to continue the case until the regular term of court. Long again denied the request, though Hall was as much entitled to it as the former suspects. Long said he "...wanted to give the defendant every benefit that the law allowed," but he saw no reason to delay. [E] Certainly Hall's request was justified. How could anyone expect an attorney to prepare a criminal defense in one day?

When that failed, Kluttz asked "that the venire be drawn from the box," but Long said, "no," it would take too long. Instead, he ordered the sheriff to summons sixty men to appear the following day when the case would be taken up. [E]

Nothing more concerning the Hall case was accomplished on August ninth—or nothing else was reported.

Near the end of his account, Bryant mentioned Sheriff Julian's condition, that he had "... been unwell for some time," and the trial was hard on him. "His nerves are unstrung. He is not himself." [E]

Before concluding his coverage for the day, Bryant scrutinized Gentle, Cress, and Bullyboy, who had sat with Hall in the "prisoner's box" throughout the proceedings. Bryant described Cress, about 44-years old, as "a long-whiskered, sharp-faced cotton mill operative." But he later corrected Cress's occupation to a lumber yard laborer.

> *He is a striking looking man. The sharpness of his face, the thinness of his nose and his restless, deep-set eyes, make him a crank, a wild fanatic. He is the oldest prisoner in the bunch. His record as a citizen does not shine. The hunted look on his face to-day made one sorry for him.* [E]

Bryant next disclosed something rather astonishing—that showed he must have *personally* known Bullyboy's role in the lynching. He said Bullyboy *was* (not, was assumed to be) "the man who sat on the limb and smoked a cigarette while Hall and others made the negroes pray." Then he said:

> *He looks the part. His face is weak and his eyes very large. He wears his hair parted in the middle and goes without a collar. His courage would not fill a thimble if it were a material thing.* [E]

Finally Bryant had to make George Gentle look bad, even though his parents, he admitted, "were very good people."

George, a young farmer, "has a bad reputation," said Bryant, "He drinks and carouses with a sorry lot of fellows." [E]

Out of the seven arrested, those actually indicted were poor working class men. Bryant's vilification of them fit the agenda of elitist Dixiecrats, who used poor whites for their dirty work, caring little for the lower classes it manipulated. And worse, they broke the fledgling bonds that had been developing between a coalition of white farmers, Republicans, Populists, and newly-freed and franchised blacks, dashing the hopes and dreams of many bent on social and economic reform. By turning these groups against each other, Dixiecrats kept control of power and suppressed the formation of labor unions. The masses, oblivious to the plan, remained in poverty, distracted by racist rhetoric that infiltrated and ruled the South.

By contrast, Bryant's description of *Mrs.* Hall was good. While in court that day, she "sat by her husband's side and conversed with him," appearing "...to be a very good woman of her class." Bryant would not likely have characterized her any other way. All white women in the South at that time, whatever their class, were represented as the personification of purity that propagandists used to incite racial fear. A little book Bryant wrote idolizing his own wife, *Little Eva*, and Thomas Dixon's, *The Clansman*, are perfect examples of how ingrained this myth had become.

Bryant had sized up all the suspects in a way that fit the view Salisbury and the state wanted the public to accept. The focus was on making these suspects appear to be part of the riffraff, and Hall fit right in. Statistics say those who generally committed the actual acts of lynchings, breaking into the jail and hanging the victims, were the poor and uneducated.

However, there were different levels of participation in mob violence, and each role contributed to the attack's success. "Not only did the onlookers make it more difficult for law-enforcement officers to stop the mob, but their presence also implied public acquiescence...and gave police officers second thoughts about interfering with the mob." [7]

Bryant said more about Cress, that he was well-liked by those in Salisbury, but didn't even mention Henry Goodman or John Cauble, both of whom were likely descendants of Rowan's pioneer property owners, i.e., "good" citizens.

There would be more arrests made the next day, Bryant said, "some charged with murder and others with rioting." He even said officers were searching for the "fine looking fellow, who wore a Panama hat," claiming now that he must have been an "interloper" because he had completely disappeared. The man several reports had earlier described as well-to-do, having the clout to disperse the crowd "with the wave of his hand," all of a sudden got demoted to an interloper, and everybody who knew so much about him before, now seemed to have forgotten his name. "The drag net will be cast out again," Bryant said, "but the court will try the men already in custody. The first step in this direction was made this afternoon." [E]

In closing, Bryant said it was generally accepted that the evidence against Hall was conclusive and "if he is not convicted the courts of the State had better discontinue trying lynchers." [E]

So it was that one did not have to be a person of color to be tried and convicted by the press. Jim Crow's society had a number of scapegoats to choose from. George Hall was just one of them.

GOVERNOR ROBERT BROADNAX GLENN

# PART TWO

By the time court reconvened on Friday, August 10th at 10 a.m., Hall had another lawyer, Walter Murphy, "employed by parties interested in Hall's case."[B] Perhaps the "decent citizens" and "men of property" who had participated were afraid a precedent might be set if Hall were to be convicted. Or maybe some felt Hall should not go down as the fall guy for thousands, without at least a proper defense.

Solicitor Hammer would prosecute with the help of Linn and Burton Craige. And, since George Hall had confessed to jail-breaking, Hammer announced right away he would pursue number 112 on the docket instead of the murder charge, which eliminated the need for the special venire ordered the day before.
[A] The docket lists number 112 as the State vs George Hall "& others unknown." The charge was "conspiracy," and the witnesses listed were: D.R. Julian, D.W. Julian, Dr. Dorsett, Lee S. Overman, A.H. Boyden, Charles A. Goodman, Tom Vanderford, A.A. Porter, Shoaf Poteat, Crawford Kennerly, and Will Thomason. Two men not listed among these witnesses, James McKinly and W.F. Jones, were recorded as grand jury witnesses. Prosecuting attorneys planned only to postpone the trial for murder, or at least give that impression. Charges of "assault with intent to kill," "resisting an officer," and two counts of "murder," remained on the dockets.[1]

The "feature of the day was the appearance of Governor Glenn as witness." Defense council hoped the governor's absence, when the special term was called, would nullify the legitimacy of the court session. Even with the governor's presence, the crowd was small, as Bryant saw it. "The multitude [was] not enthused over the case," he said.[A] Julian, however, described the courtroom as "well filled" with people who wished to see the prisoner.[B]

Glenn had stayed overnight after his arrival the previous day and spent the morning before court convened in consultation with Judge Long, Solicitor Hammer, and Sheriff Julian.[B] He had planned to leave immediately after the meeting, but missed his train, so, since he was in town anyway, he was subpoenaed to appear and confirm his whereabouts on July 17th.[A]

As soon as Hammer announced the change in charges, defense attorneys offered their plea. They argued that the special term was unlawful, according to Article 3, Section 12 of the State Constitution, and even Hammer concurred that the "commission should have been signed by the Lieutenant Governor, in the absence of the chief executive." Bryant, now leaving off his initials from the report, added that "The constitution says that the Governor is not the Governor when he is out of the State." [A] Defense next questioned Glenn to verify his absence for the record.

> *Glenn was brought into the court and sworn....*
> *"Are you the Governor of the State?" asked Mr. Kluttz of counsel for the defense.*
> *"Where were you on the 17th of July?"*

Hammer objected to the questioning, arguing that "the witness was not compelled to answer." But Glenn answered anyway and confirmed that he had indeed been in Atlantic City, New Jersey on the 17th. Then he explained his actions.

> *I issued the order by telegram and my private secretary signed the communication. My secretary could not get to the Lieutenant Governor. I sent the telegram to do what I could to stop lynching in North Carolina. I was trying to prevent the horrible thing that occurred here last Monday. This is my signature made by a stamp.*
> [A]

If the court decided in favor of defense counsel's motion, the *Post* said, Hall's case and twenty five more would have to be retried. [B] But Judge Long ruled that the court presumed "...the commission was regular and, if facts were presented to show that it had not been made regularly, he would hear the facts and pass on them." [A] With that, Long reserved his decision on the matter and went ahead with the case against Hall.

The witnesses were called, and more than a few, some from Stanly and Cabarrus Counties, didn't respond, said the *Observer*. [A] Among those listed, however, only Senator Overman's testimony was not recorded—if he testified at all.

The bulk of the testimony seemed orchestrated to focus on Hall and no one else. And all the witnesses followed the script except for one slip. A new all-white jury was there to hear the testimonies Bryant and Julian recorded, and likely more: W.H. Boggs, R.B Brittain, Joseph Mesimer, Daniel L. Eddleman, C.M. Kimball, S.H. Wiley, Charles A.W. Sloop, C.C. Boger, William G. Eagle, S.C. Karriker, J.C. Deaton and O.J. Deal. [A] Deputy D.W. Julian, the Sheriff's son and editor's brother, was the first to testify.

> *"The first time I saw the witness was on the night of the 6th. I was going down the alley of the court house with a prisoner, when I met Hall, who had a hammer and was at the head of a procession of 30 or more. Hall told me to turn the prisoner loose or he would brain me. Alex Jackson, of Faith, who was with Hall said that he liked me but I would have to turn the man loose. A third man came up and, shaking three sticks of dynamite at me, said: 'I'll throw this under you.'"* [A]

That was Bryant's version. The *Post's* differed slightly, saying it was Hall, instead of a "third man," who shook the stick of dynamite at Deputy Julian. The *Post* also changed or disguised Alex Jackson's name, printing it as Jackson Hall.

Court documents show it was Bryant who recorded the name correctly. It's in the 1900 census records as Alex P. Jackson, living in Litaker, Faith's township, among some of the area's wealthiest and most respected landowners, including the Bargers, Shupings, Earnhardts, and Holshousers. The *Post* didn't identify Jackson as the one from Faith but did say the Faith resident was the one with his hands full of dynamite—another example where the man's residence is known but, supposedly, not his name. If Jackson's name had appeared in any papers after that day, the misprint would not seem suspicious. It's likely it wasn't meant to be mentioned in the first place, though, as if only six had ever been arrested. Was it because this Jackson was a prominent Rowan citizen, perhaps related to Stonewall or Andrew Jackson? Or maybe he was a relative of G.A. Jackson, whose saloon occupied the same building as the *Post*, when the paper was first established.

Defense attorneys objected to Deputy Julian's testimony as irrelevant, but the objection was overruled, and the testimony continued with Deputy Julian explaining why he had a prisoner with him in the alley.

> *"I arrested the man for striking Mr. Tom Vanderford in the face. I got him about 60 feet from the jail.*
> *"I went out from the jail to keep the men from going up the lane. Hall went on.*
> *"I saw him later, sitting in a room in the jail, in charge of a deputy. That was about a half hour after I first saw him.*
> *"I did not see him any more until the day after he was arrested. I recognized him as the man who had stopped me and threatened to brain me."* [A]

At this point editor Julian noted Defense counsel's motion to have the deputy's testimony stricken from the record on the grounds that it was "irrelevant, immaterial, and did not connect the defendant with anything that happened at the jail." The motion was overruled, and then the court recessed. [B]

When it reconvened at 2:30, Kluttz cross-examined Deputy Julian, and the *Post* printed a choppy and at least partially paraphrased record of the examination.

Deputy Julian, again:

> *He saw defendant Monday night for first time. He saw him next in the jail, was [un]certain of man in the cell. It was dark in the cell, not sure he was same man or not. There was much excitement. Took particular notice of Hall and man with dynamite. Hall talked to them. Did not arrest Hall, because he was overpowered by Hall and others. Had one pistol. Crowd around. Pistol would shoot six times. The men were doing nothing. "One man struck T.H. Vanderford, Jr., and I arrested him."*
> *He went to get out of the lane and Julian arrested him. The crowd surged back up the lane. "Several deputies asked me to go back over the fence to the jail and argue with the crowd. Hall was in the lane and later on at the back door of the jail. He was in front of the*

*crowd in the back yard. He demanded admission. We tried to keep him from going in. He had a hammer and with profanity said he was going to lynch the negroes. He used vulgar language. I assisted and carried one man in a room in the jail building. The man had a mask and blood on his face. Hall had a hammer and was trying to get in the jail. While I was in the room Hall was brought in and I talked with him. They brought two hammers. They told Hall he ought not to do this. He said nothing. When a match was struck I could see. I showed the hammer to the solicitor. I saw Hall same night he had been turned loose. He was by the asylum."* [B]

Bryant's briefer record of Julian's cross-examination follows and mentions Alex Jackson again, by his last name. The *Post*, which gave Hall as the last name for both, didn't clarify which Hall it had referred to, though it more than likely left Jackson out of it altogether.

> *"The first time I ever saw him was that night. I know that he is the same man. I turned my man loose. They overpowered me. I had a six-shooter but Hall had a hammer over my head. Jackson had me by the arm and the other fellow had dynamite. I was helpless. They had friends around them."* [A]

Who knows why the man with the mask remained disguised after his arrest, if he did? The testimony implies that no one even tried to identify him. And it doesn't explain why Julian didn't use his six-shooter against a man armed only with a hammer.

Tom Vanderford, Jr., owner of the hotel, was up next. This is Bryant's transcript:

> *"I went over in the court yard that night, about dark, and saw people about the jail. I saw that some of them were engaged in conversation. "I heard men say, 'Those men ought to be lynched.' I argued with Hall, who seemed to be leading the mob, and told him that the negroes are in the hands of the law, and if guilty will be hung, endeavoring to get him to desist.*

*"He said: 'We will lynch them.'*
*"We were at the front gate. W.T. Porter, a deputy, advised me to come away from the fence. The crowd began to go into the lane at the side fence. Dave Julian ordered them out. I went to help Julian get them out. Before I could cross the fence a man struck me. Julian arrested the fellow. The crowd had started out. Several deputies asked me to return to the jail. I went to the building and left Julian arguing with the crowd.*
*"Hall was in the lane at the far end.*
*"I saw Hall later on at the back door of the jail. He was in front on the top step, of a crowd. This was at the back door. He was demanding admission and we were trying to keep them out. He was using profanity and declaring that they were going to lynch those negroes. The men had hammers. We carried one man in the jail. While I was in the room some one brought Hall in. I talked with him. I told him that he ought not to do what he was trying to do. The hammers were brought in.*
*"I saw Hall again that night. He was behind the jail. He said his men were cowardly sons of bitches and wouldn't stick to him. He had been turned out of the jail in my absence. He was surrounded by his men, a good sized crowd.*
*"The prisoners were taken out and lynched.*
*"My hat was broken in beating back the crowd.*
*"Hall used a blacksmith's hammer. It was small.*
*"We had three men in that room."* [A]

The *Post* ended its report at press time with a shorter version that added nothing to what the *Observer* printed of Vanderford's testimony. It did add that John Cauble and Henry Goodman were now charged with riotous conduct and released on $2500 bonds but could not say yet when their cases would be heard. [B]

Then Archibald H. Boyden, Salisbury's mayor, took the stand. According to Bryant,

*He swore: "I saw the defendant come out of the jail. There was a clamor for his release. He came out and asked to be allowed to make a speech. Some one said*

*'no, don't let him talk,' but the majority said 'let him speak.' I think Mr. Overman helped him upon the stand. He climbed up and said: 'You are a son of a bitch,' meaning his crowd.*

*"I saw a man with a black moustache. Several men tried to quiet Hall after he got out. I saw him several times after that night. The mob was commanded to leave by the sheriff, his honor and others. They did not disband.*

*"I had never seen Hall before that night."* [A]

In its next edition, the *Post* began with the mayor's statement, adding only that Boyden didn't know the man with the black mustache. And it omitted what Boyden said about Lee Overman, Salisbury's Democratic senator and advisory committee member, under whom editor Julian had studied law. Julian had also served as Overman's campaign manager, when he ran for the Senate, and briefly as his secretary in Washington. [2]

Next, according to the *Post* account, W.T. Porter (evidently the deputy Vanderford referred to as Albert Porter) spoke from the witness stand.

*W.T. Porter said: I was at the jail and saw Hall. I arrested two with Poteat. I was present when the shooting occurred, in the jail room. I went to the door and was on first step. Don't know who was arrested and did not know the defendant. Advised Mr. Vanderford to come away. The crowd rushed in the jail from the back way. This is all I know. Don't know how many came in. I do not know who was in the room. I was assisted by Deputy Poteat.* [C]

Porter didn't seem to know much at all, not even the names of the men he said he arrested, even though he was right in the middle of the ruckus. The Court Docket lists his name as A.A. Porter, which is consistent with Vanderford's reference, and it seems like Julian would have known his correct name, as well as Jackson's, but maybe since Julian was a witness, someone else did the reporting this time. Bryant added only that "If Porter knew anything he never told it."

Next, Bryant quoted John Moose Julian, who was *not* listed in the docket as a witness:

> *"The crowd was attempting to break down the jail fence when first I appeared. The officers were pleading with the crowd. I saw the defendant at the fence. He was calling to the crowd, begging white men to protect white women.*
>
> *"The next time I saw him was at the jail door just before several bullets were shot into the door. The door was closed then for the first time.*
>
> *"I saw him after he was arrested and again when he was released. I heard him make his vile speech on the steps. The crowd did not disperse when ordered to do so."*
> A

Maybe Julian confused Hall with "the man in the Panama hat." Bryant said it was this leader, also said to sport a black mustache, who called to the crowd about protecting white women. He indicated that he, not Hall, had ignited the crowd in the first place. But maybe Julian wanted Hall to take the blame for it. There seemed to be a concerted effort to protect this unnamed man, as well as Alex Jackson.

The *Post's* report of Julian's testimony added that he never saw Hall before that night and didn't hear Hall say he was going home at any time. It didn't mention that the door had been open until just before the first bullets started flying. Bryant's version of Julian's testimony supports an earlier report that the door had been standing open even as trouble outside was brewing.

Sheriff Julian, according to the *Post's* account, began by saying he "...saw the defendant at the jail the night of the lynching—saw him the first thing that night, but did not know him." C The *Post* didn't add quotations marks to this testimony.

> *One of my deputies arrested him and they were in the family rooms. Saw a hammer in the jail. Do not know who was trying to enter jail. The prisoners were taken out forcibly by the men unknown to me. Hall was*

*released. The crowd wanted the other men. I begged the crowd to go off. Judge Long ordered the crowd to leave. The crowd said they would leave if the men they arrested were turned loose. Hall cursed the crowd. I never saw Hall any more until he was in the jail. The negroes were hanged Monday night the 6th.* [C]

Bryant's version is noticeably different. He *quoted* the sheriff testifying that "His honor, the solicitor, Senator Overman, Mayor Boyden and myself begged the men to go away." Judge Long must have bristled at this, having just explained to the court that he did no such thing. Also, according to Bryant, Sheriff Julian said that "Hall cursed everybody, Judge Long, Solicitor Hammer and his followers for sons of bitches." [A]

Both papers said Deputy Arthur Thompson took the stand next, and this time Bryant paraphrased most of the testimony.

*...he was at the jail and saw Hall at the rear of the building. He had a cleaver in his hand. He cursed the officers and said they were not as good as a negro. Hall was in front of the mob.*

*He and his associates surged back and forth. The crowd made a break for the jail and came in. Shots were fired. He did not see Hall on the step or in the jail. The Witness was shot at that night. The ball went through the side of his coat tail.*

*"The man who shot me was in the hall," said Thompson. "He put the rifle against my stomach and I pushed it away."* [A]

The cleaver must have come from the kitchen in the jail, which doubled as a residence for jailer Krider and his family. Thompson said he didn't know who it was that shot him, the *Post* added. [C] It also said Thompson first saw Hall at 9 p.m, confirming how long the mob had been building before help was called in to deal with it.

Following Thompson, Sam Kenerly said he was at home, not at the jail that night. Though employed as a carpenter, he lived at Vance Cotton Mill's village, probably because his daughters worked at the mill. Kenerly said he saw Hall the next day discussing how he was going to organize a group to lynch the remaining Lyerly murder suspects that night.

> *"I noticed about a dozen men near the jail, Tuesday morning. I walked up to the crowd. I heard Hall say that he had been on the chain gang twice. The last time he went, Hammer, a vile rascal, had hired a man for $20 to swear against him.*
> *"I passed close to him. He said, 'We are going to have the others tonight. We are bound to have them.'*
> *"He said he did not know that he had so many friends as he had the night before. I went off and told some friends that the fellow, Hall, was going to have trouble.*
> *"Hall was looking over the jail grounds the next morning.*
> *"I went with the officers to identify Hall. We found him in front of the court house."* [A]

W.F. Jones, quoted next, was listed in court records as a grand jury witness.

> *"I saw Sam Kennedy [Kenerly] Tuesday morning. He pointed Hall out. I heard the defendant say, 'I got a man last night.' Later I heard Hall say that he helped to lift up one of the negroes and declare that he had confessed."* [A]

Jones and Kenerly both apparently heard Hall bragging about hanging and torturing one of the victims, because Kenerly was called back on the stand and said to corroborate Jones' testimony. The *Post* left out the part about Hall helping "lift up one of the negroes." But both Bryant and Julian omitted details about the torture Coroner Dorsett finally confirmed, which would explain any "confession" Hall may have wrung from the victim.

Dr. E. Rose Dorsett:

> *"I found the bodies hanging to a limb. They were mutilated some. Following the instruction of the*

*solicitor, I went to examine the anal opening and found a tear in Jack Dillingham.*" [A]

Then, after Dorsett's disclosure, Bryant noted that it "corroborated what Jones had said, that he had heard Hall say he had done to one of the prisoners." [A] Even this most damning testimony was not used to show Hall's involvement in the lynching, beyond his confessed crime of breaking into the jail. The other charges had been set aside for the time being.

Shoaf Poteat didn't help the State's case at all. Though he was there, acting as a deputy, he apparently couldn't make out anyone that night well enough to recognize them the next day. "It was dark and I don't know who was in the room." Poteat said.

*"You didn't recognize the defendant at any time that night, did you?" asked Mr. Kluttz.*
*" 'No, sir,' said the witness."* [A]

Vanderford and Deputy Julian had no trouble identifying Hall when they were in that room, though they seemed incapable of unmasking the faces of the other two. Deputy Poteat had been at the Lyerly murder scene on July 14th and played an active role in the investigation and arrests of Nease and his sons, according to the reports of Hammer's investigation. Poteat had also been summoned to testify in the trial on August 6th.

Deputy Pat Sloop's testimony focused on the condition of the jail and his assertion that he did not surrender the keys. The door was "torn up," the sashes and glass broken, the "lock to the door was broken and the cells were broken open," but there was no explosion, he said. "...the back door had been broken in with an axe." [A] Sloop said he saw several men but "did not see the defendant in the room." [C]

There doesn't appear to be any reason why the officers could not have shot the men inside on the narrow stairway, just as Sheriff Monroe had threatened to do in a similar situation years earlier. If the officers had simply shot anyone who entered the jail, perhaps the others would have dispersed for fear of suffering the same fate. Apparently none of them knew what effect such action would have had, because no Salisbury officer "protecting" the jail had yet fired at a would-be lyncher.

But maybe they *had* been aware of what happened in Roanoke, Virginia in 1893. To protect one of its prisoners, the Roanoke Blues fired several volleys into the threatening crowd gathered outside the jail there, and several prominent citizens were killed. While the bodies and injured were being gathered up, the prisoner was snuck out the back and to safety. But the incident so infuriated the mob, a riot in the streets ensued, and the mayor had to go into hiding to avoid being lynched himself. Then later, after officers returned the prisoner to the same jail, he was lynched after all. If the Salisbury officers, and especially the judge and the governor, knew about the Roanoke lynching, they might have been leery of firing into the crowd. However, they might also have learned a lesson from what Virginia did afterward to prevent an instant replay. In 1904, when the threat of lynching arose again, its governor sent 800 soldiers to Roanoke and had the prisoner escorted by special train to Richmond where he remained until he was tried and executed. [3] Governor Glenn could have done the same instead of pretending Sheriff Julian had accurately sized-up the situation.

After the few testimonies given during this one day of Hall's trial, the State rested, and the defense declined to introduce any witnesses or evidence at all. Neither side addressed the jury. Long instead delivered his charge to them, explaining in detail the technicalities of the law concerning conspiracy. The jury retired at 6:10 p.m. and "Twenty-five minutes later a verdict of guilty was brought in." [A]

Before Long sentenced him, "Mr. Hammer urged the judge to hear some witnesses as to the defendant's character," to which defense counsel strongly objected, saying this would be unfair and that the case had been conducted in an unusual way. Referring to Hall's crime, Hammer agreed the case was indeed unusual, but said he felt it his duty to offer testimony of character witnesses. [A]

Montgomery County's clerk of court, C.A. Armstrong, and Deputy Sheriff McKenzie, also of Montgomery, both portrayed Hall as a man with a bad reputation—a convict, a gambler, bootlegger, lawbreaker, and overall "desperate man." [A] Deputy Goodman testified that he had also heard Hall say that the officers who took the Lyerly suspects to Charlotte "were worse than the negroes," a comment apparently seen as a stain on the character of the one who made it.

Defense made a last ditch effort with two motions, one for a new trial and another for arrest of the judgment. Long overruled both and sentenced Hall to fifteen years in the State prison. Bryant noted correctly that it was the "maximum punishment under the law for lynching." Hall appealed, and then Court adjourned. It was just after 7 p.m. [A]

Senator Lee Overman probably didn't show up that day at all, even though he must have been summoned, because he's listed as a witness in the original Court Docket. Bryant didn't harp on this apparent omission, but he didn't let Overman go unscathed either. In repeating the incident of Hall's speech at the back of the jail, he made a point to include Overman's alleged role. The act proved Hall "a humorist," Bryant said.

> *He was helped upon the stand by a United States senator and properly presented by other distinguished gentlemen, who concluded their remarks by saying: "Fellow citizens! Hear him! Let him speak!"*
>
> *Having moved his horny hand, he said: "all of you is a cowardly son of a bitch."*
>
> *There was no cheering. Silence fell on this audience. No one as much as clapped his hand.*
>
> *...The court, the State, the sheriff, the mayor and others tarried at the Hotel Vanderford to discuss the speech and marvel at the nerve of the sallow young orator.*
>
> *Hall is a reckless dare-devil.* [A]

Senator Overman later wrote a lengthy letter to the *Observer*, denying he had either introduced Hall or helped him upon his perch. In the letter, found only in the *Gastonia Gazette*, Overman said: "A little fun attempted to be gotten off at my expense by a friend seems to have been taken seriously and accepted as true." "It is untrue that I 'introduced Hall to the crowd.'" [4]

Bryant's observations of Hall, as he sat in the courtroom that day, were a turnaround from what he said about him the day before.

*Hall took a keen interest in every detail of his trial to-day. He looked frightened yesterday, but he showed no signs of fear to-day. As a defendant charged with a grave crime, and with two good lawyers to represent him, he is alert, shrewd and determined. His general appearance could fool the cleverest student of human nature. He seemed to be a nonentity yesterday, when first brought into court. But, this morning, his face was animated and his eye bright. He has the cunning of the fox and the courage of the mink, which steals upon his victim and slays him in the dark. He is not far removed from an illiterate, but he has sense. Those who saw him the night that he led the mob say that he looked like a little devil. He was fearless and bold. His eyes flashed fire and his rugged, snaggled teeth pitted defiance.*

*His hands are short and his fingers stubby. He mopped his face with a dark blue and white handkerchief. At times he grinned from ear to ear and occasionally shook his head in a friendly way at a witness who claimed to have heard him say something.* [A]

At the end of the day, Hall's case would be appealed, as the *Post* explained, to challenge the original question of whether the session that convicted him was lawful in the first place.

Right after the sentencing, Hall was taken to the Rowan jail and then, shortly, moved to the Raleigh State prison for safe-keeping until his appeal was heard. [C] He must have been stunned by the outcome. Those tried for the Anson County lynching of J.V. Johnson had been acquitted on a technicality and returned home to a hero's welcome. Hall and others had probably expected the same.

Summing up the week, Bryant said it had been a great one:

*The county of Rowan and the town of Salisbury have suffered. Money-making newspaper reporters have colored their reports to increase their pay. The community rallied to the court. A few prominent individuals have sided with the lynchers. One or two educated and refined women have been heard to say it was a pity to try the members of the mob. An occasional politician has trembled lest some person or party would lose a few votes. The demagogue has expressed his opinion. But above all else law and order reign and no more trouble is anticipated. The conviction of Hall will have a good effect."* [D]

JOHN G. MITCHELL, JR.

Not everybody saw it that way though. While papers around the country congratulated Judge Long on Hall's conviction, others were not impressed at all. African American editor John Mitchell, of the *Richmond Planet,* was one of the latter.

*In the meantime, the other three thousand lynchers are in no wise uneasy. They are expecting the reversal of the decision in the case of Hall. He has been in the penitentiary before and he is used to its surroundings, but not one of those who lay claim to respectability, although guilty of murder, have been convicted and we do not believe that any of them will be. It seems to us that this conviction is one of design and Hall is taken as being a fair sample of the kind of men who engage in these nefarious and murderous practices.*

*The country seems to have been deceived and many of our own people seem to have over-looked the deep-seated purpose in this conviction.* [5]

Asheville's *Citizen* sarcastically echoed Mitchell's dissenting view the next day.

*The honor of North Carolina has been redeemed, the outraged dignity of the State has been satisfied, and the mob whereof Governor Glenn spoke has been 'arrested and identified' by the trial, conviction and sentence of one lone ex-convict named Hall. Gaze on the culprit and you will see in him the five thousand howling outlaws who defied the State soldiery, stormed the county jail, dragged out therefrom three negroes and hanged them to a tree. For doing all that alone and single-handed, Hall will go to the penitentiary for fifteen years.*

*You see, he was a jail bird any how, had no friends to speak of, and as somebody had to be made a scape goat of, he was "arrested and identified" as the mob. It was an easy matter to get a jury to convict him, and the other 4,999 'good citizens' who trampled on law and order will be lost in that indefinable haze which every now and then envelopes the judicial machinery. Oyez! Oyez! "God reigns and the law is still supreme!" Of course. And "the mills of the gods grind slowly, but they grind exceedingly fine." Tubbyshore, tubbyshore! So fine did they grind, that out of a harvest of five thousand, a mob consisting of one ex-convict was ground out.* [6]

But maybe the *Richmond News-Leader* said it best.

*Some of the more intelligent and respectable men who were in the mob should be hunted down and sent to wear stripes along with the pitiful rascal with whom they associated themselves and under whose leadership they ranged themselves. It will not do to pile the whole weight of sin on one scape-goat.* [7]

Before Hall boarded the train to leave for Raleigh, his "...wife and little son called at the jail and Mrs. Hall talked with her husband a short while. She followed him to the station and remained in conversation with him an hour. Before she left, Hall wept bitterly." [8]

# 18

# INSANITY

## FRIDAY, AUGUST 10

*Ordinarily he is insane, but he has lucid moments when he is only stupid.*

— Heinrich Heine

ROWAN COURTHOUSE SCENE

Long's court continued the day after Hall's trial ended, beginning at 9:40. More alleged lynchers remained to be dealt with, though most were quickly swept out of the way. "...almost immediately the solicitor announced that the grand jury had ignored the bill against defendants, Henry Goodman, John Cauble, and Bud Bullyboy, and moved that the defendants be discharged from custody." So Judge Long excused them—the defendants, the grand jury, and witnesses Pool and Sawyer, there to testify against Bullyboy. [A]

Attorney Walter Woodson was to represent Goodman, and John Cauble had hired E.C. Gregory from the firm of Overman & Gregory. John L. Rendleman was there to defend Cress. And he was next. After the first three defendants were set free, the court turned its attention to the charges of conspiracy, forcible trespass, and rioting against Francis M. Cress. [1] As soon as the indictment was read, "a question was raised as to Cress's mental condition. Mr. Linn, of counsel for the State, stated that he had known Cress for years, and that Cress was humble and harmless." [A]

Cress pled guilty to the charge of forcible trespass, but as soon as he did, Rendleman suggested the court inquire into the question of his sanity.

Complying, Judge Long asked for a jury investigation, "saying that if Cress was mentally irresponsible, he did not want to punish him." [A] The *Post* summed up what the jury would consider, first whether Cress was sane on the night of August 6th, and second, was he sane now? "Drs. Trantham, Dorsett, and McKenzie were summoned as experts on the question of Cress's sanity" and "A.H. Price, Esq. volunteered to represent Cress in the investigation." [A]

The *Post* didn't go into the details of the investigation, but the *Observer* did. And, though Bryant's initials aren't on this account, his mark is all over it. After A.H. Price took over, the first witness called was C.S. Nussman, Cress's employer, who said "he did not believe that the defendant could discriminate between right and wrong. He is a good man," said the witness, "if you can be with him." On cross examination by the State, Mr. Nussman admitted "he did believe that Mr. Cress had sense enough to know that it was wrong to wilfully kill a man, but when excited he was not at his best. He is very excitable," said

Nussman, adding that Cress had little more sense than that of a child. [B]

Next "John Kennerly declared that he did not believe that Cress could tell wrong from right, although at times he seems to be all right." And E.L. Heilig "said that he knew Cress to be a harmless sort of man, easily influenced and without power to reason under excitement." [B]

With Price's consent, Dr. H.T. Trantham testified for the State. He said "Cress was not insane, but not a man of sound mind; his memory is good." He felt Cress knew the difference between right and wrong, but was easily influenced. "'If warned to go away by the sheriff,'" Trantham explained, "'he would know to do that, but if backed by a crowd he would not do so.'" Cress did not have a strong mind, Trantham told Price, but not necessarily a weak one. [B] Furthermore, he "declared that he thought that Cress did not leave the jail Monday night, when appealed to by Senator Overman, Sheriff Julian and Mayor Boyden, for the reason that he wanted to remain there with the mob. He knew better," Trantham added, "but felt that the lynching party was stronger than the law." [B] Dr. W.W. McKenzie said he agreed with Trantham, but "admitted, however, to Mr. Price that under certain circumstances Cress might be temporarily deranged." [B]

Though the next to testify was also presented as a State witness, the Deputy Sheriff of Chestnut Hill, H.A. Brandon, supported the insanity plea, saying "he did not consider the defendant right bright."

Then S.B. Colly, a well-to-do farmer with a "magnificent set of whiskers," took the stand. An old confederate veteran, Colly "... carried on his watch chain bullets pumped into him by the Yankees during the war." When asked his opinion, he said Cress was prone to "crazy spells," and that his "...chief failing was making wild trades and rash promises." To explain, he related an incident where Cress had promised a $5 donation to a church organization, a lot more than anyone else had pledged, and Colly told him to give fifty cents instead. The paper said the incident was "cited as an instance of [Cress's] eccentricities," and that "Mr. Colly knew Cress to be a quiet, peaceful, harmless citizen, who had dark or cloudy intervals." [B]

Relating his dealings with Cress on the night of the murders, Mayor Boyden testified next. "He said that he saw Cress in the mob and got down [from the steps], went to him and begged him to go away. 'I said, for God's sake go away, Mr. Cress,' declared the mayor." Boyden said "Cress looked as if he had hell in him. He would listen to nothing." He felt Cress, "'would have done the bidding of the mob, that night, had it been to kill Senator Overman, the judge, the sheriff, the solicitor or anybody else.'" [B]

Sheriff Julian's testimony was less supportive of the insanity plea. "'I think Cress is a man of low order of intelligence but he knows right from wrong. I went out to try to influence him but he told me that he wanted the negroes. After begging him to go away I told him that he was having his day then, but mine would come tomorrow.'" With this, said the *Observer*, the testimony ended, and the decision was turned over to Judge Long. [B]

And Long passed it on to the jury. He told them "the law presumed a man's sanity and the burden of proof was with him," to show otherwise. After reviewing the evidence, he charged the jury to decide on the issue of Cress's sanity on the night of the lynching as well as his present mental state. Thirty minutes later, a verdict was rendered "to the effect that Cress was not responsible, on last Monday night for what he did, but that he is all right now." [B]

At this Mr. Price asked the court to dismiss Cress, but the Judge was not so sure that would be wise.

> *This Judge Long declined to do, saying that such a man is dangerous. The general impression is that the verdict of the jury is just. Cress looks like a wild man. He may be a menace to the community, but the verdict of the jury makes it difficult for the court to get rid of him. He can't be sent to the asylum for the jury has said that he is sane. If he is tried for murder it is on record that he was insane the night of the lynching.* [B]

Instead of deciding right away, Long adjourned for recess.

At 3:30 Bryant returned to cover the rest of the story on the day's proceedings. Mr. Price again requested that his client be dismissed, to which Solicitor Hammer responded that "he had another charge against Cress," a charge of conspiracy. But

"Judge Long said that if the evidence were the same as produced this morning there could be no conviction on that charge." [B]

Maybe to stall and think the matter over, Judge Long digressed for a moment.

> He declared that he had described the average lynching party last Monday, before the mob had assembled, and that the investigations that followed the affair at Henderson's ball ground had convinced him that he was right. The leader, Hall, a man who had made a grave for the sheriff of Montgomery county if ever he could kill him, was pictured as he is and has been. [B]

Then he decided what to do about Cress; "...he would put the defendant under a bond and hold him so that the solicitor and Mr. Price might study his mental gymnastics. But Mr. Price contended for a discharge. He argued eloquently for his penniless client, speaking beautifully and convincingly." [B]

But Long stood firm, putting Cress under a $500 bond "for his appearance for probable cause, at the next term of Rowan court. This, the *Observer* said, sparked "a brief, but spirited exchange," with Hammer winning the argument, insisting that he might have further evidence against Cress when the next court convened. Cress, then securing bond with the help of G.T. Kluttz and John Kennerly, was freed at 5:30 p.m. [B]

By the time the next court term convened at the end of the month, Cress had been forgotten. He could have been in Mississippi by then, but he didn't have to go anywhere, because the charges against him were eventually and quietly dropped. He showed up in Salisbury in the 1910 census, living with his wife and working at the lumber yard. For Cress, life continued as it had before.

An invisible support group, if not empire, had surrounded Cress and the other long-time Rowan residents accused of involvement in the lynching. Cress worked for Caleb Nussman, a lumber yard owner in 1906, but a farmer in 1880 and very close neighbor to Joseph Barringer, my great great grandfather and Augusta Lyerly's father. So Caleb Nussman had known Augusta since she was a girl. And his family had been involved with the Lyerly and Rendleman families since the first Nussman arrived from Germany. The only Nussmans in Rowan and Cabarrus Counties in 1906 had to have been descendants of Adolf Nussman, the first Lutheran minister in North Carolina, whom Isaac Lyerly's great grandfather, along with attorney John Rendleman's ancestor, had brought from Germany to America in 1773. When Adolf got to Rowan County, he married Rendleman's daughter, and later, when she died, he married Lyerly's daughter. The centuries-old bonds among all of these Rowan families would have been almost impossible for any outsider, especially a black one, to break. Maybe the wealthy, "good Rowan citizens," would not resort to mob violence to "protect their white women," but they would protect those who "did it" for them.

Out of all the locally-tried cases reported during the few months these tragedies occurred, the bulk involving charges against men of color, not one attorney argued for temporary or any kind of insanity on behalf of a black man. But at least two out of a handful of white men were released on this plea. Other whites charged during this time received minimal or reduced penalties, based on their "insanity."

Other indictments against Cress were expected to be heard in the afternoon session, said the Post, but that didn't happen. Apparently it was press time, and coverage of the trial ended for the Post. The next day's issue is missing from all archives, and the paper didn't mention Cress in its report of the next term of court.

Bryant finished off his report on this term with his descriptions of the accused lynchers, which had shifted with their convictions. He had first depicted Hall as a man incapable of "courage or cunning," but now alert, shrewd, fearless, and bold. Likewise, his description of Francis Cress was consistent with the jury's determination of his mental state. "The old fellow," he continued, "is a man of uncertain mind. He looks the part of a crank, who would kneel and pray in the street one moment and join a mob to cut a man's throat the next. His eyes snap and sparkle."

Since Cress had no prior record, the insanity plea was necessary. "He seems to have behaved himself up to last Monday night," Bryant wrote. [B] No "good men of Rowan" could have been involved, so there had to be an excuse for Cress. He had to have been at least a little crazy—at least on the night of the lynching.

The Charlotte report concluded with Bryant's observation of
the present state of Salisbury and more about the elusive man in
the Panama hat. Speaking of the night of the lynching, he wrote
that

> *Men who had remained at home that night realize*
> *that their county was disgraced by a lot of hoodlums.*
> *The sheriff and his deputies have furnished Mr. Hammer*
> *with his evidence. Later, more arrests may be made. The*
> *gentleman, with the Panama hat, the strong face and*
> *commanding appearance, has not been found. He*
> *promised to leave that night and maybe he kept his*
> *word. Hall was the aggressive, active leader.* [B]

"If any good men have been shielded here," Bryant
continued, "I have no knowledge of it. Monday night I was an
eye-witness to most of what went on about the jail yard. I did not
go in the jail or attend the awful ceremonies at the baseball park,
but I did see the crowd and hear the yelling and the shooting. I
believe that hundreds of those who composed the crowd are as
innocent of crime as I am." [B]

Then Bryant turned his attention again to the "man in the
Panama hat." Calling him "the unknown," he said the reason the
three arrested men had been released on the night of the lynching
was because the word of "the unknown" was believed. [B] But
maybe Senator Overman knew him, and that's why he wasn't
asked to testify in a court of law and perjure himself by saying
he didn't. Though Bryant didn't bring up the omission of
Overman's testimony, other papers did and wanted to know what
was going on. The only answer they got was the following, in
Overman's letter to the *Observer*.

> *Several came up to where I was standing and said to*
> *me privately that they had four of the crowd in jail and if*
> *they were turned out they would disperse and go home. I*
> *then asked the mob if these men were turned out would*
> *they promise to disperse. Many voices replied that they*
> *would. I replied then, "Turn them loose," and I advised*
> *that these men be discharged. I had no authority to*
> *discharge them. They were discharged by order of some*

*one who had authority. I could only advise, and did
advise this course, and I do not regret it.
...The crowd still remained, and I reminded them of
their promise. The man in the Panama hat, undoubtedly
the leader of the mob, then said: "Let's all go home and
come back to-morrow at 10 o'clock."*

Bryant did, however, emphasize that Hammer had opposed
the release of those initially arrested while breaking into the jail.
"After all is over it appears that he had the right view of it," he
said. [B] Continuing his defense of the officers' actions that night,
Bryant said he knew

*Boyden, Julian, Hammer and others believed that
when the good-looking spokesman for the mob [the man
in the Panama hat] walked out of the jail yard, taking
his personal followers with him, as he had promised to
do, the trouble was all over, for they came to the hotel
across the street and told me. But they did not know the
nature of Hall and his gang. The bloodthirsty ex-convict
and Cress, the fanatic, clamored for gore.* [B]

It seemed like years had been crammed into that one week,
and no time was left to take up George Gentle's case. So both of
the Georges were now headed for the state prison in Raleigh, one
to await the decision on his appeal, the other his trial at the
regular term of court, beginning August 27th. That Friday night
they were put on the train with the Iredell Blues company, on its
way home west to Statesville, and they would ride back east to
Raleigh the next morning, again with the Blues, who would
continue on to military camp in Morehead City on the coast.

Both Bryant and Julian seemed more than ready to report
that things were getting back to normal. Bryant assured his
readers that the "agony" was finally over—Judge Long had
completed the one-week special term, and the military
companies were leaving town. The *Post* said the Charlotte
artillery left on Saturday afternoon on the No. 7 train, and "There
is not the slightest possibility of further trouble." [A] This time the
*Post* was probably right—there were no blacks left in the county
jail to lynch.

# 19

# FANNING THE FLAMES

## THURSDAY AND FRIDAY, AUGUST 9 & 10

*...who knows how he may report Thy words by adding fuel to the flame?*

— John Milton, *Samson Agonistes*

LYERLY HOME

Just when everyone thought Hall's impending demise would put the whole horrible ordeal to rest, somebody or some group stirred things up again. It happened on the day of his trial, some time in the early daylight hours of Friday, August 9th. Later that day, while Bryant was in court, John Charles McNeill was back at Isaac's house to describe what he saw. He reported that

> *the large barn on the curtilage of the late Isaac Lyerly property was burned. Nobody has lived at the place since the recent Lyerly murder, and the barn was almost in ashes when certain of the neighbors arrived.*

The fire was discovered by farm hands who'd been working with a threshing machine, parked for the night at Joseph Lyerly's house nearby. [A] Some were sleeping outside on piles of wheat straw, when, awakened by the light from the fire, eight of them ran over to try to put it out. The barn had contained mostly hay and a thresher, among other contents worth about $800. [A]

At 4 p.m. "the ashes were still smoking," McNeill said, and "the seared condition of a great sycamore on one side and an oak on the other showed how fierce the flames had been." [A]

The barn had sheltered two horses, one of which was not expected to survive his injuries. "These horses were alive at that time. They had crossed the branch and were standing together on the opposite hillside, where half a dozen or more men were sprinkling them with linseed oil. The bay horse will recover certainly, but the black cannot live." [A]

What happened with the horses puzzled McNeill. "Contrary to the habit of horses in case of fire, they broke out of their stable instead of cowering in it; or they were driven out by somebody, after they had been burned as above described." Apparently the one that should have been the most protected from the flames had been the most injured by them. "The worst burnt of the two was not the one behind the pole, as might be expected, but the one at the door-end of the stable. They were not burned after getting into the lot, for it was a large enclosure and the horses could go far beyond reach of the flames."

Filmore Cook's son, Sam, who had worked for Isaac before the murders, was left at the home to care for the horses, McNeill explained. Cook said "...he had been feeding the horses only at noon, they being turned to pasture at other times; that at noon yesterday he fed them, shut them into a stall, with a pole for partition between them, and that he had not seen them any more until he came to the fire this morning; that he never carries matches about the barn." McNeill said "Cook and the others there could make no satisfactory explanation of it." [A]

The discussion of the horses set aside, McNeill turned his attention to the Lyerly home and the cabins formerly occupied by the now deceased and displaced tenants.

*The Lyerly residence was locked up and deserted. None of the visitors this afternoon went inside the yard, the gate of which swung wide open. The grass in the yard has run to seed, and a vine is crawling across the walk. It was a perfectly peaceful, sequestered spot, rich green woods before and a wide cornfield behind. Miss Mary Lyerly, the eldest of the surviving daughters, who is living with her neighbor, Mr. Pleasant Barber, was there, as composed in manner and gentle in speech as if nothing had happened. The fifty men and women sat on rocks or stood about in groups, having very little to say. It was a silent, mystified company, with somewhat the feeling of a funeral. Across the branch Jack Dillingham's cabin was in plain view, just as it had been left by the searchers for evidence on the day after the murder. This black mare, standing near the cabin, is the one which kicked Jack on the knee and started a quarrel between him and Mr. Lyerly. But the Gillespies' place most vividly brought to mind how rapid has been the succession of crimes: the clothes which they washed on the night of the murder still hung on the line as they hung on that memorable day: the boxes and old clothes lay scattered on the floor just as they were then. There was no sign of life about the premises, except a browsing cow in the yard.* [A]

These clothes were supposedly part of crucial evidence that implicated the Gillespies in the murders of the Lyerly family. Yet they were left hanging on the line—perhaps minus the two "wet" shirts brought to the solicitor's investigation on the 20th.

The scene supports Fannie's statement that she had simply been doing her weekly wash the day she was said to be destroying evidence. With their laundry still on the line, Fanny and Nease may not have had a change of clothes to take with them to jail, something Bryant hadn't pointed out when he noted how dirty Fannie was on the day she was questioned by Hammer.

McNeill said he wasn't able to get much out of the neighbors hanging around the property that day, but others elsewhere were willing to wager what had happened. "Of the 40 or 50 people who had gathered there none had any definite suspicion as to the incendiary; at least none which they would express." And, "there was nothing said worth quoting." However, when the people in town got wind of it, "...not a few expressed the opinion that it had been done by members of the late mob, who would expect that negroes connected with those who were lynched would be charged with this crime and that public opinion would become so inflamed against them as to leave the investigation at Salisbury a secondary matter." Some at Barber Junction agreed, according to what McNeill could gather: "those who expressed any opinion scouted the notion that the lynchers had done it" and blamed it on "Gillespie connections."

McNeill's final question to those at Barber Junction seemed to hit a nerve. When asked if any of the mob members were from this neighborhood, "they replied, emphatically, no. That mob, they said, was composed of people who had never known the Lyerlys. One man said that he happened to be in Salisbury that night and had seen the mob, and that nobody really in it was known to him."

Painting a totally different picture of the situation, Daniels' paper was apparently trying to start its own fire. It claimed "a band of negroes...bent on revenge" burned down the barn. Then it lied and said that "negroes residing in the neighborhood are charged with the crime." Including what looked like a veiled threat in a related editorial, it said the situation called for "the negroes to be quiet," because it "would be upon them that the reprisals would most heavily fall," and that "A spark may kindle a race war...." [B]

Then the *N&O* brought up the recent arrest of Caldwell Barber—the "negro" taken into custody for saying "worse calamities will befall other families than befell the Lyerlies." The paper asserted that Caldwell's statement, along with the murders, and now the barn burning, have together caused the arousal of many "good citizens," and there is talk of annihilating the negroes of the Lyerly neighborhood." [B] Of course who knows if this was true, even though McNeill, himself, had hinted that some trouble was brewing. It would now seem that the local press was contradicting itself to give the impression that the people of the neighborhood—all previously described as law-abiding, gentle, and peaceful—could now consider exterminating all the blacks in the neighborhood.

State Insurance Commissioner James R. Young sent his assistant, W.L. Scott, to Barber Junction to investigate the fire. After leaving there, he stopped by Charlotte on August 14th before returning to Raleigh. While Scott was in town, an unidentified *Observer* correspondent interviewed him to see what he found out. The interview was mostly paraphrased.

The report claimed up front that Scott felt "certain that negroes fired the barn," though "At first it was believed by Judge Long and others that the lynchers had started the fire to create feeling against the darkies and sympathy for the members of the mob." [D] It's unlikely that McNeill wrote this follow-up, because use of the word, "darkies," was not characteristic of his style. And though Bryant seemed to have no qualms about using derogatory language, his usual signature (H.E.C.B) was not added to this report.

The rest of the interview continued to contradict the impression created in the beginning. It said Scott had "worked industriously" to find some clue as to who was responsible for the arson, but "so far has not fallen on anything definite." According to the *Observer*, Scott learned that a lot of the neighborhood's black folk had been at a party at Bard Lucky's home on the night of the incendiary. Lucky's house was said to have been located about a mile from the Lyerly home. For some reason not given, a "young negro" named George Watson came under suspicion of "knowing something about the crime." Philas Culbertson, said to be a brother of Nease Gillespie's son-in-law, was questioned around one o'clock "in order to find out something of [Watson's] rambles that night." Culbertson, also "a great friend of Jack Dillingham," was described as "indignant over the arrest and then the lynching of the Gillespies and

Dillingham." However, even though Culbertson was questioned, "No one was disposed to connect him in any way with the fire." Culbertson reportedly told Scott that "he had been home early the night of the incident and had not gone to Lucky's party."

Having completed his preliminary inquiry, Scott left Barber Junction, only to return after hearing that Culbertson "had fled." The *Observer* said "He skipped between dusk and day and has not been seen nor heard of since," and added that George Watson's brother had said something that contradicted what Culbertson told the investigator. Tom Watson reportedly claimed that Culbertson was with him at Lucky's place "until nearly midnight." [D]

Even so, Scott must not have taken Culbertson's disappearance or Watson's statement as an implication of Culbertson's guilt, "realizing that all of the negroes in that community are excited and afraid," but, "he is inclined now to believe that Philas knows something about the burning." [D]

Next the writer quoted Scott:

"'Mr. Scott,' asked an *Observer* man, 'do you believe that any of the Cleveland township people, neighbors of the Lyerlys, were in the mob that lynched the negroes?'"

"'No; I do not,' was the reply. 'I saw nothing to indicate that, but I did see men up there who are ready for almost any emergency.'" [D]

The report did not elaborate on what, specifically, gave Scott this impression. But it certainly contradicted the one the *N&O* left with its readers. Scott's comments may have been meant to tone down the ones Daniels had printed, which seem unnecessarily inflammatory.

This *Observer* report on the barn burning investigation concluded with an added item about a sale held at the Lyerly home on August 14th to dispose of Isaac's personal property. It noted that Scott was there and said "...he never saw such a crowd at a sale; close to 1,000 people being there to make purchases and to look on." Mr. Lyerly's property, land and personal effects, the *Observer* reckoned, should be worth about $5,000.

The *Carolina Watchman* also commented on the "immense crowd" at the sale that day. The items "brought a good price," and "one of the horses that was singed in the fire brought $35." This reporter, who noted that the "bed on which Mr. and Mrs.

Lyerly were killed was not sold, as there was a large part of the head board burned out," had apparently not paid much attention to the evidence that said the two had slept in separate beds. But that seems to have been the norm. [E]

After these reports, the story of the barn burning investigation disappeared. I tried to find an official report of Scott's investigation and contacted everyone I could think of, including the present State Insurance Commissioner, who, by the way, is a distant relative of Judge Long's. When I discovered this relationship, I immediately wanted to know if he knew any oral history about this case. Though he was quite cordial, I never found out anything else about Long's involvement in this story or the Insurance Commissioner's report, if there was one, on the fire.

About a week after the barn burning, the *Observer* said E.A. Barber reported "that there is not the least uneasiness at Barber over the recent Salisbury troubles and everything is perfectly quiet there. The people at Barber are very anxious that the trial of the remaining negroes proceed without interruption as they are very desirous of knowing the truth of the whole matter." Constable Barber may have given an accurate assessment of the situation this time. Philas Culbertson had evidently felt secure enough to return to the neighborhood on the previous night. And Pless Barber gave him a job. [F] Pless also gave Nease Gillepsie's son, Tom, a job at some point. Barber's descendants remember Tom telling stories to them in the barn when they were kids, and census records confirm that Tom, who used the spelling, Glaspy, for his last name, was living next to Pless Barber in 1910.

The outcry over the Salisbury lynching might have died down after Hall's conviction, if the story had not been revived by the barn burning. But even though the volume of commentary increased, the tone stayed pretty much the same, the biggest concern being that society was on the brink of sinking into irretrievable depths of lawlessness and chaos. Few seemed to care about the regression of racial relations and the plight of the "colored man," though some recognized his suffering as an incidental issue of mob violence.

Finally after days of defensive editorials and weeks of duplicitous commentary, someone stopped tiptoeing around the factual issues and wrote an anonymous, critical letter to the

*Charlotte Observer.* "I have waited a week," the letter began, "for somebody to say it, and it hasn't been said. I suppose that I must say it myself." [G]

The letter examined the roles of all those involved and exonerated Long, Hammer, and Glenn, though it was particularly hard on Overman and the sheriff.

> *Judge Long did a great deal of talking the day before the lynching, quite a good deal the day after, and—sentenced Hall to the penitentiary for the limit of the law. The last item vindicated the judge.*
>
> *Solicitor Hammer voted against releasing the three murderers who were at first arrested and afterward turned loose to proceed with the crime. He also convicted Mr. Hall, and has others in soak for the penitentiary and the hangman's noose. Well done, Mr. Hammer. Here's strength to your elbow!*
>
> *Senator Overman talked some to the mob too. He also had the honor to introduce Mr. Hall when that notable gentleman made his deathless speech. The Senator's indiscretion brought its own retribution and he has paid sufficiently in humiliation for condescending to dicker with the scum of the earth who were pelting a prostrate law with dung.* [G]

The letter placed most of the blame on the officers, and it's criticism was unique. It supported what Sheriff Monroe's grandson said he'd done, pointing to

> *...the fact that the negroes who were lynched were on the third floor of the jail and that the only approach to it is by a circular stairway which at one point is not more than three feet wide. A half dozen deputies, one determined man, could have defended that pass effectually against the mob and no good citizen would have been put in jeopardy.*

And, it alluded to other lynchings. "I'm informed that this is not the first mob that has 'overpowered' this sheriff. It seems to be a habit with him." "In Rowan's sheriff, law leans upon a broken reed," the condemnation concluded, "and the prayerful efforts of Senator Overman, Judge Long and Solicitor Hammer should have been directed, not to the mob, but to the stiffening of his uncertain backbone." [G]

As far as the writer was concerned, the sheriff was the guiltiest of all, and even if Julian didn't read the letter, he likely heard about it. Though there was no such criticism printed in his son's paper, there must have been gossip circulating about his failure—a second time within four years—to protect black prisoners from a mob. The *Watchman* had certainly hinted at it. Perhaps it was the strain of the 1906 lynching that caused the sheriff, not much later, to make a mistake that could have killed him. Or maybe it wasn't a mistake.

Two months after the lynching, the *Observer* reported that Julian was recovering from the effects of accidental poisoning. "Sheriff D.R. Julian, who took by mistake a big dose of creosote for a patent cough medicine, is much improved but yet kept at his home. His mouth and throat are badly burned and he has suffered greatly." It was noted that the mistake was discovered quickly and two doctors came immediately "and undoubtably saved his life." [H]

Mayor Boyden apparently had not felt too good after his second lynching either. The September 1st *Post* said he was "...still quite weak and will not be able to resume his usual active life for a week or more," even though he had appeared back on the streets that day "... for the first time since his illness." The *Observer* blamed it on Boyden's recent vigil at the bedside of a prominent citizen Captain Hambley, who was involved in the Whitney Dam project. Hambley eventually died from typhoid fever. [I]

Boyden and Julian would recover from the criticism, if not their health. Public sentiment was, for the most part, on their side. The most widely expressed viewpoint up until the day of the fire and after, was best summarized in an *Observer* editorial on August 10th. "Too many decent citizens quietly endorse the act of the mob. Their argument is that the negroes deserved to die, that they are dead, and so they want to let it go at that." [J]

One blaring exception to that sentiment was expressed in the *Tarboro Southerner*. Tarboro is an Eastern North Carolina town, an area inland from the coast, where you can still see remnants of old plantations amid seas of white cotton—and a seasoned racial bias amid the white population. So the extinguishing tone of its August editorial stunned me.

*Lynchings are wrong, altogether wrong, demoralizing and damnable, so is capital punishment.... Making this punishment cruel and inhuman, has been shown to be not effective.... Lynching is merely a popular endorsement of the Mosaic law, an eye for an eye and tooth for a tooth, a law of vengeance and not one to protect society.... The man of Nazareth laid down a better guide, a safer rule, a more effective method, mercy to the evil doer.... Where life is cheap crime is plentiful, abounding. Let us all learn this lesson.* [K]

# 20

## A SHORT CHAPTER

### ENDING AUGUST 31, 1906

*Violence and injury enclose in their net all that do such things,
and generally return upon him who began.*
— Titus Lucretius Carus

WHITEHEAD-STOKES SANATORIUM, BY THEO. BUERBAUM

Besides the prisoners who were hanged and mutilated, others were injured during the mob violence on August 6th. The most publicized was J.C. McClendon, a 37-year-old switch engineer on the Spencer-Salisbury yards, who had a wife and four children living in Macon, Georgia. Shot in the thigh that night, he was operated on and left in serious condition the following day. Everyone seemed upset about this collateral damage. "The deepest regret," said the *Post,* "is felt on all sides at his injury." [A] The paper, however, did not convey any regret over the murder of Nease, John, or Jack.

The next day, the *Observer* indicated that McClendon had been more than just an innocent bystander. "It is not known who shot McLendon," it said, "but some of his friends charge Jailer Hodge Krider with it. When shot McLendon was beating in a window with a hammer. He is very dangerously ill." [B] The *Washington Post* also suggested that McLendon may have participated in the mob. And, though erroneously reporting he had been shot in the mouth, it agreed he was in critical condition. It was believed, said the Washington paper, that an officer "shot the engineer as he was battering a window," though others said "he was merely a spectator." [C] The *Salisbury Post*, in a progress report, said McLendon was "resting comfortably this afternoon, though he has some fever." [D]

Nobody said *who* accused Krider of shooting the gun that wounded McClendon. But when rumors spread that someone seeking revenge would go after Krider, J.S. Hall (the grand jury foreman) defended him. He said he was with the jailer all night, and insisted Krider "did not attempt at any time to use his gun." [A] Hall's statement, ironically, convicted Krider of failing to try to protect the prisoners. And the *Post's* assertion that Krider had "...been quite a sick man for a week," [A] made me question why he was put in charge of the jail in the first place.

There was only a brief mention of the others wounded that night. Private Maxwell of the Rowan Rifles was reportedly shot in the foot. Also two men from Spencer, Fireman Sells and Brakeman Mauney, were shot by stray bullets, one in the arm and the other in the leg, according to the *Post.* Two other men were reported slightly injured, also by stray bullets. Both of these tried to remain anonymous, perhaps wanting to conceal their participation in the riot. John Henderson, however, revealed one name, Hannah, the next day in a letter to his wife. Another, or perhaps Hannah, was treated at the hospital and adamantly refused to disclose his identity. The report that Will Troutman, a black drayman, was shot in the stomach that night, got no attention after initial lynching accounts were published. A few sources, including the *Mooresville Enterprise*, said both Troutman and McLendon were wounded by "weapons of the mob." [A, E, F]

About a month after the lynching, the *Carolina Watchman* commented on the incident after learning McLendon had "confessed to Solicitor Hammer that he was standing on the back steps of the jail at the time the door was being broken down and where he was shot." If true, the *Watchman* said, he got what he deserved and "should not have expected better treatment." In almost the same breath, the paper said the man who shot McLendon "...ought to be indicted like any other criminal because no proclamation warning people to keep off the jail lot, at the peril of their lives, had been issued." [G]

On another page of the same issue, the *Watchman* gave more detail. The bullet that injured McLendon had "entered his left thigh, passing through the limb. On examination of the wound at the sanitarium, the prognosis was serious," but "the attending physicians believed there was a chance for the unfortunate man." However, amputation became necessary, and after the procedure, his condition grew worse, "...so serious that it was evident his death was only a matter of a short time." [H]

On his deathbed, McLendon amended the "confession," that had circulated in the press. The *Watchman* explained here that, even though McLendon had admitted to being on the steps at the back of the jail, he "denied emphatically being one of the mob, and said he was with the crowd merely through curiosity," that he took no part "whatever" in the "hammering on the door." [H]

McLendon became the fourth known victim of the Salisbury lynching on August 31st. With him, as "...he breathed his last were his wife, his brother and two sisters." [H] No one was ever charged with McLendon's death. Since it now seemed clear that neither the officers nor the militia fired that night, McLendon may well have been killed by the mob he was a part of.

# 2 1

# WHITE LIES

## SEPTEMBER 5

*And so this trial was a mockery, but nobody seemed to mind.* *
— Bob Dylan

JUDGE GARLAND S. FERGUSON

R owan County's regular term of court began on August 27th. It was the day the Lyerly case would have begun had Governor Glenn not tried so hard to prevent the lynching—as he put it. Now it would continue with the case against the remaining three suspects, Della, George, and Henry Lee. But George Gentle's case would precede theirs, and they would stay in Charlotte until its conclusion. Just to make sure, Solicitor Hammer had new bills drawn—the extra precaution taken in case Glenn's special term turned out *not* to be legit after all.

Of all the arrested lynching suspects, only George Gentle's and Alex Jackson's cases were still pending. Alex Jackson was out on bond. His charge of rioting remained on court dockets for months, along with George Hall's other charges. If Long or his successor, Ferguson, ever even mentioned Jackson's name, there's no record of it. Hall was in the Raleigh prison for "safekeeping," awaiting his appeal, and Gentle, in Raleigh also, was to be brought back to Salisbury soon, supposed to face a murder charge. But that would change.

On September 1st Gentle was finally arraigned, and afterward he had a few words to say to the press. To represent Gentle, Judge Ferguson appointed Attorney Pritchard Carlton, to be assisted by A.H. Price, the one who helped get Cress off the hook. L.H. Clement would join Solicitor Hammer in the prosecution. [A] Though the charge had not yet been announced, the reporter Gentle spoke to after the arraignment might have known. As if preparing the public for what had been predetermined, he described Gentle as "above the average in looks," and said there was "a well-founded doubt as to his guilt." [B]

> *Gentle says he is up against it. His people have not taken any interest in him and he is not able to employ counsel. He has a young wife and three children but he appears to be a bit shy of aggressive friends. This seems to be the fault and the fate of those who took part in the demonstration that night. They were great on protecting 'our women' but left their own at home.* [A]

The same report disclosed contents of a letter counselor Carlton had received concerning his defense of the accused mob leaders.

*Some time ago Mr. Carlton received a well-written anonymous letter from a Texas woman praising him for his defense of these men who were indicted for lynching the negroes. She assumed that they were the kind that chivalry resides in solely and every one a Chesterfield and a knight.* [A]

Before any other items on the court's agenda were addressed, the new judge, like Long, first had a lot to say about lynching. Judge Garland S. Ferguson hailed from Waynesboro in Haywood County in western North Carolina near Cold Mountain. In this, his first visit to Rowan County, he was described as "not a harsh man," but one that didn't allow any "monkeying in his courts," and "when guilt is pronounced, he does his part." [1] Long's speeches were long, but Ferguson's were "exhaustive"—so much so "that the smallest thing did not escape him." [2] The *N&O* must have obtained a copy of the address from the judge afterward; published in its September 2nd edition, it filled more than two full columns.

At first it sounded like Ferguson was going to fire Sheriff Julian. Speaking of the sheriff's duties in general, he said they were "assigned by law," and the sheriff "is amenable to the courts for misfeasance or malfeasance in office, for the omission of duty—and for a willful omission of the duties of his office, he may be removed from office by judgment of the court." Ferguson said it was the sheriff's duty "to suppress riots and arrest rioters...to prevent the commission of a felony," and "to prevent rescue and escape." In fulfilling this obligation, however, the sheriff also had the right to call on anyone in the county to help him. And anyone who refused such a legal request was guilty of a misdemeanor. The way Ferguson saw it, if a sheriff failed to do his duty, it was the result of one of two possible scenarios. Either the sheriff did not have "the moral and physical courage to execute the duties of his office," or "the citizenship neglect[ed] or refuse[d] to aid him." [B]

The judge didn't say outright which one of these failures he thought led to the lynching. But he expressed serious concern about the "decay" of the "moral and physical courage of the citizen...." He said he feared this decay or indifference would lead to a reliance on "the military forces of the State." And these, he added, were under command of the Governor, with the Sheriff in charge of giving orders to shoot. He stressed a "serious cause for alarm, lest, between the lawless and violent on the one hand and the arbitrary military forces on the other, we lose our civil, political and religious liberties." [B]

Then Ferguson recognized the double tragedy, the Lyerly murders and the lynching, in a way most hadn't done so far—focusing on the vulnerability of both sets of victims. Acknowledging that two shocking crimes were committed, he empathized first with the Lyerly family. "...a citizen had retired for the night and was unconscious and helpless from sleep, his home was broken into, and he and several members of his family murdered, and an attempt made to burn his dwelling and thus cover up the crime." Then he pointed out that the prisoners accused of the murders had also been helpless. "In obedience to the command of the law, they had been arrested, disarmed and imprisoned. The law had placed them in a position from which they could not flee, in a condition in which they could not defend themselves.... Every voter in North Carolina had taken the oath that he would support and maintain the Constitution and laws of North Carolina. The pledge for their protection was as sacred as the pledge made by the signers of the Mecklenburg or Philadelphia Declaration of Independence. The whole power of the State stood pledged for their protection." [B]

Ferguson made no excuses for the officers' failure to fire into the crowd. "If those attempting to break the jail and thus commit a felony, had been killed in the necessary defense of the prisoners, or necessarily in an effort to arrest the rioters, it would have been justifiable homicide. If the officer or any of his assistants had been killed, the killing would have been murder in all the participants." [B]

Outrage must have been evident in Ferguson's voice as he spoke the next words. "Yet there was—there was a military company armed and under orders of the sheriff. Yet with all this...the jail was broken into, three of the prisoners taken therefrom, and without trial, contrary to law, and in violation of the Constitution, put to death in such a brutal manner that if it had been done pursuant to the judgment of a court, and in accordance with the law of any nation on earth, such nation would be denied treaty relations with the civilized world. Not only the parties who did the killing, but every one who aided and abetted are guilty of murder in the first degree." [B]

He criticized the highly-publicized explanation for the officers' failure to shoot into the crowd. The "excuse," as he called it, "that the law-abiding citizens were so mixed with the mob that to shoot would endanger the lives of the innocent," didn't hold up in the aftermath, in his opinion. "If such is the fact, and those who mixed with the crowd were not in sympathy with the rioters," then they ought to be able to figure out who those rioters were, he insisted. And if they couldn't do that, then they weren't innocent themselves.

> *If those who go under cover of darkness, and murder their victims without being seen or heard can be ascertained, and their guilt established by proof, will not the same vigilance—when the murderers of the prisoners assemble under electric lights fire guns and pistols, use dynamite, break jails, carry their victims for a mile, and in the presence of a multitude put to death their helpless victims—ascertain who are the guilty parties. Those who committed that high crime calculated beforehand, that they would not be prevented or punished. They calculated first on what they believed to be a morbid and lawless public sentiment. They calculated on the timidity and passiveness of the law-abiding citizen and their own vicious courage. They calculated on the perjury of witnesses and corruption of juries, and timidity of courts. Whatever may be the conditions in other sections of the State, the time is now here for the law-abiding citizens of Rowan county to array themselves on the side of law, and order, and aid the officers of the law and the courts in bringing all the guilty parties to trial and punishment.* " [B]

Ferguson's words were fearless, and if Gentle's case had been heard immediately after the address, they might have had more impact. But, there was a delay of days, as the judge went ahead and got the less notable matters out of the way. The docket wasn't cleared of these until the afternoon of September 5th, when Gentle's case finally began.

Though no detailed report for the first part of Gentle's trial could be found, the *Observer* recapped it in its coverage of the following day's proceedings. By now, Kluttz had joined Carlton in Gentle's defense. The charge, not yet specified, was apparently jail-breaking.

THEODORE FRANKLIN
(THEO F.) KLUTTZ

*The trial was amusing without being designedly so, a farce-comedy carried on in utter seriousness. The State relied upon Deputy Sheriff H.C. Kenerly, to whom Gentle told the story of his part in the crime, to give the evidence that would send the fellow to the penitentiary and the defense depended entirely upon Gentle's reputation to save him from the trouble that he brought upon himself by wild talking. It admits Mr. Kenerly's statement but denies that Gentle was telling the truth when he made it.* [C]

It took only ten minutes to select the jury, and only the *Carolina Watchman* listed their names: A.L. Hall; H.I. Hoffner; John A. Sloop; L.D.H. Brown; J.R. Guffey; W.L. Steele; A.J. Cauble; Jas. G. Hoffner; W.M. Jamison; J.F. Ritchie; E.W. Kerr; and G.E. Moore. [3] It's not certain if A.J. Cauble was related to the John Cauble who had recently been released. A.L. Hall, if related to George Hall, was probably no more than a distant relative.

Only two witnesses were listed in the court records: Deputy Crawford Kenerly and Will Thomason. [4] This Kenerly was Crawford H. from the Franklin township near Isaac's place, not the same person as carpenter Samuel Kenerly who had testified against George Hall. The case evidently hinged upon Kenerly's testimony, recorded first.

*"I was in Salisbury the night of August the 6th. I saw the defendant that night out where the negroes were*

*lynched. I don't know anything except what he told me. Gentle came up to me in the streets, as well as I remember, and was going in the direction of the negroes. He seemed to be sober and said the reason that it took them so long to get the negroes was because they were not all in the same cell. 'As soon as I got in the cell,' Gentle said to me, 'I saw old Nease Gillespie, who said he knew me and said "Boss, I used to work for your daddy and you ought not to do this." He wouldn't confess anything until we got him out to the grounds and then I asked him if he did that up yonder and he said he did. Then we swung him up.'"*

This recording of Kenerly's testimony makes it sound like Kenerly spoke to Gentle out in the street right after the prisoners were kidnapped, but before they were killed. But he also said he saw Gentle at the lynching site but couldn't describe his role, if any, in the crime. He only knew, he said, what Gentle told him. Gentle's alleged statements to Kenerly places Gentle in the cell, participating in the kidnapping and at Henderson Park, involved in the actual hanging as well. The paper's failure to record the cross-examination didn't help clear up this confusion. It said only that the questioning "did little good or harm for anybody. Mr. Kluttz announced that he would object to nothing brought out but that, as there was no charge against his client further than jail breaking, the story about what took place at the place of execution could serve no purpose further than impeachment of the man." The judge allowed the testimony to stand. [C]

Kluttz's strategy was to establish Gentle's tendency to exaggerate, particularly his role in certain events. When he asked Kenerly "if he did not know that Gentle has a reputation for 'blowing and talking big,'" the State objected to that line of questioning, citing the "State against Lewis." As it happened, Ferguson was familiar with this case, he said, because he had been overruled on it himself. So Ferguson overruled Hammer's objection, and Kenerly answered. He had not heard anything about Gentle's reputation for exaggeration until recently, he said. [C]

Next W.F. Sloop, *not* in the court records as a witness for this case, was put on the stand. His purpose was simply to

establish that the prisoners had been illegally removed from the
jail and lynched. "He told of three shots that came close to this
head and of the battering down of the jail door. He did not see
the defendant and did not know him," he claimed. [C]

Then another surprise witness, W. Thomas Bost, testified for
the State. He was the *Observer's* Salisbury correspondent and
first cousin to Chief of Police Frank Miller. He told the court he
"saw Gentle twice" on the day of the lynching, but Gentle told
him since then that he was there but had not taken any part in the
killing. "'I saw him at first at the session of the special term of
court and later in the crowd going to the lynching,'" Bost
testified.

Something rather unusual followed. "...the direct testimony
was dropped here by both sides and the newspaper
correspondent" was "made to rehearse the affair from the
standpoint of the press." Here's how the *Observer* paraphrased
this "rehearsal" by its own correspondent.

> *He said he was with the crowd that made up the jail-*
> *breaking party until it shot the last time into the bodies*
> *of the dead negroes. He recognized two men who took*
> *part in the lawlessness but does not know their names.*
> *One of these he interviewed after the affair was over and*
> *saw him at 3 o'clock in the morning in the T.W. Grimes*
> *drug store. He saw another man whom he has since seen*
> *on the streets and he ran when McLendon was shot.*
> *None of these men had he ever seen before and none was*
> *Gentle. Here Judge Ferguson asked if the reporter knew*
> *the man up the tree who manipulated the rope. This was*
> *answered negatively and followed with the declaration*
> *that many of the men who were actually taking part in*
> *the killing were masked with spotted blue handkerchiefs*
> *over their mouths. The man on the limb was not. It has*
> *been said that Tom Brown, who was released from a cell*
> *by the mob and tried last week for burglary, handled the*
> *rope, but this was denied. The lawyers hauled the*
> *reporter over the coals, extracting from him the*
> *admission that he was under the tree and with pencil and*
> *notebook in hand, wrote the account for some daily*
> *papers. He saw W.J. McMahon, who strove so hard with*

*the mob for time for which to gain the truth about the murder and was close enough to hear the negroes talk. The rope that strung Jack Dillingham up broke and the negro dropped almost on him when he fell to the ground. The crowd was composed entirely of strangers, and he took particular care to see if there were any Rowan people in it.* [C]

Bost must have known Gentle; they were both long-time residents of Rowan's Franklin Township. His testimony, or the paper's version of it, contains the only mention of any attempt by the lynchers to conceal themselves. Did Bost have to come up with some excuse for not recognizing anyone despite his presence at the very site and moment of the victims' hanging?

And why weren't Bryant and Julian put on the stand? Bryant had stated in one of his initialed reports that Bullyboy was the one who sat on the limb and blew smoke circles while the victims prayed. Bryant had at least given the impression that he had followed the mob to the ballpark. In addition to writing like he knew for a fact what Bullyboy's role was, he included other information as if he'd observed the lynching himself. He had described how McMahon had tried to persuade the mob to postpone the hanging and how "Little John clung to his arm and begged him to save his life." If he knew all this, he should have been able to testify against Bullyboy and others. And clearly Julian, said to know everyone in Rowan County by name, could have named a few there that night. Mayor Boyden had told the *Observer* when he was trying to deny the rumor of prominent citizens' involvement, that he knew no more than a dozen involved. So why didn't he own up to more than two of those?

Perhaps Bost was the one who actually witnessed and reported the story that Bryant took credit for. But surely Bost was not the only reporter who witnessed the lynching. An *N&O* newsman must have been there. He had described the rope breaking and the victim falling to the ground before being strung up again. So why wasn't *he* interrogated? At any rate, Bryant and Julian seemed to be laying low during this trial.

Nothing came of any of the State's witness accounts anyway. After the lawyers were through with Bost, the State rested. Whoever the other listed witness, Will Thomason, was, if he was called to the stand, his testimony wasn't recorded or even mentioned in the papers.

Then came the case for the defense, and Gentle was called as the first witness. The *Observer* paraphrased his testimony, saying "he sustained his reputation admirably."

> *He came here late that evening and got drunk after he had smoked a cigar. After taking the liquor and the cigar he followed the crowd for a while and soon was lost in that lingering twilight between memory and oblivion. Mr. Clement noticed this and said: "After you got that licker and cigar, oblivion seized you, did it?" Gentle did not know how to answer this and Mr. Clement was asked to talk in simpler terms. Then Gentle declared: "If I told Mr. Kenerly them things, I don't remember it; honest to God I don't. It weren't so, anyway."*
>
> *The cross-examination of Gentle was directed with a purpose to prove him inaccurate in his declarations, the very thing that the defense demonstrated in another way. Gentle corroborated his record which had beaten him here, very finely.* <sup>C</sup>

For the defendant, the trial was a win-win situation. The Defense's job was to prove he was a liar, and the State's cross-examination had the same goal. Nevertheless, the defense introduced other witnesses to clarify Gentle's particular style of lying—to show "Gentle's Munchausen proclivities," as the reporter put it. [5] In other words, "Gentle would not lie to get himself out of trouble, but would do it to get into a predicament." The writer concluded that "Whether lie or the truth got him into this, he would have had no trouble had he kept his mouth shut." <sup>C</sup> Another paper said both Hall and Gentle would have been fine had they kept quiet and suggested others should take notice for future reference.

Here court adjourned until the following morning.

Nothing else about the first part of Gentle's trial was recorded. But from what was reported the following day, at some point two of Gentle's friends or cohorts, Dave Athey and Pat

Lucas, had been questioned, and both swore they and Gentle were not near the jail when the mob leaders broke in.

The first thing the State did when the session reopened was try to prove these guys were lying, that Gentle had, indeed, participated in the break-in. Captain Max Barker was asked to confirm the time the Rowan Rifles abandoned the jail, in an attempt to discredit Lucas and Athey's version of when they moved away, a time the report did not specify. "Barker testified that the Rifles were back at the armory at 11 p.m., a perfectly correct statement, the halting of the soldiers in front of Grimes drug store for two minutes not being taken into account." [C] It's impossible to determine from the report whether Gentle's buddies helped his case or not.

The evidence ended with Barker's statement, and then closing arguments began. Prosecutor Clement opened with a 50-minute argument. Failing to record any of Clement's words, the *Observer* only described the address as a "splendid speech," considering the handicap under which he spoke, "the difficulty being the lack of evidence to support the indictment." [C] The reporter portrayed Kenerly's testimony as not having provided any evidence that Gentle had conspired to break into the jail. This was the reasoning:

> *The testimony of Deputy Kenerly was conclusive as a declaration from the prisoner off-hand. Gentle had said he helped swing the men up, but did not tell of any jail-breaking nor of any conspiracy to break the jail. The indictment incorporated these things in it.* [C]

But didn't Kenerly just say, under oath the previous day, that Gentle told him Nease spoke to him directly as soon as he got into the cell that night? Could Gentle have gotten inside that cell without breaking into the jail or aiding those who did?

After Clement concluded his argument, Defense Attorney Pritchard Carlton rose to address the jury. "His speech would have brought laughter and applause outside the court," said the *Observer*, "His digs at Mr. Clement were exceedingly amusing." [C] Carlton contended that Gentle's presence in the crowd did not, in and of itself, prove his participation in attacking the jail or his engagement in any other work of the mob.

*"Mr Kenerly" he said, "declares that Gentle said he was in the mob. Why there were 4,000 in the mob, and some of the best people in the town and county were there. I don't know whether Brother Clement was there or not, but Solicitor Hammer, Senator Overman, Sheriff Julian, Mayor Boyden, Judge Long and Mr. Bost were in it. Mr. Bost says he was under the tree and that when Jack Dillingham fell he touched him. Why, if these men were in the mob, don't you indict them and not jerk up some pauper here and try him?"* [C]

Carlton did have a point, but Hammer didn't think so. The solicitor, said to be a very large man, reportedly jumped up immediately to object to Carlton's argument. But, as he began to elaborate, "Kluttz came out from the smoking room and told him that he had a right to object but not to make a speech while Mr. Carlton had the floor." Hammer responded that "Carlton was reflecting upon the officers and 'his speech is unworthy of him because he is a very honorable man and doesn't mean to say what he is saying.'" But Judge Ferguson said Carlton could continue—and without interruption. [C]

Hammer was not to be undone. While "the young lawyer" continued his address, Hammer issued a subpoena for him to "appear before the grand jury and tell of those 'prominent citizens who were in the mob.'" This would mean that, along with the others, Senator Overman might have to appear before the grand jury. [C]

No more of Carlton's speech was recorded by the newspaper. Instead, the report moved on to Kluttz's 45-minute closing argument.

*He maintained that the story that Gentle helped swing the negroes up told nothing that could possibly bear upon the question of guilt or innocence of the charge against Gentle. "There is not a scintilla of evidence that he was at or near the jail. Mr Kenerly, whom everybody will believe, says he did not see him and he was there. Pat Sloop says he was there and bullets flew over his head, that he saw the crowd come in and George Gentle was not in the crowd. Tom Bost said he was at the foot of the jail steps, saw the man go upstairs and come down with the men, recognizing even the prisoners, but no George Gentle there. These are the State's witnesses and they utterly fail to tell one word that tends to fasten guilt upon my client of the charge against him. Dave Athey and Pat Lucas were with him and say he was not there. Everybody but Gentle's maudlin, drunken vaporing says he was not there. Gentle, sober, told State's witnesses that he was not in the lynching party. Drunken Gentle told Mr. Kenerly that he was in the party and took a part, but sober Gentle told Mr. Bost that he was not there. But drunken Gentle on one side and sober Gentle on the other, Gentle drunk and Gentle sober, which will you believe?"*

*Mr. Kluttz did not go into the sentimental side of the case and ended his argument without having gone into any matter not at issue. "I have set the solicitor a good example and hope he will profit by it," he said.* [C]

The next thing covered in the report was Solicitor Hammer's closing arguments. His speech began about 12:45, but was disrupted by the lunch recess. He continued it just before 3 p.m. and made it through about thirty minutes before Kluttz interrupted him again. He said there was no need to discuss whether or not Gentle had made a declaration to Kenerly, because the defendant had admitted that he had done so.

The reporter must have understood the meaning of the next argument, because he didn't elaborate.

*Then, "Hammer read another opinion on the question of weight to be given a confession not forced or procured by promise. The point had been made that Gentle was a man who told of great things he did and would make up the wildest stories therefore. Mr. Kluttz reminded the prosecution that he had asked that a witness be allowed to give an instance of this kind and the State had not allowed it. Attorneys differed as to who and what brought this out.* [C]

Hammer next addressed Defense attorneys about the subpoena he had just issued for Carlton. He admitted he believed Carlton had made his statements about the "best people in town" being in the crowd that night in desperation. Nevertheless, Hammer continued, "'since Mr. Carlton knows so much, I have had him subpoenaed and he will have to appear before the grand jury and tell what he knows.'" [C]

Kluttz "was up in a second," not about to let Hammer get away with it. "May it please the court; the solicitor knows that it is improper for him to testify, and I object to it."

"Mr. Hammer," warned the judge, "do not mention this again."

"If it is improper, your honor, I will withdraw it," Hammer replied.

"'Oh, yes,' said Mr. Kluttz, 'you withdraw it after it has gone into the jury box. You knew it was improper when you made it.'"

"'You can't make me mad nor can you swerve me from my purpose,'" Hammer fired back. "'I am going to finish my speech and every time there is an interruption I want the jury to know why I take so long to complete my argument. I do not intend to be threatened or intimidated'" [C]

The *Observer* didn't comment further on Hammer's argument, except to say that it was "exhaustive," and that no more incidents occurred while he finished it. The reporter did add that the "moralist" could not "discount the effort made by the Solicitor and Mr. Clement to serve the State" that day. "Both made tremendous speeches and after Mr. Hammer closed, so well had he handled the case that many thought the jury would hang or convict Gentle." [C]

It didn't. Even though the "alacrity with which they agreed upon a verdict was a surprise, and bets could have been had that it was conviction," George Gentle was acquitted. "It took that body of men exactly 21 minutes to come to the conclusion that George Gentle told a falsehood when he declared to Deputy Crawford Kenerly that he had aided in the lynching of the Gillespie murderers." [C]

With Gentle's acquittal, the press's coverage of Rowan's lynching suspects ended, for good. But the coverage of the assumed guilt of Della Dillingham, Henry Gillespie, and George

Erwin would continue. Gentle's guilt had been questioned from the start, but the lynching victims, who never got a trial, would be convicted as murderers, again and again, as they are still today.

Everyone except the prosecution seemed happy with the results. The reporter said the verdict met "almost universal approval. Lack of evidence was plainly the cause" of the verdict. "It was a jury of splendid men, and the State has no kick at all." [C] Another paper agreed with that assessment. "About all the evidence there was against Gentle was his statement to Mr. Kenerly and others as to what he did on the night of the lynching." [6] Right after his acquittal, George Gentle told the press:

> *"I will go home to-night if it takes me till mid-night, and sleep the first time in peace since I have been in jail."* [C]

Hammer won despite this defeat. "The solicitor has received at this court the highest praise that he has yet had as an officer. All of the bar took occasion to pay tribute to him and say the district has never been more ably represented. His thankless job is made tolerable by it." [C] Certainly Hammer found this praise useful when he ran again for the office of Solicitor that November, and later, in his campaign for Congressman.

The *Carolina Watchman* briefly summed up the proceedings in its first edition printed after the trial. It said the "jury evidently believed that Gentle was so full of bad booze and hot air on the night in question that he did not know what he was talking about." The *Watchman* also included one additional remark Gentle made after his acquittal, that he would "remain at home in the future and endeavor to cultivate closer intimacy with the soil on his farm." [6]

But could anyone believe it?

# 22

## ABOUT FACE

### SEPTEMBER 6 & 7

*What does the Negro want? His answer is very simple. He wants only what all other Americans want. He wants opportunity to make real what the Declaration of Independence and the Constitution and the Bill of Rights say, what the Four Freedoms establish. While he knows these ideals are open to no man completely, he wants only his equal chance to obtain them.*

— Mary McLeod Bethune [1]

GEORGE ERVIN AND HENRY LEE GILLESPIE

George Gentle didn't go home the night of his acquittal after all. The judge wasn't finished with him yet. He had been cleared of only the conspiracy charge, and Ferguson hadn't dropped the others, one being murder.

While he was chewing on what to do about Gentle, Ferguson finally, on September 6th, decided to deal with the remaining suspects in the Lyerly murder case. Attorney Williams was now in charge of the defense. No one mentioned Jake Newell's absence, but perhaps the threats against his life were still out there. Bryant, for one, had been enjoying Newell's predicament. Since the lynching he'd written several anecdotes poking fun at him, as if the threats to his life were something to joke about. [2]

As soon as the bill of indictment was read in court that day, Della Dillingham, Henry Lee Gillespie, and George Ervin were brought in and arraigned on murder charges. The report said each stood up separately and entered a plea of not guilty, but judging by earlier descriptions of Della's beatings, she may have had a hard time doing so. As was later rumored, Della may have been pregnant at the time of that beating.

After the arraignment, Williams got down to business and requested a change of venue. The prisoners, the affidavit said, feared they could not get a fair trial in Rowan County.

> *Mr. Williams spoke briefly in support of the motion. He said the newspapers had kept the public so well informed of the murder and had treated the prisoners as convicted so consistently that he thought popular sentiment was certainly against his clients. He referred to the demonstration of the mob on Saturday night, July 14th, and declared that it would have lynched them if they had not been removed.* [A]

The press had indeed continued to portray the accused as murderers, even in the reports of Gentle's trial. Of course this time there was a new and deadlier incident to add to the rationale for a change of venue. Williams reminded the court "of the actual killing of the prisoners here during the sitting of a court called to investigate the murder. He considered the risk too great."

But Hammer didn't let it go without an argument. He claimed "there had been no evidence lately" that the prisoners were in any danger. "Turning to the crowd behind him, he said that, at no time during the sitting of this court, had there been any interest in it." Though he conceded that the prisoners' "fright and uneasiness was natural," he thought there was reason to believe they needn't be afraid any longer—not in "good ole Rowan."

> "Rowan county is an unusually intelligent one," he added "and there is an illiteracy of but 11 per cent. Its juries are proverbially fair and impartial and I think there is no doubt that a fair trial can be had. We have every reason to believe that the members of the mob that first stormed the jail and later lynched the prisoners was composed of people from other counties and I fail to see what advantages there can be in taking them from one county and run the risk of taking them into the very dangers that we had attempted to avoid. There is no longer feeling against these prisoners. The excitement had died out and any one can see there is little interest in the trial now on. At no time has the court room been full. Yesterday we finished a trial in which a supposed member of the party of lynchers was indicted. The crowd then was smaller even than it is now." [A]

Though the irony in Hammer's statement is obvious, let me indulge briefly. First, the defendants' head lawyer, a prominent white man, apparently didn't feel safe enough to show up for court that day. Second, that "supposed member" of the lynching party was not just indicted; he was acquitted. If not for Ferguson's wisdom in holding Gentle to face other charges, he would now be free—and possibly drunk again, doing more things he would later be unable to recall. And he *was* freed soon, probably that very day, for nothing was heard about any charges against him after this day in court. Third, Alex Jackson, who no one had mentioned since Deputy Julian implicated him, *was* free, as were the roughly 1,000-4,000 others who had participated in the lynching. Jackson was from Litaker, Faith's township, and so were some of the jurymen, and Faith had just bragged about its total absence of African American citizens, and how none were welcome there. Anyone in those defendants' shoes would not have wanted these white men deciding their fate. Luckily for the defendants, Judge Ferguson was equally empathetic.

> *"Taking into consideration what appears in the affidavit and the statement of the solicitor, it is very apparent that, if the officers of the law and the good citizens of the county could not find out who took the prisoners' co-defendants from the jail and killed them, it is impossible for the prisoners to do so, and it seems to me that they have good grounds to fear that they cannot have a fair trial in this county."* [A]

Kluttz, hired by the Lyerly family and now assisting the prosecution, objected, reminding the court that the same mob had spared the remaining prisoners now on trial. This, he suggested, was evidence "that there was no feeling against the trio which is here." It was as if Kluttz didn't see Della's bruised body there before his very eyes.

Ferguson, not oblivious to Della's plight, continued as if Kluttz was the invisible one.

> *"It seems to me that the public mind as to this case is not normal, and I seriously doubt if a jury could hear the testimony and weigh it unbiased. At any rate I am not willing to put the defendants on trial in this county. They are entitled to all of the privileges that the law allows them and, although it is possible that there is not danger if tried here, if they fear it, it is our duty to give the benefit of the law on this point."* [A]

No matter how rational Ferguson's response, Hammer was unmoved by it. Trying another tactic, he argued that the State still had a consideration in the matter, that the case "go where it would receive justice." [A]

With what the *Observer* described as a wise observation, Ferguson ended the debate. "The State could live even though a criminal might escape," he persisted, but "a man caught by a mob and taken out of a jail could not live." [A]

That settled, the discussion turned to which county the case should be removed. The decision to go to Stanly was not explained; it would delay the trial at least until late January, putting the prisoners back into jail for nearly another five months. It hardly seemed fair, but it couldn't have been worse than facing the threat of another Salisbury mob.

The next day, with the Lyerly case resolved for the time being, Ferguson turned his attention back to George Gentle's fate. Gentle was brought into court that morning, and the solicitor addressed the remaining charges related to his alleged involvement in the lynching. Ferguson said his concern should not be construed to mean he thought the jury "had blundered" in its decision on the conspiracy charge. However, he pointed out, "a good citizen has said Gentle declared that he was a big man at the lynching, tied one of the knots around Nease Gillespie's neck and took an active part." With that justification, Ferguson decided to continue the murder charge against Gentle. [A]

Kluttz, opposed to dragging out the matter, didn't hide his displeasure. For good reason, Kluttz was satisfied with the sitting jury and didn't want to risk having another decide the next case. "If there was any other count against the young fellow, he thought it should come out and he believed the trial should begin right away as his client could not give a bond." [A]

"I see no necessity to try the other charges right away," Ferguson responded.

"This is a matter for the discretion of the court," Kluttz asserted.

"I have the authority in all cases to grant bail," Ferguson shot back, reading the statutes. Then he added: "...and without expressing any opinion one way or another (I do not wish to do so) I think the charge should be investigated, and Gentle should be tried as any other defendant. This charge is a capital crime." [A]

"I thought the case had been tried, your honor, and that the investigation was made. I thought the solicitor had brought out all the testimony he had and the matter was tried before an intelligent jury, drawn regularly, a jury from which we did not even take off a single man. I felt so confident about it that I made a short speech about it." [A]

Ferguson remained firm and patiently elaborated on the reasons for his decision.

*"Without expressing an opinion as to the unfortunate circumstances that occurred here a short time ago, I think I said in my charge to the grand jury that those who frame our government and laws acted wisely in providing every remedy for crimes affecting society. I call attention to these things because, when they occur, they sometimes put us to thinking and it is necessary to see what remedies we have got." He then read the oath of constables, sheriffs and judges and solicitors. He continued: "These duties are enjoined, it seems to me, and when a bill for murder is found, there is but one course left open and without reference to any evidence showing guilt or innocence of the defendant, I think the case should be tried and that there is no necessity for evading it. Without expressing any opinion as to what evidence may be disclosed I have power to grant bail and order the defendant to give bond in the sum of $2,500 and be held until it is justified and approved by the clerk."* [A]

In the end, Gentle had no trouble at all with the bond. The *Observer* noted that three "good citizens" got together and came up with the money. They were John F. Ludwick, James H. McKenzie, and P.A. Hartman, all from Salisbury, the latter a county commissioner. None claimed to know Gentle or have any other interest in the case except a "...feeling that the investigation has gone to the point of worrying to death a harmless, lying, bragging boy." [A]

There was no such help available for the darker-skinned prisoners to be tried on the same charge Gentle now faced. They had been in jail, with no means of providing for their loved ones, since July 14th. Mrs. Gentle had appealed to the board of commissioners that week for help because she was in great financial need. [A] There was no mention of what became of Jack and Della Dillingham's young child or of Henry Gillespie's wife, Emma. Nor was there word about Fannie Gillespie or Henry Mayhew. Though not even charged with a crime, they too had been incarcerated since July 14th. By law, both Della and Fannie, family members of the lynching victims, were now entitled to compensation from the county. There is no direct evidence they received it.

Gentle and Cress had both been easily acquitted of conspiracy. Both now had other charges pending against them, and yet they were free. If they had been black men, they would more likely have been swinging freely from a rope on a tree.

All of the charges against both were eventually and quietly dropped. *Nol pros* was abbreviated in the docket beside their case numbers. Short for *nolle prosequi*, it means: "to be unwilling to pursue" or is defined as "an entry on the record of a legal action denoting that the prosecutor or plaintiff will proceed no further in an action or suit...." [3] The riot charge against Alex Jackson, and all other remaining charges against George Hall were dropped as well.

There would be no such mercy for Della, Henry, or George. They would remain in jail until the end of January, when they would finally get a chance to face and respond to accusations against them.

Based on reviews of other convictions against African Americans around 1906, Judge Ferguson's actions concerning the most notable cases in this term of court seem exceptionally fair. However, without reviewing his entire record, it's hard to judge the judge from this one performance, especially considering the publicity of this case. Eyes beyond the county, and even the state, were fixed on it.

Leon Litwack illustrates in his book, *Trouble in Mind*, just how sheer Justice's blindfold was, as a rule, during Jim Crow's reign. At the time, the courts "regularly excluded blacks from juries, disregarded black testimony, sometimes denied counsel to the accused, and meted out disproportionately severe sentences to black defendants. Not only did whites assume black guilt in most cases, but they also often held the entire race responsible." [B]

I wondered if Litwack's observation held true for North Carolina in 1906. Though I couldn't view all the court reports from that year, it was impossible to ignore the numerous headlines of executions and lynchings for black "crimes" of all descriptions, carried out during this time. Also I did examine a few county court reports and compared the sentences by "race" in this small sample. First, I found, in the *Carolina Watchman*, the sentences Ferguson gave to both blacks and whites in the smaller cases he presided over that September before he took on the more notable trials of Gentle and the Lyerly defendants. Here are the details of that report:

A white man, Tom Brown, who allegedly entered a room of a Mr. Davis and robbed him, was found guilty and sentenced by Ferguson to "ten years on the public roads," a crime for which blacks were often hanged or lynched, even without successfully stealing anything. [C] Brown was one of those who had been freed from jail by the lynching party, at first rumored to be he who sat on the limb and blew smoke circles while the victims prayed.

Another white man, Walter Forrest, was found guilty of larceny and sentenced to four months on county roads. But a black man named Oscar Holmes, also found guilty of larceny, got ten *years* on the county roads. [C]

Charges against Ernest Darr, Ernest Mauney, John McClamrock, and Ernest Dack, all for assault with a deadly weapon, were all "suspended upon payment of costs," except for Mauney, whose case was dropped. None of these four were designated as "colored" or "negro," which would have been noted if they had been. [C] This Mauney, by the way, may have been the Mauney reported to be shot during the jail-breaking on August 6th.

Another white man, Joe Hughes, was charged "with carrying concealed weapons" and found guilty. "Judgement was suspended in his case." [C]

The *Observer's* report of the proceedings in nearby Union County on January 31, 1907, provides another example for comparison. Five months after Rowan's August term, things seemed back to normal, with African Americans thrown in jail for minor offenses, while whites committing worse offenses were treated with leniency. The subheading for that report reads: "Judge Council Makes a Fine Impression on the Folks— Numerous Terms of 12 to 30 Months on the Roads Meted Out to Colored Offenders." [D]

"Frank Jackson, a young negro who stole a pair of shoes from a car on the Seaboard Railway, was sentenced to 12 months on the roads." And, "George Jones, colored, was found guilty of stealing bacon from the store of Mr. J.A. Lingle and got 8 months on the chain-gang." [D] HBO recently aired a documentary with African American actors reciting testimonies of former slaves, recorded by the U.S. government in the 1930s. Though he knew it was wrong to steal, one admitted, he sometimes took food because he was starving. Eight months on the chain-gang for stealing bacon is reminiscent of the harshness of the French penal system described by Victor Hugo in the 1700s. Or the English one, described by Dickens about the same time. That's how the British populated Australia.

"Henry Walter, a negro found guilty of selling liquor, was sentenced to 12 months on one charge and judgement was suspended on three others." [D] George Hall, it is recalled, was sentenced to three months for his first offense of selling liquor after running from the law for years, then he was caught again later and sentenced to only nine months.

"The longest sentence given so far," said the report, "is that of Manuel Wilson, for shooting another negro, Jim Gillespie. Gillespie was not seriously wounded, but Wilson got two and a half years on the roads." [D] If Gillespie had been a white man, Wilson might not have lived to see his trial.

"In the case of W.E. Griffin, alias Ellis Crook, a young white man, who was charged with stealing $8 from Mrs. Tomberlin, for whom he was working, it came out that Griffin is mentally weak. Mrs. Tomberlin and several witnesses corroborated this, and a plea was made for leniency by the prisoner's attorney. Judge Council made an order that Griffin be hired out to work off the sentence of 4 months." [D] So Lingle, a black man, got eight months on the chain-gang for stealing food, and Crook, a white man, would only have to work off a four-month sentence for stealing what would be the equivalent of $50 or more today.

"Thurlow Alsobrooks, colored," was "sent to the roads for 4 months," for "sporting a pair of knucks." The reporter characterized another black defendant, Gary Goins, as a "darky, who seemed to think the proceedings against him for selling whiskey were largely in the nature of a joke." His sentence, twelve months on the chain gang, was more than Hall served for the same offense, even on his second conviction. [D]

Another "white boy," Neil Marsh, "had been indicted for arson." Like the other white boy, Marsh "showed such clear indications of being mentally unsound that Solicitor Robinson moved to change the indictment to forcible trespass. The prosecuting witness in this case was palpably weak minded, also. Young Marsh was sentenced to 4 months, and arrangements were made to have him work out the term." [D] In several instances in that time period, blacks were lynched for arson.

Finally, "Seth Hough, colored, was sentenced to 6 months on the roads for the larceny of $2.45." [D] The white boy Crook got less time for stealing $8.00, and he didn't have to do that time on the chain gang.

No other Union County cases were reported for that term, so apparently one hundred percent of the white people convicted in that session in January, 1907 were mentally unstable.

My extensive review of North Carolina press coverage from 1902 to 1907 revealed several cases of African Americans legally hanged for burglary or even attempting, but failing, at other crimes like assault. But I found no case of a white man hanged for anything other than murder. These few examples indicate that Leon Litwack's findings likely held true for North Carolina, at least in 1906 and 1907.

All of this probably went virtually unnoticed by those in the white community. But black Americans were well aware of the blatant injustices, and where they had a voice, they spoke out about it. The *Afro-American-Ledger* in Baltimore did so on August 11th right after the Salisbury lynching. "Suppose He Had Been a Negro?," the writer asked in the title to his commentary, which began with: "The spasms of virtue which strike the white man from time to time is something awful."

*A white miscreant attempted to assault a little daughter of a minister in a church in Connecticut almost before the eyes of the enraged parent. Possibly there would have been a lynching, but the minister persuaded the crowd to let the law take its course.*

*How different this would have been had the occurrence taken place in the South, the minister likely would have led the mob and helped to do the lynching had the miscreant been a Negro. What a funny thing the white man's idea of justice is.* [E]

# ASHEVILLE BOUND

## WEDNESDAY, JANUARY 31, 1907

*All my trials, Lord, soon be over.*

— Bahamian Lullaby

IREDELL COUNTY COURTHOUSE

Right after George Gentle was acquitted, and the three Lyerly murder suspects got their change of venue, is when all hell broke loose in Atlanta. The *Observer* called it a "Race War." It was Wilmington all over again, and the massacre there served to further fan the flames of hatred toward people of color. So Della, Henry, and George might have expected the worst as their next day in court got underway.

There was little coverage to be found of their appearance in Stanly County, and none explained why the venue and date was moved again after that. Covering the Stanly session on January 16th, the *Washington Post* reported only the change of venue, with no details. [A] It was decided they would go next to Iredell County.

On Wednesday, January 31st, Della, George, and Henry left the Charlotte train depot in the custody of Sheriff Deaton and headed toward Statesville, Iredell's county seat. The three would finally face the charges against them.

The "Silver-Haired Orator," Jake Newell, appeared at the courthouse that day on behalf of the prisoners. That was a good sign. Mary Lyerly and Henry Mayhew were listed as State's witnesses. E.A. Barber, W.P. (Pless) Barber, Phillip Lyerly, R.F. Cook, and E.B. Walton were also subpoenaed to testify. Presiding was Fred Moore, a judge who, if you believe Josephus Daniels, approved of whippings at the post—not a good sign. Theo Kluttz was on hand once again to assist Solicitor Hammer in the prosecution, and H.S. Williams of Concord joined Newell for the defense. This time a stenographer, Nora Sherrill, was paid to record the testimony.

In addition to Sherrill's handwritten account of the trial, we have the *Statesville Landmark's* coverage of the day's proceedings and a few other summaries, including one in the *Charlotte Observer*. The press and the court records complemented and sometimes contradicted each other, and without both, there would be significant holes in the story.

Timothy Dearman, current publisher of the *Statesville Record & Landmark*, says his paper, known as the *Statesville Landmark* in 1902, was previously owned and published by Joseph Caldwell and Rufus Reid Clark. Like the *Observer*, which Caldwell later took over, the *Landmark* reflected the Democratic party's sentiments. Caldwell sold his interest in the

Statesville newspaper to Clark when he moved on to the *Observer* in 1892. [1]

Unlike all the earlier reports published about the case, the ones covering this event were quite low-key. Though the story of the Lyerly murders and the lynching had made front page headline news everywhere, the *Landmark's* story of this trial was found on page three of the February 1st edition. It was so inconspicuous I almost overlooked it.

The trial was held up by the delayed arrival of the train bearing the prisoners from Charlotte, so jury selection didn't begin until noon. The *Landmark* said a "good many Rowan people" attended the trial, "...and the court house was packed during the hearing Wednesday afternoon. But there was at no time any indication of an outbreak," it reassured. [B]

The *Charlotte Observer* added that "...most all are of the opinion that the negroes were implicated in the murders." [C] Even though it had asserted, throughout the previous July, that Ervin and Henry Lee were thought to be innocent, it failed to bring this up now or mention what it had earlier deemed to be the worthlessness of the "evidence" against any of the suspects. Both the *Observer* and the *Gastonia Gazette* had printed Newell's statement after the lynching, which concluded as follows:

> *"I believe...that not sufficient evidence had been introduced to have sent the case to a jury and in any other county than Rowan, an acquittal would have been the result.*[2]

But none of that was being discussed now.

The following jurors, all white according to census records, were selected "in a short time and without summoning a special venire," said the *Landmark*, which also listed their names: A.R. Reece, W.O. Goodin, T. Scott Harkley, J.W. Hampton, W.A. Campbell, A.A. Murdoch, J.M. Sides, Arthur Craven, C.S. King, Henry Morrison, Obas A. Shook, and J.A. Lippard. [B]

Mary Lyerly, now a student at Crescent Academy in Faith, was sworn in as the State's first witness. Before the questioning began, a large wall map was brought into the courtroom so she could point out the location of the Lyerly house and its rooms.

Her testimony was mostly paraphrased by the *Landmark* and is the same, in essence, she gave to Solicitor Hammer on July 20th, with one exception. The paper quoted her as saying, "All had wounds on the head made with *some blunt instrument.*" [B]

If we can trust the accuracy of the *Landmark's* record, it's the first time, since this whole ordeal began, that any of the main witnesses gave the impression that the weapon was anything but an axe. The use of a club had been reported in the earliest accounts published in the Winston-Salem *Journal* and picked up by a few other out-of-state papers, but the prevailing impression had been that the Lyerlys were all killed by two axes. If the weapon was not an axe, then the descriptions J.C. McNeill gave of the murder scene had to have been embellished. Why did the *Landmark* print it, unless that's actually what Mary said, and why had Sherrill and everyone else failed to record her testimony that way?

It's possible both weapons were used or both sides of the axe blade. Sherrill quoted Mary as saying that her brother's head had been cut with an axe, but that her father's "face was smashed in." [D] She also said she saw "an axe next morning when they brought it to cook's." Mary identified it as theirs, and said it "had blood on it." [D] She said again, as she had before, that it was the axe she had seen at their wood pile earlier on the night of the murders. But there was no testimony at all recorded about another axe, the one said to be Nease's. And no source reported an axe brought into the courtroom for Mary to identify as the one in question. Given the testimony in the official record, it's strange that the *Landmark* would mention only a blunt weapon and not address that inconsistency. The media's record of Solicitor Hammer's July 20th investigation reported no statements by Mary or Addie about what weapon might have been used to kill their parents and siblings.

Sherrill's transcript included a couple of minor details about another matter not mentioned before. Hammer or Kluttz must have asked Mary why neither she nor her sisters had heard anything while their family members were being murdered. According to Sherrill, Mary told the court the girls' bedroom was not above her parents' room; it was above the parlor across the hall. Mary also told the court her father, who was sixty-eight, could not hear well.

One response from Mary's cross examination was also included in the court transcript. "I did not understand from what Della said that she meant to kill my mother but understood that she meant to do something to her," Mary said. [D] Apparently it was the only question Newell asked her.

The *Landmark* next paraphrased the testimony of Constable Ed (E.A.) Barber. According to this account,

> *He reached the Lyerly home about daylight but did not go in the house, as there was talk of sending for blood hounds. He went over to Jack Dillingham's house and told Jack and Della that the Lyerlys were murdered and he wanted them to go with him over there. Della cursed him and told him she wasn't going.* [B]

Barber had said all this before, but what had been withheld at Hammer's investigation, or at least not reported by the press, was the following, found in the *Landmark's* account:

> *He told her if they didn't come out of the house and go* [to the Lyerly place with him] *he would burn the house. They then came out and went with him. After going back to the Lyerly house he went in and saw the bodies."* [B]

Sherrill, the stenographer, omitted Barber's threat to burn down the Dillingham's house, but earlier reports substantiated that Barber had threatened the couple in some way. His statements about the blood hounds made me wonder about his motives for dragging Della and Jack down to the main house. According to his testimony, Barber apparently didn't go inside the Lyerly home at first because he didn't want to interfere with the dogs' ability to pick up the murderer's scent. But, it seems clear he wanted the Dillinghams there before anyone else arrived. Were the Dillinghams reluctant to comply because they guessed Barber's intent, because they were guilty, or because they feared they would be lynched on the spot?

The *Landmark* continued Barber's testimony, with him describing "the wounds found on the bodies and the condition of the premises," but it left out the details. [B] They weren't in

Sherrill's "transcript" either, maybe because nothing new was said. But had either recorded the details of that testimony here, they might have cleared up the issue of what weapon or weapons were used. Barber, the one said to be describing the scene this time, had not been quoted before about his observations, and being the first or one of the first on the scene, his might have been the most accurate.

Both records show that Barber repeated some statements he made earlier. He retold his stories about the burned spots allegedly found between the well and Nease's house and the tracks supposedly found leading from the branch to both Nease's and Jack's houses. There was no record that any of the material evidence mentioned earlier was brought into the courtroom to verify this testimony. Apparently no photographs were taken of the tracks or burned spots, though there were plenty published of the lynching. Evidence of that crime remains over a hundred years later, and the Lyerlys' gravestone marks the crime committed against them, but none of the "evidence" or photos of evidence linking the accused to the latter crime exists anywhere. If photos could be taken of the lynched bodies, why couldn't they be taken of the "evidence" or even of a crowd threatening to break in a jail?

Judging from Barber's next statement, defense attorneys must have questioned his authority to order the Dillinghams out of their house. Barber answered: "I did not tell Jack or Della that I was an officer or had a warrant." [D] He was apparently asked about the tracks and the burned spots as well. "I saw only two fresh burned places at Nease's," he told the court, and the tracks "were fresh." [D] The next question about the weather must have had something to do with the tracks. Barber said he thought the weather had been dry, though he wasn't sure. [D]

The Statesville paper paraphrased Pless Barber's statement, adding that he was the administrator of the Lyerly estate.

*Mr. Cook came after him and he went to Barber Junction and telegraphed to the sheriff and to Winston [Winston-Salem] for blood hounds. He then went to the Lyerly home. The witness described conditions there much as had been done by others. Showed lamp which had been found to Phillip Lyerly, colored, and saw the*

*axe which had been found under the porch. It was*
*bloody.* [B]

The court's record adds only that Barber said he saw "tracks
in corn field." [D] Nothing about the axes. Since the use of the map
was reported, physical evidence would likely have been reported
as well, if there had been any. The *Landmark* briefly summed up Phillip Lyerly's and
Filmore Cook's testimonies. Lyerly indicated that "the lamp
which was found, in his opinion, belonged to the negro church
about one-fourth of a mile away." This Lyerly is listed as
"colored" in the court records, which also uses the word
"colored" instead of "negro" to describe the church. According
to Sherril's record, Cook said he lived one-half or three-fourths
mile from the Lyerly home.

The next testimony, the most important given at any time
during this case, was omitted from the *Landmark* and every other
newspaper. This was the man whose testimony was only
mentioned, without details, in July, and only by John Moose
Julian, when he covered Solicitor Hammer's investigation. Julian
had said that Emanuel, or Mann, Walton's testimony was heard
that day but not recorded with the others, and he would explain
later. Perhaps that was because it would have made liars of
almost everybody who'd made assumptions about the case.
Walton was the man to whom Henry Mayhew supposedly went,
first thing, after being told the Lyerlys had been killed. Mayhew,
it was said more than once, told Walton that morning that his
"Pa" and the rest of the accused had murdered the Lyerlys. But
this day in court, E.A. Walton, under oath, said no such thing—
at least according to Sherrill's report, the only source that even
mentioned his *presence* in court that day. This is all she
recorded:

*"Henry Mayhew came to my field about nine o'clock*
*next morning after killing. He went to house with John.*
*They went off together in direction of Barber Junction."*
[D]

Certainly if Walton had said anything that defended what the
papers had dramatized for two months on front pages all over the

country, the *N&O* would have broadcast it in huge type. Walton made frauds out of them all, with testimony showing that much of Henry's "confession" was a fabrication, if not all of it. Furthermore, it indicated that John Gillespie had been at Walton's house that morning, and perhaps all night, what Fannie told Hammer on July 20th. From Walton's testimony, it appears that Mayhew had come to his house looking for John to tell him what had happened. Perhaps he came to tell him that maybe they should get away before they ended up at the end of a noose. Walton may have said so this day, but nobody recorded it if he did. It could no longer save John's life anyway, as it might have earlier, if the papers had printed it. Walton said nothing to corroborate Henry's famous "confession."

Despite the obvious impact of Walton's testimony, Hammer didn't quit. He must have sprung to his feet enthusiastically to introduce his star witness. He confidently stated that he intended to prove "the story of the killing" was told to Mayhew "by his grandfather, Nease Gillespie, and his uncle, John Gillespie, on the night of the murder." Mayhew would show, Hammer assured the court, "that by their story they implicated the prisoners now on trial." But Nease Gillespie was dead, and there would be no corroboration of Henry's statement from him.

Newell and Williams, acutely aware that Hammer had no leg to stand on, objected to the introduction of Henry Mayhew's testimony. Then "the jury retired while the competency of this evidence was being discussed." [B] The *N&O* elaborated, saying "The jury and the boy were taken from the court room and the solicitor told the court about what the evidence of the boy would be, how Nease Gillespie had confessed the crime before he was lynched, etc., and it was decided by Judge Moore, the solicitor and the defense that all this evidence was now incompetent, Nease being deceased." [E] When the reporter mentioned Nease's "confession," it referred to what he allegedly said on the night of the murder, not anything said under duress from the mob, though it might have been taken that way by the reader.

The court records end here. Sherrill wrote Henry Mayhew's name, followed by a colon, as the last entry on her list of witnesses and testimonies, and then the rest of the page was left blank. The court had not allowed Mayhew's testimony. The

*Observer* and the *N&O* both explained that the lynching of Nease and John Gillespie had rendered it incompetent.

Then Hammer said he thought he could find more witnesses, but he was pretending. And the judge played along to give the prisoners time to get out of town, presumably, before most of the crowd realized they'd already been acquitted. After Hammer's "request" was granted, court adjourned until the next morning. "Up to this time nothing whatever had developed connecting Henry Gillespie and Geo. Erwin with the murder," the *Landmark* added. [B]

This report, which didn't run until the following day, explained what was really going on. Hammer had known at that point that the case was over, "but it was thought best not to turn the negroes loose then." So the defendants were sent back to jail and the jury held until the following morning. [B]

"Soon after dark," on Wednesday,

> *officers took the three prisoners—the Dillingham woman being accompanied by a child two or three years old—to the south side of town and told them to go. They were given a small amount of money, but they said they preferred to walk out of town rather than ride on a train. It is understood that they went toward Asheville. They didn't want to go back to Rowan.* [B]

Evidently, no one told Della she was entitled to more than a small amount of money from Rowan County for failing to protect her husband from the lynch mob. It would have come in handy at the moment.

In its follow-up of the trial, the *Raleigh N&O* continued to convict those who were now acquitted. Was Daniels trying to get the released prisoners lynched, or just trying to defend the irresponsible stand his paper had taken throughout the ordeal, or both? It said Hammer had "...known all along that his case against the surviving negroes was weak, but he felt sure, as does the court, that the negroes were implicated and might possibly be convicted. [E] This paper never admitted its reporting errors or gave any attention to the case for the prisoners' innocence. Certainly all the reporters could understand the implications of Walton's inability to corroborate Henry's story, but they didn't mention what he had to say, before or after the lynching. And it's unlikely that Judge Moore, referred to in Daniels' paper as "the court" would have tainted the proceedings and his reputation by indicating to Hammer or to the *N&O* that he was convinced of the now acquitted suspects' guilt. This "opinion of the court" was not mentioned in any other paper except Daniels'. The *N&O* also reiterated that Hammer had discussed that day how "Nease Gillespie had confessed the crime before he was lynched," [E] implying he confessed it to the mob. And, again, there was no mention of this in the *Landmark*, the *Watchman*, or the *Observer*. Within months of provoking one lynching, was Daniels trying to incite another?

Though Daniels was the only one putting words into Judge Moore's mouth, he wasn't alone in his continued condemnation of these newly-freed citizens. Having just exposed the holes in the Prosecution's case, the *Landmark* also closed its report with condemnation of the defendants. It even attacked Fannie, who had not even been accused. "While it is generally believed that the Dillingham woman and Fan Gillespie, and possibly the others, were implicated in the murder," said the Landmark, "evidence sufficient to secure an indictment against Fan could not be procured."

Despite the admitted lack of evidence, the paper's attack on her continued:

> She is a notoriously mean negro. The truth is, when the mob lynched Nease and John Gillespie and Jack Dillingham at Salisbury last summer the evidence died with them. Had all the defendants been brought to trial the State was satisfied that sufficient evidence could have been secured from the three named to convict all of the defendants and possibly to implicate Fan Gillespie." [B]

Why did the reporter believe the State could have procured this information, when torture had not, officially, wrung a confession out of any of them, including fifteen-year-old John?

With the prisoners now released, court re-adjourned on Thursday and formally finalized the case against Henry, George, and Della. The *Landmark* said the "jury was instructed to render a verdict of not guilty, and thus ended the famous case." [B] The report of the climactic outcome of this "famous case" was hidden on a back page of the newspaper. There were no huge headlines anywhere broadcasting the actual acquittal.

There may have been a noble reason for downplaying the acquittal—the released prisoners' safety may have depended upon it. But, by the time the *Landmark* and the *Observer* reported the outcome, Daniels had already canceled out any good the other papers might have been attempting. The *N&O* warned any would-be lynchers ahead of time that the three remaining suspects would likely be released, and the announcement was placed right in the center of its January 31$^{st}$ (Wednesday's) front page. "Acquittal is Certain," it blared boldly in all caps, and yet presumed, again, that there was evidence against all three: "Evidence Raises a Suspicion of Their Guilt, But Does Not Connect Them With the Crime." It was the very thing that made would-be lynchers' blood boil—that guilty *blacks* might go free on a legal technicality—the reason most gave for supporting lynching. But no such protest was reported after Cress's and Gentle's acquittals.

Before finishing with Della, George, and Henry, the press, in general, trivialized their ordeal and may have further jeopardized their safety. Instead of exposing the errors that led to their six-month nightmare, either the officers or the papers or both made a joke of their release, disclosing their intended destination. The *Carolina Watchman* wrote that they were advised by the officers "to set sail for South Carolina. When released, however, the three negroes chose a different route and the last time they were seen they were hustling up the railroad on foot bound presumably for Asheville." [F] Solicitor Hammer, who knew the most about this case, also didn't publicize Walton's testimony. Instead, his own paper, the *Courier*, said that when the three asked the officers for advice as to where they should go, they were told to "go back to Africa." [G]

Concluding its report on the story, the *Landmark* discussed the previous day's decisions, adding Hammer's thoughts on the case. Speaking for the Solicitor, the paper said, despite the weakness of the case, the solicitor had "hoped something might transpire to strengthen it. When the evidence of Henry Mayhew as to the confession of Nease and John Gillespie was ruled out as incompetent, the last vestige of evidence had disappeared. The only evidence against any of the defendants was that the

Dillingham woman and Mrs. Lyerly had quarreled the day before the murder." [B] No one replayed Della's opinion about that incident.

This same report told exclusively what had become of Fannie Gillespie and Henry Mayhew while the three surviving defendants in the Lyerly case were awaiting trial. It confirmed that Fannie Gillespie and Henry Mayhew had been in the Mecklenburg jail the whole time. "They were turned loose yesterday," noted the paper. [B] It didn't say if they were given any money or where they were released, but by 1910, Fannie, now Fannie Steele, was living in Statesville with Henry Mayhew. Census records show she was married at the time, but no husband was listed. Instead she was shown as head of that household and a home owner. Had Fannie secretly received compensation from Rowan County because of Nease's lynching?

Inconspicuously placed on page four was the *Observer's* announcement of the acquittal, under the heading, "The Negroes Liberated." This report, like all the others, implied that the outcome of the trial would have been different if the lynching had not occurred. There was no use of "allegedly" in its continued assertion that Henry Mayhew "heard the discussion of the murder between John and Nease Gillespie." And it assumed the testimony was now considered incompetent, *only* "because the men are deceased." [C] Again, Walton's testimony was ignored.

The *Observer's* version of the release presented the officers in a more compassionate light, though who knows what really happened? "It was decided to quietly free the defendants at night, the report said, and "let them get out of this section as soon as possible." Money was raised for railroad tickets but the three said they preferred to "leave by foot and take the money in hand." Deputy Deaton then took them to the south side of town and "told [them] to look out for themselves." [C] The report said Hammer explained that the case had been weak since the lynching, but the Rowan people were willing to bear the cost of an investigation and "...he had devoted much time to the case and did all in his power to try to get at the negroes not lynched." [C] This the Solicitor certainly did, apparently ignoring any other leads, as well as the case for their innocence.

The *Watchman* made Hammer look even worse. It said it was thought that the trial was held "more for the purpose of quieting the sentiment that the negroes might have been implicated than anything else." [F] In other words these two men and a new mother were kept in prison to placate the mob, despite the fact that there was no evidence against them, and Hammer knew it as soon as the lynching occurred, maybe earlier. According to the *Observer*, Hammer said the case so far had cost Rowan County $4,000, not counting the cost of the trial at Statesville. No speculation was made about the cost to the accused. If the surviving relatives of the lynching victims had not been black and had access to an equitable legal system, it would have cost Rowan County far more than $4,000.

There was no other mention of the Mecklenburg jail inmates who had allegedly overheard Jack Dillingham confess to the murders, ruling out all the other defendants and implicating Jim Taylor. However, had they been brought to Statesville as witnesses, their testimony probably would have been deemed incompetent due to Jack Dillingham's death, or simply because they had African blood.

It was a miracle that Henry, George, and Della survived—if they did. There's no assurance that the Judge's scheme worked as planned. With the papers continuing to find them guilty, even after their acquittal, the group may have been targeted. Walking, they may not have gotten far.

TRAIN BY THE FRENCH BROAD RIVER, ASHEVILLE

About forty years later, Joseph Lyerly's son, Earl, told my
aunt that Della Dillingham had been pregnant when she was
pushed off a train into the French Broad River in Asheville.
Years after that, Earl was hit and killed by a train on Barringer
Road.

# BOOK THREE

## ORIGINAL SIN

SLAVE TRADERS

# 24

# TO HEAVEN WHEN I DIE

## JUNE & JULY, 1902

*A lie can travel half way around the world, while the truth is still putting on its shoes.*

— Mark Twain

BENSON FAMILY, CIRCA 1898: WILL AND CORNELIA,
SECOND AND THIRD FROM RIGHT

# INTRODUCTION

*A Girl Murdered: Supposed That an Outrage Was Committed.*
*Raleigh News and Observer, 10 June 1902.*

*Woman Outraged and Killed: Double Crime in Rowan County.*
*Charlotte Observer, 10 June 1902.*

If Karl Marx was right—that history repeats itself first as a tragedy and then as a farce—then Salisbury's real tragedy happened in 1902. Documentation of the events of 1902 was far less widespread compared to 1906, nevertheless, the local press covered the story from beginning to end, and then closed the book on it until 1957, when the *Post* printed a recap. Even so, Salisbury has yet to face all the facts of this heart-wrenching tragedy.

The first victim, Cornelia Benson, was not a girl. She was twenty-seven years old. And, contrary to what the initial headlines said, she was not outraged (raped). But once this lie got out, there was no hope for the two Gillespie boys, eleven and thirteen years old, blamed for her death.

In 1902 North Carolina was still reeling from a second vicious and concerted attack on blacks by the press, again led by Josephus Daniels. The first, in 1898, was launched to regain control of the state from the Populists, and the second, in 1900, sealed the deal. Cartoonist Norman Jennett, living then in New York, had returned to assist Daniels in his aim to convince whites to legalize the disfranchisement of most black North Carolinians. His dehumanizing images of black folk were still fresh in the minds of North Carolinians when Cornelia's body was found.

# Part One

William Alexander Benson was one of the all-white jurors selected in 1906 to help decide the fate of the Lyerly murder suspects. Benson was from the Scotch Irish Township of Rowan County, located between the two small communities of Woodleaf and Mt. Vernon, just a few miles northwest of Isaac Lyerly's property. Four years earlier, he was living with his wife and two young sons on his farm on Cool Springs Road, when his own family tragedy occurred—the accidental death, or murder, of his sister Cornelia.

The farm had been the home of Will's parents, Samuel and Nancy Benson, and the home where he and Cornelia had grown up. Having died two years earlier, Samuel was the only family member gone in 1902; Will's mother and sister remained in the old house with Will and his wife and kids. They all worked on the farm and kept it running and the fields productive, with the help of tenant farmers like Stokes Cowan.

Stokes, born in 1865, also grew up in Rowan County. His parents, Henry and Jane, had likely been slaves, and Stokes probably inherited his surname from one of the prominent white Cowan families that had been in the county as long as the Barringers and Lyerlys. Stokes, the oldest of eight children, was raised in the same neighborhood as the Bensons, not far from where Nease and Fannie Gillespie grew up. Though the Gillespies were a few years older than Stokes, they had to have at least been acquainted with each other. Most of the "colored" folk in that area probably attended Cedar Grove A.M.E. Zion Church, established not long after the end of the Civil War. It remains, housed in a newer structure, near Barber Junction today. Its present congregation welcomed me warmly a few years ago when I showed up there looking for Nease Gillespie's descendants.

Some time between 1890 and 1900, Stokes Cowan married Anna Gillespie, who he'd probably known most of his life. In 1880 Anna lived with her parents, Samuel and Maria, and several siblings in Stokes' neighborhood. By 1900 Stokes, Anna, and her sister, Sarah Gillespie, all lived in the same household, along with two boys, James and Harrison Gillespie. [A] Whatever their relationship to Stokes, Gillespie is the last name all the news reports gave both boys, even though Harrison was listed as Stokes' son in the census records and James as his nephew. James was probably Sarah's son, and Harrison was likely Anna's, and, according to the press, the younger boy, James, was the uncle of the older. Their ages in 1902 were eleven and thirteen. Sarah's three-year-old daughter, Susanne Gillespie, also lived with Stokes, Anna, and the rest in that one tenant house.

In June, 1902 the press was speculating about the relationship between James and Harrison because, like the other Gillespies in 1906, they had just made front page headlines on papers across the country. They were accused of raping and killing Will Benson's sister, Cornelia, and before the press could correct these headlined assumptions, James and Harrison were photographed hanging from an oak tree in Henderson Park, on the outskirts of Salisbury. Neither Joseph Caldwell nor Josephus Daniels apologized for their papers'
fatal errors when they corrected their accounts the next day—when it was too late. Even then, they both perpetuated a gross distortion of what actually happened after Cornelia's dead body was discovered. How she died may never be known for sure, because, as with the 1906 case, nobody seemed to suspect anyone other than the African descendants who lived closest to the home of the victim.

CORNELIA BENSON

Most sources, however, agree about what happened just before Cornelia's death on June 9th. Will's wife, Laura Benson, retold that story in 1957 to the *Salisbury Post*.

The Benson place still sits atop a rather steep hill, with corn fields in front and in back of it, both bordered by woods and streams, the one in the rear a bit farther from the house than the one in front. Cornelia, or Neely, was said to be hoeing corn in the bottom land near the branch when tragedy struck. She must have been working near the stream in back, because a descendant of Will's said the site was "quite aways, about a quarter mile" from the house. The corn would have been no more than six or so inches high at the time, says my mother, who grew up nearby, because, she says, "you don't hoe corn after it gets much taller." Laura Benson said she wasn't working in the fields along with Cornelia because her hands were full, taking care of the housework and her kids.

All of the family ate lunch together that day. After lunch, as Cornelia started back to the fields, her mother, Nancy, told her "she would come down to the branch bottom later in the afternoon and bring some fresh water." Nancy planned to take the cow with her and stake it to graze.

While Cornelia was working in the bottom land, her brother was "plowing the field near the house, opposite the barn." And this is what Laura remembers next.

> "As I was washing up the dishes from the noon meal, Ed Dickey walked through the yard going toward the Cowan house. Dickey was Cowan's half brother.
>
> "Mother Benson found Cornelia bloody and dead in a ditch where the murderers had dragged her. She set up an outcry and ran back up the hill and called to William. This was about 2 or 2:30 in the afternoon. William sent our Sammy [their older child] to the home of Jack Benson, William's uncle. Jack sent for the officers at Salisbury. [A]

As soon as the *Charlotte Observer* got wind of the story, it rushed to print the article that assumed Cornelia had been raped, which was equal to sending out an invitation to the mob to lynch whoever it guessed was responsible. The headline stated outright that she had been raped, though the report itself admitted: "No examination of the remains had been made up to the time the information reached the city...." Citing a downed phone line to Woodleaf as a reason for not having all the known details of the murder, the report, nevertheless, assumed it appeared "certain that two crimes were committed." [C]

The June 10th *N&O* did the same damned thing: "No particulars of the murder have been received," it said, "but it is supposed that an outrage was committed...." [B] Not only that, it downplayed the age of the victim, calling her a girl, then later exaggerated the ages of the suspects by several years.

The *Statesville Landmark* was one of several papers to report Sheriff Julian's receipt of a telegram "asking for bloodhounds," the same request he got four years later. The response was the same both times: "...it was impossible to secure them either here or in adjoining towns." General Superintendent Sands, of Southern Railway, had even offered to stop train No. 29 at Thomasville to take on the dogs there, but he was told those bloodhounds were sick. [D] Four years later, the bloodhound situation hadn't improved. It was as if the 1902 case set the precedent for how the Lyerly murder investigation would be conducted. Instead of sending bloodhounds in 1902, the sheriff dispatched from Salisbury Deputies Rice and Julian by buggy and Deputy Hodge Krider from Barber Junction. [C] A gang of armed men followed.

Unbeknownst to a correspondent reporting from Mooresville, a consensus among officers at the murder scene that night had already placed blame on the young Gillespie boys, just as the Mooresville writer was sending out reports that "...a suspicious character in the neighborhood of Woodleaf was under surveillance as a suspect." [C] So, the "suspicious character" was not mentioned again. Though the boys never got a trial, and there was no formal investigation of the murder, the *Observer*'s Salisbury correspondent concluded, on June 10th, that the murderers were "known" to have been James and Harrison Gillespie. [E]

There was no *Salisbury Post* in 1902, so the *Sun* offered the town's most complete summary of what was believed to have happened after Nancy discovered Cornelia's body. It said when she finished driving the cows to pasture, she headed down to where Cornelia was hoeing but couldn't find her. Not having considered the possibility of murder, she was shocked to finally find her daughter lying in a ditch, her face "covered with blood" and her brains "oozing out." [D] Seeing Cornelia in this condition,

> *Mrs. Benson, in agony of mind, ran to the house and told in broken sentences of the tragedy. The news quickly spread and every citizen of that sturdy, conservative Scotch-Irish settlement was on the alert in search of the perpetrators of the crime.*
>
> *When the officers and citizens arrived on the spot where the crime had been committed they began*

*searching for a clue. The ground had been freshly broken and footprints were distinct on the sod. Suspicion pointed to Harris and James Gillespie, two negro boys, and they were immediately taken to the spot. Their footprints fitted exactly in the impressions left on the ground and they were taken in charge by the officers and brought to Salisbury.* [D]

The 1957 account of the actual arrest might have come from Laura's recollection, because none of the original news sources available today carried it. Whatever the origin, the report said "Deputy Sheriff Krider wasted no time in arresting the two boys...." and he "tied them up which was in the manner and custom of that day."

*Then Ann Cowan shouted her protest. Next she called to her husband: "Stokes, he's tying up these boys. You tell him he ain't got no right to tie 'um up."*

*Stokes Cowan came running and said: "Mr. Krider, you got any right to tie 'um up?"*

*Deputy Krider's voice was scarcely audible, nor did he look up from his task when he answered: "Oh yes, oh yes."* [A]

After being bound, the boys were carried in separate conveyances to the Rowan County Jail in Salisbury. Maybe Krider had a right to tie them up, but there was no justification for what happened afterward.

*On their way here they were followed by about 50 Salisburians, who had left this city immediately on receipt of the news of the murder, armed to the teeth. No attempt was made to injure the prisoners, but the frequent discharge of firearms so terrified the older of the two that he volunteered a confession to Deputy Julian. The officers reached Salisbury about 12 o'clock and landed their prisoners safely in jail.* [D]

The following versions explain how the officers arrived at the conclusion of guilt, thereafter printed as fact. First was the *Observer's*:

> *When the officers arrived on the scene last night and joined the citizens already engaged in endeavoring to find a clue to the murderers, they were for some time at a loss. But when Dr. Henderson, of Woodleaf, who had been summoned to examine the remains, announced his conclusion that there had been no attempt made to commit a criminal assault, suspicion began to be directed toward Harrison and James Gillespie, two negro boys, who lived a quarter of a mile from the Benson place. It was recalled, among other circumstances, that these boys had had difficulties with the Bensons, especially the deceased and her brother, Mr. Will Benson, because of thieving habits, of which the Bensons were the principal sufferers, and that they had been seen going into the bottom where the killing occurred, about the time the crime was committed.* [E]

The 1957 version said "a crowd was gathering" at the scene *before* the officers arrived, which was also *before* the medical exam that turned their attention toward the two young boys. [A]

Once the officers convinced themselves of the validity of the presumed scenario, they created the rest of the story that came to be known as the "facts" surrounding Cornelia Benson's murder. This version was printed in the *Sun*.

> *The officers say that a stone with blood on it was found about forty feet from the spot where the body had been taken and that near by was discovered a dozen or more stones where the unfortunate woman had been beaten to death. After killing her the boys had carried her dead body to the gully near by and carelessly thrown it in. Her skull was crushed in several places and her brains were oozing out when she was found....*
>
> *...the boys were involved in words with the young woman. It is believed, however, that improper*

*suggestions were made and resented, culminating in the deadly assault of the two boys.* [D]

Theo F. Kluttz, Jr, the Congressman's son and Caldwell's nephew, was the *Observer's* Salisbury correspondent at the time.

THEODORE F. KLUTTZ,

He wrote about the incident like he'd been at the murder scene himself, though he indicated he got his information second-hand from one of the deputies. If he *had* been on the scene, he would have known no rape was involved, and the headline condemning the boys *might* not have been printed. Kluttz's report, and the *Post* article written 55 years later, both failed to disclose who it was who "saw" the boys going into or coming out of the area where Cornelia was working. Kluttz said, again as though he'd seen them himself, it was "evident that the tracks about the body were those of the two boys. The surface of the ground being wet, the tracks were well marked and the boys' feet fitted them exactly." [E] This conflicted with the *Sun* report that said tracks were evident because the ground had been recently hoed, and it's unlikely Cornelia would be out hoeing in the rain or muddy ground.

Furthermore, Kluttz said the officers *arrived* at night. So how were they able to see well enough to properly judge how well the tracks fit the boys' feet? And, how many others had been walking around the area between 2:30 that afternoon and later that night, when the footprints were supposedly inspected?

The *Sun's* and Kluttz's reports clearly conflicted on other points. The *Sun* claimed Harrison's "confession" was "volunteered," but Kluttz offered another explanation. He said the boys had been "terrified at the fusillade on the road" on their way to Salisbury after the arrest. "In the most abject terror

Harrison Gillespie, the older boy, confessed his guilt and begged the officer who held him in charge to save him from being lynched." [E] Kluttz said he had interviewed one of the deputies the following morning about the incident.

The *Sun* praised the "coolness and soberness of the people who were present when the two boys were captured," and how this alleged restraint "prevented any demonstration." [D] But Kluttz got a completely different story. The deputy he interviewed told him "…it would not be the least exaggeration to state that 1,500 shots were fired into the air about them on the way, mostly by 30 or 40 people from Salisbury who went armed to assist in the search." [E]

It appears the press, in general, tried to justify backing the officers' guilt theory by exaggerating the boys' ages and emphasizing Harrison's "muscular build." Almost all the papers consistently recorded Harrison's age as sixteen or seventeen and James', fourteen or fifteen. Only the *Sun* said James appeared to be "hardly more than 11 years old," then exaggerated Harrison's age by two years. Kluttz described Harrison as "a well grown, muscular boy and quite capable of committing the crime," while disclosing that James was "probably within the 14 years of age limit of legal presumptive innocence."

It may have been the boys' youth, after all, that sealed their fate. The crowd that lynched these boys was believed to have come predominantly or partially from Benson's and Cowan's neighborhood, where the people would have known that both were too young to face the death penalty.

The *Sun* and the *Observer* agreed that James insisted on his innocence. Yet both assumed he was lying. When a *Sun* reporter visited the jail the morning after the boys were locked up, James, "between sobs, declared he had nothing to do with the murder of Miss Benson. 'I was at home nursing the baby,' he said." [C] Kluttz said while James was being carried to Salisbury, separated from Harrison, he told the officers "Harrison had committed the crime alone and had come to the house, where he had remained with his baby sister, and told him of having done so." [E] When Kluttz visited the boys in jail, he said Harrison outlined the details of *both* of the boys' involvement. "Harrison says that he and James each threw a rock at Miss Benson, both striking her. He says that after this she walked off, not badly hurt, and he and

James went home." Kluttz explained that the boys were confined in separate cells, across the hall from each other and could hear what the other was saying. "As the writer questioned one of the prisoners the other would enter vehement contradictions of his story.... [E]

Throughout its coverage, the press failed to consider any option besides murder as the cause of Cornelia's death—or any scenario other than the officers' guess as to how it occurred. It was, after all, all speculation.

So why limit it to the Gillespie boys' involvement? Why not consider Cornelia's brother as a suspect? What stopped him from taking a break from plowing his field to come up from behind his sister and hit her on the back of the head? After all, he apparently had the most to gain, financially, from her demise. Already considered a spinster by the day's standards, Cornelia may have had no plans to marry. In that case, she'd surely be expecting her share of the estate as soon as her mother died. That would mean Will might either have to buy her out or sell the place, unless she was eliminated. That theory, however, doesn't fit with what I learned from Will Benson's descendant—one who asked me to withhold his name. He told me that Will had to have someone come and plow up the blood-stained ground where Cornelia had lain. He had been too overcome by grief to do it himself.

But there were other possibilities. Since there was no indication that Cornelia was engaged, perhaps she had rejected any number of proposals. This kind of thing often didn't go over well with male egos at that time, judging by news reports of the day. It wasn't uncommon to see stories about young men who killed their objects of desire, their families, and themselves, in these kinds of situations.

It's possible that one or both of the boys were throwing rocks and saw one hit Cornelia in the head so hard she began to stumble and fall. It would not have been safe for them to just run away and leave things as they were, that is, if Cornelia saw who did it. Given the times and the climate of racial hatred, the boys, or at least the older one, probably knew that *any* harm a black boy caused a white woman would certainly result in a lynching or a sentence spending the rest of his youth on the chain gang. Nearly every parent of African descent living in the South from the 1890s to more than a half decade later, sat her sons down and gave them "the talk" early on— "you never touch a white woman, and you never even look her in the eye, or you can be lynched," she would say, or something to that effect. Current Supreme Court Justice Clarence Thomas told "60 Minutes" interviewer, Steve Croft, how his grandfather had given him that very warning as soon as he was old enough to understand. Any hint of an assault on a white woman would be classified as outrage or rape. The only way the Gillespie boys could have escaped, under these circumstances, would have been to finish Cornelia off. So perhaps they or Harrison did just that. If not in this case, certainly in other situations during Jim Crow rule, murder became more common out of necessity than it would have under normal circumstances— because blacks had no legal recourse or protection.

Just as likely, one or both of the boys had indeed thrown a rock at Cornelia, and that one blow to her head caused her to slip on what one report described as wet ground, which was very near to the branch where she was hoeing. As she stumbled or slipped, she fell down the bank and into the stream, with its slippery stones, hitting her head and splitting it open upon a larger rock. Or maybe Cornelia stumbled, herself, and slid downhill into the ditch where her mother found her dead body.

Of course this is all guesswork. But so was the officers' theory about what happened. And nobody today would put any stock in a confession taken from two frightened boys, surrounded by a gang of pistol-toting, shotgun-firing rednecks.

Whatever happened, the press didn't stretch its analysis or investigation beyond the officers' assumptions; it seemed interested only in supporting them. Despite his disclosure about the circumstances surrounding the "confession," Kluttz was one of several reporters who went into white-supremacist mode to maintain the myth. He put it this way:

> *The theory of the crime formulated by the officers is as follows: The two boys were passing through the field where Miss Benson was working and were spoken to sharply by her about trespassing on the farm. One of them, thereupon, threw a rock, knocking her down. Then the two little fiends, in access of brute ferocity, attacked her with rocks, knocking her down again after she had risen and attempted to escape, and pounded her face and*

*head into a pulp with rocks held in their hands. Near the*
*body half a dozen bloody rocks were found.* [E]

Benson's neighbors, Kluttz pointed out, were already angry
over another situation. Recently there had been an alleged
outrage upon another neighbor, Mrs. Belle Livengood, and two
black men were scheduled to hang for it. However, the
possibility of a pardon for one of them was in the works, and
nothing besides the suspicion of black on white rape made white
southerners more angry than a black man being pardoned for
anything. Never mind that many white men were never even
arrested for committing the same offense. The existence of a
large population of mulattos in the area (and it was unusually
large there) provided substantial proof of those offenses.

With all the publicity stacking the deck against the boys, and
with two papers' assumption of rape already irretrievably out
there, it's no wonder James and Harrison were lynched before
anyone could find out the truth. Afterward, few seemed to care.

The only known account of the 1902 Salisbury lynching was
written by Theo Kluttz, Jr., reporting on June 11, 1902. The
same story was reprinted in Statesville's *Ledger* and probably
other state papers. The *Sun's* coverage is missing from the
filmed archives, and there is no *Sun* office morgue to search. The
*Observer* noted that the report resulted from "...the untiring
efforts" of their "wide-awake Salisbury correspondent, Mr.
Theodore F. Kluttz, Jr., who sat up all night with the tragic
occurrence." His story of that night's deviltry sounds all too
familiar.

It was, after all, the same old game, practice for the one
played in 1906. The mayor pleaded in vain with the mob leaders
to go home and let the law take its course—the same mayor that
twice begged the mob to disperse in 1906. Hodge Krider, as in
1906, was "guarding" the jail when it was overtaken by the mob
leaders. The same sheriff and his deputy son were in office,
though it's not clear where they were on this night. This time
things happened too fast for a judge or term of court to be called.
Perhaps only the governor was a different player in 1902. This
time the revered "education governor" Aycock, who had used his
eloquent voice to help Joe Daniels crown Jim Crow in North
Carolina, sent a telegram about midnight, authorizing the use of

the military company." <sup>E</sup> In 1906, not one paper openly discussed the eerie parallels between the two lynchings.

Judging by his description, Kluttz must have witnessed the 1902 events from beginning to end. Early on the night of June 10<sup>th</sup> he noted the "presence of a number of young people from Mt. Vernon" on the streets. But, he said, no one expected "...they would proceed to take any violent steps." <sup>E</sup> Some time later, Kluttz said, Mayor Boyden confronted several "masked" men, heading toward the jail.

> *Mayor Boyden met the men and endeavored to persuade them from their purpose, but without result. They entered the jail and proceeded to break down the doors of the building. The officers suspecting such an attack, had concealed the negroes in the attic of the jail, but the mob with scarcely any hesitation, dragged them from their place of concealment, carried them out to Main street, crossed over to the right of way of the North Carolina Railroad and a short distance from the city limits hanged them to a tree. The older one, Harrison Gillespie, was dragged up with a rope around the neck. The younger one, James Gillespie, was made to climb the tree and leap. He wept just before being made to jump, which was the only evidence of emotion by either.*
> *After the hanging the bodies were riddled with bullets....*
> *They then, after making sure of death by applying lighted splinters to the extremities, broke up quietly, leaving the bodies hanging on the trees.* <sup>E</sup>

The almost immediate discovery of the hiding place is suspicious, especially in light of Krider's later testimony at the trial of one alleged lyncher. The deputy reportedly stated under oath that he had received a call at the jail earlier in the day from residents of the Woodleaf area asking to see the prisoners, and yet he had not read anything into that phone call concerning the safety of the boys. Someone in the mob must have had inside knowledge about where they were hidden.

Before the lynchers took over the jail, the officers and military were fooled into thinking the trouble was all over.

Governor Aycock had called out the military, but soon afterward, "everything seemed to grow quiet and the military was disbanded." [E] That calm, however, had been like the eye of a hurricane. The back side of the storm soon blew in with a vengeance, just as it did in 1906, when, by then, they all should have known better.

Kluttz didn't say for sure when the mayor confronted those "masked" men, whether it was before or after the military company disbanded. He said only that shots were fired from the jail after "Mayor Boyden's vain appeal to the mob," and it was assumed this was some kind of signal to the others. Immediately after the gunfire, "a hundred men came from the direction of the passenger station, having previously assembled in the old J. D. Lanier canning factory, a large building." [E]

> *About half of these were masked. The masked men, about 50 in all, were the only ones who took active steps in the lynching. Other men joined the mob coming from different directions. Attracted by the firing, a large crowd had assembled by this time, which was just 20 minutes till 2 o'clock.* [E]

Kluttz never referred to the lynchers as criminals or in any other degrading way. But, he made a point to convict the two young black boys as "murderers" several times within his account of *their* murder by this pack of white cowards. Damning descriptions of these two defenseless children mingled with the reporter's words, even as they were being terrorized: "The two terrified little criminals were taken from the jail, placed in a carriage and driven rapidly down the street, the crowd following and firing as it went."

Josephus Daniels may have driven Raleigh and eastern North Carolina into the depths of sin in 1898, but the night of June 10, 1902 was the beginning of Salisbury's decent into hell.

And some of the details behind this wickedness are yet to surface. Before the lynching trial unearthed them, little more about this tragedy was revealed. Kluttz added only that the mob headed toward the lynching site with its victims, not realizing a light was needed. The problem was resolved, he explained, when a few members of the mob secured a torch from one of the yard engines. Since the lynching was carried out at the north end of the railroad yard, it served as a form of entertainment for some of the railroad crews who backed up two of the large engines so their workers could watch the torture. [E]

The 1957 account revealed a few more details, with only a slight change in tone. The boys were not called criminals or fiends or described as capable of brute force in the text of the article. They were described only as the "murderers of Cornelia Benson" in the caption of the lynching photo documenting their own murders. James was said to be "little more than a child," though he was *only* a child, period. In 1957, there was no discussion of presumption of innocence either.

This account more closely defined the route of the march and site of the lynching. It said the "mob carried the terrified boys up Main Street and crossed the railroad near the Cartex Mill, and the Gillespies were hung from the limbs of an oak off Long Street. [A] This would put the site very close to the one used in 1906, if not the very same tree.

1902 LYNCHING OF JAMES AND HARRISON GILLESPIE

The next morning, Salisbury's Tuesday night sin was exposed for outsiders to see and scorn. "Passengers on the four early trains crowded to the windows and steps to get a view of the bodies hanging...near the track, on the north extremity of the railroad yard."

> *The trains pass this point with diminished speed and a good view was afforded. Doubtless passengers on the three through trains from the North were highly edified at the exhibition. The scene of the hanging is only about*

*200 yards in the rear of Hon. John S. Henderson's*
*residence and just beyond the corporate limits.* ᶠ

Kluttz concluded his coverage of the lynching with the usual disclaimer. Although the "occurrence was deeply felt by the citizens of Salisbury," he said, it was at least a "satisfaction" that no men from Salisbury were known to be in the mob. Unlike the press in 1906, Kluttz didn't rule out Rowan County altogether. He said it was "known" that a number in the mob came from the eastern part of the county, far from where the Bensons lived, but

he didn't say who knew it or if they planned to testify to what they knew. Reports in other papers contradicted Kluttz, stating the "boys were hung by about fifty men from the vicinity of the crime...," a number of those from the Mt. Vernon and Unity section of the county..., the Bensons' and Lyerlys' neighborhoods. F, F1

The Benson descendant I talked to named one of the lynchers—Will Wetmore of Woodleaf. He was certain of it, he said over his wife's "Are you sure's?" Pictured in the *Post's* recap of the story, Wetmore points out the spot where Cornelia was found.

WILL WETMORE, ALLEGED LYNCHER, POINTS OUT SITE WHERE CORNELIA'S BODY WAS FOUND

After publishing one of the most damning headlines about Cornelia's death, one that certainly helped lynch James and Harrison, Daniels took the moral high road, or at least pretended to. His paper assumed a familiar role, with its mixed messages, condemning the lynching and finding and convicting the lynchers.

The *N&O* was more than complimentary of Governor Aycock's response. Aycock was governor, partly because Daniels had arranged it, and the *N&O* consistently made Aycock look good. Its June 19<sup>th</sup> edition headlined the Governor's reward offer in one-inch bold letters: "GOVERNOR AYCOCK OFFERS $30,000 FOR LYNCHERS." Actually the offer was $400 for each of the suspected 75 participants, and the paper did the math, noting it was "an entirely unprecedented sum for the chief executive to offer, and it looks as if he were determined to do everything to the uttermost to arrest those who flagrantly disregarded law and order." [G]

Even so, the *N&O* published letters by some who weren't impressed with Aycock's offer, perhaps because those letters fit in so well with the rest of the paper's agenda. W.C. Munroe of Goldsboro, Daniels' birthplace, tempered his criticism with praise of Aycock as a "great" and "good" man and "wise governor," just doing his duty, but also stated bluntly that "no body expects the lynchers to be punished." He said "the penalty due to their crime is death, and those seventy-five of the best citizens of Rowan, hung in a line would be a notable and most unexpected spectacle." The "powers of no governor, king nor potentate is sufficient to correct this evil...," he added. The trouble, he said, lay "in the people and in the laws themselves." [S] Munroe expressed the popular sentiment that the law needed to be changed, but with a kind of sick twist to it. His idea of a penalty was brutal, but at least he thought it should be administered indiscriminately.

> *Let an assault on a white woman by a negro man be presumptive evidence of an intent to ravish. Let the punishment for such an assault be, among other things, use of the knife; and I can see no good reason why the law should not be the same as to an assault by a white man on a negro woman. If for rape, the punishment of death, is not sufficient, let the law prescribe what additional tortures should be inflicted, and let the jury fix the punishment.* [S]

"The negroes ought to know," Munroe continued, "that the white women are sacred to our race, not the refined and educated, not the virtuous and good only, but all, absolutely all." He suggested that "Negroes who have any influence with their race might do much to impress this truth upon the more brutal of their race." [S] He offered no ideas about how to educate the more brutal of his own race.

J.J. Laughinghouse, state legislator and future superintendent of North Carolina's penitentiary system, had this to say about Aycock's reward:

> *It looks big, thirty thousand dollars reward for the Salisbury lynchers. Tempting to the detective service, but not one of them will touch it. Why? Because it is not safe. I know twelve men that a few years ago lynched a villain, and if the Governor were to offer one hundred thousand dollars for the names of each one of them, and I was without character, I would [still] not inform against them. Why? Because I would not care to be lynched myself."* [2]

Laughinghouse's letter addressed the truth behind the state's veil of civility. It wasn't just fear of retribution from the mob keeping Laughinghouse and others from squealing. He and others approved of their actions. "Lynching parties are generally composed of the bravest and best men," he argued, "men who regret sorely the necessity of such action and do it solely because they know that our present system of court procedure does not offer protection to the public against the criminal classes." [2] He continued:

> *I don't know much about the Salisbury people, North Carolinians are very much alike all over the State. If the Governor wants to precipitate another lynching, let him offer a big reward for those who lynched the fiend that poisoned Dr. Tayloe and family and induce some one to go to Washington [N.C.] to ferret it out, and let the lynching party find out his business. I'll wager a nice plantation against a nickel that there will be more hemp used. One might suppose I was one of the party, but I was not, simply because I was not invited. The boys thought I was too old, and I approved of their action.*

Wanting to know more about the "fiend" in the Washington incident, I located a descendant of Dr. Tayloe, who kindly mailed me a copy of the story of the poisoning, as it appeared in the local paper, and a transcript of the *N&O's* brief report of that lynching. James Walker (alias Jim Boston) was described as "a young negro, eighteen years old from Plymouth." He worked as Dr. D.T. Tayloe's driver and was accused of poisoning the coffee and hash served to Tayloe's family on the morning of March 17, 1902. The entire family, except for one of the children, suffered for days from arsenic poisoning, but all recovered within a week or so. Arrested in Washington on the day of the poisoning, James was moved that evening to the Williamston jail in the next county. On the night of March 25th, that jail was broken into "and the prisoner carried back to Washington where he was lynched from a gum tree on the Greenville Road." [1]

But James Walker was not eighteen. A more detailed report of the lynching in the Washington *Progress* gave his age as seventeen or eighteen, but also said the boy weighed about 110 pounds. Knowing no boys that age who weighed so little, I searched for James in the census records. The only youthful James Walker recorded in North Carolina in 1900 was ten years old, living in Plymouth with his mother, Ida, and step-father, a bricklayer named William Pettiford. An Ida Boston, living in nearby Jamesville in 1880, might explain James' alias. The absence of others by the same name living in North Carolina in 1900, together with his weight, convinced me that James Walker was actually about twelve years old when he was lynched. The brief report of his lynching said "His neck was not broken, but he was choked to death. There was some lint cotton nearby and strips of yellow homespun, which must have been used as a bandage over his mouth." [1]

When Dick Fleming (the man accused of assaulting Belle Livengood near the Benson home) and another man were executed by Sheriff Julian in July that same year, the *Observer* made a point to note how humanely the operation had been carried out. Both of the men, definitely older than twenty, reportedly died within eleven minutes of the drop (still far too long for a "humane execution"). "When the black caps were removed by the physicians it was seen that there were present on the faces of the dead men none of the frightful marks left by a death in which even partial strangulation plays a part." [1] But none of the boys, James Walker, James Gillespie, or Harrison Gillespie was "spared" as these grown men were. Surely aware of Walker's true age, Laughinghouse, nevertheless, approved of this cruel lynching and had no qualms about saying so. He exemplified the kind of person who could and did go far in North Carolina during Jim Crow's reign.

Attempting to justify his views on the Tayloe incident and another, more personal, experience, Laughinghouse said a good friend of his had been murdered, and the one responsible was acquitted by the jury, after the case was removed to another county. He admitted his desire to lynch the man from the beginning, but said older citizens had talked him into letting the law take its course. The man he blamed for the murder, he said, left the state after his release, but when he returned eight years later, he was lynched. [2] Though Laughinghouse did not admit to participating in that lynching, a descendant says he definitely did. The good friend Laughinghouse referred to in his letter was former Major General Bryan Grimes, allegedly murdered by a hit man named Parker, believed to have been hired by a pair of alleged barn-burning well-poisoners, the Paramour brothers. [3]

Glenn's successor, Governor Kitchin gave Laughinghouse his job as penitentiary superintendent, even after Laughinghouse publicly admitted he had withheld and would continue to withhold information about twelve individuals who had committed a lynching. Kitchin was also the one who pardoned George Hall. Having lost his appeal, Hall went to prison in June, 1907 and was freed October, 1911.

Clearly, some prominent people felt more at ease to openly express their prejudices in 1902, than in 1906. That may have had something to do with the Supreme Court's involvement in the March, 1906 Chattanooga lynching. Chattanooga's Sheriff Shipp would eventually serve time for his role in that lawlessness.

Though Laughinghouse and others revealed the futility of Aycock's reward, Aycock, himself, may have tried to do the right thing after all. One report indicated he put forth an extra effort to investigate the Benson case soon after the lynching. Though no details were provided, the *N&O* said Aycock issued the proclamation of his reward right after returning to Raleigh from his trip to Cooleemee, a tiny mill community, located not

far from the area where Cornelia Benson was murdered. [G] Had
Aycock personally investigated the murder and the question of
the boys' guilt? Did the discovery of their true ages and
likelihood of innocence prompt him to place such a high price on
the lynchers' heads?

The *N&O* didn't reveal Aycock's take on the question of
guilt, but it included an opinion of a "gentleman from Salisbury"
that did address it. He said "there was very grave doubt as to the
guilt of the younger of the two...that the parents of the two boys
affirmed all the time that the younger boy was at home at the
moment of the commission of the crime, while they readily
agreed that the elder one was from home." [G] Likewise, the *Star
of Zion*, one of the very few African American papers still
publishing in North Carolina, said in an editorial on June 26th
that there was a growing belief "now among the whites that the
two boys were innocent."

The "Salisbury gentleman" also revealed something later
confirmed at the trial.

> *He states that the younger boy died protesting his
> innocence and singing, 'I want to go to heaven when I
> die.' The Gentleman making this statement is a man well
> known in the State and has held responsible positions.
> He says moreover that there was only one track at the
> scene of the murder and this track corresponded with the
> track of the elder, and not of the younger. If these
> statements turn out to be true the lynching becomes all
> the more horrible. It is high time for the public opinion
> of the State to rise up and put a stop to this form of
> lawlessness.* [G]

This came from the newspaper that, just a few days earlier,
convicted James and Harrison of murder and rape, dehumanizing
them in the process. It portrayed them as animals on June 12th,
with its headline: "Young Tigers Attacked Miss Benson with
Stones Beating Out Her Brains," [H] perhaps inspiring North
Carolina writer Thomas Wolfe's title, "The Child By Tiger." In
its continued attack on the boys, it described the murder as a
"Deed of Fiendish Ferocity." [H] Its editorial in the same edition
said it "deplored" the lynching, but it mostly condemned the

victims, rather than what was done to them, and focused on the gruesome details of Cornelia's death. All the while the commentary denounced the boys, whose guilt was never questioned, as "inhuman beasts" and "vicious young brutes." [4]

The *N&O's* premature rape charge is even more damning when viewed in light of the paper's June 19th editorial, in which it minced no words in its support of lynching in the case of rape. For the boys, it had an impact similar to what the WMD implications had for Saddam Hussein. The *Charlotte Observer*, as bad as its offense was, didn't print editorials justifying the lynching of rape suspects.

The *N&O* further echoed the sentiment expressed in Laughinghouse's letter.

> *There is one crime in North Carolina that will always be followed by lynching if the indignant neighborhood catches the brute who is guilty of it before he is put in jail. Every good citizen deplores the lynching, but he deplores ten thousand times more the infamous crime that causes its exercise. But that is the only crime that excuses any people for taking the law into their own hands....*
>
> *These "mobs" who punish for that crime are not the worst citizens. In such cases, they are often composed of good citizens, who are moved to take the law in their hands because of the terrible character of the crime. In Anson county, at the latest lynching for rape...the men who joined the lynching party were as good citizens as any who live in that community. If the Governor had offered a reward for the capture of these men, his act would have been universally and properly condemned. He was too wise to offer a reward for the men who had protected their homes by violating the law.* [J]

In short, the editorial condemned the lynching of James and Harrison, only because they had been suspected of murder, not rape. The men in the lynching party "committed a crime against civilization, not directed at the protection of the home," it said, "It was such a crime as makes men stand aghast that it could happen in one of the most intelligent communities in North Carolina."[J]

One black voice's response to all this rhetoric was found. Though it spoke out strongly, it was probably heard by few in North Carolina. And it would not have been safe for any "colored" man in North Carolina to repeat it. The *Richmond Planet's* John Mitchell warned what would happen if this vigilante justice continued. "It will finally result in persons charged with crime resisting arrest as was done by Will Reynolds at Tuscumbia, Alabama, and Will Richardson at Atlanta, Georgia."

> *It may be all right for theorizing critics to talk about surrendering to the officers of the law, but when it is realized that in most cases, these officers are but the advance agents of the mob-leaders, sensible colored men will take the chances of dying with a rifle in their hands rather than by the slow torture of an agonizing death.*[5]

It was an incredibly risky statement for a southern black man to make in 1902. That kind of talk got Alex Manly run out of Wilmington and his newspaper office burned to the ground, just four years earlier. If any man of color living in North Carolina during this time had made such a statement he would likely have been hanging, full of bullets, on a tree limb or stretched over a bench and beaten within and inch of his life, as in an incident to which Salisbury's former Sheriff later testified. But Mitchell didn't back down; he concluded his commentary with even stronger words.

> *For our part, we prefer the route taken by Will Reynolds and Will Richardson rather than that traversed by the unfortunate Harrison and James Gillespie, who must be presumed innocent until they have been proven guilty in accordance with our forms of legal procedures. Lynch law must go!*[5]

Something must have later occurred in Mitchell's life that led to the tempering of this strong, courageous voice. Its diminished volume after 1902, along with the silencing of courageous white men like Trinity's John Spenser Bassett, left a huge void of sound reasoning amid all the high-pitched propaganda that continued for a long, long time. Neither open or silent endorsement of lynching seemed to hurt anyone's political career. On June 13th, the *N&O* reported the outcome of Rowan's Democratic County Conventions, held in Salisbury two days after the lynching. It was called to order by Chairman John M. Julian.

> *E.C. Gregory, Esq., was elected chairman of the convention. The following nominations were made: For State Senator, Hon. John S. Henderson; for the House, Walter Murphy and Burton Craige; Sheriff, D.R. Julian;...Coroner, E. Rose Dorsett; Commissioners, C.T. Bernhardt, W.L. Kluttz, P.D. Linn, J.S. Hall and H.C. Lentz. The course of Hon. Theo. F. Kluttz in Congress was unanimously endorsed. Hon. Lee S. Overman was endorsed by acclamation for United States Senator. John M. Julian was re-elected chairman of the executive committee.*

A week after the lynching, an editorial in Daniels paper ended as follows:

> *The Southern People are the truest and best friends of the negro as some incident every day demonstrates.* [6]

# PART TWO

Only one man was charged with participating in the lynching of James and Harrison Gillespie. Though the specific charge wasn't stated, a thirty-five-year-old Salisbury bartender named Tom Sparnell was arrested a month after the incident. The *Observer's* report on this arrest and trial repeatedly referred to the Gillespies as "the murderers of Miss Cornelia Benson," while the headline for Sparnell's story read: "An Alleged Lyncher Jailed." [N]

It was the thirteenth of July, the same date the Lyerlys were murdered four years later, when Judge Thomas J. Shaw of

Greensboro issued a bench warrant for Sparnell. It was Shaw who would later drop the case against the alleged Anson County lynchers of J.V. Johnson in 1906, his ruling based on a technicality. The decision to arrest Sparnell had been made a week earlier, but could not be carried out because Shaw was in Virginia and Hammer was away in Monroe, a small town near Charlotte. [O] Sheriff Julian jailed the defendant after the judge refused his offer of bond, and Shaw and Hammer planned an examination the next day. Sparnell claimed he had an alibi. [N] The report said fifteen subpoenas had already been issued for witnesses, and Hammer said he suspected the involvement of at least eleven other men.

Prior to the trial, an unidentified *Observer* reporter, presumed to be Kluttz, made an astonishing statement. "That this case is going to stir up a row," he said, "there can be no doubt in the world. I have it on the best authority that there are eleven other men, known to have been in the lynching, one of them a county officer, or sub-officer, and that it is expected soon to have enough legal evidence to justify their arrest." [O] This must be the basis for what the *Carolina Watchman* complained about after the 1906 lynching—that it had happened before and officers were involved. "The Solicitor is naturally reticent about it," the report said, "and when asked about this last piece of information declined to deny or affirm its accuracy, but saying that it was the hardest matter in the world to get a shred of legal testimony against any but the man arrested." The newsman said Hammer defended the "better element" of Salisbury in one respect: "not a single one" he claimed, "was directly implicated in the lynching..." But, evidently less guarded in his statements then, than in 1906, Hammer added that "a great many know who was, and won't tell." [O]

Sparnell's trial began on Monday, July 14th and was, essentially, over before it began. The *Observer* covered the developments in detail, printing quoted and paraphrased accounts of testimony. However, since no other record exists, it's impossible to judge how accurate or complete this one is. Therefore, everything said here about the trial should be understood as "allegedly" or "reportedly" —what witnesses told the court and how the reporter heard it and related it to the public. Furthermore it becomes obvious that what was recorded is mostly hearsay. Defense attorneys, unlike Hammer, subpoenaed the necessary witnesses to prevent problems with hearsay. They, however, had a much easier job than Hammer did—people were more likely to testify in defense of a suspected lyncher, than risk their lives accusing one.

Several witnesses were subpoenaed, and, given the nature of the trial, attendance was surprisingly low. Sparnell was represented by the newly appointed Senator, Lee Slater Overman, of the firm of Overman & Gregory, and by Walter Murphy, who, incredibly, would be named as a witness in the Mayor's testimony.

The preliminary hearing moved quickly, followed by the State's first witness. Mayor Boyden testified as follows:

> *"I was near the corner of Main and Council Streets at nearly 1 o'clock, Officer Eagle with me. I met Mr. Walter Murphy, who said all seemed quiet. Presently I saw a mob coming up Council Street and started for them to endeavor to quiet them. When I got within a few feet of the mob, whose members were masked, they ordered me to halt and all drew pistols. Then I spoke briefly to the mob, entreating them not to have a lynching in glorious old Rowan and to let the law take its course. Then one man, who seemed to be doing most of the talking for the mob, said, with an oath, that they were going to take the law into their own hands. While I was still entreating them to desist, the same voice said, 'stand out of the way,' and they made a dash for the jail, firing pistols as they went. I made a special effort to single out a man to whom I might address a personal appeal, but could recognize no one. After they had gone to the jail, Mr. Murphy suggested that the voice of the spokesman was a certain man's and I thought I recognized it. I believed it to be the voice of Thomas Sparnell. There were 50 or 60 masked men in the mob and a crowd of 300 or 400 people had also gathered."* [P]

Failing to comment on Murphy's apparent conflict of interest, the report continued with Boyden's testimony. "'I stood by the gate of the jail yard as the negroes were brought out and again urged the members of the mob to give up their purpose. After they had reached Kerr Street, two blocks down Main, I ceased observing them and went home.'" [P]

During cross examination, Boyden admitted he was not absolutely sure it was Sparnell's voice he'd heard, though "he believed it was." [P]

If the report recorded the proceedings sequentially, that was apparently all the State had, for the time being. No one explained why Hammer didn't subpoena Eagle, who Boyden said was with him that night. Would Eagle have been able to positively identify some of the lynchers?

Introduced to substantiate Sparnell's alibi, Mr. I.A. Peebles was Defense's first witness.

> *He testified that he saw the mob approach from the courthouse steps where he was sitting, and that Tom Sparnell was sitting beside him and not participating in the mob. They both heard Boyden address the mob. Sparnell, Peebles testified, was not masked, and the two men went together to the sidewalk to watch the mob as it came out of the jail with the Gillespie boys. After that, Peebles continued, Sparnell left, and he said he did not see him again that night. Peebles added that another man named T. L. Foster had also been sitting on the steps with them. The witness stated that he was "in the whiskey business" when asked about his occupation. "Mr. Peebles character was proved good by Messrs. D.M. Miller, Jno. J. Rendleman, Wyatt and other witnesses."* [P]

During the 1906 lynching trials, John Rendleman was the one who suggested that Cress's sanity be investigated. Foster would later corroborate Peebles' testimony.

After Peebles testified, Hammer offered, as contradictory evidence, an affidavit made by Sparnell. Overman and Hammer argued about the competency of the affidavit, Overman "declaring that if it was used to contradict the defendant's witness, the effect would be the equivalent to forcing him to testify against himself—that it would be doing indirectly what could not be done directly." [P]

But Shaw didn't rule on the matter right away. He explained his decision "would be governed by an important exception to the rules of evidence, created by the act of 1893 under which the investigation was to be held. Then he "announced that no witness would be excused from testifying on the ground that he might incriminate himself, since all participants in the crime who became State's witnesses are pardoned by the operation of the statute, which contains a specific clause to this effect." He said he was "inclined to hold with the defendant on Overman's point," but he instead reserved judgment and called a recess. [P]

M.L. Bean, Sr. was first to testify after the recess. "Bean told the court that, on the morning after the lynching, he heard a man named T.J. [the reporter meant to say Will, not T.J.] Rabe say that he saw Dick Sparnell, Tom's brother, tie the rope around the boys' necks." After Bean finished, Mr. C.F. Atwell swore he heard Rabe say the same thing.

But, when Will Rabe got on the stand, the picture changed.

*He said that he was on the scene before the lynching began. He said that he did not recognize Dick Sparnell as one of the two men who climbed the tree and tied the ropes and had not said that he did, but only that he had heard some one say that the man who climbed the tree on the side towards the railroad and who did not wear a mask was Dick Sparnell. He saw the man in the tree, but did not know who he was. Witness said that he had heard some wild rumors, but had no fear of harm for telling all he knew. He was near the Mt. Vernon Hotel when the main body of the mob first emerged from the old Lanier canning factory and started towards the jail. After the mob had passed Poole's saloon, at the corner of Lee Street, he saw several try to drop out but a man displaying a pistol compelled them to get back into the ranks.* [P]

Mr. T.J. Rabe, Will's father and a proprietor of Carolina Marble Works, took the stand next. Regarding what Will told Bean and Atwell, Rabe confirmed his son's story. Was Will responding to questions about threats on his life when he said he had "heard wild rumors?"

M.C. Torrence testified to what Jim Hodges told him he saw that night, though Hodges wasn't questioned to corroborate it. According to Torrence, Hodges said he had seen some youths who had composed part of the mob in an alley and not yet wearing masks, and they put on the masks just before entering the street. If Hodges had been brought before the court, perhaps he could have named names, but no one, so far, was naming any name other than Sparnell.

Coroner E. Rose Dorsett's testimony challenged earlier reports of the boys' ages and confirmed his belief in their guilt. He said he had spoken with the boys' mother, who told him Harrison was 14 and James 12. However, according to the 1900 Census, James would not have turned twelve until August and Harrison would have remained thirteen until November of 1902. "...at the inquest held over the remains of Miss Benson," Dorsett added, "the finding of the jury was that the deceased came to her death at the hands of the two boys," and that "there was no evidence before the coroner as to who participated in the lynching." [P] Dorsett, elected to his post, came to a quick and certain conclusion about the Benson murder, occurring in a field out in the middle of a rural area, and he would make an equally quick decision about the Lyerly murder, based on no substantial evidence at all. But Dorsett had no clue, out of fifty or more men who broke down the jail door right in front of the Mayor and the deputies, who was responsible for the lynching. Dorsett, like most coroners, decided the boys came to their deaths at the "hands of persons unknown."

Former Sheriff J.M. Monroe said he heard a man named Johns say a negro had been whipped near town for "talking too much about the lynching." [P] Which is irrelevant, unless the "negro" said something about seeing Sparnell and was willing to testify under oath. African descendants had good reason to fear telling what or who they saw that night. There would be no place for any of them to testify in this case. If Hammer had asked Johns, he might have learned something very relevant. But Hammer also knew this man's word would not hold any weight against a white man's. And Johns would have risked his life to testify.

Jailer Krider's testimony raises several questions. He said J.L. Thompson, John Vinson, and others from the Mt.Vernon area had called the jail just before dark to see the boys and find out if they would be willing to incriminate their mother and stepfather "'who were suspected of having incited them to commit the murder.'" Krider said the men mentioned nothing about lynching and said he had "heard some talk of lynching during the evening, but placed no belief in it, as [he had] been hearing such talk for ten or twelve years without anything ever coming of it." He also said "...he did not believe the people of Rowan would ever commit a lynching." [P]

These Benson neighbors may have tried to prevent the lynching of the children. Knowing someone would surely be lynched for Cornelia's death, perhaps they were hoping the boys would implicate Anna and Stokes. It would have been easier to get these two adults out of their cottage than to break into the jail. Just as likely, they were looking for reasons to kill them all. They were still upset over the recent "assault" on Belle Livengood. Dick Fleming had "confessed" to the "rape" but swore, at his execution, that the other accused, Rich Blanton, had nothing to do with it. Governor Aycock had granted Blanton a reprieve from execution, and the Mt. Vernon neighbors were going to make damned sure this sort of thing didn't happen again.

Deputy Krider's statement continued:

> *"When I heard the shooting in front of the jail, which was the first I knew of the approach of the lynchers, I rose, partly dressed and got out my pistol. I reached the door just as it was broken in. The mob covered me with their pistols. They were all masked and I failed to recognize anyone. I gave the keys to Deputy Ab Rice, who, with Mr. Joe Carson and my father-in-law, had entered on the heels of the mob to assist me if I should be in personal danger. Mr. Rice passed the keys to my son, who in turn hid them in the ticking of a bed. The mob forced its way upstairs and broke into the cells. There were at least 25 or 30 masked men in the party which entered the jail"* [P]

The paper does not say who Krider's father-in-law was, but if not Sheriff Julian, where was he? Julian said later he went to bed that night, assured that there was no danger of a lynching. But didn't the mayor or someone else wake him up? If it *was* Julian, then just about every officer in that jail was related to one another. Rice and Carson are the only ones mentioned in Krider's testimony with no publicized role in the 1906 events. If Carson and Rice were entering the jail "on the heels of the mob," why didn't they enter shooting? Was it because they would have shot their neighbors? Krider, Rice, and Carson were all from the area near the Benson neighborhood.

The *Observer* paraphrased the testimony of T.B. Johnson, who said he saw the mob "pass his house at the corner of Main and Kerr streets with its victims."

> *He saw four men marching in order in front. Behind them were two men with the larger boy between them. Near these were two others in charge of the younger. The remainder of the masked men were immediately behind, with the exception of a single man who patrolled the flanks of the mob, telling everybody to keep off, and endeavoring to show off, as witness thought, by cavorting about. It was on the whole a quiet and orderly procession. There was a crowd following on the sidewalks and behind in the road.* [P]

Mr. Johnson's nephew, Joe Nichols, was asked to repeat a statement he allegedly made on the morning after the lynching. When Joe said he couldn't remember it, Mr. Johnson was recalled to tell it: "'The boy said that somebody had told him that a masked man asked for a light in the jail and that the lynchers were so carelessly masked that the handkerchief on this man's face fell down when he took the lamp handed him.'" [P] If true, one man returned to the jail where the lamp was simply handed over by one of the officers still in the jail, who must have seen this man's face when his mask fell.

What was Hammer doing anyway? Why would anyone with any legal knowledge try to base a case on hearsay? Unlike 1906, this trial began a month after the lynching; Hammer had had much more time to investigate this case. Why would he put people on the stand to testify to what someone else had said and

not subpoena the one who allegedly said it? Was Hammer *trying*
to lose his case?

If so, his next witness did little other than help with that
goal. Mr. A.A. Blackwelder, a merchant in a small nearby town,
said he had telephoned Mr. Bean (not the Bean who testified
earlier) to discuss Cornelia Benson's murder and to tell him
about something he overheard regarding the lynching. The paper
said Blackwelder gave some "very material and interesting
evidence," [P] paraphrased as follows:

> *Witness called up Mr. E.H. Bean, at Salisbury and
> asked him, as a matter of interest, the details of the
> recent crime. He told Mr. Bean that a lynching crowd
> from Gold Hill was headed for Salisbury, but the latter
> pooh-poohed the idea, and refused to take it seriously.
> This information [had been] given witness over the
> phone by Dr. C.B. McNairy, of Gold Hill,
> [Blackwelder's] brother-in-law. The cause of [McNairy]
> getting this information was that Southern Railway
> Agent S.A. Robinson heard a conversation going on
> between persons in Salisbury and Gold Hill while
> waiting to talk to some ladies at Crescent. What he
> overheard prompted the further inquiries already
> mentioned. It was stated in the overheard conversation
> by Mr. Robinson, as repeated by him to the witness, that
> the Gold Hill men would be on hand for the lynching by
> 10:30 o'clock [that] night. Several names were heard
> mentioned by Mr. Robinson, but the witness did not hear
> him repeat them.* [P]

Apparently Mr. Robinson was the only one who knew the
names discussed over the phone, but for some reason he was not
called to court to either give those names or corroborate
Blackwelder's testimony. Even if Robinson had been called, his
testimony would have been hearsay, unless there was someone
else to corroborate Robinson's statements. It's not clear how
Robinson overheard the conversation. Perhaps it was on one of
the party lines so common at the time.

The *Observer*, adding that the trial would continue on
Friday, saw Blackwelder's lead as the "State's most promising

evidence for Friday, viz, the testimony of Mr. Robinson and the telephone operator." [P]

When court reconvened at 2 p.m., T.L. Foster of Spencer took the stand and supported Peebles testimony. Foster said "he was with Sparnell and Peebles on the steps of the court house," as Peebles had testified. [P]

The last recorded statement was a paraphrase of Sheriff Julian's testimony. "He said that he had heard nothing to indicate the danger of a lynching except some idle talk which he could not be expected to credit." [P] Justifying his ignorance this time, he said "There had been just such talk in connection with the Mt. Vernon criminal assault case some time before. He had his deputies make a careful inspection and patrol and nothing suspicious was brought to light. The witness went home completely assured that there was not the least real danger of lynching." [P]

After all that day's waste of time, money, and energy, Judge Shaw caught a train back home to Greensboro. When he got off the train, he went straight to the telegraph office and wired Sheriff Julian, instructing him to release Sparnell. The *Observer* said it was because "there was no positive evidence whatever against the man." [R]

A backup for Sparnell's discharge, in case the evidence against him had been substantial, was the legal loophole Overman had introduced early that day. The next day's report said the point was "so interesting and plausible," it published the section of the act for all to see—the act "found in Public Laws, ch. 461, sec. 5." [5] The judge had reserved his ruling on it, suspecting lack of evidence would make it a moot point, which turned out to be the case. The paper described the law as "An act to protect prisoners confined in jail under the charge of crime until they can be fairly tried by a jury of good and lawful men in open court." [R]

*For a month Solicitor Hammer has been examining witnesses privately before the coroner, under the authority of the act, known as the Watson Anti-lynching law, passed in 1893, and prepared by C.B. Watson, Esq. Among the men who had been examined by Solicitor Hammer before the coroner, and whose affidavit was in court yesterday, but not allowed to be introduced, was the defendant Sparnell. The point made by Mr. Overman was that the act absolutely pardoned his client, even were he guilty, not from any testimony he had given, implicating himself and others, but from the simple fact that he was called upon to make an affidavit and undergo an examination at all.* [R]

There is no indication that anyone was ever convicted for the lynching of James and Harrison Gillespie. After Sparnell's acquittal, the case was supposed to continue, to bring in Robinson, along with the telephone operator for questioning. But then the continuance was "indefinitely postponed, owing to the inability of Judge Neal, who was to have presided, to be present." [R] Explaining that the evidence already brought forth in the case was considered little more than hearsay, the *Observer* said Solicitor Hammer was left "in the same position as before—without such direct evidence as would justify further warrants of arrest." [R]

Despite his sloppy investigation and failure to bring a conviction, Hammer was praised for his efforts. The *Observer* said he "acted ably and conscientiously and the futility of his efforts thus far arises almost inevitably from the conditions with which he has had to deal, among which, however, a hostile public sentiment is not to be included. Mr. Hammer has expressed his entire satisfaction in this regard." In the end, everyone had to pretend it couldn't have had anything to do with the lack of cooperation from the public.

These last couple of reports on the lynching investigation were buried on back pages, one under a totally unrelated headline. The whole matter was soon forgotten by the legal authorities.

But the Mt. Vernon neighborhood and the mob had a much longer memory than the authorities did. They had not put it to rest yet, and the law's lenient response to the lynching now gave them license to do as they pleased. The press, with its continued inflammatory remarks, gave its own blessing. It was not long before Stokes, his wife, and the remaining members of his extended family, one a little girl, were attacked by their white neighbors.

> *Feeling in the Mt. Vernon neighborhood, the scene of the crime for which the two negro boys were lynched early Wednesday morning, is becoming very strong against Stokes Cowan and his wife, colored, the stepfather of the Gillespie boys and the mother of one of them, and the couple have been advised to leave the county. It is believed that they are indirectly concerned in the murder of Miss Benson as instigators of murderous sentiments in the boys, if, in fact, they were not near at hand and inciting them when the crime was committed. There is no positive evidence of this, however. It is known that the couple cherished a mortal feud with their white neighbors, the Bensons.* <sup>K</sup>

The *Observer* began its coverage of the attack by attacking Mr. Cowan. "Stokes is a negro of much animal courage and had never taken the threats made against him at all seriously," it said.

> *To all those who gave him friendly advice to leave, he invariably replied with an oath that he had nothing to do with the affair and would not leave. Disagreement among the mob doubtless saved them from more violence and a more expeditious trip. Some wanted to hang the whole family, others suggested the nailing of all the doors and windows so securely that when the house was fired, the negroes could not get out, still others recommended merciless beating and more conservative ones simply banishment. They could not agree.* <sup>L</sup>

Despite the lack of consensus as to how to dispatch the Cowans, a "well-armed" mob met at the house that Friday night and began shooting. Stokes didn't just sit there and take it, but unfortunately his only weapon was an "old muzzle-loader." He tried several times to return the fire coming at him from all directions, but his old gun failed. Describing the incident later, the reporter said he *heard* it said that "Stokes old sprinkle pot sounded like a cannon." <sup>L</sup> The writer didn't divulge any of the names of those who witnessed or participated in this illegal attack. But evidently no one, including Hammer, asked anyway.

Before it was all over, Anna Cowan had escaped with a wound to her arm, and the rest were run out of their home and off the land. Stokes was allowed to return later to gather the crop he had already planted, but Anna was never heard from in Rowan County again. In the end the scales of Lady Justice hung unbalanced and her blindfold was tattered. There was never any more evidence heard on the 1902 lynching case, and by 1906, it was as if none of this had ever happened. No one faced any consequences for either crime committed against the Cowan family. The damning details of these last criminal acts were totally ignored by all but the *Charlotte* press, the only one that reported them. The press, in general, never paid a penalty for its blatantly irresponsible and inflammatory headlines. But, according to the *Sun*, a black living in the county near Salisbury, was "Corrected For Talking Too Much" after the lynching. It was said the man "spoke boastfully of what he proposed to do to certain parties in the mob of Tuesday night."

*"I know some of them," he said "and I am going to pick them out when they are in the dark some night."*

*In about five minutes the would-be avenger was lying across a barrel and a paddle was being applied with considerable vigor. The negro was badly whipped but not seriously hurt.* [M]

The 1957 recap of this story concluded with a common sentiment. An old man, asked to give his opinion, said this "black chapter in Rowan history is best forgotten." For African descendants, though, forgetting isn't so easy. They never got justice, and only half-truths about what happened have since been printed. Black Rowan residents weren't even able to discuss their knowledge or opinions about these tragedies, except in whispers, for years. Nease's descendants said, growing up, they knew very little about what happened to their great grandfather and got what they did know by hiding and listening to their parents whisper about it. Current resident Henry Clement told me his older sister, now over one hundred years old, was told by her parents that "both of those little boys were innocent." These boys never got justice, and neither did Nease, Jack, or

John. The Lyerly and Benson families lost as well, because the murders were never properly investigated. To the old man who said the 1902 affair is best forgotten, I say it must be remembered, at least until it has been corrected. Had 1902 not been so swiftly swept under the rug, 1906 might have been prevented.

Two months ago, after searching for years, I found one of Will Benson's descendants. Turning on to Cool Springs Road that day, I'd hoped to locate the old Benson place where Cornelia was found dead. A long and wooded country road, circling hills and hollows, Cool Springs keeps its scattered homes well secluded, revealing no clues to the site I was seeking. Driving back and forth, from one end to another, I was finally lured into a driveway by a sign that read, "Jesus Has The Answer." A man living there directed my questions to some older neighbors nearby who he thought might have some answers. They turned out to be Cornelia's relatives.

His wife invited me in to their den and called for her husband, who slowly hobbled in with a cane. As soon as we all sat down to talk about 1902, I blurted out my first question. Did he approve of the lynching, I wanted to know?

"You mean those niggers that killed Cornelia? Sure, they got what they deserved."

"But did you realize they were just boys?" I was sure he didn't know how young they were.

He did, he said, and that didn't change his opinion.

Despite my initial shock at his response, I was made to feel at ease, and we talked for at least an hour. I told him what I'd learned, things he hadn't heard—about Daniels, the racist propaganda and its purpose, how many whites had been deceived by it—how we've all been hurt by those beliefs and deceptions. More than a few had been convinced of at least the youngest boy's innocence, I told him. We talked about a lot of other things I can't recall.

Before I left, I think he saw things differently. He and his wife seemed like "good" people.

# EPILOGUE

Main Street, Salisbury

After the lynching, authorities must have closed the case on the Lyerly murders. Other than news about the trial of the three spared by the mob, no additional information on the case was reported in the press at least up to February, 1907, when I stopped looking. None of Isaac and Augusta's direct descendants I spoke to knew of any other attempts to extend the investigation after the lynching, and they all had assumed all their lives that all of the suspects were guilty. They were, however, unaware of much of the evidence I uncovered over the past ten years, including John Gillespie's young age.

### Nease Gillespie, John Gillespie, Jack Dillingham

On the Old Concord Road in Salisbury, at the intersection of Julian Road, lies what's left of the County Home's cemetery, known as "Pauper's Field." Not too long ago, T.W. Summersett, of Summersett Funeral Home in Salisbury, compiled a list of names of those buried there before death certificate records began in 1913. But the information he was able to obtain went back only as far as 1907. Most of those listed between 1907 and 1913 were designated as "colored." But among the "white" names, one stood out—the only one that includes either Mr. or Mrs. with the name: Mrs. T.F. Kluttz.

Only five markers could be found on the site. None of these bears the name of Nease Gillespie, John Gillespie, or Jack Dillingham, whose remains probably still lie buried in one of several unmarked graves either beside or beneath Old Concord Road.

A member of Cedar Grove Church, James Ellis, helped me find Nease Gillespie's descendants. Through his son, Tom Glaspy, Nease has a long line of descendants who carry his memory with them. They have been successful in their careers and led fulfilling lives. One graduated from law school in North Carolina. She was the one who heard professor Powell tell the story of the Lyerly murders his parents had told him as a boy.

### Della Dillingham, George Ervin, Henry Lee Gillespie, and Emma Gillespie

In 1906, Greensboro native William Sidney Porter, better known as O. Henry, published his most famous short story, "The

Gift of the Magi." The main characters in the story are a young couple, the James Dillingham Youngs. Della is Mrs. Young's first name, and Della Dillingham's maiden name, in the 1906 story, was Young. I wondered if O'Henry read about Della's and Jack's tragedy and incorporated their names into his story.

I never found out for sure what happened to Della, unless Earl Lyerly's rumor is true—that someone pushed her off a train into the French Broad River. I could not find Della in the census records before or after the lynching.

I got the same results from my search for George and Henry Lee and his wife, Emma.

### Fannie Gillespie and Henry Mayhew

After I found Fannie and Henry in the 1910 census, I lost them. Maybe Henry enlisted and was killed in World War I. Fannie, perhaps did not live to be 73, the age she should have been by the time the 1920 census was taken.

### Mary, Addie, and Janie Lyerly

After the deaths of their parents, the surviving Lyerly girls stayed with close relatives briefly and then went on to live separate lives. Mary enrolled in Crescent Academy and in April, 1907, not long after testifying at the trial in Statesville, she married Matt Webb. The couple eventually moved to Davie County and had many children. Both lived long and fulfilling lives. Mary's youngest daughter, Bettie Sue, now an active, independent senior citizen, told me her mother never felt safe living in a two-story house after the murder of her parents.

Addie Lyerly studied Nursing at the normal school in Asheville, North Carolina and later married Ernest Rice. She and Ernest had a large family, and Addie worked as a midwife until she retired. In 1974 she retold the story of that horrible night in 1906 to *Salisbury Post* reporter Joe Junod. She died in 1983. Addie, like Mary, has many descendants, most of whom now carry a faint memory of what happened in 1906. All those I talked to seemed to be living happy, fulfilled lives.

Janie Lyerly taught in the Greenville, North Carolina Public School system for years. She never married.

## Joseph Lyerly

Joseph Lyerly's life seems to have been prosperous, but I'm not certain it was happy. He had one child by his first wife, who was a Lyerly before she married. With his second wife, he had ten more children. In 1908 Joseph subpoenaed his half-sisters to court and, through a special proceeding, the land they inherited from their father was ordered to be sold and the proceeds divided among the girls, Joseph, and his lawyers, one of them Theo Kluttz. Sold at auction that same year, the property went to Jed Roseman, one of Isaac's grandnephews.

In 1914, Joseph's brother-in-law, Preston Lyerly (his first wife's brother), was shot while working at a store he managed near Barber Junction. The store was set on fire, and Preston, dead already from the gunshot wound, was partially burned by the flames. Sid Finger, an 18-year-old black man, said to be of low intelligence, was arrested, convicted, and electrocuted for this murder. Thomas Bost witnessed and reported the execution. By the late 40s when my aunt dated Joseph's youngest son, Earl, Joseph was still holding a grudge about what had happened in 1906, which he transferred to my aunt. He would have nothing to do with her because of his strong dislike for his stepmother, Augusta, and wanted nothing more to do with *any* Barringers, for that matter, he told his daughter. Apparently Joseph was unaware that my aunt was not only a Barringer, but her great grandmother was a Lyerly—Isaac's first cousin.

## The Julians

It's not certain if Sheriff Julian's accidental poisoning is what led to the decline of his health, but he was not re-elected to the office of sheriff in 1906. He died in 1909.

John Moose Julian followed his father the very next year. Succumbing to pellegra, he did not live to see his 45th birthday.

## Other Officers and Attorneys

Deputy and jailer J. Hodge Krider was elected sheriff in 1906. He died of heart failure in 1909 at age 52.

William C. Hammer went on to a relatively successful political career, re-elected as solicitor and later as U.S.

Representative from North Carolina's 7$^{th}$ district. He died in office in 1930.

Though he did become well-known and admired for his actions against railroad monopolies, Judge Long did not ascend the ladder of success. He remained a Judge until his death in 1925. His son, McKendree Robbins Long and great grandson, Ben Long, both gained notoriety as artists.

Theodore F. Kluttz, Sr. continued his private law practice and never returned to Congress. He died in 1914 and was buried at Chestnut Hill Cemetery in Salisbury. Sallie Caldwell Kluttz, Theo's wife and Joseph Caldwell's sister, is also listed on that registry. Was she moved there from the pauper's plot, where she appears to have been buried? Or was there another Mrs. T.F. Kluttz in Salisbury, about Sallie's age, who died one day before Sallie's recorded date of death? If so, she's not in the census records for Rowan County.

Jake F. Newell went on to lead the state Republican Party for several years. He ran unsuccessfully for the U.S. Senate against Democratic candidate Robert Reynolds in 1932, which was no reflection on him—the Democratic hold on the state was almost impossible to break for years after the 1898 coup—and it pretty much remains so today. In his personal letters found among UNC-Chapel Hill's collections, there is no mention of the Lyerly murder case. But there are several letters discussing strategies on how to defeat the Democrats in upcoming elections.

Newell married, but he and his wife remained childless. His Charlotte home is now on the state's historical register.

I was never able to find the story behind a hit I came across on a Google search that said: "And so this defense attorney, Jake Newell, became a great hero in my mind," but I hope to one day know more about this man who was willing to risk his life and career for people who were abandoned by southern society as a whole. [1]

Lee Slater Overman was reappointed to the U.S. Senate in 1909, and in 1914, he became the first senator from North Carolina to be elected by popular vote. He and Furnifold Simmons (the third participant in Daniels' white supremacist 1898 campaign strategy), would take turns for several years as U.S. Senator from North Carolina, as part of a kind of gentlemen's agreement. During one of his terms, Overman "wrote and sponsored the Overman Act of 1918, which gave President Woodrow Wilson extraordinary powers to coordinate government agencies in wartime." After the war, he chaired a Senate committee, "...which many see as a precursor to the House UnAmerican Activities committee of the Fifties." He remained in the Senate until his death in 1930. [2] A United States liberty ship was named in his honor.

### George Hall

Prison records in the N.C. State Archives show George Hall was pardoned in October, 1911. An avid supporter of white supremacy, Glenn's successor, Governor Kitchin, pardoned him, explaining that thousands had participated in the crime, and it was unfair to punish one man alone for it. Evan Hall was recorded as the person to whom Hall was released. The prison records show Hall's term began in June, 1907, and he was listed as a resident of Rowan, not Montgomery, County.

### Francis Cress and George Gentle

The rest who were accused as participants in the lynching or breaking into the jail apparently led quiet lives after they were acquitted or pardoned. Francis Cress, acquitted of charges related to the lynching due to temporary insanity, is listed in the 1910 census records. He was working at his old job then and living with his wife. I could not find out what became of George Gentle, however, one of my aunts who grew up in Gentle's neighborhood told me she went to school with a guy named Gentle, and, she said, he seemed to never know when to be quiet.

### Jim Taylor

Jim Taylor, the one Jack supposedly implicated in the murders, could not be located. He seems to have disappeared under a sea of thousands of Taylors listed in North Carolina's census records. In the 1920s an alleged assault on the wife of a man named James Taylor led to a lynching and massacre in a small Florida town—a town called Rosewood.

### Filmore Cook

Robert Filmore Cook was living with his wife Linda Jane and children in the Steele Township of Rowan County in 1910, renting and farming, Sam still with them. By 1920, Linda Jane was a widowed resident of Cook's Crossroads in Cabarrus County. Everyone in the family was working in the mill by then except Linda Jane.

### John Redwine Barringer

The first picture I found of my great grandfather, Augusta's brother, showed him to be a tall, handsome man, with a dark mustache. A few years ago, my aunt Nellie gave me another photo of him, taken when he was older. In it, the dark hair and mustache are gone, but in his left hand, he holds a Panama hat.

LEFT: GEORGE ADAM RUFTY AND MY GRANDMOTHER, MYRTLE INEZ. RIGHT: JOHN REDWINE BARRINGER

### George Adam Rufty

My other great grandfather, my grandmother's father, was Isaac Lyerly's cousin. He was the one who kept a piece of the lynching rope, tied in a noose, in his old well house and, in his desk drawer, fingernails of one or more of the victims. He also had a photo of them hanging on the tree. At some point he loaned the photo to a man from the mountains, his only living daughter tells me, and never got it back.

Just before the state tore down George's old house, my cousin Karen and I explored the attic and found an old trunk containing papers and old school books that had belonged to my grandmother's brother, Ransom. On the cover page of one of the school books is a handwritten note, signed by Ransom Rufty. It says: "No dirty nigger better not put his hands on this book."

Because there were no blacks attending any of Ransom's schools back then, I couldn't understand the meaning of this message at first. It was not long, though, before I heard it explained on a television special about racism in the South during Jim Crow. Back then, white kids knew that blacks would eventually be getting their used books. They would write nasty notes on the front pages, knowing it would be the first thing black kids would see when they opened their books.

Certainly many who participated in the Salisbury lynchings and the assault on Della and the Cowans never paid for those crimes. However many blacks believed that neither revenge nor legal justice in these cases was always necessary—God would take care of it. And they may be right. One example of "karma" visited upon the lynchers of the earlier Davidson County incident was described in an article written by the *Lexington Dispatch* in the 1950s. One lyncher disappeared mysteriously while on a trip to Salisbury, it said. Another was plagued with sores and maggots, another was killed by a freak accident, and yet another lamented that the victim had cursed him all his life, just before he closed the door of his office and shot himself. [4]

I don't know about the other Salisbury lynching participants or souvenir keepers, but it looks like George Rufty's sins were visited upon his descendants. Following is a list of tragedies that befell George's relatives and his descendants—the ones I know about:

1. George's daughter-in-law shot and killed herself. After that George and Mary (George's wife) raised the couple's child, named Mazie. 2. Mazie later married and had a little girl who drowned in the fish pond across the street, at the home of one of George's daughters. 3. George's nephew was killed by a train when he sat down on the tracks to remove something from his shoe. 4. George's grandson, my grandmother's first born, at age six was hit by a car right in front of George's house. He died later at the hospital. The name of the man who drove the car was recorded in the papers as Dellinger. 5. George's great grandson, my grandmother's grandson, was hit and killed by a car near Salisbury when he was a young teen. 6. George's great great grandson, as a young boy, about the age of James Gillespie, developed a rare form of cancer. 7. Another great great grandson spent time in prison for a crime he did not commit. He was railroaded by the system—scared away from an innocent plea. 9. Yet another was killed in a shooting accident. 10. A great, great, great grandchild of George's, recently died of SIDS. 11. That same month, another in the same generation died in the hospital. She was only a few weeks old. 12. My children, two more of George's great great grandchildren, lost their father to agent orange when they were exactly the ages of James and Harrison Gillespie.

### J.J. Laughinghouse

J.J. Laughinghouse, who justified and participated in lynching, became superintendent of the state prison under Governor Kitchin. One of his sons, Ned, was killed at sea when the *Zamzam,* en route to Africa, was shelled by the German raider, *Atlantis.*

### John Spenser Bassett

John Spenser Bassett left the South for good and took a position in Connecticut.

### The Chattanooga Lynching Investigation

In his opinion on the case, U.S. Supreme Court Chief Justice Fuller said "statements by Sheriff Shipp and his deputies that they had no idea there would be a lynching attempt the night of March 19 were ludicrous." He also said it was "...absurd to contend that officers of the law who have been through the experiences these defendants had passed through two months prior to the actual lynching did not know that a lynching probably would be attempted on the 19$^{th}$...."

Despite the stern reprimand, the sentence for Shipp and others seemed light—90 days maximum. And though the High Court justices were equally unhappy with the judge presiding over the Johnson case— "...he had talked a great deal about justice under the law but administered very little of it"—the attorney general did not think contempt charges could be brought against him. [3]

### The *Charlotte Observer*

The *Charlotte Observer* went through major changes after August, 1906. First a beloved staff member, Mr.Abernathy, died in September after a bout with tuberculosis. In 1907 Bryant moved to Washington D.C., working there briefly as the *Observer's* correspondent. Not long after McNeill's death in 1907, Caldwell suffered a stroke and left to recuperate. In his absence, his partner, D.A. Tompkins tried to change the tone of reporting, moving it away from sensationalism and more toward progressive reporting he hoped would attract more business to the area.

### John Mitchell, Jr.

John Mitchell, editor of the *Richmond Planet*, one of few African American papers left in the South after 1898, was recently honored in a book by Ann Field Alexander titled *Race Man: The Rise and Fall of the "Fighting Editor."* After 1906 Mitchell faced some hardships, but his paper survived 113 years from the day it was founded. Fields said of Mitchell: "...he made a brave and manly protest when nearly all the odds were against him."

### Josephus Daniels

After using his paper to support Woodrow Wilson's candidacy, Daniels was paid with the position of Secretary of the Navy. Wilson had welcomed a private showing of the racist film,

*Birth of a Nation*, giving it an enthusiastic thumbs up—and showed in other ways that he was no friend to black Americans. While Daniels was in this position, government-sanctioned propaganda was used to influence Americans to support World War I. It is unknown what part, if any, Daniels played in this full-scale indoctrination effort, but he was the last cabinet official to vote for a declaration of war in 1917. After the war, Daniels supported FDR's run for the presidency, and Roosevelt, in turn, appointed Daniels Ambassador to Mexico. As soon as he showed up there, the Mexicans stoned the American Embassy. Today, a statue of Daniels stands in downtown Raleigh. An aircraft carrier was named in his honor.

### John Charles McNeill

John Charles McNeill, perhaps the kindest of all those who represented the press in this story, died very young. Not long after the lynching, he went home to his family's place in Sampson County and literally drank himself to death. A few months earlier, in May, 1907, Joseph Caldwell wrote to a family member. He was clearly concerned.

> *It's true that John Charles has been drinking more whiskey than has been good for him, and realizing this himself, said, two or three weeks ago, to one of the young men in the office...that he believed he would go home and stay about a month.... I love him dearly. All in the office are devoted to him. He is too gifted and too valuable a man to be permitted to destroy himself. We will not allow it.*

He died in October, 1907 at age 33. Some say McNeill suffered from another ailment besides alcoholism, perhaps leukemia or pernicious anemia. But maybe McNeill was just too sensitive a soul to stay long in this world.

His poem "Mr. Nigger," despite what the use of the "N word" might imply, sympathizes with the plight of the black man during that period. Before he was employed by the *Observer*, he worked briefly as a lawyer. The little personal correspondence I could find in McNeill's papers, in Wake Forest University's library, includes a letter written to Governor Aycock requesting a pardon for a black prisoner, whom he and others believed to be innocent. Aycock's response was flippant. He wrote McNeill that he'd consider the pardon if McNeill would write a poem about the prisoner's return home for Christmas. Though Aycock added that he was seriously, "disposed' to pardon the man, I could find no indication that he did.

### Henry Edward Cowan (Red Buck) Bryant

In February, 1910, Tompkins wrote Bryant saying "he wanted to avoid sensational stories based on flimsy foundations." Later reflecting on that time, Bryant said Tompkins hadn't understood what was and was not newsworthy. The clash between the two had led to Bryant's break with the *Observer*, which sent him out west for a while. Years later he returned to the *Observer*, where he wrote a column until his death in 1967.

The front page of the *Observer's* November 4, 1967 issue carries a eulogy to Red Buck Bryant. Accompanied by his small photo, the item is nearly buried amid news of a race riot in Winston-Salem and a much larger depiction of two military guardsmen, standing with guns strapped on their shoulders. The headline of an article above Bryant's head reads: "Guardsmen Don't Have Ammunition."

### William Thomas (Tom) Bost

William Thomas Bost, Isaac's former neighbor and the *Observer's* Salisbury correspondent, remained in the newspaper business and went on to high praise for his work. A *Greensboro Daily News* tribute before his death said Bost had covered 250 executions. He was against capital punishment, he explained, and he "covered them as a religious duty," reporting them in a way he hoped would make readers' skin crawl.

Years after the Salisbury lynching, Bost wrote of his experiences and views on capital punishment in an article that appeared in *The State* magazine in 1935. Below are some excepts:

It would seem that I have witnessed as many executions as any one man should be forced to see. It is not necessary to suggest that I am opposed to the whole business and I keep on going with the hope that in my own day our state will become ashamed of its cold-blooded attitude toward even the worst of its criminals.

Most of the judges, solicitors and governors with whom I have been acquainted have great doubt as to whether capital punishment really works. For if in some instances it does seem to rid the world of so much rubbish, it seems by the same token to set an example of violence to a great number of others, so that I am firmly convinced that as a corrective measure it misses more often than it hits.

I have seen men hanged with the populace of almost an entire county looking on, and I have seen other men hanged by ravening mobs. Then I have seen them electrocuted in a little dark room with only a few persons allowed admittance. All methods appear to me to be fundamentally at fault but I think perhaps the mob's way is the most rational. It doesn't pretend that it is not wreaking vengeance. It doesn't pretend that it is prematurely yanking these derelicts into paradise. It just sordidly and brutally kills with no thought other than satisfying its lust for blood. That sort of killing carries its own antidote.

THOMAS BOST,
CIRCA 1930

I am profoundly persuaded that murderers believe in capital punishment and therefore they inflict it. The state also believes in capital punishment and it inflicts it. I have often wondered if nobody believed in capital punishment under any circumstances how long it would take us to become a nation without homicides.

I am prepared to show that there is between the public legal hanging and the lynching party a subtle but an irrepressible affinity. I remember when I was a boy that a negro named Whit Ferrand killed a cousin of mine who was a deputy sheriff. Ferrand was duly convicted and sentenced to death with another negro who had killed a woman. They rode out from the jail to a sacred Rowan County spot known as "Gallows Hill."

There were 25,000 people—men, women and children—looking upon this noble spectacle. Get a picture of that crowd if you can. Pretend that you are at the Duke-Carolina football game. There is a gallows in the center of the stadium. Two huge black caps are tied over the prisoners' heads. A left-handed sheriff raises a hatchet to cut the rope that springs the trap, but it takes one, two and three blows to sever the cord. Then the black devils fall, and for fifteen minutes these babes and boobs look at two men suspended between heaven and earth. Finally they quit kicking and you know they are dead.

If you have any doubt of this event as a great social occasion read this from the front page advertisement of the *Salisbury Afternoon Herald*: "Thursday, July 24th, Will Be a Gala Day for Salisbury. In Addition to the Double Hanging on Gallows Hill There Will Be Horse-racing at the County Fair Ground and a Baseball Game at Henderson Park Between Salisbury and Concord. Come One. Come All." They came!

That isn't so bad, you say, but behold the aftermath. Two little black imps about 12 and 13 years old, are accused of stoning to death a white woman. They are taken from jail without the formality of a preliminary hearing and lynched from the limb of a tree in the yard of an ex-congressman.

A few seasons later six negroes were charged with the murder of the Lyerlys. The evidence against them depends almost entirely upon the dream of a romantic little black, mostly white, eleven years old. The

Governor of North Carolina orders a special term to try them. A grand jury brings in the bill of indictment and with judge and jury empaneled and all the machinery of the courts in operation three of these are taken from the jail and hanged on the same limb in this same distinguished citizen's yard. You may be sure that wherever a community holds human life so cheaply that it would countenance a public hanging, by the same token it will regard all human life so lightly as to make a recurrence of lynching likely for any or for no cause. For whether the demand for public execution of criminals comes reputedly from deity or from devil, whether from Russia or from Rowan, from heaven or from hell, from holy hoboes or from Hottentots, from the streets of New Jerusalem or from the Sodom of perdition, it is savagery pure and simple and all that it can possibly do is to acquaint decent people with the impulses of barbarians. [5]

# CONCLUSION

# A GAME CALLED SPIN

## 1890S TO TODAY

*As soon as men decide that all means are permitted to fight an evil, then their good becomes indistinguishable from the evil that they set out to destroy.*

– Christopher Dawson,
*The Judgment of the Nations*

*It is too often the case that border newspapers...disseminate all sorts of exaggerations and falsehoods about the Indians, which are copied in papers of high character and wide circulation, in other parts of the country, while the Indians' side of the case is rarely ever heard. In this way the people at large get false ideas with reference to the matter. Then when the outbreak does come, public attention is turned to the Indians, their crimes and atrocities are alone condemned, while the persons whose injustice has driven them to this course escape scot-free and are the loudest in their denunciations.*

– General George Crook,
*Bury My Heart at Wounded Knee* [1]

W hen I was growing up, my mother used to say we were living in the end times, with Satan loose, doing his dirty work. I'm not sure about all that, but if there's a devil and he *is* "loose," he must have escaped in the 1890s. Those were the years Jim Crow flew into the South, and America sold its soul to the god of industry. And spin convinced the public that it was good.

A decade earlier, the press made it look like Geronimo was the devil. Unscrupulous newspapers were trying to "stir up a profit-making, land-grabbing war." And so "...they made a special demon of him, inventing atrocity stories by the dozens and calling on vigilantes to hang him if the government would not." When General Crook tried to support the Apaches and speak out against the propaganda, as John Bassett did for African Americans, the newspapers turned on *him* [2] the way Daniels pounced on Bassett. Not long after the government took what it wanted from the Apache and threw Geronimo into a Florida jail, the southern Dixiecrats went after African Americans, and one president after another pretended not to notice. Three years after Nease, John, and Jack were lynched, Geronimo, the last Apache chief, died in a prison 2,000 miles away from his beloved ancestral home.

Though the demonization of American Indians and African Americans began much earlier, it accelerated after the mid 1800s. It was during this period that the "news" media really began to realize how much power it had. By the end of 1890, Sitting Bull was dead, and the massacre at Wounded Knee was over. Media tactics contributed to those atrocities, and then Daniels used the same tools to attack blacks in North Carolina. Afterward, the southern states that hadn't already cooked up their own course of white supremacy, soon followed suit, some using Daniels' unique recipe of rhetoric and race baiting.

Before the U.S. government finished off the Indians and allowed the South to bring back a system of virtual slavery, it had already begun lusting after Hawaii. The demise of the Indians was about land and gold, the attack on African Americans was mostly about cotton, but Hawaii's lure was sugar. All of it was about money—for an elite few.

Stephen Kinzer's *Overthrow* details *"America's Century of Regime Change..."* that begins with its acquisition of Hawaii. Public support for Hawaii's annexation followed America's resolve to win the Philippines conflict, a spinoff of the Spanish American War—the war spawned from yellow journalism. [A]

Industry's desire to gain control of markets abroad led to a period of U.S. imperialism, kicked off by its own "regime" change. It went from Democratic to Republican in 1897 when William McKinley succeeded the anti-imperialist president, Grover Cleveland. Right away McKinley worried about Spain's control of Cuba, where U.S. businessmen owned millions in land investments. He didn't want Cuba to become independent, because that might lead to land distribution that would benefit Cuba's inhabitants at the expense of these wealthy Americans. To exert his influence over the Cuban situation, McKinley sent the battleship *Maine* over to Havana, supposedly on a friendly visit. Shortly afterward, in February, 1898, the *Maine* mysteriously exploded. [A]

LA GUERRE A CUBA
Les insurgés revenant des Batailles et des Munitions

CUBAN WAR

Enter William Randolph Hearst, owner-editor of the *New York Journal* and a number of other papers across the country. As part of a circulation war with another prominent publisher, Pulitzer, Hearst had already begun turning public opinion against Spanish colonists by demonizing their commander, General Weyler. "Like countless others who have sought to set the United States on the path to war, he knew that he needed a villain, an individual on whom he could focus the public's outrage." [A] Sound familiar?

Hearst happily exploited the explosion of the *Maine* to support his cry for war:

> *The moment Hearst heard about the sinking of the Maine, he recognized it as a great opportunity. For weeks after the explosion, he filled page after page with mendacious "scoops," fabricated interviews with unnamed government officials, and declarations that the battleship had been "destroyed by treachery" and "split in two by an enemy's secret infernal machine." The Journal's daily circulation doubled in four weeks. Other newspapers joined the frenzy, and their campaign brought Americans to near-hysteria.*
>
> *With such intense emotion surging through the United States, it was easy for McKinley to turn aside repeated offers from the new Spanish prime minister, Praxedes Sagasta, to resolve the Cuban conflict peacefully.* [A]

Kinzer says the U.S. didn't want negotiation because it more than likely would have led to "an independent Cuba where neither the United States nor any other country would have military bases." So in April, 1898, McKinley, "... asked Congress to authorize 'forcible intervention' in Cuba. [A] But Cuba strongly opposed U.S. intervention, and Americans back then were very pro-Cuban. Therefore, McKinley had to trick Americans into supporting his plans. He lied to Congress, promising, basically, that America would be fighting to help the Cubans gain their independence—that America would "'...leave the government and control of the island to its people.'"

Congress fell for it.

It was as if they were looking for something to get excited about. Kinzer explained that the declaration of war gave Americans, recently torn apart by the Civil War, a cause to rally around. "Members of the House of Representatives celebrated their vote by breaking into rousing choruses of 'Dixie' and 'The Battle Hymn of the Republic' as they left the chamber." After lying about the intent to go to war, the imperialist propaganda machine later convinced Americans that Cubans were really not fit for self-government, and then the U. S. government went back on its promise. [A3] A lot of Americans may not understand why Cubans are mad at us now, but this looks like a pretty good reason.

Soon after the intervention in Cuba, the attack on the Philippines began—which was part of the goal to defeat Spain. During that campaign, the hatred that had been drummed up in America against Indians and African descendants was now transferred to the dark-skinned Filipinos. When American soldiers stationed in the Philippines wrote home,

> *...they told friends and relatives that they had come "to blow every nigger to nigger heaven" and vowed to fight "until the niggers are killed off like Indians."* [A]

This violence begat even worse violence. The Filipinos countered with "tactics unlike any Americans had ever seen," and the U.S. responded to that by sending Colonel Jacob Smith, who had participated in the massacre at Wounded Knee, to "do whatever was necessary to subdue the rebels." And, "American soldiers carried out these orders with gusto."

> *"I want no prisoners,"* he told them. *"I wish you to kill and burn. The more you kill and the more you burn, the better you will please me."* [A]

Americans, overall, were oblivious to the extent of the atrocities in the Philippines until eleven innocent Filipinos, working for America, were summarily executed, and the commanders demanded a court martial—which led to a cry of outrage from the American public. It was then that they became aware of the torture being used, including the "water cure," [A] which was mentioned several times in 1906 newspapers, reporting the court-martial of an officer named Glenn. It has also been in the news a hundred years later, in regard to use on Iraqi war prisoners. In this form of torture, bamboo sections "were forced down the throats of prisoners and then used to fill the prisoners' stomachs with dirty water until they swelled in torment. Soldiers would then jump on the stomach to force the water out, often repeating the process until the victim either informed or died." [A]

Mark Twain wrote, "God Damn the U.S. for its vile conduct in the Philippines." [A] He'd probably have said the same about North Carolina if he'd known the details of the Wilmington massacre, which was overshadowed by the Philippines fiasco. Some blacks had volunteered to serve during the Spanish American War, hoping it would finally gain them the respect they deserved. But those returning to North Carolina were welcomed with the Wilmington massacre and/or Jim Crow instead. And when Wilmington survivors wrote to McKinley for justice and reparations, the President ignored them. By then, McKinley "...needed the goodwill of the Southern white congressional delegation in order to obtain ratification of the Treaty of Paris, which would formally conclude..." the war. [3] Over a hundred years later, North Carolina is just beginning to discuss reparations, though the press, overall, isn't saying much about it.

Cuba, the Philippines, and Hawaii were only the beginning of "an era in which the United States has assumed the right to intervene anywhere in the world, not simply by influencing or coercing foreign governments but also by overthrowing them," Kinzer said. The "first time a president acted on his own to depose a foreign leader was in 1909, when William Howard Taft ordered the overthrow of Nicaraguan president Jose Santos Zelaya." Taft claimed "he was acting to protect American security and promote democratic principles. His true aim was to defend the right of American companies to operate as they wished in Nicaragua." And this, Kinzer said, "set a pattern. Throughout the twentieth century and into the beginning of the twenty-first, the United States repeatedly used its military power, and that of its clandestine services, to overthrow governments that refused to protect American interests. Each time, it cloaked its intervention in the rhetoric of national security and liberation." [A] And in most cases, if not all, the mainstream press promoted the rhetoric.

The United States' cotton exports helped fund its budding imperialism in its desire to scoop up markets abroad, and the South wanted a piece of that pie. That's where the oppression against blacks came in and why it remained for decades. For one thing, the South wanted to ensure "...northern investors that the southern "Negro problem" would not be a bar to progress." [B] In this way, black communities in the South were much like undeveloped or underprivileged countries abroad the U.S. sought to exploit for the sake of industry. "The whites do not wish them to progress," said a French Political Science professor, after touring the South, "for they need them to supply the lowest type of manual labour." [C]

By 1914, the propaganda tactics tested to turn public opinion against Southern blacks, Indians, Hawaiians, Cubans, and Filipinos near the turn of the century, were now tried and true and ready for the big time.

M.I.T. Professor Noam Chomsky, whose expertise, among others, is propaganda, writes about its role in World War I.

*The First World War was the first time there was highly organized state propaganda. The British had a Ministry of Information, and they really needed it; they had to get the United States into the war or else they were in bad trouble. The Ministry of Information was mainly geared to sending out propaganda, including huge fabrications about "Hun" atrocities. They targeted American intellectuals on the reasonable assumption that these were the people who were most gullible and most likely to believe propaganda. The intellectuals are also the ones who disseminate it through their own system."* [D]

It was meant to be a kind of twisted "trickle-down" effect. And it all started with the industrial revolution and creation of "the huge industries of domination and control." [D2]

However, there were obstacles impeding Britain's goal to get Americans interested in the war. Woodrow Wilson had just been elected under the slogan, "Peace without victory," and the United States was "a very pacifist country" at the time, where foreign affairs were concerned, said Chomsky. However, he explained, Wilson had "...intended to go to war all along. So the question was, how do you get the pacifist population to become raving anti-German lunatics so they want to go kill all the Germans? That requires propaganda. So they set up the first and really only major state propaganda agency in U.S. history...." Called the Creel Commission or the Committee on Public Information, its job "was to propagandize the population into a jingoist hysteria. It worked incredibly well. Within a few months there was a raving war hysteria, and the United States was able to go to war." [D]

Chomsky said World War I "...taught a lesson: State propaganda, when supported by the educated classes and when no deviation is permitted from it, can have a big effect. It was a lesson learned by Hitler and many others, and it has been pursued to this day." [D1] "Speaking of Nazi Germany," Chomsky said,

> *Joseph Goebbels, its propaganda minister, once said, "It would not be impossible to prove with sufficient repetition and a psychological understanding of the people concerned that a square is in fact a circle. They are mere words, and words can be molded until they clothe ideas in disguise." [D2]*

Isn't this, after all, what Josephus Daniels did to whites in North Carolina—convince many of them that black folk were all ravenous beasts and other things inhuman?

Neither Chomsky nor Kinzer mention that Josephus Daniels was President Wilson's Secretary of the Navy during World War I. He was also an acquaintance of William Randolph Hearst, who was apparently so impressed with Daniels' abuse of the first amendment, he wanted to add the *News and Observer* to the list of the many he already owned. When he offered him a million dollars for it, Daniels refused. Retaining control of the paper would be his ticket to even greater power. Using it to support Wilson's campaign led to his appointment to more than one government position.

In his introduction to Chomsky's book, *Letters From Lexington: Reflections on Propaganda*, Donaldo Macedo discusses propaganda tactics used recently by the Bush administration. They are not at all dissimilar to those that molded the actions by and against black Americans in 1906. This discussion of current affairs brings the 1906 story into the twenty-first century and helps us understand the roots of "racial" attitudes today—how Americans can easily become blinded by a barrage of billboard rhetoric.

Macedo, who wrote this in the early days of the current Iraqi war, talks about how easily Americans were fooled by flag-waving and other distractions, blindly supporting "...an illegal war against Iraq, allowing the jingoistic display of the American flag to 'patriotically' cage their minds...," resulting in the almost total lack of outrage in the media, the intellectual class, and a very large segment of the population toward the falsehoods that informed and shaped the rationale for the war against Iraq......the American public, in general," he said, "seemed to be unbothered by the big lies... [D]

> *Criticizing the Bush Administration policies for the war against Iraq was viewed as un-American. Questioning the Bush Administration after the war began was cleverly labeled as not supporting our troops. In fact, the media's cheerleading for the war preparation made it impossible to question Bush's motives for wanting to preemptively attack Iraq—to such an extent that even for members of Congress to criticize the president would have raised exponentially the possibility of their losing the next election.* [D]

The problem is not with the decision, either way, so much as it is the deceitful methods used to garner public support. Keeping the public focused on emotional distractions, gets in the way of attempts at honest debate of relevant issues.

Similar forces were at work in North Carolina in 1898 and afterward. White men who had voted with blacks supporting Populist reform in 1896 where accused of not supporting their white women, abandoning their manhood. John Spenser Bassett's questioning of white supremacy in 1903 nearly cost him his job. All the "cheerleading" for white supremacy in the 1898 campaign made it likewise impossible for whites opposed to the tactics to speak out against them. The same jingoism Daniels used to get whites to back or ignore atrocities committed against blacks is at work today. It's the same influence that makes Americans see casualties of the World Trade Center attack differently than casualties of war waged by America in other lands. Doesn't it all come down to the same old myth of white supremacy?

Kinzer discusses several other examples where the U.S. used questionable means to exert its power over other countries. One very timely example explains why Iran doesn't trust America today. Following is the gist of what Kinzer said happened in the 1950s—which actually began years earlier, in those days of America's "fall."

In 1901, Britain began its monopoly on the extraction of Iranian oil, on which it had become dependent by the 1950s. It relied on this oil to "project military power, fuel its industries, and give its citizens a high standard of living..." The British corporation, Anglo-Iranian Oil Company, seemed to care little about the Iranian's standard of living though. Its "grossly unequal contract, negotiated with a corrupt monarch, required it to pay Iran just 16 percent of the money it earned from selling the country's oil." "Anglo-Iranian made more profit in 1950 alone than it had paid Iran in royalties over the previous half century." [A]

Then in 1951, a western-educated Iranian, descended from royalty, who seemed to care deeply about "Iran's poverty and misery," was elected to power. Mossadegh "...was determined to expel the Anglo-Iranian Oil Company, nationalize the oil industry, and use the money it generated to develop Iran." Both houses of the Iranian Parliament unanimously supported their new leader's plan. And Iran offered "to compensate Britain for the money it had spent building its wells and refinery...." It further justified its action by pointing to Britain's own example—it had also "recently nationalized [its] coal and steel industries." [A]

That seemed fair enough. But Britain's response was reminiscent of the South's attitudes towards black Americans. "'We English have had hundreds of years of experience on how to treat the natives,' one of them scoffed. 'Socialism is all right back home, but out here you have to be the master.'" The British were incensed by this "backward" country's gall. And even though America had a more equitable agreement, fifty-fifty, with Iran's neighbors, Britain refused to accept this kind of deal with Iran. Britain's foreign secretary, Herbert Morrison, advised his leaders "to do everything possible to prevent the Persians" from getting out of the original contract. And "Over the next year, the British did just that." [A] But what does all this have to do with America? Kinzer gets to that.

First, before involving America, the British considered just about every tactic available to change Mossadegh's strategy, including "bribing" him, "assassinating him, and launching a military invasion of Iran, a plan they might have carried out if President Truman and Secretary of State Dean Acheson had not become almost apoplectic on learning of it." They even used sabotage to try to prove that the Iranians were incapable of running the industry without Britain's help. After Britain's appeals to the United Nations Security Council and the International Court of Justice were unsuccessful, they felt they had one option left. "They resolved to organize a coup." [A]

This is where the press and propaganda once again played a key role. During its domination of Iran, Britain had bought "a variety of military officers, journalists, religious leaders, and others who could help overthrow a government if the need arose. Officials in London ordered their agents in Tehran to set a plot in motion." But Mossadegh was one step ahead of them and thwarted their plans and shut down the British embassy. The British responded with personal attacks against Mossadegh, labeling him "'wild,' 'fanatical,' 'absurd,' 'gangster-like,' 'completely unscrupulous,' and 'clearly imbalanced.'" But despite its adeptness at name calling, Britain's tongue and hands were otherwise tied. [A]

Then they got a "miracle" —the help they wanted from America. Truman left office, Eisenhower took his place, and John Foster Dulles was appointed his secretary of state. Dulles was a friend to the huge corporations, and he was obsessed with protecting their rights and fighting what he believed to be the spread of Communism. For the British, Dulles was their ace in the hole. Before Eisenhower could be inaugurated, the British presented their plan to have the CIA "carry out a coup in Iran that they themselves could no longer execute...." But Britain knew its true motive for overthrowing Mossadegh—his desire to nationalize Iran's oil industry—would not fly in America. So it spun the plot to make the cause appear to be a "'rollback' of Communism." However, since the State Department "did not have the capacity to overthrow governments...Dulles would have to enlist the CIA." And it just so happens, the CIA's director was Dulles' younger brother, Allen. [A]

The Dulles brothers were ready for the takeover, but first they had to get Eisenhower to go along. John Dulles was able to win him over by convincing the president that if Mossadegh were removed from power by another force—or assassinated, it could create a political vacuum "the Communists might easily take over." And that meant Iranian oil would also "fall into Communist hands." [A]

So plan Ajax evolved. And a big part of it was molding public opinion against Mossadegh. "Under their plan, the Americans would spend $150,000 to bribe journalists, editors, Islamic preachers, and other opinion leaders to 'create, extend and enhance public hostility and distrust and fear of Mossadegh and his government.' Then they would hire thugs to carry out 'staged attacks' on religious figures and other respected Iranians, making it seem that Mossadegh had ordered them." Other monies were allocated to bribe "additional friends" and "key people." "On 'coup day,' thousands of paid demonstrators would converge on parliament to demand that it dismiss Mossadegh." [A]

The American press, for the most part, got with the program.

*A few newspapers and magazines published favorable articles about Mossadegh, but they were the exceptions. The New York Times regularly referred to him as a dictator. Other papers compared him to Hitler and Stalin. Newsweek reported that, with his help, Communists were "taking over" Iran. Time called his election "one of the worst calamities to the anti-communist world since the Red conquest of China."* [A]

Once the operation was set into motion, headed by Theodore Roosevelt's grandson, Kermit Roosevelt, "it took him just a few days to set Iran aflame.... He created an entirely artificial wave of anti-Mossadegh protest.... Newspapers were filled with articles and cartoons depicting him as everything from a homosexual to an agent of British imperialism." Mossadegh "realized that some unseen hand was directing this campaign, but because he had such an ingrained and perhaps exaggerated faith in democracy, he did nothing to repress it." [A]

To make a long story shorter, Mossadegh was finally taken down with a riot scene not unlike the one that occurred in the streets of Wilmington and Salisbury a half century earlier, followed by an attack on his personal residence. Left with no other choice, Mossadegh surrendered, and he was placed under arrest. [A] He was tried, "and found guilty of treason. He spent three years in prison and the rest of his life under house arrest." [A]

While U.S. and British forces were working on destroying Iran's hope for democracy, an American corporation, United Fruit, with connections to John Dulles, went after Guatemala. And, thanks to Dulles, the rest of America eventually followed. United Fruit had felt threatened when Guatemala turned democratic and tried to implement agrarian reform, just as the Populist reforms in the South had scared southern elites. The head of the fruit corporation, Sam Zemurray, to make "sure that American public opinion was with him," hired a public relations expert, Edward Bernays, who was a nephew of Sigmund Freud." Bernays, in turn, launched an all-out propaganda campaign "portraying Guatemala as falling victim to 'reds....'" The "Guatemalan version of Operation Ajax" followed, and President Arbenz was ousted. [A]

During this campaign the CIA used God to get to the Guatemalans—to turn them against Arbenz. Its agents wrote scripts for the Guatemalan and Catholic clergy, warning "the faithful that a demonic force called Communism was trying to destroy their homeland and called on them to 'rise...against this enemy of God and country.'" "CIA pilots dropped leaflets, like one that said: "'Fight for God, Fatherland, Freedom, Work, Truth, Justice." [A]

Kinzer says Dulles had "...truly believed that Arbenz was a tool of 'Communist imperialism' rather than what he actually was; an idealistic, reform-minded nationalist who bore Americans no ill will. By overthrowing him, the United States crushed a democratic experiment that held great promise for Latin America. As in Iran a year earlier, it deposed a regime that embraced fundamental American ideals but that had committed the sin of seeking to retake control of its own natural resources." [A] And as in North Carolina, a half century earlier, Daniels' Dixiecrats crushed an experiment in interracial cooperation and agrarian reform that had the potential to change the future of America, for the majority of Americans, for the better.

Kinzer emphasizes that "most 'regime change' operations achieved their short-term goals. But from the vantage point of history, it's clear that most of these operations actually weakened American security. They cast whole regions of the world into upheaval, creating whirlpools of instability from which undreamed-of threats arose years later." In 1979, when the U.S. embassy in Iran was seized and American diplomats taken hostage, most Americans did not know the history, and therefore "...few had any idea why Iranians were so angry at the country they called 'the great Satan.'" [A] The leader the U.S. imposed in Guatemala in 1954 after the coup, Carlos Armas, laid the foundation "for a police state that plunged Guatemala into bloody tragedy over the following decades." [A] Likewise many "white" Americans today, don't really understand why remarks recently made by Don Imus, Trent Lott, and others, and especially the display of nooses, result in such strong protests from the African American community. Propaganda like that used in 1898 to effect the coup in Wilmington, North Carolina and usher in Jim Crow throughout the South, created over a century of contaminated fallout in the form of "racial" hatred and unrest.

A news item written after a tragic train wreck in 1906 illustrates early residual effects from North Carolina's degradation of the value of African American lives. By this time, Jim Crow laws were firmly established, and all black passengers were required to ride in separate, but not nearly equal, cars. These were often of flimsy wood construction and sandwiched between the engine and the other sturdy, metal passenger cars, set aside for whites only. When two Seaboard engines collided on the night of July 22nd, the "Jim Crow Car Telescoped," killing twenty two, eighteen of which were "colored." Of the forty-six injured, forty-one were "mangled Negroes." [E]

John Charles McNeill reported public reaction to the wreck and the inequalities it exposed.

> *It is a good thing, people said today, that the Jim Crow car is carried next to the engine. It so much lessens the number of white people killed.... The mail and baggage were carried in the same car on Engineer Lewis' train and it completely telescoped the Jim Crow car.... The mail and baggage coach still stand there, driven clear through the flimsy Jim Crow car. The mass of debris of splinters and lumber is evidence of the dangerously cheap construction of these coaches. They look like they were pasteboard boxes full of shattered tin.* " [E]

Chomsky explains that the real threat to democracies based on corporate power structures is the good example. In 1898, Wilmington blacks were proving to the rest of the world that they were not savages, lazy, or stupid. Where given a respite from oppression, blacks often proved their ability to educate themselves, run successful businesses, own nice homes and property, and hold offices. With new developments in newspaper production technology in the late 1890s, this example in Wilmington might have spread to all corners of the globe if allowed to continue, and then where would the state fill its need for "slave" labor? Chomsky says of any "model for achieving modernization in a single generation," —it has to be stopped," in the view of those running the show. [D2]

> *It was the same reason that the State Department gave for supporting Hitler in the 1930s, and in fact just about every other case. Case after case after case. The threat of a good example, or it's sometimes called the virus effect. The virus of independent nationalism might succeed and inspire others. Actually, the war in Vietnam started the same way.* " [D2]

After Guatemala, it was one damned thing after another. And then there was Iraq.

As I write this conclusion to the Lyerly story on Friday, July 13, 2007, the death toll for Americans in the Iraq war is near 4,000, with an estimated 25-100 thousand Americans wounded. The number of Iraqis killed in "Operation Iraqi Freedom" is conservatively estimated at 400,000. Countless numbers of injured on both sides have lost limbs and some the will to live. Was the real cause behind this war, whatever it was, worth this sacrifice? Could another way to "freedom" have been found through honest debate, unhampered by jingoist rhetoric?

Vietnam war casualties are said to be from 2-5 million. Darfur, over 400 thousand. The estimated number of American Indians killed in wars is 45-100 thousand. The Civil War, over 600,000; WWI, 40 million; and the Nazi Holocaust, close to 6 million. Between 1882 and 1951, alone, a total of about 3,437 African Americans were lynched, and that's just the ones that got reported.

The Lyerly tragedy is just another example of the residual effects of misguided propaganda. It reveals that the forces running the show then, are still running it now. And the game will continue until the majority learns to recognize when it is being had.

Changing Minds website tells us what we know, that "propaganda and manipulation of reality continues to be used in large quantities in the modern world." It also points out what we may not know or may not wish to believe, that "...most people are taken in and see nothing of how they are manipulated." One of its goals is to help the public see beyond the rhetoric, the flag waving, and the Bible thumping. It and other websites, like Andy McDonald's on "Propaganda" at George Mason University, list seven common propaganda techniques to look for. These are based on those Boston merchant Edward Filene helped establish, along with the Institute for Propaganda Analysis, "which sought to educate Americans to recognize propaganda techniques."

> * Bandwagon: "Pump up the value of 'joining the party'"—"Creates the impression of widespread support."
>
> * Card-stacking: "build a highly-biased case for your position."

* Glittering generalities: "Use power words to evoke emotions" — "Using language associated with values and beliefs deeply held by the audience without providing supporting information or reason."

* Name-calling: "Denigrating opponents" —Used "to create fear and arouse prejudice."

* Plain folks: "Making the leader seem ordinary" —"that the spokesperson is from humble origins, someone they can trust."

* Testimonial: "The testimony of an independent person is seen as more trustworthy." —like a product endorsement without facts to back it up.

* Transfer: Associate the leader with trusted others. [E] Often involves the use of symbols "(e.g., waving the flag) to stir our emotions and win our approval." [E, F]

To this list, Aaron Delwich's website on "Propaganda" adds the tactics of "Fear" and "Euphemisms." Certainly we're all familiar with the "Fear" approach by now. Delwich gives the following examples of "Euphemisms":

> *Since war is particularly unpleasant, military discourse is full of euphemisms. In the 1940s, America changed the name of the War Department to the Department of Defense. Under the Reagan Administration, the MX-Missile was renamed "the Peacekeeper." During war-time, civilian casualties are referred to as "collateral damage," and the word "liquidation" is used as a synonym for "murder."*

And "enhanced interrogation techniques" is now used as a synonym for torture.

If we can recognize these and other tactics used to distract us from the truth or the real issues, maybe we will learn to see through them and beyond them. Chomsky seems optimistic. He says, "...despite all the propaganda, despite all the efforts to control thought and manufacture consent...people are acquiring an ability and a willingness to think things through. Skepticism about power has grown, and attitudes have changed on many,

many issues. It's kind of slow, maybe even glacial, but perceptible and important." [DI]

There is more cause for hope. According to the *Greensboro News-Record*, on August 2, 2007, just days ago, the North Carolina State Senate expressed "profound regret" for the 1898 campaign. The *News-Record* responded that it's the least they could do:

> *The success of this campaign in Wilmington inspired a white supremacy movement across the state and eventually the South, ushering in the Jim Crow era. By 1900, blacks and white Republicans were largely kept from the polls by violence and intimidation. In effect, the Wilmington coup negated the result of one election and altered the outcomes of all those to come for the next seven decades—more than regrettable.*

The paper's right, of course—it's pitifully little and ridiculously late—but it's a start.

When asked about the recent rash of apologies for slavery, professor and author Dr. John Hope Franklin said he wasn't impressed. However, his response to a 300-page report published by the 1898 Wilmington Race Riot Commission is more encouraging. He told the *Independent Weekly* in April, 2007 that those recommendations are "commendable."

> *I don't know if they go far enough; they go pretty far to the extent that they undertake to reverse the sentiments and to establish a new basis for racial harmony, not only in New Hanover County but also throughout the state. I can only hope that they do almost as much as they propose to do.*
>
> *It's a big order and I must say, if the recommendations are seriously considered by the population of this state, we will be doing a remarkable job in moving in the right direction.* [H]

CRSO

North Carolina native and singer/songwriter, James Taylor, inspires us to look beyond the hatred of the past in his *Shed A Little Light*, inviting us to "turn our thoughts to" the words and wisdom of Martin Luther King. [4]

King recognized that:

> *Even when pressed by the demands of inner truth, men do not easily assume the task of opposing their government's policy, especially in time of war. Nor does the human spirit move without great difficulty against all the apathy of conformist thought within one's own bosom and in the surrounding world.* [5]

Nevertheless, he refused

> *...to accept despair as the final response to the ambiguities of history...to accept the idea that the "isness" of man's present nature makes him morally incapable of reaching up for the eternal "oughtness" that forever confronts him...to accept the idea that man is mere flotsam and jetsam in the river of life, unable to influence the unfolding events which surround him...to accept the view that mankind is so tragically bound to the starless midnight of racism and war that the bright daybreak of peace and brotherhood can never become a reality.*

And he refused

> *...to accept the cynical notion that nation after nation must spiral down a militaristic stairway into the hell of thermonuclear destruction.*

Above all, he had the "audacity to believe"

> *...that unarmed truth and unconditional love will have the final word in reality.......that peoples everywhere can have three meals a day for their bodies, education and culture for their minds, and dignity,*

*equality and freedom for their spirits.... that what self-centered men have torn down men other-centered can build up....that one day mankind will bow before the altars of God and be crowned triumphant over war and bloodshed, and nonviolent redemptive good will proclaim the rule of the land....*

"I still believe," he said on the day he accepted the Nobel Peace Prize, "that we shall overcome." [6]

*The End*

# Acknowledgments

With so few words to adequately express gratitude, I'll simply say "thank you" to all who helped me tell this story. I was overwhelmed by the encouragement, kindness, information, and hospitality I received from many in Rowan County and others scattered across the state and elsewhere. I am grateful to you all, and I sure hope I don't make too many of you mad when you read this book. I tried to present all of the information available so everyone can better decide or debate what actually happened in Rowan County in 1902 and 1906.

In addition to those listed below, I want to particularly acknowledge some who exceeded common courtesy to share their time, expertise, oral history, and, most important, their encouragement: Glenda E. Gilmore endured the torture of my wretched rough draft and helped me understand the historical setting of this story. Cate Kozak and Winifred Golden steered my writing in the right direction. Nellie Troxell, for preserving and sharing my family history. Marilyn Harrison for her knowledge of local history you won't find in any book. Mary Olive Johnson, for a valuable critical reading. Susan Goodman Sides, for photos and more. Sandy Sanders, for hours of newspaper research in Raleigh. Joel Reese, for the same in Statesville. Phil Dayvault for leading me to the information in the first place, and Kristin Wells, for making me get on with it. And, my daughter, Jennifer, helped in too many ways to list.

Another special thanks to the pastor and congregation of Cedar Grove A.M.E. Zion Church, Barber Junction, for the warm welcome and help finding Nease's descendants.

**For oral history and more:**
Paul Barnhardt, Henry Clement, Phil Dayvault, Joe Dobbin, Dot Ellis, James Ellis, Jackie Graham, Cotrellia Hunter, Harold Gillespie, Janie Hurst, Bobby Ford Lyerly, Mary Henderson Messinger, Sharon Avery Mitchell, Bettie Sue Webb Moore, Albert Monroe, Ruby Lee Rufty Myers, Ralph Oliphant, Margaret Owen, Sara Penninger Knapp, John Robert Phipps, Anne Poole, Mrs. Cline, Ray Powlas, Carol Satterwhite, Tom Satterwhite, Eric Solomon, Edward Steele, John Thomas Steele, Karen Troxell, Bob Waller, Jim Webb, Mildred Barringer Wells, Justice Williams, Lois Work. To the kind man at the convenience store on Long Street who rode your bike to show me the lynching tree: you pedaled off before I got your name. And particular thanks to my aunts, Nellie Barringer Troxell, Hazel Barringer Oates, Faye Barringer Clontz

and to cousin Ralph Krider Barringer, for food and lodging, as well as oral history.

**Libraries and Archives:**
Barbara Allen, Naomi Rhodes, Sharon Flatt and others at Dare County Library
Dave Grabarek, Library of Virginia
Vanessa Sterling and Gretchen Witt at Rowan County Library
Wilson Library, UNC-Chapel Hill
NC State Archives
Joel Reese, Iredell County Library
Evelyn Smith, Davidson County Genealogical Society
Mecklenburg County Law and Government Library
Staff at Cleveland County Library
James Green, Womble, Carlyle, Sandridge & Rice
Lisa, Z. Smith Reynolds Library, Wake Forest University
Paul Morrison, Stanly County Library
Joseph Thomas, Joyner Library, East Carolina University
Patricia C. Grant, Colleton County, South Carolina Clerk of Court
Staff at Haywood County Library
Elizabeth Cook, editor, *Salisbury Post*
Mark Wineka and Andy Mooney, *Salisbury Post*

**Historical Background:**
Glenda Gilmore, Timothy Tyson, David Cecelski, Deborah Barnes, Michael Curriden, Staff at Rowan County Historical Museum, Nancy Dorr, Marvin Ira Dayvault, Pat Beck with Rowan County Genealogical Society, Donald Carter of Summersett Funeral Home, Bill Schafer of Southern Railway Historical Association

**Readings and Edits:**
Glenda E. Gilmore, John Harper, Marilyn Harrison, Mary Johnson, Mary Olive Johnson, Cate Kozak, Andrea Long, Mary Ellen Riddle

**Photographs:**
Janie Hurst, Sara Penninger Knapp, John Robert Phipps, Susan Goodman Sides, Nellie Troxell, Jim Webb, Mildred Wells

**Permission to use song quotation:**
Bob Dylan

**Permission to link to websites on Propaganda:**
Andrew McDonald and David Straker

**Publicity:**
Rose Post, *Salisbury Post*
Dick Gordon and Carol Jackson, *The Story*

**Computer Graphics:**
Dan Banks

Gratitude to Charles Frazier, for mentioning Salisbury three times on one page in his wonderful book, *Cold Mountain*, which I took as a sign.

A special note of thanks for *The Charlotte Observer* and *The Salisbury Post* film archives.

And finally, Clyde Overcash—thanks for nothing.

# PHOTO CREDITS

*In order of appearance*

**Map of Barber Junction**, *Courtesy Rowan County Library*
**Isaac Lyerly**, *Courtesy Jim Webb*
**Barber Junction Depot**, *Courtesy North Carolina Transportation Museum*
**John Charles McNeill**, *Courtesy NC ECHO*
**John Moose Julian**, *Courtesy Salisbury Post*
**William Thomas Bost**, *Greensboro Daily News*
**Joseph Pearson Caldwell**, *Courtesy UNC Press*
**H.E.C. Bryant**, *Courtesy Charlotte Observer*
**Isaac and Augusta Lyerly**, *Courtesy Addie Lyerly's Descendants*
**Addie Lyerly**, 1974, *Courtesy Salisbury Post*
**Janie and Mary Lyerly**, *Courtesy Nellie Barringer Troxell*
**Penninger's Sawmill**, *Courtesy Sara Penninger Knapp*
**Sheriff David R. Julian**, *Courtesy of The North Carolina State Archives*
**Josephus Daniels**, *Courtesy U.S. Navy*
**Wilmington Rioters**, *Collier's Weekly, November 26, 1898*
**Unity Presbyterian Church**, *Courtesy Crystal Earnhardt*
**William Pleasant (Pless) and Margaret Walton Barber**, *Courtesy John Robert Phipps*
**Prisoner Cage**, *Courtesy North Carolina Department of Correction*
**Central Prison in Raleigh**, *Courtesy North Carolina Department of Correction*
**John Nelson Penninger**, *Courtesy Sara Penninger Knapp*
**Solicitor William Cicero Hammer**, *Courtesy Randolph County Historical Photograph Collection*
**John Spenser Bassett**, *Duke University Archives*
**Suspects**, *Courtesy Salisbury Post*
**Rowan County Courthouse and Jail**, *Susan Goodman Sides Collection*
**Defense Attorney Jake F. Newell**, *Obituary in Greensboro Daily News, August 10, 1945*
**Salisbury Train Depot**, *Susan Goodman Sides Collection*
**Streetcar on Main Street**, *Susan Goodman Sides Collection*
**Nease Gillespie, Jack Dillingham, John Gillespie, Murdered by a Mob**, *Courtesy Salisbury Post*
**Judge Benjamin Franklin Long**, *Courtesy Iredell County Library*

**Rowan County Jail**, *Courtesy Susan Goodman Sides and Dave Graham*
**John G. Mitchell, Jr.**, *Used with Permission of Documenting the American South, The University of North Carolina at Chapel Hill Libraries*
**Lyerly Home**, *Courtesy Salisbury Post*
**Whitehead-Stokes Sanatorium**, by Theo. Buerbaum, *Courtesy Rowan Public Library*
**Judge Garland S. Ferguson**, *Courtesy of The North Carolina State Archives*
**Theodore Franklin Kluttz**, *Courtesy Salisbury Post*
**Slave Traders**, *The Mariners' Museum, Newport News, VA*
**Benson Family**, *Courtesy of a Benson Descendant*
**Cornelia Benson**, *Courtesy Salisbury Post*
**Theodore F. Kluttz, Jr.**, *North Carolina Collection, University of North Carolina Library at Chapel Hill*
**Will Wetmore, Alleged Lyncher, Points Out Site Where Cornelia's Body Was Found**, *Courtesy Salisbury Post*
**Main Street, Salisbury**, *Susan Goodman Sides Collection*
**George Adam Rufty & John Redwine Barringer**, *Collection of the Author*
**Thomas Bost, Circa 1930**, *The State* Magazine, 12 January 1935
**La Guerre A Cuba (The Cuban War)**, *Le Petit Parisien, 1898*

# END NOTES

## Introduction
**1-2.** "Play of lynching: The Leaven Works Among Our Children," *Raleigh News and Observer*, 10 August 1906, front page. Reports on this incident vary slightly; a couple say the little boy's name was Emil, but records indicate Emil was his father's name. Locals' pronunciation of Salisbury is Sawz-berry.
**3.** "Raleigh Boys Try to Lynch Negress," *Greensboro Industrial News,* 16 August 1906.
**4-5.** "Small Boys Get Lynching Mania: Think it Fine Sport to Play at Lawlessness in Emulation of Elders," *Greensboro Industrial News*, 24 August 1906.
**6.** George Cox, "Murder Lynching and Aftermath: Rowan County July 6 - August 10, 1906" (Chapel Hill: The University of North Carolina Press, no date).
**7.** Baltimore *Afro-American Ledger*, 9 August 1906, editorial page.

## Chapter 1: *Friday The Thirteenth*
**1.** Paul Jeffers, *With an Axe* (New York: Kensington Publishing Corp, 2000). Some newspapers reported that the Lyerlys were clubbed to death. All sources, considered together, indicate that both an axe and a club or handle of an axe were probably used. However, since the murders were most commonly publicized as axe murders, they will be referred to as such throughout the book.
**2.** Joel Williamson, *The Crucible of Race: Black-White Relations in the American South Since Emancipation* (New York: Oxford University Press, 1984).
**3.** Richard Wormser, *The Rise and Fall of Jim Crow* (New York: St. Martin's Press, 2003).
**4.** Glenda Gilmore, *Gender & Jim Crow* (Chapel Hill: University of North Carolina Press, 1996) 85.
**5-6.** *The Rise and Fall of Jim Crow.*
**7.** James S. Brawley, *Rowan County: A Brief History* (Raleigh: NORTH CAROLINA Division of Archives and History, 1977).
**8.** Catherine Kozak, *Virginian Pilot*, 17 December 2003.
**9.** *Raleigh News and Observer*, 15 July 1906.
**10.** *Greensboro Industrial News*, 15 July 1906.
**11.** "Four Killed While Asleep," *Charlotte Observer*, 15 July 1906. Both McNeill and another *Observer* reporter, H.E.C. Bryant, wrote separate accounts of the Lyerly murders, using subheadings under this

main headline. McNeill got the ages of the girls wrong in this account. Correct ages are 17, 14, and 11.

**Chapter 2: *An Eerie Calm***
**1.** James Brawley, *Rowan County: A Brief History*, 155.
**2.** Mark Wineka, *A Family Affair: The Life, Times and Sale of a Family-owned Newspaper* (Asheboro, North Carolina: Down Home Press, 1999) 38-39. Jack Claiborne, *The Charlotte Observer, Its Time and Place 1869-1986* (Chapel Hill: UNC Press, 1986). "Assembly Pays Tribute To Newsman Tom Bost," *Greensboro Daily News*, 28 February 1953. "Associates Praise His Integrity, Ability As Writer," *Greensboro Daily News*, 14 September 1951.
**3.** *The Charlotte Observer, Its Time and Place 1869-1986.*
**4.** "75 years of Newspapering in Charlotte, North Carolina" (*Charlotte Observer,* 1961)6.
**5.** *The Charlotte Observer, Its Time and Place 1869-1986.* "75 years of Newspapering in Charlotte, North Carolina." Glenda E. Gilmore, editorial comment.
**6.** *The Charlotte Observer, Its Time and Place 1869-1986.*
**7.** *The Charlotte Observer, Its Time and Place 1869-1986.* "75 years of Newspapering in Charlotte, North Carolina."
**8-9.** *The Charlotte Observer, Its Time and Place 1869-1986.*
**10 - 19.** "Four Killed While Asleep," *Charlotte Observer*, 15 July 1906. Both McNeill and Bryant wrote separate accounts of the Lyerly murders, using subheadings under this main headline.
**20.** McNeill's poem, "Mr. Nigger" portrays the black man as scapegoat for all the South's problems (poem published in *Lyrics from Cotton Land (*Chapel Hill: University of North Carolina Press, 1922). In 1902 attorney McNeill petitioned Governor Aycock for a pardon on behalf of Reuben Ross, who McNeill apparently believed to be innocent of the crime for which he was serving a life sentence. (Personal Correspondence in collection at Z. Smith Reynolds Library, Wake Forest University.)
**21.** "Four Killed While Asleep."
**22.** "The Law Has Its Clutches On The Lyerly Murderers," *The Carolina Watchman*, 25 July 1906, front page.
**23.** "Lyerly Axe Murders," *Salisbury Post,* 14 July 1974.

**Chapter 3: *Wheat & Chaff***
**A.** "Horrible Butchery," *Salisbury Post*, 18 June 1906, front page.
**B.** "Four Killed While Asleep," *Charlotte Observer*, 15 July 1906. Details of Henry Mayhew's testimony vary with reports.
**C.** "Lyerly Axe Murders," *Salisbury Post,* 14 July 1974.

**D.** "Crimson Horror Shocks Carolina, " *Raleigh News and Observer*, 15 July 1906.

**E.** *Greensboro Industrial News*, 21 July 1906.

**F.** "Man, Wife and 2 Children Slain," *Greensboro Industrial News,* 15 July 1906. The *Industrial News*, though a Republican paper, also refrained from the more respectful addition of "Mr" or "Mrs" when referring to people of color, following the same protocol as the Dixiecrats.

**G.** "The Lyerly Murder Case, " *Charlotte Observer*, 22 July 1906, 1, 3, 4.

**1.** "Weeping Girls Drag Out of the House the Bodies of Murdered Relatives," *Asheville Citizen*, 15 July 1906.

**2.** Conversation with current owner of Lyerly property. Map of Rowan County, drawn by C. M. Miller, 1903.

**3.** Personal conversation with relative who will remain anonymous, 2004.

**4.** David Pilgrim, "The Brute Caricature," Jim Crow Museum of Racist Memorabilia. Online at: http://www.freeis.edu/news/jimcrow/brute/

**5.** "Brained Wife and Children: Crazy Colleton Farmer Commits Horrible Deed," *Charleston News and Courier*, 12 July 1906.

**6.** H. Paul Jeffers, *With An Axe* (New York: Kensington Publishing Corp, 2000).

**7.** Patrick J. Huber, "Caught Up in the Violent Whirlwind of Lynching: The 1885 Quadruple Lynching in Chatham County, North Carolina," *The North Carolina Historical Review*, LXXV: 2 April 1998.

**8.** *Baker Street Times* 1999, online report: http://www.sherlock-holmes.co.uk/news/hound.html

**9.** *Carolina Watchman*, 22 August 1906.

**10.** "A Jack the Ripper," *Salisbury Post*, 28 August 1906.

**11.** *Remembering Jim Crow.* One woman who had lived part of her life during Jim Crow rule and had been subject to its "laws" later recalled how she had been up North for a while and forgotten this unspoken rule when she returned to the South. In a conversation with a white woman, she had referred to a black friend as Mrs. so-and-so. The white woman interrupted and corrected her, insisting that she not do it again.

**12.** Leon Litwack, *Trouble in Mind* (New York: Vintage Books, 1998).

**13.** The spelling of "Ervin" varies with reports. Ervin is used in the 1900 U.S. Census.

**Chapter 4: *The Inquest***

**A.** "Four Killed While Asleep." *Charlotte Observer*, 15 July 1906.

**B.** "Five Members of Family Are Murdered by Burglars," *Fairbanks Daily Times*, 15 August 1906.

**C.** "Salisbury Quiet," *Charlotte Observer,* 15 July 1906.

**D.** "Horrible Butchery," *Salisbury Post*, 18 June 1906, front page.

**1.** Ronald Singer, personal email communication. Singer is the Chief Criminalist at the Tarrant County Medical Examiner's Office in Fort Worth, Texas. In addition to his responsibilities there, he also maintains a private practice as a consulting forensic scientist.
**2.** Mark Twain, *Puddin'head Wilson*.
**3.** "Prisoners Were On Trial For Murder," *Richmond Times-Dispatch*, 7 August 1906.
**4.** "Some Points in Lyerly Case," *Charlotte Observer*. 16 July 1906. "The Rowan Tragedy," *Statesville Landmark*, 17 July 1906.
**5.** *Salisbury Post*, 28 October 1954. This spelling of Henry's last name may be the correct version though only the version with the "y" was used in most 1906 reports. 1910 census records show Henry Mayhew with the "y."
**6.** Conversation with Goodman's great granddaughter, Susan Goodman Sides.
**7.** "Crimson Horror Shocks Carolina," *Raleigh News and Observer*, 15 July 1906.
**8.** "Intended to Burn Surviving Girls: Such is the Frank Admission of One of the Prisoners," *Richmond Times-Dispatch*, 16 July 1906.
**9.** "Lyerly Axe Murders." *Salisbury Post,* 14 July 1974.
**10.** "Weeping Girls Drag Out of the House The Bodies of Murdered Relatives," *Asheville Citizen*, 15 July 1906.
**11.** *Raleigh News and Observer*, 15 July 1906.

### Chapter 5: *A Gathering Storm*
**A.** "Rowan Jail Attacked," *Charlotte Observer*, 15 July 1906.
**B.** *Greensboro Industrial News,* 16 July 1906.
**C.** *Charlotte Observer*, 16 July 1906.

**1.** Rowan County Criminal Docket, 1904.
**2.** Iredell County Court transcript, January, 1907.
**3.** Jack Claiborne, *The Charlotte Observer, Its Time and Place, 1869-1986.*

### Chapter 6: *The Role of the White Supremacist Press*
**A.** Ida B Wells, *Southern Horrors and Other Writings: The Anti-Lynching Campaign of Ida B. Wells, 1892-1900*, edited by Jacqueline Jones Royster. (Boston: Bedford Books, 1997) 2-4.
**B.** Michael Honey, "Class, Race, and Power," *Democracy Betrayed* (Chapel Hill: UNC Press, 1998), edited by Cecelski and Tyson, 165-179.

**C.** Gilmore, *Gender & Jim Crow: Women and the Politics of White Supremacy in North Carolina, 1896-1920*, 23, 82-92. C1. Gilmore, "The Flight of the Incubus," *Democracy Betrayed*, 79.

**D.** Kenneth Joel Zogrey, Pope Museum Website online.

**E.** Claiborne, *The Charlotte Observer: Its Time and Place*, 85,86, 105, 106, 108, 138.

**F.** http://ftp.rootsweb.com/pub/usgenweb/nc/wayne/bios/norman.txt

**G.** http://www.lib.unc.edu/mss/inv/j/Jennett,Norman_Ethre.html

**H.** Josephus Daniels, *Editor In Politics*, 147.

**I.** http://starnesjewelers.com/operahouse/shows/pmiller1.htm

**J.** "Christmas on De Ole Plantation," *Raleigh News and Observer*, August, 1906.

**K.** http://members.tripod.com/~american_almanac/griffith.htm

**L.** http://docsouth.unc.edu/dixonclan/about.html

**M.** "The Clansman Returns," *Charlotte Observer*, 19 February 1907.

**N.** *Charlotte Observer*. 15 July 1906, front page.

**O.** http://www.pbs.org/blackpress/news_bios/defender.html

**P.** "Suppose He Had Been A Negro," *Afro-American Ledger*, 11 August 1906.

## Chapter 7: *The Saddest Funeral*

**A.** "Four Laid in One Grave," *Charlotte Observer*, 16 July 1906, front page.

**B.** *Greensboro Patriot*, 18 July 1906.

**C.** *Asheville Citizen*, 15 July 1906.

**D.** Mark Wineka, *A Family Affair: The Life, Times and Sale of a Family-owned Newspaper* (Asheboro, North Carolina: Down Home Press, 1999) 34.

**E.** "Verdict of Coroner's Jury: Burial of the Four Victims of Negroes' Barbarous Hate," *Raleigh News and Observer*, 17 July 1906.

## Chapter 8: *The Prisoners Speak*

**A.** "Mob Seeks Lives," *Washington Post*, 16 July 1906. This report also added that the Rowan Rifles had showed up about midnight on Saturday night to deal with the mob at Salisbury. McNeill had failed to mention this; perhaps he didn't stick around long enough to witness the militia's arrival.

**B.** "The Special Term," *Salisbury Post*, 17 July 1906, front page.

**C.** "Boy Confesses: Five Are Murderers," *Salisbury Weekly Post*, 18 July 1906, front page.

**D.** "Gillespie's Son Talks: Says Father Killed Lyerlys," *Charlotte Observer*, 17 July 1906, front page.

**E.** "The Rowan Prisoners," *Charlotte Observer*, 17 July 1906.

**F.** *Greensboro Industrial News,* 16 July 1906.
**G.** "Aftermath of Tragedy," *Charlotte Observer,* 16 July 1906.
**H.** "Four of the Five Negroes Are Believed To Be Guilty," *Asheville Gazette,* 17 July 1906.

**1.** Letter to John Steele Henderson, found in Southern Historical Collection, Manuscripts Department, Wilson Library, The University of North Carolina at Chapel Hill, #327. The name of the author of this letter is not clearly legible, but looks like Minnie.
**2.** In North Carolina the Ku Klux Klan was known as The Invisible Empire, according to testimony taken by the U.S. Congress in February, 1872, and as recorded in its *Report of The Joint Select Committee to Inquire Into The Condition of Affairs in The Late Insurrectionary States* (Government Printing Office: Washington, 1872).
**3.** "Killed Husband and Babes," *Savannah Tribune,* September 1906.

## Chapter 9: *Foreshadows*
**A.** "Alleged Lynchers' Trial," *Charlotte Observer,* 15 July 1906.
**B.** "True bill Against Four," *Charlotte Observer,* 17 July 1906.
**C.** "Will Quash Indictment," *Charlotte Observer,* 18 July 1906.
**D.** "Motion to Quash Allowed: Lynching Cases Continued," *Charlotte Observer,* 19 July 06.
**E.** "Alleged Lynchers Cheered," *Carolina Watchman,* 25 July 1906.
**F.** *Raleigh News and Observer,* 9 August 1906, editorial page.
**G.** *Raleigh News and Observer,* 8 August 1906, editorial page.

**1.** "To Get Speedy Justice," *Salisbury Post,* 20 July 1906, 4.
**2.** *Charlotte Observer,* 19 July 1906, 12.
**3.** "Danger of Lynching," *Washington Post,* 21 July 1906, 5.
**4-5.** *Charlotte Observer,* 19 July 1906, 12.
**6.** "Lyerlys' Alleged Slayers," *Charlotte Observer,* 20 July 1906.
**7-8.** *Raleigh News and Observer,* 2 August 1906, front page.
**9.** Litwack. *Trouble In Mind: Black Southerners in the Age of Jim Crow,* 249.

## Chapter 10: *The State's Investigation*
**A.** "The Lyerly Murder Case: The State Hears Evidence," *Charlotte Observer,* 22 July 1906.
**B.** "Witnesses Talk: Solicitor Was Here," *Salisbury Weekly Post,* 25 July 1906.
**C.** "Evidence Indicates Guilt of Gillespie and Dillingham," *Asheville Gazette,* 22 July 1906.

**D.** *Charlotte Observer,* 21 July 1906. "Grand Jury Seeks Light on Murder," *Greensboro Industrial News,* 21 July 1906.
**E.** *Raleigh News and Observer,* 21 July 1906.
**F.** "Little New Evidence," *Charlotte Observer,* 21 July 1906.

**1.** The original report is identified as, "Special to The Observer," indicating, by today's practice, that Bryant, a staff writer, was not the author of this report. However, his name "H.E.C. BRYANT" is tacked on at the end of the report.

**2.** Julian added that the daughters of the murdered couple, Joseph Lyerly, and other relatives of the family, along with newspaper men crowded the narrow room. It's certain that no black reporters were in that room because Jim Crow would not allow such mingling—if there had been any black reporters in North Carolina to mingle.

**3.** Julian added that Joseph "went with them over to Mr. Cook's by Mrs. Sallie Lyerly's.... Dr. Chenault was there. I remained there until Mr. Barber [Pless] came and then went down to my father's." [B] This would perhaps explain why it took him until sunup to arrive at his father's house. Maybe he was afraid to go there alone.

There's no mention of a Mr. Watson in Julian's account of Matt's testimony. Watson was not in any other reports. There's no testimony recorded for W.P. (Pless) Barber or E.A. Barber in any account. Pless Barber is, however, listed in court records among the witnesses for this case.

Joseph's mention of going to Cook's "by" Sallie Lyerly's may solve the mystery of the direction Addie, Mary, and Janie went on the night of the murder. Census records show that by 1910, Filmore Cook had moved from the Unity Township to the Steele Township, which was just south of the old Highway 70 where Isaac's house had stood. Isaac's place had actually been located near the northern border of the Steele Township. If the girls took that route, it would have taken them by the tenant cottage (believed to have been Jack and Della's) which sat on the hill across the highway from their home. On the 1900 Census map, William C. Lyerly, who was Sallie's husband, was shown to live directly south of Isaac's house, about three-fourths of a mile away. Census records show Cook, who owned his home in 1900, was renting by 1910. So he was likely renting a place on Sallie's land in 1906—her husband William deceased by then. On the map, however, it still looks to be slightly farther away than Joseph's place—and the trip to Cook's did require that they go by Dillingham's place, whom they were said to be afraid of. This route also took them through the woods, up a hill, and across a stream and a railroad track. So it still seems that Joseph's place would have been the safest and easiest way to go. Nevertheless, if Cook was living on Sallie's property, and this is what Joseph meant when he said it was "by Mrs. Sallie Lyerly's," then the girls did go to a relative's place after all—just not their closest one. Sallie was Isaac's sister, and she had married one of their first cousins when she married William. This route, however, would not have jibed with reports that said the girls ran through their father's corn fields. Those fields were located North of the house.

**4.** There is no recorded testimony for Dr. Chenault, nor does his name appear in court records as a witness. Joseph may have taken this money and other things as well; a relative indicated he took something that didn't belong to him from the house after the murders. And he kept what he took.

**5.** Julian added that Joseph said he lived about half a mile from his father's home. He also quoted Joseph as saying that after his father ordered Nease out of the yard, "Nease's boys worked the crops since that trouble and Nease had driven a team for 12 months for J.M. Penninger. Father rented the house for them to live in to work for him. Henry and wife were living there until this spring when they went to Leroy Powlas' to make a crop." [B] Joseph Lyerly's statements recorded earlier by the press indicate that either Nease or the boys or both had done some work on a crop for Isaac that they did not receive compensation for, as Nease's new employer had covered the rent Nease had owed Isaac.

**6.** Julian wrote in an earlier report that both front windows were open about two feet. In his account of Hammer's investigation, Julian said Mary testified that the "front door was open" when she went downstairs and the other door was shut. [B] Mary doesn't explain in Bryant's report how she knew that Isaac had gone out and forgotten to re-lock the door, after saying first that she knew nothing after retiring around 9 o'clock, which was supposedly after Isaac and her mother and younger siblings had gone to bed. She may have just assumed that Isaac had gone out after retiring because it had happened before, or she had forgotten about this when she made the first statement. Or, Bryant could have recorded the conversation incorrectly. Julian's report says it this way: "I locked front door before going to bed, left key in door, but I think Papa went out afterwards, because I had locked the back door before going to bed, and when I came down I found it still locked." [B]

**7.** Julian quoted Mary saying: "I saw John and Alice cutting stove wood late the evening before." [B] So apparently these two "babies" had indeed been cutting wood, which means that the tool in question must have been a small axe—more like a hatchet.

**8.** Augusta's mother's maiden name was Cranford, so this Cranford may have been a relative. However, there is no recorded testimony from him, and he is not listed in court records as a witness. His absence on this day classifies this threat as hearsay. This testimony about Fannie fussing at Isaac is not mentioned at any other time, but it may have some significance. Fannie apparently felt comfortable "fussing" at Isaac. Hildebran, without the "d" is a small town lying about thirty miles west of Barber Junction on Highway 70. Julian said Cranford lived at Hildebrand's place rather than just Hildebrand. [B]

**9.** Julian noted that this statement was Jack's response to Isaac "getting after Jack for coming to work so late." [B] Both Taylor and Cook are listed in the court records as witnesses, but Taylor had no recorded testimony anywhere. It's not clear why Isaac was losing all of his workers at the same time. Perhaps this time of the year was normally slow, but a reported statement by Della Dillingham, as well as information from Lyerly descendants, suggests that the older girls were having to do a lot of plowing. Mary's youngest daughter told me there were some things about her mother, Augusta, that Mary did not like—one being that Augusta never did any work. My mother tells me, however, that Augusta was known for her wonderful cooking. Julian's account quoted Mary saying that "Taylor slept at our house every night, since they had been working for us until that night."[B]

**10.** Julian's report says the girls were afraid of both men: They didn't go by "Jack's or Nease's" because they were "afraid of them." Also Julian added this statement: "We went by Jack's but left the path before getting opposite the house and we slipped stealthily by. The path was about ten feet from Jack's door, and we went 25 or 30 feet from the door." [B] I believe Julian added Nease's name to this testimony, because other accounts indicate that the girls were afraid only of the Dillinghams, even though they knew that Nease had been angry over the disagreement with their father.

**11.** This information, which is the same in Julian's report, contradicts earlier stories that the girls had fled in their night clothes to Cook's house. But there is no mention in either testimony on this day that the girls checked the outbuildings, looking for the murderers. Interestingly, the two stories differ concerning the lamp.

**12.** In Julian's report, Matt Webb said he lived "one mile away from Mr. Lyerly's." Webb is also quoted as saying the following: "James

Thompson came by my house about daylight and told me to put out the word that the Lyerlys were killed. He said he heard it from Taylor and Cook. As quick as I could catch and saddle a horse I went there, got there about sun up. Sheriff Julian and a crowd of men were there." [B] Julian again printed the more damning version of what Nease had supposedly said concerning the crop: "Nease said Mr. Isaac Lyerly could cut his, Nease's wheat, but he could not live to eat it or get the money for it." [B] Webb and Jones (not James) Thompson are listed as witnesses in the court records. The wheat crop, in general, was indeed very good that year, according to another report.

**13.** At this point everyone in the room knew who Henry's father was, but none of the reporters divulged this name. It could be that a point was made of Henry's parentage to support the credibility of his testimony.

**14.** There was no mention of an actual axe brought in for the witness to identify. There's no explanation why a fire was burning in their fireplace in August. Henry would not have called Fannie "old Fannie," so this part was probably not quoted after all.

**15.** Mr. Walton's first name is recorded as Mose in Julian's report. Julian did not use any of the degrading remarks Bryant used to describe Fannie. He included a statement that she would have been living at the Lyerly place for a year come September.

**16.** Mr. Roseman, who was Isaac's grand nephew, ended up owning the Lyerly property. Alexander might have been the man who was interviewed by reporters earlier and for whom Nease had previously worked. The man's name was not mentioned in those accounts.

**17.** From what can be gleaned from all the initial reports about this matter, it was Bryant who said Fannie told this to Dick File. Bryant made several errors of fact, including treating this hearsay as fact. It comes down to File's word against Fannie's. Furthermore, Bryant did not back up his statement asserting that "Fannie had been trapped in a dozen or more instances." The only contradictions shown here are the ones with File's and Henry's stories. And Henry contradicted himself more than once.

**18.** Bridgewater, like Hildebran, is another small railroad stop right off of Highway 70. Located on a branch of the Catawba River, Bridgewater lies just west of Morganton, about 50 miles from Barber

Junction. I wondered why Taylor left town so fast, what had happened to his job at Penninger's.

**19.** Penninger's daughter, Sarah Knapp, is still alive, and I contacted her to let her know about her father's involvement in this case. She had never heard about it. When I told her I admired her father because he seemed willing to stand up for the sharecroppers, contradicting what many others believed about them, she told me she had known her father as one never afraid to tell the truth.

**20.** Julian added that Thompson said "The blood on it was rusted," and that "Both sides of he handle were projecting through the axe." [B] Miller and reporter W.T. (Tom) Bost were first cousins.

### Chapter 11: *The Flip Side*
**A.** "The Bassett Affair," Duke University Archives, 1995.
**B.** Joel Williamson, *The Crucible of Race* (New York: Oxford University Press, 1984) 263.
**C.** "Josephus Daniels," *Greensboro Industrial News*, 25 July 1906. Hicks made no secret of his affiliation with the Republican Party; his name is among those in the party's 1906 hand book.
**D.** "75 Years of Newspapering in Charlotte, North Carolina: 1886-1961," 6-7.
**E.** "Deny The Murder of The Lyerly Family," *Richmond Times-Dispatch*, 20 July 1906.
**F.** "The Story of Della Dillingham," *Charlotte Observer*, 22 July 1906.
**G.** *Salisbury Weekly Post*, 25 July 1906.
**H.** "Jack Dillingham Confesses," *Asheboro Courier*, 26 July 1906.
**J.** "Witnesses Talk," *Salisbury Weekly Post*, 25 July 1906.
**K.** *Charlotte Observer*, July 1906.
**L.** *Raleigh News and Observer*, 25 July 1906.

### Chapter 12: *Assumption of Guilt*
**A.** "Henderson Papers, #327, Southern Historical Collection, Manuscripts Department, Wilson Library, UNC-Chapel Hill.
**B.** The current owners of the Lyerly land say there was only one well on the property, and after the old house burned down, that well was filled with bricks from the chimney left standing.
**C.** "Intended to Burn Surviving Girls: Such is the Frank Admission of One of the Prisoners," *Richmond Times-Dispatch*, 16 July 1906.
**D.** "Aftermath of Tragedy," *Charlotte Observer*, 16 July 1906.

## Chapter 13: *Red Sky At Morn*
**A.** "The Prisoners in Salisbury," *Salisbury Post*, 6 August 1906, front page.
**B.** "True Bills Were Found," *Charlotte Observer*, 7 August 1906, front page. For some reason H.E.C. Bryant didn't sign his initials to this report, but it was noted in the August 10th *Mooresville Enterprise* that Bryant had been "detailed to report the trial, which was started Monday morning," August 6th.
**C.** Leon Litwack, *Trouble In Mind* (New York: Vintage Books, 1998), 257.
**D.** Andre Siegfried, *America Comes of Age* (New York: Harcourt, Brace and Company: 1927) 95.
**E.** Mark Curriden and Leroy Phillips, Jr., *Contempt of Court: The Turn-of-the-Century Lynching That Launched 100 Years of Federalism.* (New York: Anchor Books, 1999) 12, 13, 14, 49, 50, 53, 54, 59, 194.

**1.** "The Law Is Sufficient," *Salisbury Post*, 6 August 1906.
**2.** "Splits His Head Open," *Salisbury Post*, 6 August 1906, front page.
**3.** "Strong Lynching Sentiment," *Mooresville Enterprise*, 3 August, 1906.
**4.** "Mob, Defying Court, Lynches Five Negroes," *New York Times*, 7 August 1906.
**5.** George Stoney, "Suffrage in the South: Part II, The One-Party System," *Survey Graphic: Magazine of Social Interpretation*, online at http://newdeal.feri.org/survey/40c23.htm
**6.** "Progressivism and Agitation for Legal Reform in North Carolina, 1897–1917," *Essays In American History* (Greenville, North Carolina: Department of History, East Carolina College,1964) 92.
**7.** Criminal Docket, Rowan County Superior Court, 1904-1907, 225.
**8.** North Carolina State Archives, Raleigh, North Carolina.
**9.** This law which originated in 1893 is still listed in North Carolina's Statutes under Chapter 162, involving the duties of sheriffs. **162-23. Prevent entering jail for lynching; county liable http://www.ncga.state.nc.us/statutes/generalstatutes/html/bychapter/chapter%5F162.html

*INNOCENCE, PRESUMPTION OF - The indictment or formal charge against any person is not evidence of guilt. Indeed, the person is presumed by the law to be innocent. The law does not require a person to prove his innocence or produce any evidence at all. The Government has the burden of proving a person guilty beyond a reasonable doubt, and if it fails to do so the person is (so far as the law is concerned) not guilty. http://www.lectlaw.com/def/i047.htm

An interesting discussion on the History of the principle of Presumptive Innocence can be found at this website: http://www.talkleft.com/archives/001907.html It explains the precedence for presumptive innocence to be a case from 1895, Coffin vs, United States.

** § 162-23. Prevent entering jail for lynching; county liable.
"When the sheriff of any county has good reason to believe that the jail of his county is in danger of being broken or entered for the purpose of killing or injuring a prisoner placed by the law in his custody, it shall be his duty at once to call on the commissioners of the county, or some one of them, for a sufficient guard for the jail, and in such case, if the commissioner or commissioners fail to authorize the employment of
necessary guards to protect the jail, and by reason of such failure the jail is entered and a prisoner killed, the county in whose jail the prisoner is confined shall be responsible in damages, to be recovered by the personal representatives of the prisoner thus killed, by action begun and prosecuted before the superior court of any county in this State. (1893, c. 461,s. 7; Rev., s. 2825; C.S., s. 3945.)"

## Chapter 14: *Eye of the Storm*
**A.** "Mr. Newell on Lynching," *Gastonia Gazette*, 10 August 1906, front page. The *Gazette* was a bi-weekly paper.
**B.** "Last Night's Triple Lynching," *Salisbury Post*, 7 August 1906, front page.
**C.** "Mob Lynches Three," *Charlotte Observer*, 7 August 1906, front page.
**D.** "Militia Guarding the Jail," *Charlotte Observer*, 8 August 1906, front page.
**E.** Mark Wineka, *A Family Affair: The Life, Times and Sale of a Family-owned Newspaper* (Asheboro, North Carolina: Down Home Press, 1999) 34-37.
**F.** "Censure for the Mob," *Charlotte Observer*, 7 August 1906, 12.
**G.** "Four Swung Up By Mob at Salisbury," *Raleigh News and Observer*, 7 August 1906, front page.
**H.** "That Fearful Night in Rowan," *Charlotte Observer*, 17 August 1906.
**I.** "Mob Burns Three," *Washington Post*, 7 August 1906.
**J.** "Quiet Rules in Salisbury; Jail Under Guard," *Greensboro Industrial News*, 8 August 1906.
**K.** "Lynchers Murderers, Declares Judge Long," *Greensboro Industrial News*, 8 August 1906.

**1.** John S. Henderson Papers, UNC-Chapel Hill.
**2.** "Negro Workmen Strike," *Charlotte Observer*, 13 July 1906.
"Spencer Negroes Threaten Strike," *Greensboro Industrial News*, 13
July 1906. "Lynchers Foiled," *Tarboro Southerner*, 26 July 1906. "Was
Tom Uzra Lynched?" *Concord Times*, 18 May 1906.
**3.** *Richmond News-Leader*, 7 August 1906, reprinted under the
headline, "Disgrace Complete," *Mooresville Enterprise*, 17 August
1906, front page.
**4.** W.E. Hennessee, "The Klan in Carolina," *The State: A Weekly
Survey of North Carolina*, 9 November 1940, 5. Leslie Black, "The
Boydens in Rowan County," *The Genealogical Society of Rowan
County, North Carolina*, Volume 20.
**5.** "Captain Barker's Statement," *Salisbury Post*, 7 August 1906.
**6.** These two must have been men of African descent, for the paper
noted next that a white man jailed for carrying a concealed weapon left
also. His name was not disclosed, though it must have been known if
the charge was known.
**7.** *Raleigh News and Observer*, 8 August 1906. *New York Times*, 9
August 1906. *Richmond Planet*, 11 August 1906.
**8.** "To Avenge the Outraged Law," *Raleigh News and Observer*, 8
August 1906.
**9.** Julian did later "lie" about this, printing that Nease had confessed
and apparently concocted an additional story stating that Henry Lee had
implicated the others after they were lynched. Not one other paper
confirmed these stories. Several even made a special note of the
defendants insistence on innocence until the very end.
**10.** "Four Swung Up By Mob At Salisbury," *Raleigh News and
Observer*, 8 August 1906, front page.
**11.** "Mob Takes Three Negroes Accused of Murder From Jail at
Salisbury and Lynches Them," *Greensboro Industrial News*, 7 August
1906, front page.
**12.** "Lynchburg" advertisement, *Raleigh News and Observer*, 7 August
1906.

## Chapter 15: *The Morning After*
**A.** "A Blot on the State" *Charlotte Observer*, 8 August 1906.
**B.** "Militia Guarding the Jail" *Charlotte Observer*, 8 August 1906.
**C.** "Last Night's Triple Lynching," *Salisbury Post*, 7 August 1906,
front page.
**D.** "Murderers Lynched-Military Guard," *Carolina Watchman*, 8
August 1906. The *Watchman* also published a photo of the lynching.
**E.** "Attempt at Rescue," *News and Observer*, 8 August 1906.
**F.** "Description and Comment," *Charlotte Observer*, 9 August 1906.

**G.** "A Tense Calm," *Raleigh News and Observer*, 9 August 1906.
**H.** "Women Witnessed Lynching," *Charlotte Observer*, 8 August 1906.
**I.** *Carolina Watchman*, 22 August 06.
**J.** "Quiet Rules in Salisbury; Jail Under Guard," *Greensboro Industrial News*, 8 August 1906.
**K.** "Lyncher Sentenced," *Asheboro Courier*, 16 August 1906. This paper was located in Randolph County, owned by Solicitor Hammer.
**L.** "Five Arrested for Lynching at Salisbury," *Greensboro Industrial News*, 10 August 1906.

**1.** Henderson Papers, #327, Southern Historical Collection, Manuscripts Department, Wilson Library, University of North Carolina at Chapel Hill. The reference to Baldy is a nickname for either a relative named Archibald, or businessman W.S. Baldwin, with the Salisbury and Spencer Gas and Electric Company.
**2.** ibid. The note on the bottom of this August 8th letter appears to be in different handwriting than Henderson's own.
**3.** "Angry Mob Stormed Jail, Lynched 3 Suspects," *Salisbury Post*, 14 July 1974.
**4.** "Barbarism Rampant in North Carolina," *Richmond Planet*, 11 August 1906.
**5.** "Lynchers Murderers, Declares Judge Long," *Greensboro Industrial News*, 9 August 1906. "Senator Overman Writes," *Gastonia Gazette*, 21 August 1906. "The Salisbury Affair," *Charlotte Observer*, 13 August 1906.
**6.** "Forty Paupers Go on Strike," *Salisbury Post*, 20 July 1906.
**7.** "Will Try Lynchers First," *Greensboro Industrial News*, 28 August 1906.
**8.** "To Avenge the Outraged Law," *Raleigh News and Observer*, 8 August 06.
**9.** In telling this story, Bryant did not identify the one who gave the solicitor this information. Montgomery and Stanly are adjoining counties, east and southeast of Rowan.
**10.** "Negro Made Threats," *Charlotte Observer*, 8 August 1906.
**11.** *Monroe Journal*, reprinted in editorial section of *Greensboro Industrial News*, 9 August 1906, with the *News'* disapproval of and "considerable surprise" over the *Journal's* "unjust and uncalled for" "utterance."

## Chapter 16: *Reactions*
**A.** "Militia Guarding the Jail," *Charlotte Observer*, 8 August 1906.
**B.** "To Avenge the Outraged Law," *Raleigh News and Observer*, 8 August 1906.
**C.** *Salisbury Post*, 7 August 1906.

**D.** "Quiet Rules in Salisbury," *Greensboro Industrial News*, 8 August 1906.

**E.** "Aftermath of the Lynching," *Charlotte Observer*, 9 August 1906.

**F.** "A Blot on the State" *Charlotte Observer*, 8 August 1906.

**G.** "Convicting A Lyncher," *Richmond Planet*, 18 August 1906.

**H.** "Hall Is Up: Is Court Void?," *Salisbury Post*, 10 August 1906.

**1.** *Charlotte Observer*, 10 August 1906.

**2.** "Mob, Defying Court, Lynches Five Negroes," *New York Times*, 7 August 1906, 12. "Lynchers Murderers, Declares Judge Long," *Greensboro Industrial News*, 9 August 1906.

**3.** "The State Bears the Brunt," *Raleigh News and Observer*, 11 August 1906.

**4.** "Topic of the Times: Lynch Law Applied Both Ways," *The New York Times*, 9 August 1906.

**5.** "Les 'Lynchages' Aux Etats-Unis: Massacre de negres a Atlanta (Georgie)," *Le Petit Journal*, 7 October 1906. "Atlanta Mob Ridden City," Baltimore *Afro-American Ledger*, 29 September 1906. "Race War in Atlanta," *Charlotte Observer*, 23 September 1906. "Ten Known Negroes Dead," *Charlotte Observer*, 24 September 1906.

**6.** "North Carolina Mob," *Chattanooga Times*, 8 August 1906.

**7.** "Local Man Lynched For Killing Mother-In-Law," *Lexington Dispatch*, 13 December 1956.

**8.** "To Deal With Mobs," *Charlotte Observer*, 10 August 1906.

**9.** "A Crime Without Excuse," *Charlotte Observer*, 7 August 1906.

**10.** *Carolina Watchman*, 8 August 2006.

**11.** *Durham Caucasian*, 16 August 1906. *Republican Hand-Book North Carolina, Republican State Executive Committee, 1906.*

**12.** "Description and Comment," *Charlotte Observer*, 9 August 1906. "Lynchers Murderers, Declares Judge Long," *Greensboro Industrial News*, 9 August 1906. *Salisbury Sun*, reprinted in *Charlotte Observer*, 9 August 1906. *Salisbury Post*, 9 August 1906.

**13.** "Georgia Editor Approves," *Washington Post*, 8 August 1906, reprinted from *Atlanta News*.

**14.** Timothy Tyson and Glenda Gilmore, their essays on the Wilmington race riot/massacre found in *Democracy Betrayed* (Chapel Hill: UNC Press, 1998), edited by David Cecelski and Timothy Tyson.

**15.** *Chattanooga Times*, 20 March 1906.

**16.** "Negroes Call On Bryan," *Hickory Times Mercury*, 12 August 1908. "Night Riders Throughout South," and "The Night Riders," *Times Mercury*, 4 November, 1908. "Difference in Mobs," *Times Mercury*, 16 September 1908. "And They Can't, Eh?," *Times Mercury*, 30 September 1908. *Raleigh Enterprise*, comments printed in the *Caucasian*, 16 August 1906.

**17.** "Why Extend to 1920 If Unconstitutional," *Chatham Record*, editorial, reprinted in *Asheboro Courier*, 2 August 1906.
**18.** "The Salisbury Lynching," *Asheville Citizen*. 8 August 1906. The comment "you cannot hang the public" may have come from what Judge Phillips told B.F. Long at another lynching trial in 1889, in which he acted as prosecutor, assisted by then attorney, W.B. Glenn. Phillips reportedly said, "You cannot indict a county...." in Wade H. Phillips' recap of the story, "Local Man Lynched For Killing Mother-In-Law," *Lexington Dispatch*, 6 November 1889.

### Chapter 17: *Conspiracy, Part One*
**A.** "True Bill Against Hall," *Charlotte Observer*, 9 August 1906, front page.
**B.** "True Bills Were Found," *Charlotte Observer*, 7 August 1906.
**C.** "One Hundred Men May Be Indicted," *Raleigh News and Observer*, 10 August 1906, front page.
**D.** "A Tense Calm Now Reigning in Salisbury," *Raleigh News and Observer*, 9 August 1906.
**E.** "Mob Spirit Has Subsided," *Charlotte Observer*, 10 August 1906.
**F.** "Hall Is Up," *Salisbury Post*, 10 August 1906.

**1.** "Lawless Mob Lynched Three Murderers," *Asheboro Courier,* 9 August 1906, front page.
**2.** James S. Brawley, *Rowan County: A Brief History*, 117.
**3.** *Raleigh News and Observer,* 8 August, 1906.
**4.** "Mob Lynches Three," *Lexington Dispatch*, 8 August 1906, front page.
**5.** "Murderers Lynched - Military Guard," *Carolina Watchman*, 8 August 1906.
**6.** "Lynching," *Afro-American Ledger*, 11 August 1906, editorial page.
**7.** Mark Curriden and Leroy Phillips, Jr., *Contempt of Court* (New York: Anchor Books, 1999) 216.

### Chapter 17: *Conspiracy, Part Two*
**A.** "Hall Gets Fifteen," *Charlotte Observer*, 11 August 1906, front page.
**B.** "Hall is Up," *Salisbury Post*, 10 August 1906, front page.
**C.** "Is Guilty," *Salisbury Post*, 11 August 06, front page. Poteat is the correct spelling for the deputy mentioned in Porter's testimony.
**D.** "Special Term Adjourned," *Charlotte Observer*, 12 August 1906.

**1.** Rowan County Court Docket, page 414.

**2.** Mark Wineka, *A Family Affair: The Life, Times and Sale of a Family-owned Newspaper* (Asheboro, North Carolina: Down Home Press) 37.

**3.** Ann Field Alexander, "'Like An Evil Wind:' The Roanoke Riot of 1893 and the Lynching of Thomas Smith," *Virginia Magazine of History and Biography*, Vol. 100, No. 2 (April 1992).

**4.** "Senator Overman Writes," *Gastonia Gazette*, 21 August 1906, front page.

**5.** *The Richmond Planet*, 18 August 1906, editorial page.

**6.** "The 'Mob' Arrested," *Asheville Citizen*. Reprinted in *Carolina Watchman*, 22 August 1906.

**7.** "The Real North Carolina," *Richmond News-Leader*, 14 August 1906, reprinted in *Gastonia Gazette*, 17 August 1906.

**8.** "2 Taken to Raleigh," *Salisbury Post*, 13 August 1906.

## Chapter 18: *Insanity*

**A.** "Is Guilty," *Salisbury Post*, 11 August 06.

**B.** "Special Term Adjourned," *Charlotte Observer*, 12 August 1906.

**1.** Court Records for Cress show only a charge of rioting.

## Chapter 19: *Fanning the Flames*

**A.** "The Lyerly Barn Burned," *Charlotte Observer*, 10 August 1906.

**B.** "Fire Wakes Fury," *Raleigh News and Observer*, 10 August 1906, front page. "Vicious Idiocy," *Raleigh News and Observer*, 11 August 1906, editorial page.

**C.** "Mob Spirit Has Subsided," *Charlotte Observer*, 10 August 1906.

**D.** "The Lyerly Barn Fire," *Charlotte Observer*, 16 August 1906.

**E.** "The Lyerly Sale," *Carolina Watchman*, 22 August 1906.

**F.** "Negro Suspect Returns," *Charlotte Observer*, 25 August 1906.

**G.** "Fixing the Responsibility," *Charlotte Observer*, 16 August 1906.

**H.** *Charlotte Observer*, 16 October 1906.

**I.** "Mayor Boyden Ill," *Charlotte Observer*, 23 August 1906.

**J.** *Charlotte Observer*, 10 August 1906.

**K.** "That Salisbury Lynching," *Tarboro Southerner*, 16 or 23 August 1906.

## Chapter 20: *A Short Chapter*

**A.** "Last Night's Triple Lynching: Engineer Badly Shot," *Salisbury Post*, 7 August 1906.

**B.** "Bodies Horribly Mutilated," *Charlotte Observer*, 8 August 1906. Reprinted in *Gastonia Gazette*, 10 August 1906.

**C.** "Gatling Guns....," *Washington Post*, 8 August 1906.

**D.** "Engineer McLendon's Condition," *Salisbury Post*, 11 August 1906, front page.

**E.** "A Salisbury Lynching," *Mooresville Enterprise*, 10 August 1906.

**F.** "Mob Lynches Three," *Charlotte Observer*, 7 August 1906.

**G.** *Carolina Watchman*, 5 September 1906, editorial.

**H.** "Engineer Dead," *Carolina Watchman*, 5 September 1906.

## Chapter 21: *White Lies*

**A.** "George Gentle Arraigned," *Charlotte Observer*, 2 September 1906.

**B.** "Judge Ferguson on Lynch-Law," *Raleigh News and Observer*, 2 September 1906.

**C.** "Geo. Gentle Not Guilty," *Charlotte Observer*, 6 September 1906.

**1.** "Rowan Murder Trial," *Charlotte Observer*, 31 August 1906.

**2.** "Superior Court Convenes," *Charlotte Observer*, 28 August 1906.

**3.** "Negroes to be Tried," *Carolina Watchman*, 5 September 1906.

**4.** Kennerly is the spelling used in the Court Docket, but Kenerly is used by the *Observer* and is the spelling used by the census taker in 1900.

**5.** Munchausen, in this case, apparently refers simply to a tendency to exaggerate in a way that is self-destructive—from a 1797 definition found in Webster's Collegiate Dictionary, based on Baron K.F.H. von Munchausen – "German soldier and proverbial teller of exaggerated tales." Health connotations and hypochondria were not specifically associated with the term until the 1950s.

**6.** "Gentle is Acquitted," *Carolina Watchman*, 12 September 1906.

## Chapter 21: *About Face*

**A.** "To Be Tried In Stanly," *Charlotte Observer*, 7 September 1906, front page, and "Gentle Put Under Bond," 8 September 1906, front page. This chapter is based solely on the *Observer's* September 7th and September 8th reports on this term of Rowan County Court proceedings. No other detailed accounts that are not reprints of these reports could be found. Any quotes in this chapter are taken from these *Observer* reports unless noted otherwise.

**B.** Leon Litwack, *Trouble in Mind: Black Southerners in the Age of Jim Crow*, 240.

**C.** "Court Proceedings," *Carolina Watchman*, 5 September 1906.

**D.** *Charlotte Observer*, 31 January 1907.

**E.** "Suppose He Had Been A Negro," *Afro-American-Ledger*, 11 August 1906, editorial page.

**1.** "Certain Unalienable Rights," from "What the Negro Wants."

**2.** "Where is Col. Jake Newell?" *Charlotte Observer*, 23 August 1906.

**3.** *Merriam-Webster's Collegiate Dictionary, Tenth Edition* (Springfield, Massachusetts, 1997).

**Chapter 23: *Asheville Bound***
**A.** "Change of Venue Granted," *Washington Post*, 16 January 1907.
**B.** "Lyerly Prisoners Not Guilty," *Statesville Landmark*, 1 February 1907, 3.
**C.** "The Negroes Liberated," *Charlotte Observer*, 1 February 1907.
**D.** Iredell County Criminal Action Papers, 1906-1907, C.R.054.326.29, North Carolina State Archives.
**E.** "Last Chapter in Lyerly Tragedy," *Raleigh News and Observer*, 31 January 07.
**F.** "The Negroes Freed," *Carolina Watchman*, February 1907.
**G.** "Lyerly Murder," *Asheboro Courier*, 7 February 1907.

**1.** Timothy E. Dearman, email communication, 28 Jaunuary 2003. *Charlotte Observer*, 28 February 1950.
**2.** *Charlotte Observer*, 8 August 1906, reprinted under "Mr. Newell on Lynching," *Gastonia Gazette*, 10 August 1906.

**Chapter 24: *To Heaven When I Die***
**A.** "A Senseless Murder...And A Mob," *Salisbury Post*, 23 August 1957, front page.
**B.** "A Girl Murdered: Supposed That An Outrage Was Committed," *Raleigh News and Observer*, 10 June 1902.
**C.** "Woman Outraged and Killed," *Charlotte Observer*, 10 June 1902. "A Suspicious Character Being Watched," is a subheading of an addition to this report, said to come from Mooresville.
**D.** "Murder Followed by Lynching," *Statesville Landmark*, 13 June 1902, a reprint of a 10 June 1902 *Salisbury Sun* report.
**E.** "The Two Negroes Hanged: Murderers of Miss Benson Dead," *Charlotte Observer*, 12 June 1902, front page.
**F.** "Two Dangling Black Bodies: Passengers View the Ghastly Sight from Train Windows," *Davidson Dispatch*, 18 June 1902, reprinted from the *Charlotte Observer*.
**F1.** "Two Negroes Lynched: Youthful Murderers of Miss Cornelia Benson Lynched at Salisbury," *Winston-Salem Journal*, 12 June 1902, front page.
**G.** "Governor Aycock Offers $30,000 for Lynchers," *Raleigh News and Observer*, 19 June 1902, front page.
**H.** "Dragged From the Jail and Lynched," *Raleigh News and Observer*, 12 June 1902, front page.
**I.** "Lynching Brings Lawlessness," *Raleigh News and Observer*, 12 June 1902, editorial page, 4.

**J.** "Lynching Must Be Suppressed at Any Cost." *Raleigh News and Observer*, 19 June 1902.
**K.** "Parents of the Lynched Negroes Advised to Move," *Charlotte Observer*, 13 June 1902, reprinted in the 17 June 1902 *Statesville Landmark*.
**L.** "Negroes Driven Off By Mob," *Charlotte Observer*, 24 June 1902.
**N.** "An Alleged Lyncher Jailed." *Charlotte Observer*, 14 July 1902.
**O.** "Eleven Other Men to be Arrested on Charge of Being in the Mob" *Charlotte Observer*, 14 July 1902.
**P.** "Sparnell Placed on Trial," *Charlotte Observer*, 15 July 1902.
**R.** "The Lynching Investigation," *Charlotte Observer,* 16 July 1902.
**S.** "Lynchings and the Remedy," *Raleigh News and Observer*, 22 June 1902.

**1.** Transcripts provided by letter correspondence with John Tayloe, 24 February 2007. "Jim Boston Lynched," *Washington Progress*, 27 March 1902. U.S. Census Records, Townships of Plymouth and Jamesville, North Carolina, 1880 and 1900. "Fleming and Conley Hanged," *Charlotte Observer*, 9 July 1902.
**2.** "Why Lynchings Continue: Loss of Confidence in the Law-Making Powers. The Remedy," *Raleigh News and Observer*, 29 June 1902.
**3.** John Grimes. email correspondence, 10 February 2007 and 12 February 2007.
**4.** "Lynching Brings Lawlessness," *Raleigh News and Observer*, 12 June 1902, editorial page.
**5.** Public Laws, ch. 461, sec. 5: In all investigations before a justice of the peace, coroner, judge, grand jury, or courts and jury, on the trial of the cause, as authorized by this act or under existing law, no person shall be excused from testifying touching his knowledge of information in regard to the offense being investigated, upon the ground that his answer might tend to subject him to persecution, pains or penalties, or that his evidence might tend to criminate himself, but no discovery made by such witness upon any such examination shall be used against him in any court or in any penal or criminal prosecution, and he shall when so examined as a witness for the State be altogether pardoned of any and all participation in any crime arising under the provision of this act or under existing law, concerning which he is required to testify.
**6.** "Didn't Happen in the South," *Raleigh News and Observer*, 17 June 1902.

## Epilogue
**1.** The web address for that hit was:
www.dcbar.org/about_bar/charless.html-42k

**2.** "Lee Slater Overman," Wikipedia, the free encyclopedia. Overman's portrait can be viewed on this website: http://en. wikipedia.org/wiki/Lee_Slater_Overman
**3.** Mark Curriden and Leroy Phillips, Jr., *Contempt of Court* (New York: Anchor Books, 1999) 252, 330, 332.
**4.** "A Ghastly Shadow Signals Retribution Across Davidson County," *Salisbury Post*, 31 March 1957.
**5.** W. Thomas Bost, "I Have Seen 142 Electrocutions," *The State*, 12 January 1935, 3, 22.

**Conclusion:** *A Game Called Spin*
**1.** Dee Brown, *Bury My Heart at Wounded Knee* (New York: Henry Holt & Co.: 1970) 405.
**2.** ibid, 407-408, 413.
**3.** John Haley, "Race, Rhetoric, and Revolution," *Democracy Betrayed*, 211-212.
**4.** "Shed A Little Light," James Taylor.
**5.** Martin Luther King, Jr. "Beyond Vietnam: A Time to Break Silence," delivered at a meeting at Riverside Church, New York, N.Y., 4 April 1967 found on the web at http://www.ssc.msu.edu/~sw/mlk/brksInc.htm
**6.** Martin Luther King, Jr. "Acceptance Speech," on the occasion of the award of the Nobel Peace Prize in Oslo, 10 December 1964.

**A.** Stephen Kinzer, *Overthrow: Americas's Century of Regime Change from Hawaii to Iraq* (New York: Times Books, 2006) 3, 6, 36, 37, 38, 50, 53, 54, 117, 118, 122, 123, 124, 128, 134, 136, 138, 147, 202
**B.** Glenda E. Gilmore, *Gender & Jim Crow* (Chapel Hill: University of North Carolina Press, 1996) 123.
**C.** Andre Siegfried, *America Comes of Age* (New York: Harcourt, Brace & Company, 1927) 95.
**D.** Noam Chomsky, *Letters From Lexington: Reflections on Propaganda* (London: Paradigm Publishers, 2004) xi, xii, xiii, 10, 11.
**D1.** Noam Chomsky, Massachusetts Institute of Technology, Excerpted from the *Alternative Press Review*, Fall 1993.
online at:
http://www.zmag.org/chomsky/talks/9103-media-control.html
**D2.** Noam Chomsky, *Propaganda and the Public Mind* (Cambridge, Massachusetts: South End Press, 2001) 149.
**E.** "22 Are Dead; 46 Injured: Aftermath of the Hamlet Wreck." *Charlotte Observer*, 24 July 1906.
**F.** http://changingminds.org/techniques/propaganda_history.htm
**G.** Andy McDonald and Lene Palmer, "Propaganda," http://mason.gmu.edu/~amcdonal/Propganda%20Techniques.html

**H.** This past November, The *News & Observer* and other North Carolina newspapers revisited the Wilmington race riots in a 16-page supplement subtitled, "Wilmington's Race Riot and the Rise of White Supremacy," a response to a 300-page report published by the 1898 Wilmington Race Riot Commission. (Visit www.ah.dcr.state.nc.us/1898-wrrc for the full commission report or www.newsobserver.com/1370/story/511596.html for the *N&O* Wilmington Race Riot supplement.) Source: Independent Weekly website: www.indyweek.com 18 April 2007

## About the Author

An eighth-generation North Carolinian, Susan grew up in the Piedmont part of the state, where she later studied English, History, Art, Ad Design, and Environmental Health. Since then, like Forrest Gump, she's worn a lot of shoes. Few fit, and some were downright painful, but they all eventually brought her back to her roots in Salisbury.

She currently lives on the Carolina coast with her family and cats, where she works as an artist, a writer, and a nutrition specialist, occasionally fighting the good fight for environmental and social reform.

CPSIA information can be obtained at www.ICGtesting.com
Printed in the USA
BVOW06s1603300516

449560BV00023B/77/P